Israelis and Palestinians

Israelis and Palestinians

Conflict and Resolution

Moshé Machover

Haymarket Books
Chicago, Illinois

Published in 2012 by Haymarket Books
PO Box 180165
Chicago, IL 60618
www.haymarketbooks.org
773-583-7884

ISBN: 978-1-60846-148-6

Trade distribution:
In the US, Consortium Book Sales and Distribution, www.cbsd.com
In Canada, Publishers Group Canada, www.pgcbooks.ca
In the UK, Turnaround Publisher Services, www.turnaround-uk.com
In Australia, Palgrave Macmillan, www.palgravemacmillan.com.au
All other countries, Publishers Group Worldwide, www.pgw.com

Cover design by Ragina Johnson.
Cover image of devastated land in Burin in the West Bank. Zuma Wire Photo.

Published with the generous support of Lannan Foundation and the Wallace Global Fund.

Printed in the United States by union labor on FSC certified paper stock.

Library of Congress cataloging-in-publication data is available.

10 9 8 7 6 5 4 3 2 1

SUSTAINABLE FORESTRY INITIATIVE

Certified Sourcing
www.sfiprogram.org
SFI-01234

Contents

To the memory of Oded (Odik) Pilavsky—a comrade and friend

Preface

In April 2010 I was approached by a well-known British left-wing publisher with a proposal to publish my political autobiography. This flattering offer put me in a quandary.

I am a carrier of what I consider to be a valuable corpus of socialist theory and political positions on Zionism and the Israeli-Palestinian conflict, elaborated by the group that I helped to found, the Socialist Organization in Israel, better known by the name of its journal, *Matzpen*. I felt duty bound to seize the opportunity of presenting these ideas to a wider public, particularly to a new generation of socialists. But would an autobiography be the right vehicle for transmitting the message I was keen to broadcast?

By definition, an autobiography is centered around the person of the writer. If I were to write such a narrative, my life story would have to be its main theme, into which the political substance that I wish to convey would have to be slotted as a series of add-on digressions. I suppose this could be contrived somehow, but it would be unsatisfactory. My life (so far) has been interesting, in the sense that I have done things in which I had passionate interest. But my life *story* has been less than dramatic: no cliff-hangers, no great escapes, no thrilling adventures, and I am happily married to the same woman I wed in my twentieth year. I lack the talent of a fiction writer needed to embellish this tale—as some of the autobiographers whose creations I have read (and one or two I have reviewed) did to great effect. As for the political substance: it would have to be presented in a cursory manner, inadequate to its complexity.

My dilemma was happily resolved when, about four months later, I was contacted by Haymarket Books with an offer to publish a collection of my essays and articles on the Israeli-Palestinian conflict. This book is the outcome.

As I have said, the ideas, theoretical analyses, and political statements presented here are collective products of a remarkable group, Matzpen, the importance of whose heritage is disproportionate to its small size. I am not trying to hide my light under a bushel: I believe I played a significant part in producing, elaborating, and formulating these ideas, and especially in arguing publicly for them. But that is what it was: a *part* in a group dialectic, inconceivable without this collective matrix.

Matzpen was formed in 1962.* The impetus for this had little to do with the Israeli-Palestinian conflict; rather, it was a resolve to break away from the Stalinist tradition and launch an independent radical socialist organization. In this respect we were, without first realizing it, part of a 1960s-era world movement of socialist regeneration. In the early years, our main activity was propaganda for promoting workers' rights by the creation of genuine trade unions, outside the corporatist-bureaucratic stranglehold of the Histadrut.

Of course, being consistent socialists, we were anti-Zionists. But it took us some time to elaborate an independent detailed analysis of Zionism and the Israeli-Arab conflict. Fortunately, we had breathing space to do so. The early formative years of Matzpen happened to fall within a period in which the Israeli-Arab conflict was at its most quiescent: between the immediate aftermath of the 1956 Suez war and the June war of 1967. So we were able to deliberate over these issues rather than being forced to react off the cuff to a fast-moving reality under the pressure of current events.

By the time the catastrophic 1967 war broke out, we were equipped with conceptual weapons for confronting it and its consequences. Our analysis can be summarized in the following four points:

1. Zionism is a colonizing project, and Israel, its embodiment, is a settler state. The core of the Israeli-Arab conflict is the clash between Zionist colonization and the indigenous people, the Palestinian Arabs.

   This did not require great perspicacity; it was a straightforward observation of evident facts. Nevertheless, it is remarkable how few people in the West see things in these terms even today. In the Israel of the mid-1960s, Matzpen was alone in expressing this view explicitly and clearly. (The Israeli Communist Party avoided using such terms as "Zionist colonization," and confined the brunt of its critique of Zionism to the latter's alignment with Western imperialism against the Soviet Union.)

2. We pointed out that Zionist colonization belongs to a different species from, for example, that of South Africa and Algeria: rather than being based on exploiting the labor power of the indigenous people, it sought to exclude and eliminate them.

   This observation—which has profound implications regarding the nature of the conflict and its eventual resolution—came quite naturally to us, as Marxists. It was of course obvious to the Palestinian victims of Zionist colonization, and was noted also by many of their Arab and third-world supporters. But it eludes many thinkers and activists whose

---

* For material in English relating to Matzpen, see its website at http://matzpen.org/index.asp?p=100. A short history is at http://matzpen.org/index.asp?p=140.

attitude to colonialism is *purely* moral: for example, those who regard it as a *consequence* or *manifestation* of racism rather than the other way around. For many years we were virtually alone in Israel and the West in stressing the fundamental significance of this feature of Zionist colonization. In recent years it has been picked up by some academic critics of Zionism, but most of them have failed to recognize or admit that we had long anticipated them.

3. We insisted on the regional context of the Israeli-Palestinian conflict. Due to the specific features of Zionist colonization, the balance of power is heavily tilted in favor of Israel (backed by its imperialist sponsor) and against the Palestinian people. The imbalance could only be redressed, and Palestinian liberation would become possible, as part of a revolutionary transformation of the region, by an Arab revolution led by the working class, which would overthrow the repressive regimes, unify the Arab East, and put an end to imperialist domination over it.

   We were not alone in holding this view: it was shared by leftists in the Palestinian resistance movement. However, as reaction strengthened its hold on the Arab world from the 1970s, many people who initially looked forward to an Arab revolution lost hope and sought shortcuts—which, predictably, proved to be illusory—to resolving the Palestinian problem. We remained rather isolated in clinging to the revolutionary regional perspective.

   But very recently, while I was putting together the present book, the eruption of a revolutionary tempest in the Arab world has lent much greater credibility to our regional perspective. I shall return to this point below.

4. Our regional view of the Israeli-Palestinian conflict applied not only to the *process* whereby it would be resolved but extended also to the *form of the resolution itself.* Unlike almost all who addressed the issue, we did not believe that a resolution would occur within the confines of Palestine (established by the British imperialists and their French allies following the First World War). Thus, we did not advocate a so-called two-state solution in a repartitioned Palestine, nor a "one-state solution" in a unitary Palestine. Instead, we envisaged incorporation of the two national groups—the Palestinian Arabs and the Hebrews (so-called Israeli Jews)—as units with equal rights within a socialist regional union or federation of the Arab East.

◆ ◆ ◆

This book contains a selection of essays, articles, statements, and short pieces written by me, or cowritten with my comrades, over some four and a half decades, between 1966 and 2010. Inevitably, during this long and eventful period, the original ideas and insights outlined above have evolved and been modified in response to changing reality, as well as in the light of further reflection. The items are presented here as they were published originally, except for minor stylistic editing. They represent my opinions at the time of writing; and I would certainly put some things differently today, with the benefit of hindsight as well as second thoughts. Some polemical pieces may perhaps seem too acerbic after the passage of time.

Nevertheless, I believe that the reader will find a fair degree of overall consistency and continuity. Indeed, I must apologize for the fact that some items, written at very different times, overlap in content and argumentation. This is unavoidable and even deliberate: each item included in this collection, even if it repeats some ideas presented in earlier items, also contains some new arguments or analyses that would make little sense if presented on their own, in isolation from their context.

The opening item is a brief personal statement, in which I distance myself from the widespread belief—held even by many whom I regard as political allies, if not as close comrades—that the Israeli-Palestinian conflict can be addressed primarily in terms of war and peace: war is what we have now, and peace, to be achieved by a genuine "peace process," is what we need to have. This apparently innocent belief serves as ideological camouflage: it presents in symmetric terms a conflict that is profoundly asymmetric. It disguises the reality of the issue: a confrontation between past and ongoing Zionist colonization and the Israeli settler state on one side, and the indigenous Palestinian Arab people on the other.

Insistence on the colonial nature of the conflict, and elaboration of its specific features, is a leitmotif that runs through the entire book.

The remaining articles are grouped into parts by theme. Part I consists of fairly brief items expressing the Matzpen position on the Palestinian struggle, viewed in a regional context. They are arranged chronologically except for the first item: my obituary of Jabra Nicola, which is put first in acknowledgment of his important influence on what follows. The oldest item in this part dates from shortly before the 1967 war and the last substantive item was written in 1988; so the reader can assess both the continuity and the evolution in Matzpen's views over those two decades.

The items within each of the following parts are in chronological order. Part II is concerned with Hebrew (Israeli-Jewish) society. A specific feature of the type of colonization based on excluding and displacing the indigenous people (rather than exploiting their labor power) is the formation of a new settler nation. Zionist colonization is no exception to this rule. However, it has a unique feature: Zionist ideology denies the fact that a new Hebrew nation has come into existence because its self-legitimation depends on the fiction that all Jews around the world are one nation that has an eternal national right over its ancient god-promised and god-given homeland, Eretz Yisrael.

Uri Avnery, a journalist who published and edited a popular journal, *Ha'olam Hazeh* (This World), was strongly influenced by a group of intellectuals who called themselves the Young Hebrews (also known as "Canaanites," a term of mild abuse conferred on them by their Zionist critics). Founded in 1939, they denied the Zionist myth of a worldwide Jewish "nation," advocated recognition of the reality of a new

Hebrew nation, and preached a new Hebrew nationalism of a decidedly right-wing tinge. Avnery adopted their Hebrew nationalism—which of course challenged Zionism on a crucial ideological tenet—but discarded the extreme right-wing elements of their outlook. Whereas the Young Hebrews looked forward to Hebrew domination of the entire region (whose inhabitants were to be assimilated into this new nation, as they were allegedly devoid of any national identity of their own), Avnery and his co-thinkers looked forward to integration of Israel in the Arab East. Avnery also actively promoted equality of rights for Israel's Arab citizens. In 1965, he founded a new movement, and ran for the Knesset, Israel's parliament. Members of Matzpen participated as individuals in this movement, because we approved of its rejection, however partial, of Zionism, its regional outlook, and its support of equal rights.

The first two items in part II are concerned with that episode of cooperation. They make it clear why it was inevitably short-lived. The third item, dating from 1970 to 71, is a general analysis of Israeli society. It is perhaps the best known of all essays originating from Matzpen: it has been reprinted and circulated widely in several versions. Although outdated in several fundamental respects, it seems to me of sufficient historical interest to be reproduced here.

One of the facts pointed out in this analysis is the large overlap between the Hebrew working class and the Israeli Mizrahim (immigrants from mostly Muslim Asian and African countries). This aspect of Israeli society is taken up in the last item of part II. Written more than thirty-eight years later, it revisits the position of the Mizrahim in Israel and argues against the identity ideology that addresses this issue primarily as a manifestation of Zionism's Orientalist attitude.

Part III addresses the complex issues of racism and the national question in the specific context of the Israeli settler state. As a rule, colonization projects practice racism against the indigenous people and use racist ideology for self-legitimation. At the same time, the national identity of the latter is also suppressed. Zionist colonization is no exception to this rule. The second item in part III attempts to clarify the analytic difference between these two types of oppression and the way they are combined in the concrete reality of Israel.

Another aspect of the national problem arises from the crucial specific feature of Zionist colonization pointed out in point 2 above. As a rule, where the indigenous people were excluded and displaced, rather than being used as the main source of exploitable labor power, the settlers emerged as a new nation. Israel is again no exception (although, as mentioned above, Zionist ideology denies the fact that a new Hebrew nation has come into existence). The first and third items in part III argue that resolution of the Israeli-Palestinian conflict would be impossible without recognizing this fact. Following the overthrow of Zionism, the Hebrew nation must be accorded due national rights within a regional union.

Part IV is entitled "Polemics against Zionism." The brand of Zionism addressed is for the most part what is commonly known as "socialist" or "left-wing" Zionism. Except for four early items, the bulk of the material in this part, including two fairly long essays, were originally written for publication outside Israel. The reason for this is that, while "left-wing" Zionism was rapidly losing ground in Israeli politics, its ideology was still being used by the Zionist propaganda machine abroad. It had some appeal among leftists in Europe and the United States, and we saw it as our duty to confront that propaganda and enlighten the international left as to the true nature of the Zionist project and Israel. Today most of the radical left around the world is much more critical of Israeli policies and of Zionist ideology than it used to be. But battles against regressive ideologies are rarely won once and for all; they have to be refought again and again. So the material in this part can be of more than archival interest.

Part V contains book reviews written at various times since 1987. Each of them is included for a specific reason, to make some particular point. Thus, for example, the review of the book by Ze'ev Schiff and Ehud Ya'ari exposes the changes made in the English translation from the original Hebrew, to suit the convenience of Zionist propaganda abroad. The review of the book by Greg Philo and Mike Berry will, I hope, make this invaluable report of media research more widely known and read. My review of Michel Warschawski's book serves to set the record straight on the history of Matzpen and other factual and political issues.

Part VI is entitled "Final Analysis," not because it has any claim to real finality— no such thing is possible—but simply because it sums up much of the foregoing. It contains my most recent elaboration of points 1–4 outlined above. Unlike the items in earlier parts, the three items here were planned as a sequence: the second item was intended to be read as a sequel to the first, and the third item was meant to round off the analysis.

When I started putting together the material for this collection, on the one hand I felt like a Cassandra: my comrades and I were pretty accurate in foretelling the moves made by the forces of oppression, we expected the worst from their side, and we warned against trusting in illusory "peace processes" manipulated by them. But few people believed our predictions. On the other hand, I was disappointed by what appeared to be the failure of the forces of our side, those of progressive transformation and regional revolution, to manifest themselves as we had expected and predicted. While never losing faith in the ultimate victory of the forces of progress, and eventually of socialism, I felt that this was a vision for the very long term.

This somewhat wistful mood changed while I was still busy gathering the material for this book, with the eruption of the Arab revolution, which seemed to presage the developments that our theoretical analysis had pointed toward.

Of course, it would be very naïve to expect the present upheaval to lead to a decisive victory of the revolution in the near future. Setbacks and counterrevolutionary reactions are most likely. But a victorious Arab revolution is no longer an abstract projection: the events of the Arab Awakening of 2011 make it a tangible potentiality. And these events also demonstrate the necessary connection between the revolutionary liberation of the masses of the region and the decline and eventual demise of imperialist hegemony over it.

1

Why I Am Not
an Israeli Peace Activist

As the desultory "peace process" meanders from pointless appointment to meaningless meeting between heads of the Israeli settler state and the authority-less Palestinian Authority, with the United States playing the part of dishonest broker, there can no longer be any lingering doubt that this is a charade staged by charlatans.

But behind and beyond this fairly obvious confidence trick there is a much more subtle deception or self-deception: it is widely assumed—even taken for granted—that "peace" is what it would take to resolve the Israeli-Palestinian conflict. In other words: that what is needed is a genuine peace process instead of the present fake one.

This belief is held by almost all decent enlightened Israelis (the so-called Israeli left)—which is why they refer to themselves collectively as "the peace camp" and individually as "peace activists"—and it is shared by their friends and supporters in the West.

The "left" Zionists of Peace Now as well as the "soft" Zionists and semi-Zionists of Gush Shalom (the Peace Bloc) display this self-deception on their name tags. The non-Zionist Stalinist-turned-reformist Israeli CP insists on giving top prominence to peace slogans. Many of the activities in which these good people engage are highly commendable: dissent from oppressive policies and actions of the Israeli authorities, and in particular opposition to the post-1967 occupation. Some of them show real moral and physical courage in various acts of solidarity with the oppressed Palestinians.

Nevertheless, their self-description as "peace activists" reveals a profound misapprehension of the nature of the Israeli-Palestinian conflict and a delusion as to how it might be resolved. The image it evokes is essentially symmetric: two sides, two nations, at war with each other, locked in a series of battles over a piece of disputed turf. To end the conflict, the two sides need to end the war, sit down together, and make peace.

This article was originally published in *Weekly Worker* 836, October 7, 2010.

In fact, this is also the image promoted by Israeli *hasbarah* (propaganda). It likes to speak the symmetric language of "war" and "peace." Thus, Israel and its friends describe the assault on Gaza in the winter of 2008–09, code-named Operation Cast Lead, as a "war."[1] In reality, it was not a war: there was virtually no fighting. It was a one-sided massacre. Similarly, Israeli diplomacy insists on referring to the territories seized by Israel in 1967 as "disputed"—a deliberately symmetric description—rather than *occupied*.

As for peace: none wish for it more ardently than most of Israel's leaders. I am saying this with hardly a trace of irony. It is the truth. Only very few people—psychopaths, arms dealers, and other war profiteers, as well as some cynical careerist demagogues and military officers eager for fast-track promotion—actually prefer war per se to any kind of peace. I suppose that a few Israeli political and military leaders do belong to each of these exceptional categories. But most Israeli leaders genuinely wish for peace—peace on Israel's terms: their cherished wish is that the Palestinian people, dispossessed and subjugated, would peacefully accept their lot and give up the struggle.

Colonial Conflict

The key to a proper understanding of the conflict is that it is an extremely asymmetric one: between settlers-colonizers and the indigenous people. It is about dispossession and oppression. As was the case in other colonial conflicts, the Israeli-Palestinian conflict has involved real wars between Israel and the neighboring states; but these were spin-offs, consequences of the fundamental cause: the Zionist colonization of Palestine. As this colonization proceeds and expands, Israel will need to maintain its regional hegemony as Western imperialism's local subcontractor, and new wars will no doubt be provoked.

In colonial conflicts, the colonizers always regard themselves as coming in peace, bearing the gifts of enlightenment and progress. It is the benighted natives who are the aggressors, resorting to violence against their benefactors. This compels the colonizers to use their superior force in order to put down the native aggressors.[2] The latter have only themselves to blame.

I suppose this is the kind of thing my late friend, the socialist poet Erich Fried, had in mind when he wrote this poem:

Clean Sweep

The causes
now fight
their effects,

so that one can no longer
hold them
responsible for the effects;

for even
to make them responsible
is part of the effects

and effects are forbidden
and punished
by the causes themselves.

They do not wish
any longer
to know about such effects.

Anyone who sees
how diligently
they pursue the effects

and still says
that they are
closely connected with them

will now have to
blame
only himself.

While the colonizers' aim is to impose peace—on their own terms and, if necessary, by force—the indigenous people tend to have a rather different view of the matter. Their concern is not to make peace with their dispossessors but to resist being dispossessed. To this end they often need to come bearing not peace but the sword.

This is why one would be hard put to find peace activists among the Native Americans or Australian Aborigines resisting colonization in the nineteenth century, or among Algerian liberation fighters or anti-apartheid militants in the twentieth century.

Of course, the Israeli peace activists do not support *all* the harsh "peace" terms that their government wishes to impose on the Palestinian people. (Although some of them do not object to some of these unequal terms.) But by their reductive definition of the issue as being all about peace, they knowingly or unwittingly accept a point of view biased in favor of the colonizers.

This biased viewpoint is inconsistent with internationalism. So Israeli self-proclaimed peace activists cannot be genuine socialists. Israeli socialists, whether Hebrew or Arab, fight against the Zionist project and its practices: colonization, dispossession, discrimination, and for equal rights and universal liberation.

Peace will be an outcome of liberation, not its starting point.

Part I

THE PALESTINIAN STRUGGLE AND THE ARAB EAST; JABRA NICOLA AND HIS HERITAGE

2

Comrade Jabra Nicola (1912–74)

On December 25, 1974, Comrade Jabra Nicola passed away following a long illness. He died, at age sixty-three, of cerebral hemorrhage in his home in London.

Jabra was born in Haifa. At the beginning of the 1930s he joined the Palestine Communist Party and soon became a leading member of the party. He grew critical of Stalinism, which at the time totally dominated the international communist movement. The first impetus for this came from an article by Trotsky against the catastrophic Stalinist policy regarding Germany. An Arabic translation of that article appeared in an Egyptian paper, and so came to Jabra's notice. This is how he was attracted to the Trotskyist outlook, which he upheld to the end of his life.

At the outbreak of the Second World War, Jabra was arrested [by the British Mandate authorities] together with other communist activists, and imprisoned in an administrative detention camp as "suspected of sympathizing with the enemy." This was bitterly ironic because right from the beginning of the war Jabra was for supporting the antifascist side—contrary to the position of the official communist movement, as well as to that of most Trotskyists. Following the Hitlerite invasion of the Soviet Union, the communist detainees, including Jabra, were released.

In the 1940s Jabra officially joined the Trotskyist Fourth International, and eventually became a member of its leadership. The position of the world Trotskyist movement on the problems of the Middle East was formed largely under his influence. At the same time he remained a member of the Communist Party. Although he did not keep his Trotskyist views secret, the leaders of the party—intellectual Lilliputians compared to him—did not dare expel him. But they gradually removed him from all positions of direct political influence and confined him to literary work. Even subject to this restriction, Jabra found an outlet for his talents: he published important

This obituary was published in *Matzpen* 73, March–April 1975. Translated from the Hebrew by the author.

articles and studies on Arab history and Arabic literature, as well as translating literary classics into Arabic. He was particularly proud of his translation of Tolstoy's *Kreutzer Sonata*.

In the beginning of 1963, Jabra came across one of the early issues of *Matzpen* (which started publication in the autumn of 1962); this soon led to contacts between us and him. It transpired that his views and ours had much in common, and he began to draw close to our organization. His first article in *Matzpen* (about the situation in Iraq following the coup of Abd as-Salam Arif) was published in issue number 5, in April 1963. Jabra started to collaborate closely with our organization, and formally joined it at the end of 1963.

Jabra had a major profound influence on the direction taken by Matzpen, especially regarding the Arab East and Zionism. On this, I take the liberty of quoting from an interview I gave in 1972 to the Italian journal *Quaderni del Medio Oriente*.

> He was much older than us, the founders of the group: about twenty to twenty-five years older. He had gone through the earlier thirty years of the history of the world revolutionary movement, but was not soiled with all the Stalinist shit. He remembered from his own experience things we knew only from books. In particular, a vital period of the Zionist colonization process was for him a living memory. But more important than this: he had exactly what we lacked—a coherent conception of the Zionist colonization process, and in particular the way it affected the Arab society in Palestine. From him we got a much better and deeper understanding of Israel as an embodiment of Zionist colonization. Also, he had a conception of the Arab revolution as one and indivisible process. Matzpen's positions on all these matters were adopted essentially under his influence. Some of his points we adopted almost at once, because we saw immediately that they were plausible. Other points we accepted after a longer period, with some modifications, perhaps. Of course, it was not a mechanical or completely one-sided process but a dialectical one. Anyway, his influence is clearly discernible in practically all our documents on Zionism and the Arab East.

I thought it right to quote these words, precisely because they were not said after his death, but when he was still alive; moreover, they were said shortly after a painful split, in which we found ourselves on different sides.

Jabra's thinking was always remarkable for its independence, originality, and consistency. He was not in the habit of deferring to intellectual authority, not even that of people he most respected and esteemed. Let me note briefly his main views on the Arab East—views that he instilled in many people in this country, in the region, and around the world.

First, as mentioned above, he instilled in us the view of the unity of the Arab revolution. This unity is twofold: in both time and place.

Unity in time, because he resolutely rejected the idea that the Arab revolution must go through two separate stages, a bourgeois-democratic stage followed only later by a separate socialist stage. His profound historical analysis of the Arab world showed that in this region, unlike Europe, there did not exist and had not developed in the past a bourgeois class *distinct* from the big landlords, which alone could lead the bourgeois-democratic revolution in a struggle against the feudal landlords. Regional and global conditions prevailing in our time no longer allow the rise of a *progressive* bourgeoisie able to carry out the classical tasks of the bourgeois revolution. Therefore these tasks too are left for the socialist revolution, led by the working class.

Unity in place, because the Arabs throughout the Arab East are one nation in the process of crystallization, but divided by imperialism following the First World War, whose unification is vital for the advancement and development of the region. This national unification is one of the democratic tasks that the bourgeoisie is unable to carry out, and so it too remains as a mission of the socialist revolution. On this issue, the unity of the Arab East, Jabra kept alive the tradition of the revolutionary movement prior to the Stalinist degeneration, and was a link between it and revolutionaries of the present generation.

Second, Jabra was uncompromisingly an internationalist. One of the expressions of his internationalism was his staunch support for the right of the Israeli-Jewish people to self-determination. In his and our view, the regional socialist revolution will overthrow the Zionist regime, and integrate the Israeli people as a partner in the future united socialist state of the Arab East. However, this partnership must not and cannot come about through national coercion by the Arab majority against the Israeli-Jewish minority, but only through free choice and self-determination. Jabra fought like a lion for this principle (which was not popular among the majority of the Arab left) and absolutely insisted on including the recognition of the right of the region's non-Arab peoples to self-determination as one of the pillars of the program of the socialist Arab revolution.

Third, he criticized mercilessly all manifestations of opportunism of the left in the region. In particular, he often stressed the need to wage a vigorous struggle of ideas against the reactionary influence of religion and for women's liberation. He severely criticized the majority of the Arab left, which behaves hesitantly and opportunistically on these two interconnected issues.

Of course, these few remarks cannot possibly exhaust Jabra's world outlook. We have mentioned only those issues that he regarded as most important for the revolution in our region.

◆ ◆ ◆

Jabra was not a complaisant person; he was stubborn and uncompromising. Nevertheless, he maintained fruitful and comradely collaboration even with people with whom he had serious disagreements. When he joined our organization, we knew he belonged to the Trotskyist Fourth International, while we had no wish to join that international. Any worries that his membership in our organization could lead to a conflict of divided loyalties proved to be unfounded. Jabra always put the good of the revolutionary endeavor above all else, especially above narrow organizational interest. He was absolutely untainted by the slightest smidgen of manipulativeness and uncomradely intrigue. In all my political life I have never met anyone more honest, politically and personally.

His death is a heavy loss to the revolutionary movement in this country, in the region, and the world, and a hard blow to those who knew him closely. But his ideas have become inalienable assets of an important part of the revolutionary socialist movement; and through them he will live posthumously.

3

The Palestine Problem
and the Israeli-Arab Conflict

he nineteenth anniversary of the establishment of the State of Israel will occur
this month. During these nineteen years the Israeli-Arab conflict has not come
nearer to a solution. The Palestine problem is still an open wound in the body of
the Middle East: an incessant source of bloodshed, suffering, and wrongs; a heavy
burden on the economic resources of the region; a pretext for imperialist aggression
and military intervention; and a grave threat to world peace.

Especially grave is the state of the Palestinian Arabs—the direct victims of the
1948 war and of the collusion between "the friendly enemies," Ben-Gurion and
Abdullah. The majority of Palestine's Arabs were dispossessed of their homes and
fields during and after the 1948 war, and have since been living as refugees, in
suffering and distress, outside Israel. The leaders of Israel emphatically refuse to recognize their elementary right to be repatriated. The Arabs who were left in Israel
are victims of severe economic, civil, and national oppression.

During these nineteen years, Israel has been an isolated island in the Middle
East, a state that is independent only in the formal sense, being economically and
politically dependent on the imperialist powers, especially the United States. It has
continually served as a tool of these powers against the Arab nation, against the
progressive forces in the Arab world. The clearest manifestation (but not the only
one) of this role of official Israeli policy was in 1956, when the Israeli government

---

This statement was written jointly with Jabra Nicola and adopted by Matzpen as its official position in
early May 1967, before the beginning of the 1967 crisis. It was read at a public meeting held in Paris
on May 18, 1967, sponsored by Arab and Palestinian student organizations. The meeting was reported
in *Le Monde* on May 20, 1967. The statement, first published in *World Outlook*, May 18, 1967, has
been revised to correct minor stylistic errors and replace "dispute" with "conflict," which is a better translation of the original Hebrew.

joined Anglo-French imperialism in an aggressive collusion against Egypt, and even furnished these powers with a pretext for military intervention.

The state of war and hostility between Israel and her Arab neighbors has continued for nineteen years, and Israel's Zionist leadership has no real prospect of changing this situation. Israeli policy is a cul-de-sac.

The present economic crisis in Israel, which has caused grave unemployment of the workers and great hardship to the popular masses, also serves to underline the fact that Israel cannot long continue to exist in its present form, as a Zionist state, cut off from the region in which it is located.

Thus, the present state of affairs is against the interests of the Arab masses: Israel, in its present form, constitutes a grave obstacle for the struggle of these masses against imperialism and for a socialist Arab unity. The continuation of the present state of affairs is also against the interests of the Israeli masses.

The Israeli Socialist Organization, in whose ranks are both Arabs and Jews, holds that the Palestine problem and the Israeli-Arab conflict can and should be solved in a socialist and internationalist way, taking into consideration the unique features of this complex problem. This is not an ordinary conflict between two nations. Therefore it is not enough to call for coexistence based on mutual recognition of the just national rights of the two peoples.

The State of Israel is the outcome of the colonization of Palestine by the Zionist movement, at the expense of the Arab people and under the auspices of imperialism. In its present Zionist form, Israel is also a tool for the continuation of "the Zionist endeavor." The Arab world cannot acquiesce in the existence in its midst of a Zionist state, whose declared purpose is not to serve as a political expression of its own population but as a bridgehead, a political instrument and a destination for Jewish immigration from all over the world. Israel's Zionist character is also opposed to the true interests of the Israeli masses, because it means constant dependence of the country upon external forces.

We therefore hold that a solution of the problem necessitates the de-Zionization of Israel. The State of Israel must undergo a deep revolutionary change that will transform it from a Zionist state (i.e., a state of the Jews all over the world) into a socialist state that represents the interests of the masses who live in it. In particular, the Law of Return (which grants every Jew in the world an absolute and automatic right to immigrate to Israel and become a citizen) must be abolished. Each request to immigrate to Israel will then be decided separately on its own merits, without any discrimination of a racial or religious nature.

The Palestine Arab refugee problem is the most painful part of the Israeli-Arab conflict. We therefore hold that every refugee who wants to return to Israel must be enabled to do so; he should then obtain full economic and social rehabilitation. Those refugees who will freely choose not to be repatriated should be fully compensated for loss of property and for the personal suffering they have endured.

In addition, all the laws and regulations aimed at discriminating against and oppressing the Arab population of Israel and expropriating its lands must be abolished. All expropriations and damages (to land, property, and person) caused under these laws and regulations must be fully compensated.

The de-Zionization of Israel implies also putting an end to the Zionist foreign policy, which serves imperialism. Israel must take an active part in the struggle of the Arabs against imperialism and for the establishment of a socialist Arab unity.

The Zionist colonization of Palestine differs in one basic respect from the colonization of other countries: whereas in other countries the settlers established their economy upon the exploitation of the labor of the indigenous inhabitants, the colonization of Palestine was carried out through the replacement and expulsion of the indigenous population.

This fact has caused a unique complication of the Palestine problem. As a result of Zionist colonization, a Hebrew nation with its own national characteristics (common language, separate economy, etc.) has been formed in Palestine. Moreover, this nation has a capitalist class structure—it is divided into exploiters and exploited, a bourgeoisie and a proletariat.

The argument that this nation has been formed artificially and at the expense of the indigenous Arab population does not change the fact that the Hebrew nation now exists. It would be a disastrous error to ignore this fact.

The solution of the Palestine problem must not only redress the wrong done to the Palestinian Arabs, but also ensure the national future of the Hebrew masses. These masses were brought to Palestine by Zionism—but they are not responsible for the deeds of Zionism. The attempt to penalize the Israeli workers and popular masses for the sins of Zionism cannot solve the Palestinian problem but will only bring about new misfortunes.

Those nationalist Arab leaders who call for a jihad for the liberation of Palestine ignore the fact that even if Israel would be defeated militarily and cease to exist as a state, the Hebrew nation will still exist. If the problem of the existence of this nation is not solved correctly, a situation of dangerous and prolonged national conflict will be re-created, which will cause endless bloodshed and suffering and will serve as a new pretext for imperialist intervention. It is no coincidence that the leaders who advocate such a "solution" are also not capable of solving the Kurdish problem.

In addition it should be understood that the Israeli masses will not be liberated from the influence of Zionism and will not struggle against it unless the progressive forces in the Arab world present them with a prospect of coexistence without national oppression. The Israeli Socialist Organization therefore holds that a true solution of the Palestine problem necessitates the recognition of the right of the Hebrew nation to self-determination.

Self-determination does not necessarily mean separation. On the contrary, we hold that a small country such as Israel, which is poor in natural resources, cannot exist as a separate entity. It is faced with two alternatives only—to continue to depend on foreign powers or to integrate itself in a regional union.

It follows that the only solution consistent with the interests of both Arab and Israeli masses is the integration of Israel as a unit in an economic and political union of the Middle East, on the basis of socialism. In such a framework the Hebrew nation will be able to carry on its own national and cultural life without endangering the Arab world and without a threat to its own existence by the Arabs. The forces of the Israeli masses will join those of the Arab masses in a common struggle for progress and prosperity.

We therefore hold that the Palestine problem—like other central problems of the Middle East—can only be solved in the framework of a Middle Eastern union. Theoretical analysis and practical experience alike show that Arab unity can be formed and exist in a stable way only if it has a socialist character.

One can therefore sum up the solution that we propose by the formula: de-Zionization of Israel and its integration in a socialist Middle Eastern union. We hold that the problem of the political future of the Palestinian Arabs should also be solved within the framework described above.

There are people who think that justice necessitates the establishment of a special Palestinian Arab political entity. Our view is that this question must be decided by the Palestinian Arabs, without outside interference. However, we think that it would be a grave error to pose the problem of the political future of the Palestinian Arabs separately from and independently of the question of socialist Arab union. At present the Palestinian Arabs are in the first ranks of the struggle for unity. If they were to be presented with a separate and independent aim, the cause of Arab unity may suffer grave damage. Also, the establishment of a small separate Arab state is not consistent with the interests of the Arab nation, including the Palestinian Arab people.

We therefore hold that if the Palestinian Arabs decide in favor of establishing a political entity of their own, the necessary political and territorial arrangements should be made within the framework of establishing a socialist union of the Middle East. The countries that now hold parts of the territory of Palestine—Israel, Jordan, and Egypt—should particularly contribute to such a settlement.

We call upon the revolutionary socialist forces in the Arab countries and in other countries to consider our present program and to start a wide discussion aimed at working out a common position on the problems of the Middle East.

4

Palestinian Struggle and Middle East Revolution

The Middle East is approaching a crossroads. The four great powers are conferring in an attempt to reach an agreed "solution," which they will then proceed to impose on the inhabitants of the region, and which they hope will restore the stability that was shaken by the June 1967 war and its aftermath. Our aim here is to analyze the dangers that wait at this crossroads and that threaten the future of the revolution in the Middle East.

A new force has appeared on the Middle Eastern political stage: the Palestinians. True, they had taken action into their own hands a few years before the June war, but the real impetus came only afterwards. But now Palestinian action has transformed a struggle formerly between governments into a mass struggle. For nearly twenty years the Palestinians had been an object of history, passively awaiting salvation by the Arab states in general, or by the "progressive" Arab states, in particular Nasser's Egypt.

The 1948 war exposed the bankruptcy of the old middle-class and landowners' leadership of the Arab national movement. As a result, a new leadership—petit bourgeois in class—came to the forefront; it overthrew the old regime in several Arab countries and scored considerable successes in the anti-imperialist struggle.

But the June 1967 war revealed the limitations of this leadership: limitations resulting from its class nature and its nationalist ideology. Among other things it proved its total inability to solve the Palestinian question. Despite Soviet support, Nasserism and Ba'athism are in a state of political bankruptcy.

This article, cowritten with A. Sa'id (Jabra Nicola), originated as a position paper adopted by Matzpen. It was first published under a somewhat different title ("The Struggle in Palestine Must Lead to Arab Revolution"), and without the one-paragraph preamble, in the *Black Dwarf* 14, no. 19 (June 14, 1969). A Hebrew version under the present title was published in *Matzpen* in August 1969.

The emergence of this new political and military force is a positive phenomenon, but within it are dangerous and negative trends. Some sections of the movement have adopted the view that the Palestinian masses can and should "go it alone" and solve their problem by themselves, in separation from the all-Arab revolutionary struggle. They present the problem solely as a Palestinian one, which can be solved in a purely Palestinian framework. The old passivity risks being replaced by a narrow localist attitude. The only help that is demanded from the rest of the Arab world is aid to the Palestinian front itself. This attitude disregards the connection between the Palestinian struggle and the struggle in the Arab world as a whole, and it therefore advocates "non-intervention in the internal affairs of the Arab states."

The Arab governments encourage this attitude. The very mobilization of the masses in the Arab countries—even if only for the Palestinian cause—threatens the existing regimes. These regimes therefore wish to isolate the Palestinian struggle and to leave it entirely to the Palestinians. The Arab governments—both reactionary and "progressive"—are trying to buy stability for their regimes with a ransom to the Palestinian organizations. Moreover, the governments want to use this financial aid to direct the Palestinian struggle along their own politically convenient lines, to manipulate it and to utilize it merely as a means of bargaining for a political solution acceptable to them. The Egyptian, Syrian, and Jordanian governments are mainly interested in regaining the territories they lost in the June war (thereby regaining their lost prestige and consolidating their authority) while the Palestinian cause is, from their point of view, only secondary, a means rather than an aim. This is what the Arab governments mean when they call for "liquidating the results of aggression."

The four great powers are now meeting to reach an agreed solution that will then be imposed on the region. If the Arab governments achieve their aim through this solution, they will be prepared to desert the Palestinians, and even take an active part in a political and physical liquidation of the Palestinian movement. The four powers will probably insist on this as a condition for a political settlement.

As the consequences of the 1948 war provided the background for the downfall of the old national leadership in the Arab world and for the emergence of the petit bourgeois leadership—so the consequences of the 1967 war have set the stage for replacing this leadership by a new one, representing a new class. Since the propertied classes proved unable to solve the social, political, and national problems of the Arab world, it has become apparent that only the exploited masses themselves, under a working-class leadership, are capable of solving their historic problems. But the existence of suitable objective conditions does not mean that this new leadership will automatically emerge. For this further requires a subjective factor—a political organization with a revolutionary theory and a revolutionary all-Arab strategy.

However, it is precisely this need for political work and for an all-Arab revolutionary strategy that is explicitly rejected by some important sectors of the Palestinian movement. They advocate confinement of the struggle to the Palestinian front alone and its limitation to armed operations without a political program.

But the balance of forces, as well as theoretical considerations, show the impossibility of confining the struggle to one country.

What is the balance of forces? The Palestinian people are waging a battle where they confront Zionism, which is supported by imperialism; from the rear they are menaced by the Arab regimes and by Arab reaction, which is also supported by imperialism. As long as imperialism has a real stake in the Middle East, it is unlikely to withdraw its support for Zionism, its natural ally, and to permit its overthrow; it will defend it to the last drop of Arab oil. On the other hand, imperialist interests and domination in the region cannot be shattered without overthrowing those junior partners of imperialist exploitation, the ruling classes in the Arab world. The conclusion that must be drawn is not that the Palestinian people should wait quietly until imperialist domination is overthrown throughout the region but that it must rally to itself a wider struggle for the political and social liberation of the Middle East as a whole.

Just as it is impossible in practice to defeat Zionism without overthrowing imperialist domination throughout the region, so it is theoretically absurd to present formulas for solving the problem within the territory of Palestine alone. If one speaks about the situation existing before the overthrow of imperialism in the entire region— then the de-Zionization of Israel and the establishment of a Palestine without Zionism is quite impossible. And if one thinks of the situation after the overthrow of imperialism—then what is the sense of a formula that refers to Palestine alone, without taking into account the necessary changes that would take place in the whole region?

The formula that restricts itself to Palestine alone, despite its revolutionary appearance, derives from a reformist attitude that seeks partial solutions, within the framework of conditions now existing in the region. In fact, partial solutions can only be implemented through a compromise with imperialism and Zionism.

In addition, the solutions that are limited to Palestine cannot grapple successfully with the national problem. The formulas that speak of "an independent democratic Palestine all of whose citizens, irrespective of religion, will enjoy equal rights" have two defects. On the one hand, they imply the creation of a new separate "Palestinian" nation whose members do not differ from one another nationally but only by religion. The authors of these formulas are themselves aware of the absurdity of separating the Palestinians from the general Arab nation: they therefore hasten to add that "Palestine is part of the Arab fatherland." This looks suspiciously like the old slogan of "Arab Palestine" dressed up in new—and more nebulous—garb.

This attitude results from a misapprehension of the national problem in general and of Israeli reality in particular. It is true that the Jews living in Israel came to settle there under the influence and leadership of Zionism, and that they—as a community—have oppressed and are still oppressing the Palestinians.

But it is impossible to ignore the patent fact that today this community constitutes a national entity (which differs from world Jewry on the one hand, and from the Palestinian Arabs on the other) having its own language and economic and cultural life.

In order to solve the Palestinian problem, this community (or at least a substantial part of it) must be severed from the influence of Zionism and attracted to a joint struggle with the revolutionary forces in the Arab world for the national and social liberation of the entire region. But clearly this cannot be achieved by ignoring the existence of that community as a national entity.

This problem cannot be solved within the narrow framework of Palestine. If one is thinking of a democratic state pure and simple—"one man, one vote"—then in fact it will be a state with a Jewish majority, and there is nothing to prevent it from being like the present State of Israel, but having a larger territory and bigger Arab minority. If one is thinking of a binational state, then it will be an artificial creation separating the Palestinian Arabs from the rest of the Arab world and from the revolutionary process taking place in it. Besides, in a binational structure there are no inherent guarantees that one of the two national groups would not dominate the other. All this refers to proposed solutions that can be considered as feasible within the present condition of the Middle East, that is, which do not presuppose a comprehensive social revolution.

On the other hand, if one considers the situation that will exist after a victorious social revolution, after imperialism and Zionism are defeated, then there will not exist a separate Palestinian problem but rather the problem of the various national groups living within the Arab world (Kurds, Israeli Jews, South-Sudanese). This problem can only be solved by granting these nationalities the right to self-determination. Of course, recognition of the right to self-determination does not mean encouragement to separation; on the contrary, it provides the correct basis for integration without compulsion or repression. Moreover, self-determination in the Middle East is impossible so long as that region is under direct or indirect imperialist domination. It is possible only after the region is liberated, only after a victorious socialist revolution. In particular, this situation presupposes the overthrow of Zionism.

To sum up: the existing objective conditions enable and require the creation of a revolutionary mass movement, led by the working class, guided by a revolutionary Marxist theory and acting according to an all-Arab strategy that will recognize the national rights of the non-Arab nationalities living within the Arab world and is capable of attracting their masses to a common struggle for the national and social liberation of the entire region.

5

Arab Revolution and
National Problems in the Arab East

I t is not our intention in this article to discuss the national question in general,
or to develop the subject from first principles. Our general point of departure is
the revolutionary Marxist position on the national question. Moreover, we are here
concerned with this question only in so far as it is connected with the problematic
of the Arab socialist revolution; our main interest is the impact of the national question on the revolutionary movement in the Mashreq (Arab East).[1] The Arab East
has, in fact, not one but several intertwined national problems.

First of all, there is the national problem of the Arabs themselves, who constitute
the overwhelming majority of the population of that area. In addition, there are
the problems of the various non-Arab nationalities living there.

Let us start by analyzing the national problem of the majority—the Arab nation.
Only a small part of this nation is at present subject to direct foreign domination
and oppression: the Palestinian Arabs, living under Israeli occupation or exiled by
Israel. We shall return later to this aspect of the problem, which is of very great political importance although it involves directly only a small part of the Arab nation.
With the above-mentioned exception, the Mashreq has achieved political independence—but under conditions of extreme balkanization. *The national problem
of the Arab nation is thus primarily that of national unification.*

National unification is necessary not simply because the Arabs of the Mashreq
share a long common history, a language, and a cultural heritage. It is necessary primarily because the present political fragmentation of the Mashreq is a huge obstacle
in the way of development of the productive forces, and facilitates imperialist exploitation and domination. In fact, the Arab East was in the first place balkanized by the
imperialist powers, in their own interest. Dividing the region between them, they
were able more easily to dominate each part separately and use one part against an-

---

This article was cowritten with A. Sa'id (Jabra Nicola), and was published in the *International,* Summer 1973.

other. But from the point of view of economic development this fragmentation is an obstacle, because the various parts are mutually complementary, each lacking what the others possess in abundance. The main natural wealth of the region is oil. But most of the oil is concentrated in tiny and backward ministates with small populations. (Even Libya, which looks vast on the map, is really small; most of it is uninhabitable desert, and its population is about 1.5 million. The same is true of Saudi Arabia; although its population is about 6 million, this is in a country more than four times the size of France). These oil states are the most backward parts of the region, and have no economy to speak of other than that of oil. The huge oil revenues are shared between imperialism and a small ruling clique that spends its share on lavish luxuries. Hardly a penny of this fabulous wealth is invested in building up the local economy. (What the oil sheikhs do invest, they invest not locally but in the West). When finally the time comes when the oil reserves are exhausted, the oil states will remain without any sort of productive economy, like an oasis whose spring has dried up. All the wealth that had been extracted in the meantime will have been wasted as far as the regional economy is concerned. On the other hand, countries such as Egypt and Syria are forced, in order to develop their economy, to incur huge foreign debts—a bitter irony, in view of the fact that the annual oil profits would have sufficed to finance the building of three Aswan dams. A similar complementarity also exists in terms of availability of arable land in one Arab country and a surplus rural population in another.

All these historical, cultural, and economic factors are vividly reflected in the consciousness of the Arab masses throughout the region. The aspiration for Arab national unification is one of the most deeply rooted ideas in the minds of these masses. But Arab national unification is impossible without a struggle to overthrow imperialist domination, which is the root cause of the present balkanization. And genuine anti-imperialist struggle means at the same time struggle also against the ruling classes in the Arab countries.

The political independence of the Arab countries was achieved as a result not of a victorious popular revolution but of inter-imperialist rivalry and a compromise between the imperialist powers and the local ruling classes. As a result of this compromise, the local ruling classes have achieved the maximum concession they could get from imperialism. Direct foreign political rule was ended and has been replaced by a neocolonialist arrangement, consisting of an alliance between imperialism and the local ruling classes in which the latter have become junior partners in exploiting the working masses of the region. Both sides are interested in keeping this alliance, since both are afraid of a socialist revolution that would put an end to their profits and privileges. Thus both imperialism and its local junior partners have a stake in the continuation of the status quo and are ready to defend it tooth and nail.

The local ruling classes have also developed their own localist economic interests, those of one country competing with those of another. This economic rivalry has led to political contradictions and conflicts, encouraged by imperialism. All these economic and political conflicts, as well as the fact that national unification requires an anti-imperialist struggle and a mobilization of the masses, make the local ruling classes not only incapable of achieving national unification but actually opposed to it—though they pay lip-service to it in order to deceive the masses. It follows from all this that national unification—the main national problem of the Arabs in the Mashreq—cannot be achieved without overthrowing the present ruling classes, that is, a socialist revolution.

In Europe, the solution of the national problem was part and parcel of the tasks of the bourgeois revolution. But in the third world, the local propertied classes have proved incapable of carrying out a bourgeois-democratic revolution. Therefore, the unfulfilled tasks of such a revolution have been left to the proletariat to solve in a socialist revolution. The coming revolution in the Arab East cannot be a national-democratic but only a socialist one—led by the working class, relying on an alliance with the peasantry. It must be either a proletarian socialist revolution or none at all.

By the very nature of its tasks, this socialist revolution can be conceived only as a revolution of the whole Mashreq. This does not mean that it must occur simultaneously in all parts of the region; what it does mean is that even if it starts in one part of the region it must be conducted under the banner of an all-Arab revolution, because its immediate political aim will be to establish a united socialist Mashreq. Moreover, a revolution in one Arab country will draw an immediate intervention by the ruling classes of the whole region, supported by imperialism. (This is not merely a theoretical prognostication: in the pact establishing the so-called confederation between Syria, Egypt, and Libya there is an explicit clause to this effect!) Under these circumstances there can be only two possible outcomes—either a victorious revolution in the whole area or a crushing of the revolution wherever it may start.

The revolution in the Mashreq is thus necessarily one and indivisible—it cannot have a preliminary separate national-democratic stage, and it cannot be victorious in each country separately. Its immediate outcome must be the establishment of a united socialist Mashreq.

The Palestinian Struggle

The Palestinian Arabs are the only part of the Arab nation that is under direct foreign rule. The Palestinian armed resistance movement, which developed after the 1967 war, regarded its task as confined to Palestine alone; it saw itself as a national liberation movement of the Palestinians alone. Even those Palestinian left-wing groups that favored the idea of a socialist revolution relegated it to a separate second stage.

At the time we criticized this tendency, and pointed to the dangers inherent in it. In an article entitled "The Struggle in Palestine Must Lead to Arab Revolution," published in *Black Dwarf* (June 14, 1969),* we stated:

> The balance of forces, as well as theoretical considerations, show the impossibility of confining the struggle to one country. What is the balance of forces? The Palestinian people are waging a battle where they confront Zionism, which is supported

---

* See chapter 4 in this book.

by imperialism; from the rear they are menaced by the Arab regimes and by Arab reaction, which is also supported by imperialism. As long as imperialism has a real stake
in the Middle East, it is unlikely to withdraw its support for Zionism, its natural ally,
and to permit its overthrow; it will defend it to the last drop of Arab oil. On the other
hand imperialist interests and domination in the region cannot be shattered without
overthrowing those junior partners of imperialist exploitation, the ruling classes in the
Arab world. The conclusion that must be drawn is not that the Palestinian people should
wait quietly until imperialist domination is overthrown throughout the region, but that
it must rally to itself a wider struggle for the political and social liberation of the Middle
East as a whole. . . . The formula that restricts itself to Palestine alone, despite its revolutionary appearance, derives from a reformist attitude that seeks partial solutions,
within the framework of conditions now existing in the region. In fact, partial solutions
can only be implemented through a compromise with imperialism and Zionism.

In the same article we pointed out why the Arab governments encouraged the
attitude prevailing among the Palestinian groups, according to which they were to
confine their struggle to Palestinian issues only:

The very mobilization of the masses in the Arab countries—even if only for the
Palestinian cause—threatens the existing regimes. These regimes therefore wish to
isolate the Palestinian struggle and to leave it entirely to the Palestinians. The Arab
governments—both reactionary and "progressive"—are trying to buy stability for
their regimes with a ransom to the Palestinian organizations. Moreover, the governments want to use this financial aid to direct the Palestinian struggle along their
own politically convenient lines, to manipulate it and to utilize it merely as a means
of bargaining for a political solution acceptable to them. . . . The four great powers
are now meeting to reach an agreed solution that will then be imposed on the region.
If the Arab governments achieve their aim through this solution, they will be prepared to desert the Palestinians, and even take an active part in a political and physical liquidation of the Palestinian movement. The four powers will probably insist
on this as a condition for a political settlement.

This analysis and prognosis was proved to be correct to the letter by subsequent
events, especially the smashing of the guerrilla forces in Jordan by the Hashemite
regime in September 1970,* with the complicity of the other Arab regimes and the
support of imperialism and Israel. We can only reiterate the conclusion that we
drew in that article. The Palestinian problem can only be solved through an all-
Arab socialist revolution, and within the framework of a united socialist Arab East.

The Problem of the Israeli Nation

In addition to the national problem of the Arabs themselves, there exists also the problem of the non-Arab national communities living in the Mashreq: the Kurds in Iraq,
the South-Sudanese, and the Israeli Jews. The solution to this problem too is among
the tasks of the coming all-Arab socialist revolution. It therefore should be considered
in the context of the united socialist Arab East that that revolution will set up.

---

* Known as "Black September."

As for the Kurds and the South-Sudanese, there is a wide agreement throughout the Arab left that these, as oppressed nationalities, should be granted the right to self-determination. The case on which there is no such agreement is that of the Is- raeli Jews. The main arguments against granting them the right of self-determina- tion are (a) that they are not a nation, and (b) that even if they are a nation, they are an oppressing one. Sometimes it is also argued that to grant them the right to self-determination means to accept Zionism and recognize the State of Israel.

The idea that the Israeli Jews do not constitute a nation is a myth, a piece of wishful thinking based on lack of familiarity with the actual facts. In reality, they satisfy all the generally accepted criteria for nationhood. First, they live concentrated on a continuous territory. It is true that they obtained this territory unjustly, by a process of colonization at the expense of another people. But there are many other nations that developed as such on a territory conquered from others. One can, and should, condemn such depredations; but value judgments are irrelevant to the ob- jective question of defining nationhood.

Second, they have a common language, Hebrew. It is true that Hebrew had been for centuries a dead language and has been revived artificially for political mo- tives. But the objective result is nevertheless that the Israeli Jews have Hebrew as their common language, which they use both in literature and in daily life. In this language they have developed a new culture that is quite specific and different from the cultures of the various Jewish communities in the East or West.

Third, the Israeli Jewish community has its own common socioeconomic struc- ture, with its own class differentiation, as in other capitalist societies. That the Israeli economy is heavily subsidized by imperialism does not change the basic fact that the Israeli socioeconomic system exists as a real and specific entity.

Finally, all these factors have helped to create an Israeli national consciousness. It is true that Zionist ideology has helped the formation of this consciousness by artificially fostering a synthetic "Jewish national consciousness," which is supposed to embrace not just the Israeli Jews but all Jews around the world. The means used by Zionism have been self-contradictory. It revived Hebrew in order to foster the attachment of the various Jewish communities to each other and to their ancient history. But since this revival succeeded only in Palestine, the actual result was to *sever* the cultural ties of the Israeli Jews to the Jewish communities in their various places of origin. Similarly, in order to encourage the immigration of Jews to Pales- tine, Zionism struggled against the culture and mentality of the Jewish commu- nities in the Diaspora; in this too it helped to create a *separate* Israeli culture and mentality. But since the aim of Zionism is the ingathering of all Jews into Israel, and since it needs the material and moral help of world Jewry, Zionism is at the same time doing its best to combat this feeling of separateness of the Israeli Jews and to strengthen their feeling of identity with all Jews around the world. Thus under the pressures of Zionist ideology on the one hand and the influence of their real material conditions on the other, the Israeli Jews find themselves in a psycho- logical conflict between a Zionist all-Jewish "national consciousness" and an Israeli national consciousness. When Zionism is defeated, the Israeli Jews will not lose all national consciousness; while their synthetic all-Jewish "national consciousness" will tend to wither away, their specific Israeli national consciousness will on the contrary tend to be reinforced.

It is sometimes argued that the Israeli Jews cannot be a nation, since there is a constant stream of immigration to Israel, so that at any given time a considerable proportion of the Jews there are new arrivals, with their own language, culture, and so on. But in this the Israeli Jews are no different from any other nation created by immigrant settlers. In all such cases, once the national character of the older settlers crystallized, the new immigrants were soon assimilated. Mass immigration did not have to be stopped before an American nation was created.

Israel and the Arab Socialist Revolution

As to argument (b) above, it is true that it is ridiculous to talk about granting the right of self-determination to an oppressing nation. An oppressing nation is in no need of being granted such a right: it has not only appropriated this right for itself, but is denying it to others!

Clearly, the right to self-determination is meaningful only in the case of a nation that is denied, or in danger of being denied, such a right.

At present, the Israeli Jews are an oppressing nation. This is so because of certain conditions: the domination of Zionism, its connections with imperialism, the aggressive and colonizing role it is playing in the Mashreq. But what is being discussed here is not the right of self-determination for the Israeli Jews now, in the present context. What is under discussion is the program of the socialist Arab revolution. A victorious Arab socialist revolution implies the overthrow of Zionism and of the entire Zionist state structure, together with the liquidation of imperialist domination in the Mashreq. Under such circumstances the Israeli Jews would not remain an oppressor nation; they would become a small national minority in the Arab East. The question that we are raising, and that all revolutionaries of the region must raise, is how this national minority should be dealt with.

There are only three possibilities: expulsion from the region, forcible annexation or, finally, granting them the right to self-determination. As socialists, we are totally opposed to the first and second possibilities. There remains only the third possibility: self-determination. To deny them this right would *in itself* reduce them to the status of an oppressed nation, and the maintenance of a proletarian state is not compatible with the oppression of national minorities.

It should be stressed that the status of being oppressed or an oppressor is not immutable; being oppressed is no guarantee against becoming an oppressor. The Jews have been oppressed, but those of them who have immigrated to Palestine have become part of Zionist oppression. Similarly the Arabs, who are now oppressed, would by denying the Israeli Jews the right to self-determination become themselves oppressors.

It must be clearly understood that self-determination does not automatically mean separation. What it does mean is that the decision whether to separate or to remain in the same state is to be taken by the minority nation, not imposed on it by the majority. In the specific case of the Israeli Jews we do not recommend a Jewish state separate from the socialist Arab union. Such a separate state would not in fact be viable economically, militarily, or politically. If Israel has existed so far, that is only thanks to imperialist support. Liberated from Zionism and imperialism, the Israeli Jews will have no viable alternative other than to integrate (preserving only some degree of autonomy) in the socialist union of the Mashreq. But in our view, the chances for a successful integration of this kind will be considerably increased if the decision about it is left to the Israeli Jews themselves. Conversely, denying them the right to self-determination will tend to strengthen their separatism and create a problem of an oppressed national minority struggling for separation. The task of struggling for integration is primarily that of the revolutionaries of the national minority. The revolutionaries belonging to the national majority should not try to enforce a decision on the minority.

Our position is not abstract; it does not consider the national problem per se but is completely determined by our understanding of the strategy of the socialist revolution in the Arab East. The inclusion of the right of self-determination for the Israeli Jews in the program of the revolution will help the course of that revolution. It presents to the Israeli masses an alternative to Zionism, and thus makes it possible to attract sections of these masses to the side of the revolution. It is true that it is not impossible for the socialist revolution to triumph in the Mashreq even without the support of any section of the Israeli masses. But without such support, the course of the revolution will certainly be much more difficult and bloody. Denying them the right to self-determination will push all Israeli Jews to the side of counterrevolution: they will fight to the bitter end because they will not see any acceptable alternative to Zionism.

Finally, does not granting the right of self-determination to the Israeli Jews mean accepting Zionism and recognizing Israel? On the contrary, it means just the opposite. Such a right can only be granted, will only become meaningful, when Zionism and the present Israeli state are overthrown.

But what about the borders within which the Israeli Jews will be allowed to exercise their right to self-determination? And does not this right conflict with the rights of the Palestinian Arab refugees? The answers to these two questions are interconnected. Of course, the Israeli Jews' right to self-determination must not infringe upon the right of the Palestinian Arabs to be repatriated and rehabilitated. But even after their repatriation and rehabilitation, there will still be a continuous territory inhabited by an overwhelming majority of Israeli Jews. In that territory they will exercise the right to self-determination. The right of self-determination has nothing to do with the borders of Israel, or with any other borders that can be drawn on the map at this moment.

6

The National Movement in the Arab East at the End of the Road

T he aim of these theses is to analyze the turn in Middle Eastern dynamics (particularly in regard to the Palestinian question) due to the [civil] war in Lebanon and the Syrian challenge and to characterize the struggle for the rights of the Palestinian people in the coming historical period.

A. The Turn

1. The main characteristics of the line of developments in the region since the October 1973 war have been: intense acceleration of the Arab East's integration in the global capitalist order under direct US political hegemony, and a gradual drive toward "settlement" of the Israeli-Arab conflict. The continuity of this line has not been broken, but it is nevertheless taking an important turn due to the war in Lebanon.

2. The war in Lebanon is driven *primarily* by two motive forces. *First*, the internal antagonisms that existed in the Lebanese society and state irrespective of the Palestinian problem, but have been further complicated by the active presence of the Palestinian movement in Lebanon. *Second*, Syria's interests, which drove it to an active military intervention and turned the civil war into a war of intervention.

In the present document we will not go into an analysis of the former factor (the internal antagonisms in Lebanon) but address only the latter.

This article was cowritten with Emmanuel Farjoun, August 8, 1976. It was published in *Matzpen* 80, February 1977. Translated from the Hebrew by the author. Explanatory remarks in brackets have been inserted in translation.

B. The Syrian Challenge

1. The Syrian Ba'ath regime does not differ in its fundamental essence from the Egyptian regime, just as in the 1950s and '60s there was no essential difference between Ba'athism and Nasserism. In both cases we have a current originating in the petite bourgeoisie, that while holding state power underwent a process of bourgeoisification and helped to create a new bourgeois class.

   The fact that the Syrian regime still relies to some extent on Soviet diplomatic and military assistance does not disprove its basic similarity to the Egyptian regime.

2. The antagonisms between Syria and Egypt are neither ones between two regimes having different class characters nor between two fundamentally different political lines, but ones of rivalry between two similar and parallel models of the regime of the new Arab bourgeoisie. Their rivalry is mainly about predominance in the Arab East.

3. This predominance has a double implication. *First*, the predominant Arab state can influence the internal Arab market, and in particular the movement of Arab capital; and is able to direct the political steps of the other Arab regimes. *Second*, the predominant Arab state serves as the main link between the local regimes and global capitalism. As the main Arab agent of American policy, Egypt has so far been predominant; but now Syria is trying to gain, or at least share, this position. This also fits into the long-term plans for establishing a "Greater Syria"—a state or federation that would include Syria, Lebanon, the East Bank of the Jordan [the Kingdom of Jordan], and areas west of the Jordan River, under the leadership of the Syrian bourgeoisie.

4. The price paid by Egypt to the Americans for its present position has included, among other things: *first*, giving up its freedom of maneuver in the international arena (a freeze in relations with the Soviet Union) and, *second*, giving up the military option against Israel, at least for the foreseeable future. The price that Syria will pay for sharing the position of predominance cannot be a loss of the military option, because Syria in any case has no credible military option separately from Egypt. However, Syria can serve American interests (while also advancing its own long-term plans) by seizing total control of the Palestinian movement, turning it from a protégé into a hostage, from a popular movement with a considerable measure of independence into an abject handmaiden of the Syrian master.

C. The Settlement and the Palestinian State

1. Liquidation of the Palestinian national movement as an independent actor is desirable to the Americans, because their basic policy in the region is incompatible with a compromise that would satisfy even the most moderate current in the independent Palestinian movement.

2. The minimal demand, which even the most moderate current in the Palestine Liberation Organization (PLO) cannot give up (so long as it exists as an independent actor), is the establishment of a sovereign Palestinian state in the Occupied Territories, which would exist for an entire historical period alongside the Zionist State of Israel.

3. The Americans for their own part could accept this demand in order to tranquilize the national ferment. From a purely American viewpoint, as from that of the moderate current in the PLO, a compromise that includes the establishment of a sovereign Palestinian state under US protection would be acceptable. But in practice such a compromise is precluded by the resolute Zionist position and the special position of Israel in the American setup in the region.

4. The decisive majority of the Zionist leadership, both in the government and in the right-wing opposition, is resolutely opposed, as a matter of fundamental principle, to the establishment of any kind of independent Palestinian state.

   First, the Zionist legitimation for the existence of the State of Israel as an exclusive Jewish state has always been entirely based not on the right to self-determination of the Jews who live in this country but on the alleged "historical right" of all Jews around the world over the whole of the "Land of Israel." From this viewpoint, recognition of the existence in Palestine of another people, the Palestinian Arab people, which has a legitimate claim in it would undermine Zionism's legitimation and self-justification.

   Second, the Zionist leadership indeed takes into account the eventuality that within the framework of a settlement Israel would be obliged to withdraw also from parts of its conquests west of the Jordan River. But from a Zionist viewpoint any withdrawal from any part whatsoever of "the historical Land of Israel," especially west of the Jordan, is—in principle—temporary and contingent on transient conditions. From this viewpoint, Israel must reserve the ability and right to reconquer these territories, if that becomes politically possible or militarily necessary. But in international politics there is a huge difference between conquering part of another state and conquering the whole of a "third state" [i.e., a Palestinian state between Israel and Jordan]. The world would be much more likely to accept, under certain conditions, an Israeli reconquest of part of Jordan (or of Greater Syria), than the total erasure of a sovereign Palestinian state. The establishment of such a state would therefore impose a severe constraint on Israel's political and military strategy.

Third, the Zionist leadership is worried that the establishment of an independent Palestinian state, however small, may be the starting point of a historical process whereby that state would expand step-by-step at Israel's expense. The Zionists in fact know from their own experience all about a process of this kind: at first they agreed to the establishment of a small Jewish state within the borders recommended [in 1937] by the Peel Commission, and later within the borders of the [UN] Partition Plan of 1947, but they expanded the borders further and further, step by step.

In this context it is worth quoting Moshe Dayan (*Ha'aretz*, December 12, 1975):

> Fundamentally a Palestinian state is an antithesis of the State of Israel. . . . The basic and naked truth is that there is no fundamental difference between the relation of the Arabs of Nablus to Nablus and that of the Arabs of Jaffa to Jaffa. . . . And if today we set out on this road and say that the Palestinians are entitled to their own state because they are natives of the same country and have the same rights, then it will not end with the West Bank. The West Bank together with the Gaza Strip do not amount to a state. . . . The establishment of such a Palestinian state would lay a cornerstone to something else. . . . Either the State of Israel—or a Palestinian state.

5. Since the October 1973 war, Israel is no longer the exclusive ally of the United States in the region; but it is still the surest and closest ally. Now the United States has other allies, namely the regimes of the Arab countries, but the relations between the United States and the Arab countries are always fundamentally exploitative. Therefore, even if the regime of a given Arab country is ready to collaborate with the United States, there exist important social forces, historical forces, that threaten to change the policy of that country in an anti-imperialist direction. Besides, there is always the possibility of a conflict between the American senior partner and the junior partner, the local ruling class, over division of the spoils of the exploitation of the Arab workers. In conflicts of this kind the Americans have no real substitute for the Israeli watchdog.

Israel is not economically exploited by imperialism but is subsidized by it. So long as imperialism dominates the region and is capable of keeping Israel, the latter is its sure and vital ally. (This truth is adverted to in Joseph Alsop's "open letter" to Amos Eran—which is in reality a letter from Kissinger to Rabin*—whose Hebrew translation appeared in *Ha'aretz*

---

* Joseph Alsop was close to Secretary of State Henry Kissinger. Amos Eran was from 1975 to 1977 senior political adviser to Prime Minister Yitzhak Rabin. He took active part in negotiations with Kissinger on Israel's interim agreements with Egypt and Syria following the 1973 war. Alsop's "Open Letter to an Israeli Friend" was originally published in the *New York Times Magazine* on December 14, 1975.

on December 19, 1975. Although the letter was written when US-Israel relations were very tense, and its main purpose was to warn the Rabin government that Israel cannot dictate detailed conditions to the US, just as the tail cannot wag the dog, it ends with the words: "[N]othing that I've said alters my belief, already noted, that Israel's ruin may well bring our own ruin in its train.") Therefore, even if the United States is prepared to apply pressure to Israel's government and impose on it concessions here and there, this pressure cannot be expected to reach the point of forcing a concession over what is considered to be an existential interest of the Zionist State of Israel. Preventing the establishment of a sovereign "third state" [between Israel and Jordan] is one such "existential interest."

D. Other Parties Stirring the Lebanese Cauldron

1. *The United States* is coordinating the offensive against the Lebanese left and the Palestinians, and dictates how far the Syrian intervention army is allowed to go.

2. *The Soviet Union* has lost almost all remnants of its influence in the region. It grasps at the Syrian straw, but its position is so weak that it has no means of applying pressure on Syria. Soviet arms continue to flow to Syria while the Syrian army is fighting against the Palestinian movement and the Lebanese left front, which includes the Lebanese Communist Party: in this war the arms supplied by the Soviet Union are deployed on the same side of the barricade as the arms supplied by the United States and Israel.

3. *The Arab countries* are exploiting the Syrian intervention to advance their own interests in the inter-Arab struggles. Libya and Iraq are trying to replace Syria in its former role as supposed defender of the Palestinians, but since their policies and regimes are not essentially different from those of Syria, it can be predicted with certainty that they too will turn out to be like the proverbial "staff of broken reed, whereon if a man lean, it will go into his hand, and pierce it." The other Arab countries do not even pretend to be defenders of the Palestinians. The true role of the inter-Arab force is to serve as cover for the Syrian intervention.

4. *Israel* is serving as a whip in the hands of the United States. By cracking this whip, the US draws the "red line," the permitted limit of the Syrian intervention; this line varies according to current needs, and by this means the US is able to regulate the rate and scope of the Syrian intervention. Along with Syria, Israel participates in the naval blockade preventing shipment of arms to the Palestinians and the forces of the left.

Meanwhile Israel is preparing the ground for seizing the south of Lebanon up to the Litani River, in case suitable conditions arise (such as a terminal disintegration and division of Lebanon). The fairground show of the "good fence" [between Israel and Lebanon] is part of these preparations.*

E. Lessons Regarding the Palestinian Struggle

1. The Syrian intervention vindicates once again the assertion of the Israeli Socialist Organization (Matzpen) that liberation of the Palestinian people requires struggle not only against Zionism, or Zionism and imperialism, but also against the ruling classes in all the Arab states. Liberation of the Palestinian people can only be achieved as part of a socialist revolution in the entire region, led by the working classes.

2. Already in the [1964] Palestinian National Covenant, the PLO asserted the principle of non-intervention in the internal struggles in the Arab countries. Ever since then, the Palestinian movement tried to abide by this principle—unsuccessfully, because events kept hitting it in the face and proving again and again that it is impossible to separate the Palestinian struggle and the class struggles in the Arab countries. In practice, the principle of non-intervention has meant that all sections of the Palestinian movement, without exception, allied themselves with one Arab regime or another and accepted its patronage.

3. In consequence of the alliance that existed between the PLO and Syria, Al-Sa'iqa—an organization always known to be an obedient instrument of the Syrian regime—was awarded a respectable position in the PLO and was thereby legitimized as though it were a genuine Palestinian organization. Wishing to keep its rotten alliance with Syria, the Palestinian leadership agreed to admit this Trojan horse into the movement. Only at a later stage, when Al-Sa'iqa resorted to armed struggle alongside Syria and against the Palestinian movement, did the PLO turn against it.

4. At first the leadership of the Palestinian movement tried to keep a position of non-intervention in the Lebanese civil war. Later it was compelled to get involved, which proved once again that the Palestinian struggle is inseparable from the internal struggles within the Arab world. No ruling class can acquiesce for long in the presence of a serious focus of force (especially an armed force) that is not under its control. Hence the active presence of the Palestinian movement in Lebanon was itself one of the causes of the outbreak of the civil war. This fact had not been understood in time or sufficiently clearly by the Palestinian leadership.

---

* Israel in fact invaded Lebanon up to the Litani River for seven days in March 1978. It reinvaded Lebanon in 1982 and remained in occupation of the south up to the Litani River until 2000, when it was forced by local resistance to withdraw.

5. When the Palestinian movement was sucked into the war, there were many cases in which Palestinian forces were drawn into behaving as an army of occupation toward the Christian masses, and to acts of revenge along sectarian lines.

6. All the weaknesses, errors, and faults listed above follow from a common source: the character of the Palestinian national movement as an all-class alliance, with petit-bourgeois leadership and ideology.

7. Militarily, the Palestinian movement has withstood the Syrian challenge more successfully than had been predicted, and with many manifestations of heroism. This however is but a short-term success. In our region—in which exploitation, poverty, and disease hold sway; in which the ruling classes impose on the masses ignorance, stupidity, and religious obscurantism; and in which class antagonisms are intensifying—no movement can have long-term success without positioning itself clearly on one side or another of the class barricade.

F. A New Era

1. Current events herald the end of an era and the beginning of a new one. The era in which it has been possible to win the masses, if only in the short term, for a purely national struggle, not organically connected to the class struggle, is approaching its end. The coming era is that of explicitly class struggles.

2. This does not mean that from now on the Palestinian struggle must cease and wait for an upsurge of the forces of socialist revolution in the entire Arab East; rather, the Palestinian struggle must see itself in advance as an organic part of the social struggle in the region, against all its existing regimes.

G. Consequences for Our Activity

1. We, members of the Israeli Socialist Organization (Matzpen), propose to those Palestinian masses with whom we can have direct contact (that is, mainly those within the border of the State of Israel) a road that differs in essence both from that proposed by the PLO and that proposed by Rakah [the Israeli CP].

2. The road proposed by the PLO is external to the struggle taking place inside Israel. The actions of the PLO have no organic connection with the daily problems encountered by the Arab and Jewish workers in Israel.

3. Rakah's situation is more complex. Regarding general political questions (resolution of the Israeli-Arab conflict and the Palestinian problem)

Rakah mainly relies not on mass struggle but on the actions of a coalition of external forces, headed by the Soviet Union, that also includes what Rakah regards as the "progressive Arab regimes."

As far as the daily problems of the Palestinian masses in Israel are concerned, Rakah does not have an "external" stance but is involved directly in the struggle and even leads it. It is not for nothing that Rakah has so far won a great deal of confidence on the part of the best among the Arab community in Israel.

But growing parts of the politically conscious Palestinian community are gradually discovering (especially following Land Day*) the limitations of Rakah, which is fundamentally a reformist party. Rakah bases its program and activity on acceptance of the continued existence of the present regimes in the region—both the Arab regimes and the Zionist regime. Rakah therefore tries to restrain or prevent struggles and demands that may be seen as calling into question the continued existence of these regimes, including the Zionist regime.

4. Also, on general political questions as well, Rakah cannot arouse full confidence, because its supreme loyalty is given to the foreign policy of the Soviet Union. Past experience suggests that it is possible that the Soviet Union may change its policy line, due to internal reasons or its global interests—and Rakah's leadership will then follow in its footsteps. Rakah's loyalty to the Soviet Union also explains the confusion in the position of this party regarding the Syrian invasion of Lebanon, for the Soviet Union regards itself as a friend both of the Syrian regime and of the PLO.

5. We, members of Matzpen, regard the daily struggle of the workers in Israel—as well as in the surrounding countries—as actively and necessarily connected to the general political problems. We envisage the resolution of the region's general problems as resulting not from the action of a coalition of global diplomatic forces but from the struggle of the masses in the region. We stress the continuity between the daily struggle and revolutionary struggle. It is not accidental that a strike [on Land Day] against the expropriation of some thousands of *dunams* of land boiled over immediately into a confrontation that challenged the entire Zionist regime.

6. Although under present conditions the Palestinian masses struggling against their national oppression in Israel constitute the most active protagonist in the struggle for the overthrow of the Zionist regime, in its profound essence it is not a supra-class national struggle but a supranational class struggle.

---

* This refers to the bloody events of March 30, 1976.

7. We regard the struggle for democratic rights for all the citizens of Israel as an aspect of the general struggle for social liberation; and in the colonial reality of Israel it is necessarily connected with the struggle against Zionism.

8. A necessary condition for the success of any struggle against Israel's regime—including the struggle for democratic rights—is that it is a joint Jewish-Arab struggle. It is therefore the duty of the Israeli Socialist Organization (Matzpen) to create frameworks in which this joint struggle can develop, on the basis of the joint historical interest of the workers of both peoples.

7

Following the Israeli-Egyptian Treaty: Against the Autonomy!

O ne of the central and most consequential questions in assessing the Israeli-Egyptian peace treaty is whether Israel's policy has come out relatively better or worse off as a result of the agreement just signed. This question is hotly disputed among the Israeli public, and it seems that also in our organization (Matzpen) opinions about it are divided.

It is my impression that some comrades believe that Israeli policy has suffered a relative defeat. In fact, if we examine the *text* of the Camp David Accords (and of the other documents pursuant to them) it would appear that Israel has hardly made any important concession on the most consequential issue, the Palestinian issue. But if I have understood correctly the position of these comrades, they believe that what is significant is not the literal text. That text is supposedly only a sugaring of the bitter pill (bitter for Zionism). The accords speak of some fuzzy and limited autonomy, but *in practice* this autonomy will be but an initial stage of a process leading to the creation of an independent Palestinian state. If I have indeed understood correctly the assessment of these comrades, then I completely disagree with it.

But a totally opposite position is also possible: the agreement constitutes a crushing victory for Zionism, and (among other things) entombs the Palestinian people and its right to self-determination for the foreseeable future. The autonomy is in reality exactly what it looks like on paper—an alibi and cover not for the creation of a Palestinian state but for more or less rapid colonization and annexation to Israel of the West Bank and Gaza Strip.

Pursuant to the Camp David Accords (September 17, 1978), Israel's prime minister Begin and Egypt's president Anwar Sadat concluded a peace treaty on March 26, 1979. This article was written in late March 1979, in immediate reaction to the signing of the treaty, and was published in issue 87 of *Matzpen* (August–September 1979). It addresses in particular the agreement to establish a Palestinian autonomy in the West Bank and Gaza Strip (as "framework for peace in the Middle-East"), which had been part of the Camp David Accords, but which in the event was quietly shelved. Translated by the author.

I must say that I tend more toward the latter assessment. It seems to me that in the recent agreements Zionist policy has scored a major success. Begin has achieved a peace treaty with Egypt without making any significant concession on the Palestinian issue (although on the Israeli-Egyptian issue, that of Sinai, he conceded more than what the Labor Alignment government had been ready to do); whereas Sadat has given up all his initial demands, virtually without exception.

True, *in a certain sense* the autonomy may in the end bring about the creation of a sovereign Palestinian state; however, that would not be because this autonomy is by its very nature and purpose a kind of germ of self-determination, but for a different, almost opposite reason. The attempt to impose the autonomy may lead to unprecedented intensification of the struggle in the West Bank and Gaza Strip. So long as the moves of the accord were in a preparatory stage, the Palestinian struggle (especially that of the population in the Occupied Territories) was partly paralyzed, because many people were waiting for the situation to become clearer. The more moderate, in other words, more conservative, elements were hoping that perhaps there would be the kind of settlement that would accommodate them. It has now transpired that there is no question even of the minimal rights of a genuine autonomy. In addition, Jordan too has been kept out of the loop of the accord, so the supporters of King Hussein have also been pushed into the camp of the resistance.

The recent meeting of Hussein and Arafat signifies *not only* the backsliding of the present Palestinian movement but also confirmation and recognition that in the present situation both the Palestinians and the Jordanian regime find themselves in the front of opposition to the accord. On the other hand, the signing of the accord removes one of the temporary brakes on the momentum of Israeli colonization in the Occupied Territories. It can be predicted with certainty that the camp represented in the government by Ariel Sharon will now launch an unprecedented colonization drive. Now that the accord has been signed, there is no longer any real reason for Begin and Sharon to hold back; they can now show their cards and make it crystal clear that the "autonomy" in question is in fact vacuous, and its real meaning is a *worsening* of the Palestinians' situation. And as Dayan has hinted, even if the United States or Egypt doesn't like it, there is little they can do about it. Sadat has already demonstrated that he is not very tenacious as far as Palestinian interests are concerned.

So in my opinion we can expect major intensification on both sides: intensification of the Palestinian struggle in the face of intensification of the pressure of colonization and Israeli oppression. Attempts to implement the fake autonomy will only exacerbate the situation and intensify the struggle. One reason for this is that the election of any representative bodies, even if they have no real authority whatsoever, would introduce an element of instability, and create foci of struggle (in this connection recall the effect of the election of pro-PLO mayors in consolidating the struggle in the West Bank, despite the fact that these mayors have no political power). In my opinion the fake autonomy will be an important cause of instability, not because it is a sort of germ of Palestinian sovereignty, but precisely because it is not.

If this prognosis is correct, then we can expect a long period, lasting more than a few years, of intensifying struggle. And *at the end of it* a sovereign Palestinian state may perhaps be established in the Occupied Territories. But even if that will come about, it will not be a natural outgrowth of the autonomy germ but precisely the opposite: the outcome of an intensive struggle *against* the autonomy. Therefore our support for the Palestinian people's right to self-determination obliges us to take a *most adamant position* against the autonomy, and to condemn it as worse even than South Africa's bantustans.

Of course, this condemnation is mainly directed against Israel's policy in the Occupied Territories. If among the leaders in the West Bank and Gaza Strip there will be persons who would agree to collaborate with the autonomy (whether out of corrupt personal motives, or as a tactical move aiming to extract every possible benefit out of the few rights offered to the Palestinians), then it is certainly not our business to attack them and denounce them as "traitors." We can leave that to the [Israeli] Trotskyists, who like preaching to all and sundry how they ought to behave. Our struggle is mainly against Zionist policy, against the Israeli regime.

As I said, I think we should forcefully denounce the autonomy plan. In doing so, a slogan that we should *counterpose* to it is the Palestinian people's right to self-determination, including the right to establish its own sovereign state. This brings me to another matter, which has only an indirect connection to the accord. I am referring to the improvement in the attitude of the Communist Party* to our organization.

I hope that within our organization there is no support for an aloof sectarian stance, whereby we should reject the CP's courting and continue in splendid isolation. Clearly, we must welcome these advances, and cooperate with the CP on all matters where such cooperation is possible. The CP is not the enemy but an ally on a whole range of topics. However, I think we must be very careful that our approval of the positive turn in the CP's attitude toward us will not go to our heads and will not lead us to give up our principles. The CP has not managed to kill us with blows, and we have no reason to allow it to kill us (or to assist us to commit political suicide) with embraces.

One of the points on which we have always had a principled difference with the CP, and on which in my opinion we must not make any concession, is the attitude to the creation of a Palestinian state in the Occupied Territories and the existence of the Zionist State of Israel.

For the CP, the creation of a Palestinian state alongside Israel (even in the latter's present, Zionist form) would actually constitute a solution of the national problem and a realization of "the just national rights of both peoples." We have always emphasized that we do not regard the creation of a Palestinian state as a solution, still less as an ideal. The creation of such a state is a *right* of the Palestinian people, and any attempt by Israel to prevent it doing so constitutes grievous national oppression.

---

* In the Hebrew original the CP is referred to as "Rakah," the acronym of its parliamentary faction.

But we do not acquiesce in the existence of a Zionist state, and in our view the national problems of this region cannot be solved short of a revolution that will overthrow all its present regimes, including the Zionist regime. In my opinion we must not soften our position on these questions.

Of course, these differences need not prevent useful collaboration between us and the CP on many important issues.

To sum up: as a direct and legitimate extension of our organization's past position, all of whose main elements have in my opinion proved to be correct, I think that our position following the signing of the Israeli-Egyptian peace agreement should focus on the following points:

- Continued opposition to the occupation, also in its new—and more grievous—form, dubbed "autonomy."
- Support for the Palestinian people's right to self-determination, including the right to establish its own sovereign state.
- Denying the right of the State of Israel to exist as a Zionist state.
- Rejection of the "stage theory" that envisages a "bourgeois-democratic" stage, in which the region's national problems would be solved while the present regimes continue to exist, separate from the stage of the socialist revolution.

8

The Middle East—Still at the Crossroads: A Socialist Position on the Palestinian Problem

Foreword

This article was written in September 1988, in anticipation of the Palestinian declaration of independence, which was in fact promulgated by the Palestinian National Council a few weeks later (November 15, 1988). Quite a long time before that declaration, it had become clear that the majority of the PLO, led by Yasser Arafat, is resolved to propose the creation of an independent Palestinian state in the Occupied Territories, alongside Israel. This gave rise to a debate among socialists, both in the Middle East and elsewhere, as to what attitude should be taken toward this demand. The debate will no doubt go on.

However, it seemed to me that both those socialists who supported the demand for a Palestinian state alongside Israel and those who opposed it were doing so for the wrong reasons.

Most supporters of the new moderate PLO demand, including the official Communist Parties, argue in effect that a repartition of Palestine into two independent states (Israel in something like the pre-1967 borders, and a new Palestinian Arab state in the remainder) would solve the "Palestine problem."

Contrariwise, most socialists (mainly of the extreme left) who condemn the new PLO line do so because they adhere to the older PLO position, formulated a year or two after the 1967 war, according to which the only solution to the "Palestine problem" is the creation of a unitary "secular-democratic" state in the whole of Palestine.

I have long believed that both positions are based on a common error: both approach the Palestinian problem within an essentially petit-bourgeois ideological framework, instead of trying to rethink the whole problem in socialist terms.

Originally published in *Khamsin Bulletin* no. 5, January 1989. Reproduced here with some minor corrections.

The present article is an attempt to amplify and elaborate on this critique. The main ideas on which it is based are far from new: they can be found in an article written about twenty years ago by A. Sa'id and me. I believe that that old article, which is no longer in print, has more than purely archival interest, and I have therefore appended it below.*

I hope that the publication of the new article, and the republication of the old, will help to advance a serious discussion among socialists on the problems of the Middle East.

Socialism or Nationalism?

It is an unfortunate fact of political life that fundamental principles, however self-evident, need to be reiterated over and over again; they must continually be shored up against erosion by the prevailing currents of opportunism, the tides of forgetfulness, and the decay of mental laziness.

One such principle of socialism is internationalism: *Die Arbeiter haben kein Vaterland.* Marx and Engels affirm that the first thing that distinguishes their own brand of proletarian revolutionism from other working-class parties is that the former always "point out and bring to the front the common interests of the entire proletariat, independently of all nationality."

Internationalism is incompatible with nationalism. Consequently, socialists are put under great ideological pressure. Throughout the world, nationalism is part of the dominant ideology; the temptation of succumbing to it is great, and the peril of falling inadvertently into its many traps is greater still. The danger is particularly grave because many, perhaps most, present-day liberation struggles are not, in any direct sense, class struggles, but are fought for patriotic aims, under nationalist banners, led by bourgeois or petit-bourgeois nationalists and informed by nationalist ideology. Clearly, socialists have a duty to support these national liberation struggles; equally clearly, they must beware of adopting the nationalist ideology of the patriotic protagonists. At the level of political action there is all the difference in the world between the aggressive nationalism of an oppressing nation and the defensive nationalism of the oppressed. But at the doctrinal level both are equally inconsistent with a socialist worldview.

It seems that many socialists often find it difficult to maintain this absolutely vital distinction between supporting a national liberation struggle and accepting the ideological viewpoint of those who lead it. In their zeal for aiding a just cause, they swallow the nationalist ideas and phraseology of its protagonists. Worse still, some socialists try to outdo the bourgeois patriots in nationalist extremism.

It is easy to see how they fall into this grave error. These socialists know that socialism is supposed to be more radical than liberation nationalism; they do not like

---

* The article referred to was reprinted in the same issue of *Khamsin Bulletin*. It is reprinted in this book as chapter 4.

to be seen as tailing behind common or garden-variety petit-bourgeois nationalists; they wish to prove that they are far more radical than the latter. For this purpose they adopt a more fundamentalist patriotism.

What they fail to understand is that the sense in which socialists ought to be "more radical" than liberation nationalists is not in vying with the latter's nationalism but in putting forward revolutionary *social* aims. Liberation nationalists do not propose to overthrow the existing social order; what they want is just to put an end to the oppression of *their own* nation. (In order to attract the working classes, these nationalists often masquerade as "socialists" and swear that they are also against class exploitation; but invariably they claim that the class struggle and social liberation must be shelved until the achievement of national liberation, which requires national unity irrespective of class.) Socialists, on the contrary, must seek to promote in every national liberation struggle the aim of overthrowing the existing order of class exploitation.

Fatherland Fetishism

An important ingredient of bourgeois nationalism is its fetishist attitude to the national soil, the Homeland, the Motherland, the Fatherland. This attitude has some interesting parallels with the way bourgeois ideology mystifies private property.

Just as, to the bourgeois mind, private property is sacred, so the Homeland is the sacrosanct Real Estate of the Nation; it is absolute, eternal, and inalienable.

The nation's ownership over its homeland is regarded as part of a divine or natural order of things, established in the dawn of the mythical past. (Almost every nation invents a distant mythical past that long antedates its actual historical beginning as a nation.) Members of any other nationality or ethnic group who also happen to be living in that territory, no matter how many they are or how long established, are seen as intruders, interlopers, who may at best be tolerated but never accorded national rights there.

Just as, to the mind afflicted by commodity fetishism, human beings become appendages of things, so to the nationalist the Homeland is not merely the place where the nation happens to be but a Divine Mistress that must be served.

This fetishism is characteristic of all bourgeois nationalism, including that of oppressed nations. Thus, to bourgeois and petit-bourgeois liberation nationalism, it is not so much the people that have to be freed, but the Homeland. The point of departure of such nationalist liberation programs is the Homeland and the goal of "liberating" it; what to do about the peoples living in and around that territory is considered only secondarily.

Socialists should beware of sliding into this mode of thinking and even of using such language. Of course, there is no great harm in talking of "liberating" a country or a territory, if it is clearly understood that this is merely a figure of speech, and that the concept of liberty is human and can only apply to human beings, not to stretches of land. However, unthinking and habitual use of such figures of speech is dangerous, because the mind often follows the tongue.

The Land and the Peoples

I have so far spoken in general terms, because those characteristics of bourgeois nationalism, as well as the mistaken attitudes of many socialists, are indeed ubiquitous. But I should now like to confine myself to the specific issue of the Palestinian problem and the Israeli-Arab conflict.

I must insist right at the outset that what socialists should be addressing is indeed the *Palestinian*, rather than a *Palestine*, problem. This may seem a mere pedantic quibble, but it is in fact quite important to realize that the entity whose present oppression and future well-being should concern us is not a territory, a country called "Palestine," but the Palestinian people.

Talk of a *Palestine* problem tends to give the discussion a false point of departure and to reinforce the presupposition—an implicit presupposition, but all the more dangerous for that—that the issue should be addressed by considering Palestine as a given (perhaps God-given) entity and by trying to think of the best way in which it ought to be disposed and governed.

This is precisely the way the issue is approached both by Palestinian nationalists and by Zionists, except that the latter call the country Eretz Yisrael (the Land of Israel) rather than Palestine.[1]

At this point it may be of interest to observe in passing that since the end of antiquity there was only one historically brief period of some twenty-five years (1923–48) when Palestine was in reality a single unitary and separate political entity, rather than an ideological Judeo-Christian construct (the "Holy Land"). During the long centuries of Muslim rule, it was never a single coherent administrative province, let alone a separate political entity; and indeed classical Arab geographical texts—such as al-Idrisi's *Nuzhat al-mushtaq* (written for Roger II of Sicily in the mid-twelfth century) and the geographical survey in Ibn Khaldun's masterpiece, the *Muqaddimah* (late fourteenth century)—do not even regard Palestine as a geographic unit but refer to the area in question as part of Syria. Of course, this does not necessarily mean that Palestine should not be a unitary or separate political entity in the future; but it suggests that that cannot, at any rate, be taken for granted without argument.

It is far better to start by considering not the land but the peoples involved in the conflict. Let us do so briefly.

The two central national protagonists are the Palestinian Arabs and the Hebrews (or Israeli Jews),[2] both of whom are newly created national entities, whose process of national formation is in fact still ongoing.

Like almost all statements about the Middle East, the statements made in the last paragraph are far from being noncontroversial. Mainstream Zionist ideology denies the very existence of the Palestinians as a national entity but regards them merely as "the Arabs of the Land of Israel." Zionist propaganda can be paraphrased somewhat as follows:

"First, the country in which we Zionists settled was virtually empty. Second, we did not dispossess or displace anyone; the people, who were not really there in the first place, simply ran away. Third, we dispossessed and displaced merely a relatively small part of a large nation (the Arab nation), rather than an entire small nation (the Palestinian nation), which does not exist anyway."

At the same time, Zionist ideology also denies the existence of a separate Israeli Jewish nation; for this ideology adheres to the myth that all the Jews around the world constitute, and have always constituted, one nation whose homeland is and always has been the Land of Israel. The Israeli Jews are considered to be merely one part of that nation, the part that has "returned" to the homeland. The Israeli Jewish community is therefore subject to a peculiar state of collective schizophrenia: it knows very well, it feels in its very bones, that it is a separate nation with its own language and other national characteristics (even its own style of pop music); but its official ideology denies this fact.

Zionism finds it very hard to accept the historical irony that, as a quite unintended result of its own activity—Zionist colonization—two new national entities have come into existence. Both these nations have been formed through the experience of the colonization process and by it—as two dialectical opposites, inseparable and at the same time mutually antagonistic, like prey and predator. The Palestinian nation has come into being through the shared formative reality of being individually and collectively the victim of a peculiar colonization project, as well as by the experience of struggle against it.[3] And the Hebrew nation has been formed at the same time and through the very same process but as its opposite pole, as a colonizing settler-nation.

Nevertheless, these facts, particularly the existence of the Palestinians as a national entity, have lately been recognized by some Zionist fringe groups.

Palestinian nationalist ideology, on the other hand, insists that the Palestinian nation had been long established; after all, the Palestinians have been there for centuries and centuries, unlike the Johnnies-come-lately Jewish settlers. It does not like to remember that, before they had been subjected to the unique realities of Zionist colonization, there was virtually nothing to distinguish the Palestinian Arab population from that of the rest of Greater Syria. Many Palestinian nationalists may even be somewhat offended by the suggestion that their nation owes its very existence to an external factor that has, moreover, been the author of its terrible calamity.

At the same time, many (perhaps most) Palestinian nationalists—and, more generally, Arab nationalists—deny the existence of the Hebrew nation. They point out that the Israeli Jewish community is a recent creation, put together artificially (that is, by conscious design) out of many heterogeneous groups of immigrants. How can such a recent, artificially created hotchpotch be described as a "nation"? Implicit in this argument is the widespread nationalist myth that "true" nations are somehow "natural" creations, formed over long centuries. Marxists know, of course, that nations, in the modern sense of the term, are creations of the development of capitalism; and, as the example of other immigrant societies shows, under appropriate material conditions immigrants from various different backgrounds can rather quickly forge themselves into a nation, particularly if a suitable ideological cement is produced to bind them together.

One reason why Arab nationalists find it difficult to regard the Israeli Jews as a nation is historical. For centuries, Jewish communities have existed throughout the Arab world. They were always regarded as a *millah*, an ethno-religious community, alongside a host of other such minority communities. They were not in any sense a national minority, and were certainly never regarded as such. It is difficult to accept that these people, or their children, have "suddenly," by the mere act of immigration, become part of a separate nation.

But undoubtedly the main reason for refusing to accept the existence of the Hebrew nation is ideological convenience. All bourgeois and petit-bourgeois nationalism—including that of oppressed nations—tends to exclusivism; it wishes to demand exclusive national rights over what it regards as its historical homeland. And it cannot be denied that the existence of another, Hebrew, nation makes the Palestinian problem vastly more complicated. The majority of Palestinian nationalists have by now come to accept that the Israeli Jews, or at least most of them, are there to stay,[4] and must be accorded equality of *individual* rights in the future liberated Palestine. But to recognize them as a *national* entity would imply that they should be accorded some collective national rights. This is much harder to accept, especially for the more radical Palestinian nationalists.

Nevertheless, quite a few Palestinian nationalists have, to their credit, overcome these serious psychological and ideological barriers and have accepted the fact that an Israeli Jewish nation does exist.

I do not propose to waste paper and the reader's time on proving here that the Palestinian Arabs and the Israeli Jews do indeed constitute two national entities, brought into being by the dynamic of Zionist colonization and the struggle against it. These facts are very clear to anyone prepared to examine the reality of the matter rationally with unbiased eyes. And long experience has shown me that virtually all who deny these facts do so because of ideological preconceptions, to which they cling even if they fly in the face of reality. Argument with such people is as futile as debating with flat-earthers.

The Arab Context

The Palestinian national problem has a special aspect, of which few outsiders are sufficiently aware. This arises from the unique formation of the Arab world, in which there are two tiers of nationhood.

Because of historical, linguistic, and cultural factors, the Arab world is in many ways a single national domain, divided into two large regions: the Maghreb, or Arab

West, consisting of North Africa to the west of Libya; and the Mashreq, or Arab East, consisting of all the remaining Arab countries to the east of Libya. (Libya itself straddles this division, and is the connecting link between the Maghreb and the Mashreq.) With the exception of Egypt, all Arab states are recent creations, whose borders were for the most part drawn by foreign imperialist powers to suit their own convenience.

Internal political division is of course nothing new in the Arab world. After a relatively brief period of political unity, the original Arab empire, set up in the seventh century, disintegrated into a number of units. But these Arab states kept changing, dissolving and re-forming, and the borders between them were continually shifting. In the sixteenth century, the Arab world was incorporated in the Ottoman Turkish empire, within which the various Arab regions became so many provinces. Although some of these provinces—notably Egypt—gradually acquired a large measure of de facto independence, the lines dividing one Arab province from another were in principle, and often also in practice, no more than administrative boundaries.

The Arab world has always shared one literary language—the classical Arabic of the Qur'an—and one "high" culture, which nonetheless coexisted with a great diversity of regional spoken Arabic dialects and local popular cultures. But in modern times the linguistic and cultural unity of the Arab world has been greatly enhanced by the cinema, radio, and television. The language of these media—usually a modernized and somewhat vulgarized version of classical Arabic—is heard and understood throughout the Arab world, so that today a Moroccan and an Iraqi who have little formal education can nevertheless converse with each other, something that would have been quite difficult for their counterparts two or three generations ago. Popular culture too has largely broken out of its parochial confines.

In view of this, virtually all Arabs regard the present boundaries between the Arab states not so much as international borders in the proper sense but more as internal division lines within one homeland. This attitude may perhaps be compared to the attitude of the Italians or Germans in the first half of the nineteenth century toward the fragmentation of their countries.

Objectively, it can be said that the Arabs are a nation in the process of formation. This is reflected in Arab consciousness as a widespread popular aspiration to political unification of the Arab world.

Of course, the road to the actual implementation of Arab unification is neither short nor easy. (Note that while the unification of Italy was wholly successful, that of Germany has proved to be much more problematic, so that today [1989] there are three German states: two Germanies and Austria.)

Moreover, due to the sheer size of the Arab world, the important material and historical differences between its various parts, and the diversity of the spoken Arabic dialects, the people of each Arab region constitute a distinct national entity. This is evidently true of Egypt, which has always been a distinct geopolitical unit. The Palestinians too have been formed into a quite distinct national entity, as a result of their unique recent history. Similarly one can talk, for example, of a Syrian, an Iraqi, or an Algerian national entity, which have achieved varying degrees of national crystallization.

Thus every Arab has a dual, or two-tier, national identity: as member of the greater Arab nation, and at the same time also a member of a component subnationality—Egyptian, Palestinian, Iraqi, Algerian, and so forth. To most Arabs these two levels of national affiliation seem quite "natural" and mutually compatible, even complementary. This is greatly aided by the fact that in Arabic each of the two levels of nationhood, as well as the patriotic sentiments and nationalist ideology associated with them, are denoted by quite different terms.[5] In practice there is of course a dialectical tension between the two kinds of nationalism: the centripetal force of all-Arab nationalism and the centrifugal forces of local patriotism. The relative emphasis given to one or the other level of nationalism varies in place and in time, as well as according to class affiliation and individual convictions.

It can hardly be doubted that an ardent aspiration to Arab political unification is deeply implanted in the masses throughout the Arab world. On the other hand, the rulers of the Arab countries have been unwilling or unable to implement this task. The more traditional conservative Arab regimes are happy to mouth slogans about Arab unity but in practice prefer to hold on to their local power and privilege, which they do not wish to risk by unification adventures. The petit-bourgeois populist movements, Nasserism and Ba'thism, which rose to prominence and achieved power in several Arab countries during the 1950s and 1960s, seemed at first to be more genuine about unification; but the few actual attempts in this direction proved to be dismal abortive failures. The 1958 Nasserist union of Egypt and Syria soon collapsed because the new Egyptian ruling class tried to use it to its own narrow advantage, at the expense of its Syrian counterpart. Ba'thism, which was if anything even more fanatically committed to Arab unity, ended up by splitting into two hostile factions, presiding over extremely repressive regimes in Syria and Iraq respectively, and are too much at each other's throats to bother about unity. There is every reason to believe that the existing ruling classes in the Arab world will not be able to do any better in the future.

The question of Arab national unification therefore remains very much an open one. It follows that the Palestinian issue is by no means the only unsolved national problem in which the Palestinian Arab people is directly involved. Clearly, then, it is a grave theoretical and political error for socialists to formulate their position on the Palestinian problem without placing it in the larger context of a socialist attitude to the issues of the Arab world as a whole, and in particular to the question of Arab national unification.

Should Socialists Support Arab Unification?

What has been the attitude of Middle Eastern revolutionary socialists toward the demand for Arab national unification? On the whole, they—and this includes the Arab Communist Parties prior to their total corruption by Stalinism—have concurred in supporting and upholding it. In this they were motivated not by a romantic inclination to pan-Arabist nostalgia but by two quite different reasons.

First, there is the general socialist principle that, other things being equal, bigger states are preferable to smaller ones, because big states afford indisputable advantages, both from the standpoint of economic progress and from that of the interests of the masses and, furthermore, these advantages increase with the growth of capitalism. Therefore socialists must, wherever possible, encourage the unification of smaller national subgroups into larger national entities, and discourage the centrifugal tendencies of local particularism and separatism. All this is of course subject to the vital condition that unification must proceed in a consistently democratic way, without any national coercion, and must ensure equality to all national subgroups, without any special privileges. Separation is to be encouraged when, and only when, there is no other way to guarantee equality and prevent national oppression.

Since the demand for Arab unification is in any case supported by the masses throughout the Arab world, and it is the existing regimes and ruling classes who either oppose this demand outright or are congenitally unable to implement it, socialists would be acting very foolishly indeed if they failed to uphold this cause.

Second, the specific geographic, economic, and demographic configuration of the Arab world is such that its unification is a necessary condition for progress and development. The present political fragmentation—largely imposed by Western imperialism—constitutes an enormous obstacle to economic development under capitalism, and would be totally absurd under a future socialist social order. At present, the main socioeconomic resources are divided extremely unevenly between the various Arab states.

One Arab country has an enormous density of population but no spare land and few other natural resources; another has large reserves of good arable land but a sparse population and virtually no energy resources; and a third has a miniscule population and almost no fresh water or arable land but vast quantities of the most precious subterranean treasure—oil. Clearly, unification is demanded by the most elementary logic of social and economic progress. For these reasons, revolutionary Marxists have long recognized that the program of a socialist transformation of that region must uphold the aim of setting up a united socialist Arab world.

In order to accommodate the great internal diversity of the Arab world, and in particular the existence of distinct subnationalities within the Arab nation, it is vital that the proposed socialist union should have a federal structure, allowing the greatest possible degree of autonomy to each of its constituent parts.[6]

Because a socialist program for the Arab world must obviously form a coherent whole, it is quite absurd to formulate a programmatic position on the Palestinian problem, proposing a long-term solution to it, without relating the proposed solution to the broader socialist aim of creating a united socialist Arab world. Yet, this is precisely what many socialists (not to mention would-be socialists), both in and outside the Middle East, have been doing.

A False Dichotomy

In the public discourse among those who support the right of the Palestinian people to self-determination, an almost universally accepted tacit assumption is that there are two and only two formulas for solving the "Palestine problem."

First, there is the program proposing the creation of a unitary "secular democratic Palestine," which the PLO adopted a few years after the June war of 1967, and which is still upheld by some diminishing radical sections of the PLO and by their non-Palestinian supporters.

Second, there is the "two-state solution," which proposes the partition of Palestine in two, by creating a Palestinian national state alongside Israel, on a territory consisting more or less of the West Bank and the Gaza Strip. This is the solution proposed by the Israeli Communist Party, as well as by various Zionist peace groups (but not by any major Zionist party). It is also supported in fact by the mainstream sections of the PLO, although most of them continue in theory to uphold the idea of a secular democratic Palestine as an aim for the remote future.

Internationally, this plan has the support of many governments, including the Soviet Union and its allies as well as of most third-world and some developed capitalist countries.

Among those who seem to have accepted without question the tacit assumption that these two are the only conceivable solutions, there are quite a few revolutionary socialists. Faced with a choice between the two formulas, which they suppose to be the only possible ones, most of these socialists opt for the secular democratic formula, which is more radical inasmuch as it implies the overthrow of Zionism, and is indeed upheld by the more radical Palestinian nationalists.

However, in light of what has been stated above, it is quite clear that neither formula can possibly serve as a socialist program for solving the Palestinian problem. In both formulas, the Palestinian people is treated as a totally separate national entity, in isolation from the Arab nation. And Palestine is treated as a separate entity, which is to form a unitary state or partitioned in two, but in either case is seen in isolation from the context of the Arab world.

Associated with this is another feature shared by both formulas: they are bourgeois in the sense that they envisage a solution of the Palestinian problem within the present capitalist order, rather than in the context of a socialist transformation. Now, I do not wish to claim in general that every national problem requires, for its solution, a socialist revolution. But, for particular reasons that will be explained later on, I do argue that an ultimate, entirely satisfactory solution to the Palestinian problem is very unlikely to be achieved within the present social order. If this be granted, then it is an error for socialists to advocate a formula for solving the Palestinian problem that does not explicitly connect it with a program for a socialist revolution.

Such errors are inevitable when socialists accept the terms of the discourse as defined by nationalists, instead of rethinking the whole issue ab initio in socialist terms. A revolutionary socialist position on the Palestinian question should start from the programmatic aim of creating a united socialist Arab world, or at least a united socialist Arab East, and proceed to provide within this framework a solution to the particular national problem of the Palestinian people.

In addition to the fundamental defects already mentioned, which are common to both bourgeois formulas, each one of the two has additional grave defects of its own.

When one reads the small-print explanations of the secular democratic scheme,[7] it transpires that one of the basic aims of this old PLO formula was to evade the difficulty posed for Palestinian nationalism by the existence of the Hebrew nation. This difficulty is "solved" by the fiction that the Jews of Palestine constitute not a national entity but a religious denomination. The phrase "secular democratic Palestine" is in fact an abbreviation of the full formula, which reads: "a democratic, non-sectarian Palestine where Christians, Jews and Muslims can live, work and worship without discrimination." Here the Israeli Jews are clearly regarded as a religious community, on a par with Christians and Muslims, rather than a national entity on a par with Palestinian Arabs. This is indeed the meaning that the authors of the formula encoded in the word "secular."

But what national entities are there in Palestine? The authors of this formula claim that "the majority of Jews in Palestine today are Arab Jews—euphemistically called Oriental Jews by the Zionists. Therefore, Palestine combines Jewish, Christian, and Muslim Arabs as well as non-Arab Jews (Western Jews)."

This piece of ideology ignores several facts. First, not all so-called Oriental Israeli Jews originate in Arab countries; for example, Israelis of Iranian and Turkish origin are also classed as "Oriental" or "Mizrahim."* Second, while the Jewish communities that existed in some Arab countries, such as Iraq, may perhaps be described as "Arab Jews,"† this is certainly not the case for most of the Jews in some other Arab countries, such as Egypt and Algeria, who did not speak Arabic and did not share in Arab culture. Third, by now the great majority of Mizrahi Israeli Jews are not the original immigrants that were brought there in the 1950s but their children and grandchildren, whose first language is Hebrew and who for the most part do not speak or even understand the languages of the original immigrants. The Israeli descendant of Iraqi immigrants can no more be described as an Arab Jew than an American descendant of Italian immigrants can be said to belong to the Italian nation. All these are objective facts, to which must be added the subjective, but no less important, fact that the people in question, almost without exception, regard themselves as part of the Israeli Jewish nation and not as Arab Jews.

The true meaning of the secular democratic formula now becomes quite clear. In the future liberated Palestine, the Jews will be granted equal individual rights,

---

* In Israel, Jews originating from Muslim countries are referred to—by others as well as by themselves—as "Mizrahim," which is Hebrew for "Orientals"; see also endnote 1 to chapter 14 in this book.

† See, however, a detailed discussion of this question in "Zionism and Oriental Jews: Dialectic of Exploitation and Co-optation" by Ehud Ein-Gil and Moshé Machover, chapter 14 in this book.

including religious freedom, but they will not be recognized as a nationality and will therefore have no national rights. The only national entity in Palestine, according to this nationalist Palestinian ideology, is Arab—comprising Christians, Muslims, and most of the Jews. The remaining Jews, those of European origin, apparently do not belong to any nationality. The future secular democratic Palestine will therefore be an Arab country, in which no other national group shall be recognized.

While this position is quite typical of bourgeois and petit-bourgeois nationalism, which is exclusivist and only cares about its own nation, it is totally unacceptable to socialists, who must insist on equality of rights for all nations.

Some people who consider themselves Marxists protest at this point that socialists should only demand national rights for oppressed nations, while the Israeli Jews, if they are a nation at all, are clearly an oppressing one. This argument is sheer sophism. It is certainly true that the Hebrew nation is now an oppressing one and therefore it would be wrong to demand any national rights for it at present. At this moment it is not the Hebrew nation that is deprived of national rights; on the contrary, it has usurped national privileges at the expense of the Palestinian people. But in the future state proposed by the authors of the secular democratic formula, the Israeli Jews would become an oppressed nation, whose very existence is denied. Some Palestinian nationalists may well think that this would be a just retribution to be meted to the Israelis for their past and present crimes. But it would be absurd for socialist internationalists to support such a program that proposes to "solve" a national problem by reversing the roles of oppressor and oppressed.

The defects of the two-state formula, as a solution to the Palestinian problem, are even more glaring. The root cause of the whole problem is Zionist colonization, and therefore the problem cannot be solved completely without the overthrow of Zionism.

Israel is, and has been since its foundation, a Zionist state, and as such it is a structurally racist settlers' state. This was the case even before 1967, and will continue to be the case if Israel were to withdraw back to its pre-1967 borders.

Since the foundation of Israel, its Palestinian Arab minority (within the pre-1967 Green Line) have been severely oppressed: denied many individual civil rights as well as all rights pertaining to a national minority. Most of their lands have been expropriated by various forms of legalized robbery, and they have been subjected to economic discrimination, social persecution, and individual humiliation. All this is unlikely to change, so long as Israel remains a Zionist state, even if a Palestinian state is set up in the West Bank and Gaza Strip. On the contrary, the Palestinian minority inside Israel may be put at greater risk: the pressure for their "transfer"— that is, deportation—which is quite strong already, is likely to grow, as every complaint by them will be met with the reply, "You have your own state now, so if you don't like it here, you can go there."

In addition, the two-state formula fails to address the rights of the Palestinian refugees expelled from the pre-1967 Israeli territory.

Finally, given the disparity in area, resources, economic development, and military power between a Zionist racist Israel (even reduced back to the [pre-1967] Green Line) and a Palestinian state in the West Bank and Gaza Strip, the relations between the two states is likely to be somewhat similar to those between the Republic of South Africa [under apartheid] and Lesotho or Swaziland.

For these reasons, it is quite out of the question for socialists to advocate the two-state formula as a solution to the Palestinian problem.

Long-Term Program and Interim Demands

For the reasons just explained, a genuine solution to the Palestinian national problem requires not merely the withdrawal of Israel from its 1967 conquests but the overthrow of Zionism in Israel itself. (This much is indeed presupposed also by the secular democratic Palestine formula, which is however unacceptable for other reasons, as I have argued.)

But the numerical, political, and technical relations of forces are such that the Palestinian people on its own, even if fully mobilized, are highly unlikely to be able to achieve the total overthrow of Zionism. Nor are the Arab states, under their present regimes, able to do so.

The overthrow of Zionism will become possible only through a deep social and political transformation of the Arab world, or at the very least the Mashreq, which will not only unite it but also infuse it with new revolutionary social energies.

Moreover, because of the partnership between Zionism and Western, particularly American, imperialism, and because of the political, financial, and military protection that the former receives from the latter, the overthrow of Zionism is inseparable from the uprooting of imperialist domination over the Arab world.

All this points to the conclusion that an ultimate thorough solution of the Palestinian problem can be achieved only as part of a socialist revolution throughout the entire region, leading in particular to the overthrow of Zionism. Socialists who fail to make this conclusion clear, and who support various bourgeois nationalist formulas that obscure it, are guilty of gross dereliction of duty and are indeed acting in a self-defeating way.

A socialist program must therefore be along the following lines. A united socialist Arab world—or at least, in the first instance, Arab East—with a federal structure, reflecting the two-tier structure of the Arab nation. The Palestinian problem would be solved within this union by incorporating in it a part of Palestine as one or more autonomous Palestinian Arab cantons. The remaining part of Palestine will also be incorporated in the union, as one or more autonomous Hebrew national cantons. Thus the whole of Palestine's territory is to be included in the union, but as two or more cantons rather than as one country. The boundaries between the Palestinian Arab and Hebrew cantons are to be determined not on the basis of the present or past borders of Israel but according to economic, geographical, and demographic criteria, a principal criterion being which national group—Palestinian Arab or Hebrew—is the majority of the population in a given district.

Naturally, the socialist union is to be formed in a democratic way, by voluntary accession rather than by coercion. In particular, the Hebrew nation (as well as the other non-Arab nationalities in the Arab world) will be invited to join freely; that is, on the basis of the right to self-determination. This is absolutely vital for two reasons. First, it is in any case unthinkable for socialist relations between nations to be established on any other basis. Second, the task of a socialist revolution in the whole area will become immeasurably easier if at least part of the Israeli masses, of the working class in particular, would be attracted away from Zionism into the camp of the revolution. This cannot possibly be achieved without guaranteeing to respect their Hebrew national identity.

Obviously, the program just outlined is very much a long-term one. It would be foolish to pretend that it is capable of being realized in the near future, and it is vain to speculate how many decades will elapse before it can become a reality. But only a crass pragmatist can think that for this reason there is no point in putting forward such a program and trying to mobilize support for it. Without the light, albeit distant, of a long-term program to guide it, political activity is blind and ends up by falling into the trap of opportunism.

It is equally obvious, however, that a long-term program alone is insufficient. If all that we had to tell the Palestinian masses was that their national problem would be, and can only be, fully solved by a socialist revolution in the entire Arab East, then they would rightly dismiss us as irrelevant loonies. We must put forward not only a long-term program but also immediate and interim demands for the short and middle term. At the same time, socialists must also formulate an attitude to the various plans, demands, and proposals put forward by other parties, inside and outside the region.

One immediate demand that is indisputably vital is the demand to put an end to the Israeli occupation of the West Bank and Gaza Strip. This has been the demand of all true socialists—indeed of all true democrats—ever since 1967, but it has acquired added impetus with the Palestinian uprising that started in December 1987 and is still going strong at the time of writing (September 1988).

In this connection, we must also formulate an attitude toward an interim demand that has received wide support among the Palestinians in the Occupied Territories, namely the demand to set up a Palestinian national state in these territories.

I have argued in detail that the creation of a Palestinian ministate alongside Israel can in no way be considered a complete solution to the Palestinian problem and is even fraught with some dangers. But this does not mean that socialists should *oppose* the demand for such a state. On the contrary, it seems to me that subject to certain provisos, a Palestinian state in the West Bank and Gaza Strip may well represent a definite step forward, a definite improvement compared to the present situation.

I therefore believe that the right position is to support this demand with due reservation, while explaining very carefully and patiently that its implementation would fall far short of solving the Palestinian problem. In other words, what should be opposed in the two-state formula is not the demand itself, which in the present conditions is actually correct, but the pretension that this is The Solution to the Palestinian problem.

On the other hand, a situation may arise in the future in which some variant of the secular democratic formula may become appropriate, not as a long-term solution of the problem but as an interim demand.

Imagine, for example, a rather pessimistic scenario, which unfortunately cannot be ruled out entirely, in which the Palestinian uprising is eventually suppressed and the creeping de facto annexation of the Occupied Territories to Israel is resumed and proceeds to such an extent that the creation of a Palestinian state in these territories comes to be regarded, by the Palestinian masses themselves, as altogether impracticable. In such a hypothetical situation,[8] it may be correct to demand that the state of occupation be ended by according equal rights—both individual civil rights and collective rights as a national group—to the Palestinians under Israeli rule. The implementation of such a demand would tend to produce an approximation to a democratic binational state.

Yet other, hitherto unforeseen, situations may arise in which entirely new immediate and interim demands would have to be raised.

The point is not to speculate what these situations and demands might be. What is important is to stress that socialists must be prepared to be flexible and responsive to the changing situation and to the mood of the masses in formulating immediate and interim demands, while at all times upholding the long-term socialist solution to the problems of the peoples of the region as a whole.

9

Sharon's Agenda and Arafat's Irrelevance

What is [Ariel] Sharon trying to achieve by the massive devastation of the Occupied Territories, the widespread humiliation of the Palestinian population, and the brutal bloodshed? Surely, as antiterrorist strategy this is patently counterproductive: it can only engender hundreds of new suicidal would-be martyrs, who—reversing Samson's last words—will pray to their merciful and compassionate god: "Let me die with the Jews, and take with me as many of them as you please." Any fool can see this; and Sharon is certainly no fool.

Another, apparently unconnected, curious fact: a few weeks ago Sharon called Yasser Arafat "irrelevant." What did he mean? As a term of abuse, "irrelevant" would be rather weak, certainly by Israeli standards; and Sharon is anything but weak. It could of course be interpreted as a subtle insult; but Sharon is not a subtle man—cunning, yes, but this is quite a different matter.

No, Sharon's description of Arafat was in fact chillingly literal. It can best be understood as addressed not to Arafat himself or to the outside world but in the context of an internal discourse within the Israeli leadership. In order to decode Sharon's deeds and words, we have to go back to the early 1990s. The first intifada, which erupted in late 1987 and went on for several years, had by 1991 taught the Israeli leadership that Israel could not long continue its direct rule over the Palestinians: keeping "order" in the Occupied Territories was just too costly—not only in economic terms but also in its adverse effects on Israel's army and society. Shimon Peres concluded that a way must be found to get the Palestinians to police themselves. This of course meant giving them some degree of autonomy. It also required a willing Palestinian partner, who would be ready to lead an autonomous Palestinian Authority—on Israeli terms. These terms include bearing sole responsibility for

---

Circulated by email, March 11, 2002. Ariel Sharon was prime minister of Israel from March 7, 2001, until April 14, 2006; he was incapacitated by a stroke on January 4, 2006.

preventing any attack on Israeli soldiers, settlers, or civilians—and taking full blame for any attacks that do occur.

As it happened, such a partner was found in the apparently unlikely shape of Yasser Arafat, who was desperate for a deal at almost any price. His feeble bargaining position was of his own making. By foolishly siding with Saddam Hussein in the Gulf War (instead of taking the morally justified and politically astute position of "a plague a' both your houses"), Arafat cut the financial branch on which he had been sitting so comfortably. Until the Gulf War, he had maintained his control of the PLO and manipulation of its personnel by means of ample funds flowing from Saudi Arabia and the Gulf States, both as direct government subventions and as taxes he was allowed to levy on the large Palestinian refugee community profitably employed there. Suddenly the funds were cut off, and Arafat was left bereft of his means of control.

No wonder he was ready to accept Israel's terms at Oslo, without—so insiders report—even bothering to read the small print. For Peres's plan, which he eventually managed to sell to an initially reluctant Rabin, this was a very "relevant" Arafat. In fact, he was vital.

But other Israeli leaders—some in the Labor Party, but most in the Likud and its far-right allies—drew a different lesson from the first intifada. Yes, Israel cannot indefinitely subdue an oppressed Palestinian population. But allowing the Palestinians to do it on a DIY basis was too risky: it may start as a bantustan, but who knows where it might lead, given time? After all, had not Zionist colonization of Palestine also started from modest beginnings, under foreign control? The only alternative is to complete the ethnic cleansing—or, to use the Israeli term: "transfer"—that had been massively begun during the 1948 war and in its immediate aftermath, and attempted again, with much less success, in the wake of the 1967 war.

For this transfer plan, now supported by 46 percent of Israel's Jewish citizens and openly advocated by several of Sharon's ministers, Arafat is indeed highly irrelevant. If the Palestinians are to be stampeded across the Jordan, even his feeble and corrupt leadership is merely an obstacle. For a stampede, you don't need any leader; what you do need is to terrorize the Palestinians into becoming a frightened herd. If some become frenzied suicide bombers, this is a price worth paying for the greater national good.

This is what Sharon is attempting to do. His plan is not new: it long predates Oslo. It is part of a breathtakingly grandiose plan to rearrange the whole Middle East under Israeli hegemony, with client Arab states in all parts of the region, including a Palestinian bantustan—not in Cisjordanian Palestine [west of the Jordan], but across the river, in what is now Hashemite Jordan. It was this plan he was trying to implement in 1982, when he deceived the Begin cabinet into supporting his Lebanese adventure.* Nor is Sharon's Grand Plan a deeply held secret: at the time of the Lebanese war it was openly and widely discussed in the Israeli press.

---

* Sharon was defense minister in the Begin cabinet.

That time it failed. But Ariel "the Bulldozer" Sharon is nothing if not dogged. He will try it again; he is trying it again. Yes, he will promise the Americans that he would behave; he will agree to cease fire; he will consent to negotiate. But he will break any promise, violate any agreement, and torpedo any talks—if they stand in the way of his plan.

An excellent opportunity will arise if and when Bush II starts another large-scale "antiterrorist" war on Iraq.*

And after that? The next item in the grand plan is Iran, which is the only serious potential obstacle to Israeli regional hegemony.

Will Sharon's grand plan succeed? Will he be able to implement even its first stage, the "transfer" of the Palestinians? He may well do, if the world lets him.†

---

* The predicted war broke out almost exactly one year after this article was written. However, its conventional phase, ending with George W. Bush's declaration of "victory," was too brief to serve as smoke screen under which massive "transfer" could be implemented.

† Arafat died on November 11, 2004, at the age of seventy-five, following a mysterious illness. The cause of death was never conclusively determined, but there are strong rumors that he was poisoned by the Mossad, Israel's national intelligence and special operations agency. Sharon was then still in office as prime minister.

10

A FAQ: What Do You Think about Suicide Bombers?

The common motivation behind this frequently asked question is by no means an innocent one. In fact, the question itself is quite strange: why ask about *suicide* bombers rather than about bombers *simpliciter*? Is the questioner interested in our view about suicide bombers as distinct from *non-suicide* ones? Surely, whether a perpetrator of a bombing commits suicide in the act is—morally speaking—not the principal issue: what matters most is the bombing. And why confine the question to *bombing*? Can our judgment about firing a machine-gun indiscriminately into a crowd differ from that about detonating a bomb in a crowded place?

I will therefore start by considering the principal issue raised by the question: that of indiscriminate killing. Yet, the secondary issue of suicide committed in such an act is nevertheless of some importance, and I do not wish to evade it. I will deal with it later on.

Indiscriminate Killing

Indiscriminate killing of persons who are non-combatants and who may well be innocent is an abhorrent atrocity and must be condemned without reservation. Where the intention or the likely effect is the murder of *many* innocent non-combatants, the act is all the more heinous. This is so irrespective of the larger goal in the name of which the act is perpetrated. An atrocity can in no way be justified or excused even if committed in the course of a just war or a struggle for liberation from oppression.

Yet, the aims and circumstances do make a difference—not to the culpability of the act itself but with respect to *additional* blame that may be associated with it. An

---

This article was written in March 2005 and circulated by email.

atrocity committed in an unjust war or in the service of oppression is *doubly* damnable: for its aim as well as the means. But where an evil is committed by those who resist oppression and in the course of struggle for liberation, the oppressor must be regarded as an accessory to the outrage. This is because the oppressor must know that those driven to despair and outrage by their miserable condition are likely to respond by deranged desperate outrageous acts; this in no way exculpates the latter, but it does make the former a causative contributor to evildoing. Oppression is the root cause.

Does a Perpetrator's Suicide Make a Difference?

Within an armed conflict, suicide killing—whether by bombing or by other means—is in almost all cases perpetrated by the weaker side, often by the downtrodden. So the hidden agenda behind the question posed at the outset, asking us to comment on suicide bombings, is to make us focus on the violence of the oppressed and turn our attention away from that of the oppressor. We must not fall into this trap. Yet the question deserves a straight answer.

In a case of indiscriminate killing of random victims, the suicide of the perpetrator does make some difference. However, the difference does not concern the degree of abhorrence or culpability of the act but the character of the perpetrator. It is this: a soldier firing a missile from the safety of a helicopter or a tank into a densely populated area is not only a war criminal but also a coward. An officer or politician ordering such acts from the safety of an office is a war arch-criminal and an arch-coward. But suicide bombing—however abhorrent—is clearly not a cowardly act. In some limited sense—which in no way implies moral approval!—it may even be regarded as heroic. (One of the definitions of "heroic" in the WordNet Dictionary of Princeton University is "showing extreme courage; especially of actions courageously undertaken in desperation as a last resort." And in the Shorter Oxford Dictionary one of the definitions is "having recourse to bold, daring, or extreme measures." Courage has no moral value whatsoever in itself; it is only laudable when in the service of good.)

Eyeless in Gaza

Contrary to the propaganda spread by some Western politicians and their media lackeys, suicide killing is by no means an invention of Islamic fanatics, nor is it unique to them. In fact, it is widespread in many cultures. In modern times it has been practiced, for example, by the Tamil Tigers in Sri Lanka. Kamikaze bombing by Japanese pilots in the Second World War is also similar in many respects.

But it is important to point out the positive attitude to an extreme act of this sort in the Judeo-Christian tradition. I am referring to the story about Samson in the biblical Book of Judges.

Samson, who terrorized the Philistines, was captured by them (using his lover Delilah as honey trap, in a ruse reminiscent of the capture of the nuclear whistleblower Mordechai Vanunu using an attractive Mossad agent). This is how the story ends (Judges 16:21–30):

> But the Philistines took him, and put out his eyes, and brought him down to Gaza, and bound him with fetters of brass; and he did grind in the prison house. . . . Then the lords of the Philistines gathered them together for to offer a great sacrifice unto Dagon their god, and to rejoice: for they said, Our god hath delivered Samson our enemy into our hand. And when the people saw him, they praised their god: for they said, Our god hath delivered into our hands our enemy, and the destroyer of our country, which slew many of us. And it came to pass, when their hearts were merry, that they said, Call for Samson, that he may make us sport. And they called for Samson out of the prison house; and he made them sport: and they set him between the pillars. And Samson said unto the lad that held him by the hand, Suffer me that I may feel the pillars whereupon the house standeth, that I may lean upon them. Now the house was full of men and women; and all the lords of the Philistines [were] there; and [there were] upon the roof about three thousand men and women, that beheld while Samson made sport. And Samson called unto the LORD, and said, O Lord GOD, remember me, I pray thee, and strengthen me, I pray thee, only this once, O God, that I may be at once avenged of the Philistines for my two eyes. And Samson took hold of the two middle pillars upon which the house stood, and on which it was borne up, of the one with his right hand, and of the other with his left. And Samson said, Let me die with the Philistines. And he bowed himself with [all his] might; and the house fell upon the lords, and upon all the people that [were] therein. So the dead which he slew at his death were more than [they] which he slew in his life.

This story of the suicidal killing of thousands of men and women, most of them no doubt innocent, by the blinded and humiliated Samson, is taught approvingly to present-day Israeli children. The protagonist is conventionally referred to as "Samson the Hero" (Shimshon Haggibbor).

The seventeenth-century revolutionary English poet John Milton, a devout Christian, is even more panegyrical in his glorification of this suicide killing. At the end of his great poem *Samson Agonistes* (verses 1664–1672) he says:

> *O dearly-bought revenge, yet glorious!*
> *Living or dying thou hast fulfill'd*
> *The work for which thou wast foretold*
> *To Israel, and now ly'st victorious*
> *Among thy slain, self-killed;*
> *Not willingly, but tangled in the fold*
> *Of dire necessity, whose law in death conjoin'd*
> *Thee with thy slaughtered foes, in number more*
>   *Than all thy life hath slain before.*

Of course, we need not accept the judgment of the Book of Judges (any more than the creationist story of Genesis). Nor should we blindly follow Milton in this matter. But let us beware of facile one-sided lack of compassion toward the miserable wretches driven by oppression and humiliation to horrendous deeds.

Part II
ISRAELI SOCIETY

11

Matzpen and Ha'olam Hazeh–New Force

Foreword*

In 1965, toward the elections to the sixth Knesset (Israel's parliament), the editors and coproprietors of the weekly *Ha'olam Hazeh*, Uri Avnery and Shalom Cohen, started a movement called Ha'olam Hazeh–New Force, which raised anti-establishment slogans, did not regard itself as Zionist, and called for recognition of the Palestinian people and integration of Israel in the Middle East. This attracted support among varied sections of the Israeli public, including some young Arabs.

Matzpen did not join this movement as a group, but some of our militants joined it as individuals, worked energetically in the election campaign and thereby helped Avnery to get elected to the Knesset.[†]

The movement had virtually no formal structure or detailed program until December 1966. Then, more than a year after the election, it held what was in effect its formal founding conference, which was expected to adopt a draft program ("Principles"), proposed by Avnery and his confidants.

The seventeen amendments ("reservations") proposed by me to this draft had two aims. First, to make the program consistently non-Zionist, by eliminating the draft's concessions to Zionist ideology. Second, to make it minimally acceptable to socialists, by eliminating statements and expressions on socioeconomic matters that no socialist could support.

I knew there was little chance of getting my amendments adopted. But I hoped they would serve to rally the minority of leftists in the movement. In the event, this is what happened. During the conference, we were expelled from the movement,

---

* This foreword was added in 2011 for this book.

† The 120 members of the Knesset are elected by the party-list proportional representation system. The HHNF list got 14,124 votes, 1.2 percent of the total: more than enough for one seat, but not for two.

61

not only because of the political differences but also because of Avnery's authoritarianism: he regarded the movement virtually as his private property, and was not going to tolerate any challenge, let alone opposition to his absolute leadership. But on our way out we were joined by a few new members.

In a duplicated document distributed at the start of the conference, I explained my "reservations" in some detail. This text is deliberately as moderate as it was possible to make it, consistent with the aim of the amendments. It has never been published in print*; I have made the translation below from the original typescript.

The "chapters" and "articles" referred to in this document are those of the draft Principles.

Reasons for my reservations about the draft Principles presented to the first conference of the Ha'olam Hazeh–New Force movement

In order not to take up too much time during the oral debate in the conference, I have chosen to put in writing the arguments for the seventeen amendments I tabled to the draft Principles.

Reservations to Chapter I

Article 1, as it stands, is so badly phrased that in part it is meaningless and in part factually incorrect.

According to the draft, "The independent and sovereign State of Israel, in its existing borders, is the possession of all its citizens, irrespective of nationality, ethnicity, religion, origin and language."

If we take this sentence literally, it contains hardly a single truth. The State of Israel is not entirely *independent and sovereign*; it has no *borders* recognized by the international community or set in an international treaty, but *armistice demarcation* lines (which, as the armistice agreements† explicitly state, are not political borders); it *does not* at present belong to all its citizens irrespective of nationality, etc.

So what is apparently intended is to assert that the State of Israel *will* or *should* be independent, sovereign, etc. So instead of "is," it should say "will be."

But this necessary emendation brings out another serious fault in the phrasing of the article. If we read "The independent and sovereign State of Israel, in its existing borders, will be the possession of all its citizens, . . ." then this raises immediately the following question. In a properly phrased sentence, each part ought to

---

* An electronic version of the Hebrew original is posted on the Matzpen website: www.matzpen.org/index.asp?p=haolam-1966.

† Agreements signed in 1949 between Israel and its neighbors (Egypt, Jordan, Syria, and Lebanon) following the 1948–49 war.

add something to the meaning of the sentence as a whole, to extend or qualify its sense; so what extension or qualification is intended by the words "in its existing borders"? Is this supposed to imply that if the borders of the State of Israel were to change to some extent, then it will *not* be the possession of all its citizens? Clearly such an interpretation is absurd.

Therefore the inescapable conclusion is that what we have here is a faulty formulation of quite a different idea. Apparently the intended meaning is "the State of Israel must remain in its present borders."

In the 1948 war certain facts were created, which constitute the *status quo*— the status quo to which the present regime adheres and which it wishes to extend forever, and has made into a cornerstone of its policy. As a result of the war the territory allotted by the UN to the Palestinian Arabs was split equally between Transjordan and Israel. To be precise, this was not only the result of the war but also of the secret bargain between King Abdullah and Ben-Gurion. Another consequence of the war was that the majority of the Palestinian Arabs became refugees.

The proposed draft asserts, in effect, that while we ought to support changing the status quo regarding the refugee question, we must consent as a matter of principle to the perpetuation of the territorial situation created as a result of the war and the agreement between Abdullah and Ben-Gurion.

I am opposed to the adoption of such a principle by the movement. In order to prevent misunderstanding let me add at once that I am not in favor of adopting an opposite principle, of advocating some *other* boundaries for Israel. But insisting, as a matter of principle, on the existing boundaries is mistaken in my opinion.

If it were a matter of listing not *principles* but *practical demands* that we would wish to present for negotiation with the Arab world today, it could be argued that keeping the status quo is simpler than changing it; and therefore it should be kept. (This argument may not be justified but at least would be logical.)

But what we have here is not a proposed bargaining position in negotiations that are about to start right now but our principled position. I think that even a devout optimist does not believe that our principles can be implemented in the immediate future. That will necessarily take several years at least—and in the meantime the situation (including the territorial situation) in the region may change to some extent.

The present boundaries of Israel have no priority, as a matter of principle, over any other boundaries, whether those that have been proposed at one time (the lines of the Peel Plan,* those of the UN Partition Plan, the lines of Jehovah's promise to Abraham), or just any more-or-less-arbitrary lines that can be drawn on the map. The present boundaries have no metaphysical significance and do not constitute "natural" borders, geographically or in any other sense. They reflect only the position of the fighting forces at the end of the 1948 war.

---

* The Palestine Royal Commission, headed by Lord William Peel, proposed in 1937 the partition of Palestine.

Of course, at this moment they have one enormous advantage: they exist, whereas any other line is merely hypothetical. But this advantage is a matter of fact rather than principle, and will disappear at once if the territorial situation were to change for one reason or another.

To make this more concrete, let us suppose that (perish the thought!) a war will break out in the coming year, following which an Arab territory would be held by Israel, or an Israeli territory by an Arab state. Or suppose that during this year the Great Powers will impose a territorial change. How would we have to interpret the words "in its existing borders" in the proposed principle?

Two interpretations are possible—and both are implausible.

First interpretation: the "existing borders" are those that existed at the time of the first conference of New Force, in December 1966. In other words, whatever the real situation in a year, two years, five or ten years—we must strive to bring back the borders that existed in the reality of 1966. Clearly, a commitment as a matter of principle to insist on such a demand is illogical.

Second interpretation: the "existing borders" are those that will exist next year. In other words, we commit ourselves as a matter of principle to support whatever border would exist at any given moment. It must be admitted that this interpretation—however absurd it is—would be consistent if we adopt here and now the principle of "existing borders." Indeed, suppose the Israeli government will annex Nablus and hold it for a number of years, the status of Nablus at that time will be like that of any territory conquered by the IDF in 1948—so if today we agree to accept, as a matter of *principle*, the border that exists *right now*, why should we not accept in the future any border that would exist then?*

In my opinion, it is unnecessary and impossible to turn a border into a principle. When we [our movement] are in power and negotiate with the Arab world, we will no doubt put forward a practical proposal for permanent borders. That proposal may or may not be congruent with the lines that exist now. That will depend on the situation at the time of the negotiations, as well as on various practical considerations. But to adopt right now a particular border as a matter of principle—this is an illogical error. On the question of borders it is possible, at most, to assert two general principles. First, Israel's borders must be mutually agreed upon. Second, the borders must be such as to enable the existence of a State of Israel integrated in the region. (Without integration in the region Israel would not be viable in the long term even within borders that are larger than the present ones.) But these things are so obvious that it is doubtful whether they need to be included as explicit principles.

---

* In the event, Israel started a war a few months after the conference, in June 1967. During the war, Avnery adopted an ultrapatriotic stance, and called in print for the Israeli armed forces to go "forward to Damascus!" Immediately following the war, he voted in the Knesset for the annexation of East Jerusalem to Israel. However, he has opposed the annexation of other territories occupied in that war, and has supported the creation of a Palestinian state in the Gaza Strip and the West Bank.

Instead of adopting illogical "principles" on the question of borders, it would be better in my opinion to explain to the public that it is not the border question that is the key to the existence of Israel and to the resolution of its conflict with the Arab world. Rather, the key is integration in the region. If integration of Israel is achieved, the border question will surely become much less important and will be regarded—by both sides—as a secondary matter.

◆ ◆ ◆

In Chapter I of the draft (one of whose topics is "equality") there is no mention of *equal rights for women*. It seems to me self-evident that such a principle is essential.

Reservations to Chapter V

Article 35 speaks about "integration of the Arab citizens in the state and public apparatus." The qualification, "according to their relative number" is no doubt well intentioned, but is liable to be interpreted as indicating a *numerus clausus* (i.e., there will not be more Arab civil servants than the Arabs "deserve" according to their relative weight in the population); or perhaps as a binational principle (filling positions according to a precise national formula). In a pluralist state such a qualification is neither needed nor desirable.

Article 37 promises that public institutions will help the Arabs in Israel to rid themselves of backward social patterns. This reeks of condescension. Do not backward social patterns exist among various Jewish strata and ethnic groups? It should be stated in general terms that public institutions will help all the country's inhabitants to rid themselves of such patterns.

Article 38 promises to equalize the status of Arab women to that of their Jewish sisters. Is the status of women among, say, [Jewish] immigrants from Kurdistan so high that Arab women should regard reaching it as their heart's desire? Here again there is condescension (unintended, no doubt), due to the fact that the authors of the draft belong to the educated strata and are not sufficiently aware of the situation among the broad strata of the Hebrew population.

In my opinion it should be sufficient to assert a general principle of equal rights for women, as I mentioned in connection with Chapter I of the draft Principles.

Reservations to Chapter VII

Article 51 of the draft claims that the mutual affinity between Israel and Jews around the world is an actual and positive fact. There is no doubt that the affinity exists. But is it right to assert in a sweeping and casual way that it is *positive*? Do Israeli Arabs also have to think that this affinity is "positive"? This formulation implies that the affinity, *in its existing form*, is desirable. I disagree.

In my opinion it should be asserted that Jews *around the world* have *no special national rights* over Palestine (and not merely, as Article 52 asserts, that they have no right to interfere in Israel's internal affairs).

Zionist ideology is based crucially on the idea that the world's Jews (rather than just the Hebrew nation in this country) have special national rights in Palestine; any formulation that speaks one-sidedly of "Jewish affinity" is a concession to Zionism.

Is the affinity of all Arabs around the world (not only the Palestinian Arabs) to Palestine inferior to that of Jews around the world to the State of Israel? So why mention one "affinity"—and go so far as asserting that it is "positive"—and ignore the other? Is the religious affinity of Christians and Muslims to this country not a fact? Is it less "positive" than the religious affinity of the Jews?

Article 53 demands that Israel welcome immigration of Jews, as well as that of non-Jews who can contribute to the strengthening and prosperity of the country. This formulation implies that Jewish immigration would be "welcome" unconditionally, whereas other immigrants would be "welcome" only if they contribute to strengthening the country. The title of this article ("Jewish immigration") also displays a different attitude to immigrants according to racial origin.

This is a clear climb down from the principle of a *pluralist* country. It is inconceivable that we adopt a principle that prescribes a difference—however slight—in the attitude to immigrants according to their racial origin or religious affiliation. The attitude [to immigrants] should be according to character, skills, and age, as well as humanitarian considerations (granting asylum to persecuted persons).

Can we accept that questionnaires of the state's immigration department include sections regarding racial origin and religious views?

Reservations to Chapter IX

Article 60 asserts that Israel's main aim ought to be integration in the region. But why should the region be described as "multinational"? How many nations are there in it? In fact there are three: Arabs, Jews, and Kurds. Do three make "many" [multi]?

Perhaps the authors of the article mean to include Iran and Turkey et cetera as well in their concept of the "multinational region." But should Israel's "main aim" be integration with Iran and Turkey? Of course not. In order to secure its existence Israel must integrate with its Arab neighbors, with whom it is in conflict, and it is its relations with them that will determine its future. Moreover, in reality there exists a movement for unification of the Arab world—it has real roots and prospects. But (if we dismiss the idea of a "Muslim World League" mooted by Faisal* and his Western masters) there exists no movement for a "multinational" union of Arabs, Persians, Turks, and so on; this is not on any real agenda.

---

* Faisal bin Abdul-Aziz, King of Saudi Arabia, 1964–75.

In fact, the region in which we ought to integrate is Arab—in terms of the language and nationality of the overwhelming majority of its inhabitants. It would have been most correct to speak of integration in the *Arab East*. But in case one is worried that this might be misinterpreted as though we are advocating "Arabization" of Israel, it would be best to speak simply of integration in the region, without the mistaken and misleading adjective "multinational."

Article 62 speaks of "support for the aspiration of the Arab nations." Most Arabs believe there is a *single* Arab nation. Do we have to assert the opposite, as though out of spite? In my opinion it is correct to speak of "the aspiration of the Arab nation"—but if we do not wish to go into the question as to how many Arab nations there are (and indeed there is no need to do so in the present context), one can say simply "aspiration of the Arab world."

This article is also deficient in that it fails to mention the main aspiration of the Arab masses in our time: socialist Arab unity.

Reservations to Chapter XI

Article 73 overstates the case in asserting that Israel's supreme economic goal (economic independence, welfare, equitable income distribution) would be *fully* realized by integration in a regional common market. Such integration is a necessary condition for achieving this goal, but not a sufficient one.

Article 77 demands minimizing the physical intervention of the state in the economy. This means, among other things, opposition to nationalization and expansion of the state-owned sector (except for the "minimum necessary" required for implementation of the national economic plan).

Persons of a socialist persuasion cannot accept such a demand; but, on the contrary, would support the opposite tendency: nationalization of enterprises and expansion of the state and public sector of the economy to the maximum extent compatible with economic advantage. Had this article demanded that the state should not physically intervene in the economy in cases where that would harm the supreme economic goal (as defined in Article 72), then it would have been acceptable to socialists. But the present formulation in the draft can put every socialist off our movement. Is this what we wish?

Article 78 demands nationalization of every monopolistic enterprise. In my opinion this demand is mistaken. Even a strict socialist would not insist on nationalizing cooperative enterprises (such as [the transport companies] EGED and Hammeqasher) even though they are monopolistic. Clearly such enterprises must be *supervised* by the state. But demanding nationalization of Hammeqasher while at he same time *opposing* nationalization of Bank Leumi (because that would amount to physical intervention in the economy!)—this is a very odd position.

Article 81 demands that economic enterprises should not be preferred "due to organizational form or on political grounds." Here there is a double error. First, economics cannot be disconnected from politics. To demand that the state should not prefer any economic enterprise on political grounds is an absurdity that cannot be implemented in any sovereign regime. Suppose that two companies compete for a license to import wheat: one importing from Canada, the other from the United States. Suppose the state is politically interested in promoting trade with Canada. Would it then be debarred from taking this into consideration when awarding the contract? This would clearly be absurd. Of course, it is possible (and necessary) to demand that there should be no preference on *party-political* grounds.

Second, according to this article the government should not be allowed to prefer cooperative enterprises (for example, in agriculture) over private ones. Suppose that a kibbutz competes with a private company for a given tract of land, and that both can cultivate it equally efficiently. Would it be wrong to grant the franchise to the kibbutz in order to encourage cooperative agriculture?

Just as political considerations cannot be ignored in economics, so also it is unnecessary and impossible to ignore social considerations. The attempt to reduce economic policy to considerations of mere "economic efficiency" is in general due to a backward social outlook—and at best to naïvety and pseudoscientific superficiality.

In connection with this chapter, a general consideration should be added: if we wish to integrate in the region, we must recognize that the aspiration for socialism has taken deep roots among the Arab masses around us. Any real step toward solution of the region's problems and its unification will necessarily take a socialist turn. It would be unpardonable if our principles on economics would have an antisocialist hue.

12

The Social Identity
of Ha'olam Hazeh

I t is common knowledge that parties and movements differ from one another in their political views and attitudes to political and economic problems. But we Marxists do not stop at this point: we expose the *source* of these differences of opinion. Scientific analysis shows that in general (and almost without exception) differences of political opinion are a result and reflection of class oppositions within society.

Each class (or social stratum) has its special interests, which decisively determine the views and demands of its political representatives. In many cases the connection between interest and corresponding view is simple and transparent. For example, a party of property owners would uphold the "sanctity of private property" and fight for the "freedom of private enterprise"—in other words, for creating conditions favorable to accumulation of private profits, to exploitation of workers by capitalists. A farmers' party would extol the virtues of agriculture.

There are also subtler and less overt connections between the social background of a party and its views and ideological character. It is well known that a person's living conditions and experiences largely determine his mental makeup, his psychology. This applies also on a social scale: the living conditions of a social stratum, following from its role and position in the economic processes, largely determine the political style and psychology of a party that gives voice to that social stratum. And just as in the case of an individual, so also for an entire party: this connection between social background and mental makeup is neither simple nor automatic; it is not quite overt, and is certainly not clearly conscious. But it always exists, and it is important to uncover it.

◆ ◆ ◆

Hebrew original published in *Matzpen* 32, January 1967. Translated by the author.

Anyone familiar with *Ha'olam Hazeh*—the journal and the movement—would not have any difficulty in detecting their social background, the social origin from which they derive their mental makeup: it is the world of the lower middle class, particularly the stratum of clerks, owners of mini-capital, and to some extent members of the liberal professions. To this must be added an important qualification: in the present case we are not talking about the strata of the Jewish lower middle class as it exists in various countries abroad, parts of which have arrived in this country with the waves of immigration while retaining their previous class character. We are talking about strata that have come into being or have crystallized in this country, against the background of local reality. The readership of *Ha'olam Hazeh* and Avnery's followers are a relatively young group, made up, generally speaking, of people who were born in this country or acquired their main education, professional qualification, and social status here rather than abroad.

(Of course, these are general statements, regarding the collective, average makeup of this group and do not apply to each and every individual in the movement and its leadership. In every political movement there are some individuals whose social background is atypical of the generality of its membership.)

Hebrew Nationalism

In almost all peoples, the lower strata of the middle class are especially and outstandingly inclined to nationalist views (and in general also to deference—even reverence—toward the army. The petite bourgeoisie is often the principal mainstay of militarism). These phenomena have several causes, inherent in the position of these strata in economic and social reality. This is not the place to dwell on these causes in detail. We will mention only one explanation, derived from social psychology.

Along with the working class, the lower middle strata are the first to be seriously hit by the various afflictions of the capitalist system. Every crisis or "recession" may impoverish and ruin large masses among these strata, which even in normal times have only modest means and lack a robust base. Economic insecurity leads to a tendency to identify with a large group, which gives the individual a sense of belonging and security, helping him to overcome the feeling of alienation caused by the anarchy of capitalist economic reality.

A wage worker spends at least eight hours a day, six days a week,* together with a more or less large group of members of his own class; he cooperates with them in the labor process, eats together with them, and struggles shoulder-to-shoulder with them. Thus for the worker there exists the possibility of developing a class consciousness, identification with the class collective to which he belongs.

---

* A six-day workweek was the norm in Israel and many other countries at the time of writing.

Such a possibility does not really exist for the middle strata. Therefore their feeling of estrangement and insecurity finds an outlet in a more or less powerful nationalist sentiment.

In this country a new Israeli-Jewish nation is coming into existence and crystallizing. On one hand, this nation is part of the world Jewish ethnos; but on the other hand it constitutes a separate group of people living in a specific territory, leading a common economic life, speaking a separate language, and so on. Against this background, a clash is waged between religious and Zionist ideology on one side and the new Hebrew nationalism on the other. The former emphasize the affiliation of Israel's Jews to world Jewry; whereas the latter, on the contrary, emphasizes the national specificity of the Hebrew nation, and its relative disconnection from Judaism and world Jewry.

What was said above about the class makeup of the Ha'olam Hazeh movement makes it clear why it is precisely this movement that is the main standard-bearer and mouthpiece of the new Hebrew nationalism. From this point of view it would be wrong to regard Ha'olam Hazeh as an ephemeral, accidental, and fleeting phenomenon. Its political achievements will largely depend on the quality of its leadership and on other somewhat accidental factors. But its very existence reflects—in the specific form appropriate to certain social strata—actual objective facts. Its nationalist ideology serves deep psychosocial needs of these strata.

Socialism versus Nationalism

Our socialist outlook is a fundamentally supranational one. Our political path corresponds to the historical interest of the working class, and our ideology aims to strengthen the workers' class feeling as opposed to nationalism.

In this sense we oppose in principle any nationalism whatsoever—be it Arab, French, Russian, Chinese . . . or Hebrew. Yet we judge each national movement *on its merits*, according to the interest of socialism. We admit the possibility of aims common to us and a given national movement (in the short or medium term), and we are prepared to accept collaboration based on such common and agreed upon aims. For example, under conditions existing in colonies, there generally forms a partnership of struggle between nationalists, whose sole aim is *national* liberation, and socialists, for whom the anti-imperialist struggle aims at *social* liberation and is the opening move of a social revolution.

Under the conditions of this country, we consider Zionism to be the main obstacle to the integration of Israel in a socialist regional union. Securing the future of our people, as well as the general interest of socialism in the Middle East, demands a resolute struggle against Zionism. (This is not the place to go into the details of this issue; we have done so several times before, and shall return to it in the future.) Likewise, we are opposed to theocracy, all the more so because here religion is closely associated with Zionism.

So in this context there exists a possibility of partnership between socialists and Hebrew nationalists in the struggle against Zionism. This explains our past participation in the Ha'olam Hazeh movement. Yet the split that occurred in the Ha'olam Hazeh conference is not accidental: because we have never ceased—and shall never cease—to point out the negative aspects of Hebrew nationalism, namely:

First, Hebrew nationalism is able to struggle against Zionism, which, as mentioned above, is the main obstacle to the integration of Israel in the region. But Hebrew nationalism cannot serve as a positive platform on the basis of which such integration will be put into effect. The regional union will be a socialist one, and Israel will only be able to integrate in it on the basis of a socialist platform.

Second, Hebrew nationalism is indeed opposed to Zionism; but it is incapable of confronting Zionism thoroughly and repudiating it *radically*, root and branch. For the Hebrew nation has come into being as a result of the Zionist colonization of Palestine, and therefore the nationalist outlook, for which this nation is an absolute and supreme value, cannot radically repudiate Zionism, its progenitor. Hebrew nationalism can only claim that Zionism is outdated, no longer suited to present conditions, and Hebrew nationalism ought to be embraced in its place. Thus Hebrew nationalism gets into a contradiction: on the one hand it repudiates Zionism, and on the other it regards itself as Zionism's legitimate heir.

This explains the Zionist (or quasi-Zionist) position of Avnery and his followers on the question of borders, the affinity between the State of Israel and world Jewry, and encouragement of Jewish immigration. (We shall not elaborate on this issue here, but merely mention it in passing.)

Third, like any nationalism, Hebrew nationalism contains within it a seed of a new national clash with the neighboring peoples. A nationalism that can dwell for long in tranquility alongside another nationalism exists only in fables, like the leopard that shall lie down with the kid.*

Toward an Israeli Poujadism?

Let us have a look at the views of Ha'olam Hazeh on matters of economy, society, and administration. The lower middle strata in capitalist society have a split psyche: on the one hand (as we mentioned above) they are severely afflicted by the scourges of capitalism's anarchic economy; yet on the other hand they enjoy certain privileges and advantages within this social order, which follow from ownership of property (albeit petty property) and from a relatively respectable social status (this applies in particular to white-collar workers and members of the liberal professions).

Consequently, these strata vacillate between progressive and conservative moods, between support for social reforms (sometimes quite radical ones) and fanatic defense of the existing order. On the one hand they can regard the working class as a

---

* Isaiah 11:6.

fellow-sufferer and ally; yet on the other hand they are terrified of shocks in the existing social order and the property relations on which it is based. It is indeed the owners of petty property—whose hold on it is shaky and insecure—who are the most fanatic believers in the sanctity of private property; it is indeed they—who must toil hard to accumulate petty capital so as to enjoy its fruits, who wear themselves out in straining to climb the ladder of an anarchic society (that in general appears to them alien and hostile)—who are the most enthusiastic supporters of the "freedom of private enterprise."

These dispositions found full expression in the conference of Ha'olam Hazeh. It is difficult to describe the vehemence with which the movement's centrists and rightists—who now, following the split, constitute its decisive majority—attacked socialism.

This is not the place to set forth a detailed account of the differences between our socialist outlook and the petit-bourgeois economic views prevailing in the Ha'olam Hazeh movement. Let us just mention that among the principles approved in the conference there is an article (§77) that demands "*reducing to the minimum the physical intervention*" of the government in the economy; and another article (§80) calling for encouragement of private enterprise. The latter article also speaks of encouraging cooperative enterprise, but its title is "*encouragement of private enterprise.*" This is no accident: it seems that cooperative property emerged unscathed by the fury of the rightists because they regard it as a kind of variant—a bastard form—of private property. Without any protest, the conference heard proposed amendments demanding that "*the government will strive to minimize its ownership of economic enterprises*" and that "*the number of state enterprises will be reduced, and will be restricted mainly to services that cannot be operated by a person or a private firm.*" Likewise it was proposed that "*the rights of a person or firm to manage businesses or enterprises as they see fit, without restrictive interference of economic planning, will be guaranteed by the constitution*"(!). That these proposed amendments were not approved is mainly due to the voting procedure employed in the conference, which made it extremely difficult to amend the text proposed by movement's ruling bodies.

There are some further, albeit less essential, points that reveal the unmistakable class character of Ha'olam Hazeh. Let us have a brief look at some of these.

Being "above class." We pointed out earlier that the lower middle strata lack a consciousness of belonging to a class. A view widespread among them is that all that "class" talk is nonsense or a fiendish invention concocted by subversives in order to divide the nation artificially. Also typical of these strata is a denial of the usual left/right classification of political outlooks and parties. Mr. Avnery understands quite well this psychology of his present and potential followers, and from the conference's rostrum he very insistently rejected any attempt to attach a "class label" to himself and to his movement, or to label the latter as being on the right or left.

"War against corruption." No decent person likes corruption or is happy to tolerate it. But making the fight against corruption and maladministration a *central* political slogan is one of the *most typical* symptoms of lower middle-class movements. This follows from the special social psychology of that class: by nature it is incapable of making an *essential* critique of the capitalist social order, and it therefore attributes its various afflictions to maladministration and corruption.

Every reader of the weekly *Ha'olam Hazeh* knows what a central role this topic plays in that journal. During the Ha'olam Hazeh movement conference, no less than nine special articles dealing with corruption were approved, constituting a separate chapter in the movement's principles. (Article 50, the last in that chapter, is notable and typical: "*The state will compensate citizens for damages due to hooliganism and for any other damage due to the authorities' neglect.*" This demand is particularly fitting for the stratum of small-car owners,* just as the demonstrations Mr. Avnery organizes—protest convoys of cars—are made to measure for that stratum.)

To prevent misunderstanding, let us repeat that the demands raised by Ha'olam Hazeh against corruption are, generally speaking, justified and correct, and we have nothing against them. We are only pointing out the social roots of the *great importance* that Mr. Avnery and his followers attribute to this issue.

Complaints against taxes. Again, there is hardly anyone who does not grumble against high taxes. But this issue is very central precisely for parties of the lower middle class. The reason for this is simple: the small proprietor is in constant danger of economic ruin by bankruptcy. Whereas for the hired employee taxes appear as abstract numbers on a paystub, and never take a concrete form of notes and coins, for the small self-employed person tax is a physical payment made to the state treasury; and this sum is a substantial part of his expenses.

Ha'olam Hazeh's conference was presented by the movement's ruling bodies with three proposed articles dealing with taxation. (In the conference itself, two further amendments were proposed, supported mainly by the left wing.) Of these three articles, one (§85) demands progressive taxation. This demand is common to both workers and the self-employed. Another article (§87) demands the "*abolition of methods of taxation that increase the cost of production and impair national saving.*" This demand has no direct relevance to workers, and is typical of all strata of the middle class. The third article (§86) demands that "*all systems of taxation, at all levels of public administration, should be unified as far as possible.*" This demand is specifically typical of a petty property owner, who drowns in a sea of tax-demand forms arriving on papers of various colors, sent to him by various authorities, and who is nearly driven mad by the exertion of dealing with them and filling out all the many forms. A worker is not greatly concerned by the number of rubrics appearing on his paystub; what matters is only the sum appearing at the bottom line as "net pay."

Yearning for a "strong authority." Of all tendencies characterizing the lower strata of the middle class, this is perhaps the most dangerous. It derives from the

---

* In the 1960s only rich Israelis could afford a large car, and most workers could not afford even a small one.

same psychosocial source as nationalism and the overconcern, not to say obsession, with corruption and maladministration.

Against this background we can make sense of Mr. Avnery's proposed demand that Israel should adopt a presidential form of government, and his articles in his weekly journal in which he heaps praise on de Gaulle.* Although this proposal was rejected by the conference (largely due to the vigorous opposition of the left), he repeated the demand for "*strong authority*" in an article published under this title in the December 28, 1966, issue of his weekly. (In the middle of the article there is a picture of President Lincoln, and next to the article's heading—a picture of Mr. Avnery himself; the similarity between the two visages is so noticeable that the choice of the American president can hardly be random.)

This political tendency goes together with the special organizational structure of the Ha'olam Hazeh movement—a structure on which Mr. Avnery himself strongly insisted. At his insistence, the movement has no right to interfere with the contents of his appearances in the Knesset and of his articles in the *Ha'olam Hazeh* weekly. The movement's executive body (the "Management") is *appointed* by Mr. Avnery. Although the movement's Center, a large body without any executive authority, is—theoretically—entitled to pass a resolution of no-confidence in the Management, such a resolution is in practice almost impossible, because it constitutes a vote of no-confidence in the leader himself. And even if such a resolution is passed, the leader is entitled to manage the movement by means of appointees for a further period of six months.

◆ ◆ ◆

These elements—hatred of socialism; a pretension of being "above class"; along with the ingredients of emphasizing the fight against corruption (which is turned into a central slogan); excessive grumbling against the taxation system; and last but not least the demand for "strong authority"—these are precisely the hallmarks of a majority of the most reactionary demagogic movements of the lower middle class. The most well-known movement of this kind in recent times was that of Poujade in the Fourth French Republic—hence the name by which these movements are known nowadays: *Poujadism.*

Following the exit of the left, Mr. Avnery's movement is almost certain to turn toward the right. In this case there is a danger (not certain, but nevertheless possible) that the movement will gradually take on a pronounced Poujadist character.

* Charles de Gaulle was president of France from January 8, 1959, to April 28, 1969. The constitution of the Fifth Republic gave him great power.

13

The Class Nature of Israeli Society

Haim Hanegbi, Moshé Machover, and Akiva Orr

I sraeli society, like all other class societies, contains conflicting social interests—class interests that give rise to an internal class struggle. Yet Israeli society as a whole has been engaged, for the last fifty years, in a continuous external conflict: the conflict between Zionism and the Arab world, particularly the Palestinians. Which of these two conflicts is dominant and which is subordinate? What is the nature of this subordination and what is its dynamic? These are questions that everyone involved with Israeli society and politics must answer.

For revolutionaries inside Israel these questions are not academic. The answers given determine the strategy of the revolutionary struggle. Those who consider the internal class conflict to be the dominant one concentrate their efforts on the Israeli working class and attach secondary importance to the struggle against the colonizing, nationalistic, and discriminatory character of the Zionist state. This position sees the external conflict as a derivative of the internal one. Moreover, in this perspective, the internal dynamics of Israeli society will lead to a revolution in Israel, without this necessarily depending on a social revolution in the Arab world.

The experience of classical capitalist countries has often demonstrated that internal class conflicts and interests dominate external conflicts and interests. However this theory fails to hold in certain specific cases. For example, in a colonized country under the direct rule of a foreign power, the dynamics of the colonized society cannot be deduced simply from the internal conflicts of that society, since the conflict with the colonizing power is dominant. Israel is neither a classic capitalist country

This article was cowritten with Haim Hanegbi and Akiva Orr, and appeared in various publications in several slightly differing versions. The present chapter is based on the version in *New Left Review* 65, January–February 1971. Since this article was written, Israel has undergone fundamental socioeconomic changes. For a brief outline of these changes, see my article "Israel Rocked by Protests," *Weekly Worker* 879, September 1, 2011.

nor is it a classic colony. Its economic, social, and political features are so unique that any attempt to analyze it through the application of theories or analogies evolved for different societies will be a caricature. An analysis must rather be based on the specific characteristics and specific history of Israeli society.

A Society of Immigrants

The first crucial characteristic of Israeli society is that the majority of the population are either immigrants or the children of immigrants. In 1968 the adult (that is, over fifteen) Jewish population of Israel numbered 1,689,286 of whom only 24 percent were Israeli-born and only 4 percent of Israeli-born parents.[1] Israeli society today is still an immigrant society and has many features typical of such a community.* In such a society classes themselves, not to mention class consciousness, are still in a formative stage. Immigration produces an experience, and a mentality, of having "turned over a new page in life." As a rule the immigrant has changed his occupation, social role, and class. In the case of Israel the majority of the immigrants come from the petite bourgeoisie, whether they are from urban areas in Central and Eastern Europe or from towns and cities in the Arab world. The new immigrant looks forward to changing his place in society. Moreover he sees that all the advantageous positions in the new society are filled by earlier immigrants and this enhances his ambition to climb the social ladder presumably through long, hard work. The immigrant considers the actual social role he occupies as transitional. This applies to Israeli workers as well. His father was rarely a worker, and he himself lives in the hope that he too will one day become independent, or at least that his son will be able to do so. The class consciousness and pride that exist among the British and French proletariats do not exist in Israel, and appear odd to many Israeli workers. An English worker, if asked about his origins, will almost automatically reply in class terms ("I'm working class"), and will define his attitudes to other people in terms of similar class concepts; an Israeli worker, however, will use ethnic categories and consider himself and others in terms of being "Polish," "Mizrahi," and so on. Most people in Israel still consider their social position in terms of their ethnic and geographic origins, and such a social consciousness is obviously a barrier hindering the working class from playing an independent role, let alone a revolutionary one aiming at a total transformation of society.

No working class can play a revolutionary role in society while the majority of its members desire to improve their situation individually, within the framework of the existing society, by leaving the ranks of their class. This truth is reinforced when the proletariat does not recognize itself as a stable social class with its own group interests and its own value system in conflict with those of the existing social order. The impulse toward a total transformation of society does not arise easily in

---

* In 2010 the Jewish population of Israel (of all ages) numbered about 5,795,000, of whom 68.8 percent were Israeli-born.

a community of immigrants who have just changed their social and political status and who are still living in conditions of high social mobility. This does not mean that the Israeli working class cannot become a revolutionary force in the future; it merely implies that today political activity inside this class cannot proceed from the same assumptions and expectations as apply in a classic capitalist country.

A Society of Settlers

If the uniqueness of the Israeli working class consisted only in the fact that it was composed mainly of immigrants, then it could still be assumed that through time and patient socialist propaganda it would start to play an independent, possibly revolutionary, role. In such a situation patient educational work would not differ much from similar work elsewhere. However, Israeli society is not merely a society of immigrants; it is one of settlers. This society, including its working class, was shaped through a process of colonization. This process, which has been going on for eighty years, was not carried out in a vacuum but in a country populated by another people. The permanent conflict between the settlers' society and the indigenous, displaced Palestinian Arabs has never stopped and it has shaped the very structure of Israeli sociology, politics, and economics. The second generation of Israeli leaders is fully aware of this. In a famous speech at the burial of Roy Rutberg, a kibbutz member killed by Palestinian guerrillas in 1956, General Moshe Dayan declared: "We are a settler generation, and without the steel helmet and the cannon we cannot plant a tree or build a house. Let us not flinch from the hatred enflaming hundreds of thousands of Arabs around us. Let us not turn our head away lest our hand tremble. It is our generation's destiny, our life's alternative, to be prepared and armed, strong and harsh, lest the sword drop from our fist and our life cease."[2] This clear evaluation stands in sharp contrast to official Zionist mythology about "making the desert bloom," and Dayan brought this out by going on to say that the Palestinians had a very good case since "their fields are cultivated by us in front of their very eyes."

When Marx made the famous statement that "a people oppressing another cannot itself be free" he did not mean this merely as a moral judgment. He also meant that in a society whose rulers oppress another people the exploited class that does not actively oppose this oppression inevitably becomes an accomplice in it. Even when this class does not directly gain anything from this oppression it becomes susceptible to the illusion that it shares a common interest with its own rulers in perpetuating this oppression. Such a class tends to trail behind its rulers rather than to challenge their rule. This, furthermore, is even truer when the oppression takes place not in a faraway country, but "at home," and when national oppression and expropriation form the very conditions for the emergence and existence of the oppressing society. Revolutionary organizations have operated within the Jewish community in Palestine since the 1920s and have accumulated considerable experience from such practical activity; this experience provides clear proof of the dictum that "a people oppressing another cannot itself be free." In the context of Israeli society it means that as long as Zionism is politically and ideologically dominant within that society, and forms the accepted framework of politics, there is no chance whatsoever of the Israeli working class becoming a revolutionary class. The experience of fifty years does not contain a single example of Israeli workers being mobilized on material or trade union issues to challenge the Israeli regime itself; it is impossible to mobilize even a minority of the proletariat in this way. On the contrary, Israeli workers nearly always put their national loyalties before their class loyalties. Although this may change in the future, this does not remove the need for us to analyze why it has been so for the last fifty years.

Ethnic Diversity

A third crucial factor is the ethnic character of the Israeli proletariat. The majority of the most exploited strata within the Israeli working class are immigrants from Asia and Africa.[3] At first sight it might appear as if the reduplication of class divisions by ethnic divisions might sharpen internal class conflicts within Israeli society. There has been a certain tendency in this direction. Yet the ethnic factor has worked mainly in the opposite direction over the past twenty years. There are a number of reasons for this. First, many of the immigrants from Asia and Africa improved their standard of living by becoming proletarians in a modern capitalist society. Their discontent was not directed against their condition as proletarians but against their condition as "Mizrahim," that is, against the fact that they were looked down upon, and sometimes even discriminated against, by those of European origin. The Zionist rulers have taken measures to try to fuse the two groups together. But, in spite of these, the differences remained clear: in the mid-sixties, two-thirds of those doing unskilled work were Mizrahim; 38 percent of Mizrahim lived three or more people to a room, whereas only 7 percent of those from Europe did so; and in the Knesset only 16 of the 120 members were Mizrahim before 1965 and only 21 after it. However, such social differences are interpreted by the Mizrahim in ethnic terms; they do not say, "I am exploited and discriminated against because I am a worker," but "I am exploited and discriminated against because I am a Mizrahi." Second, in the present context of colonial Israeli society the Mizrahi workers are a group whose equivalent would be the "poor whites" of the United States of America or the Algerian *pied noirs*. Such groups resent being identified with Arabs, blacks, and natives of any kind, who are considered as "inferior" by these settlers. Their response is to side with the most chauvinist, racialist, and discriminatory elements in the establishment; most supporters of the semi-fascist Herut party are Jewish immigrants from Asia and Africa, and this must be borne in mind by those whose revolutionary strategy for Israeli society is based upon a future alliance of Arab Palestinians and Mizrahi Jews, whether on the basis of their common exploited condition or on the basis of a putative cultural affinity they might have as a result of the Mizrahi Jews having come from Arab countries. This does not mean that these strata of the Israeli proletariat are reactionary by "their very nature"; their present reactionary character is merely a product of rule by political Zionism. These strata could become the agents of socially revolutionary processes in Israeli society if the Zionist establishment itself has been shattered. It is doubtful, however, whether they will spearhead the movement to shatter it.

A Privileged Society: Capital Inflow

Israeli society is not only a settlers' society shaped by a process of colonizing an already populated country, it is also a society that benefits from unique privileges. It enjoys an influx of material resources from the outside of unparalleled quantity and quality; indeed it has been calculated that in 1968 Israel received 10 percent of all aid given to underdeveloped countries.[4] Israel is a unique case in the Middle East; it is financed by imperialism without being economically exploited by it. This has always been the case in the past: imperialism used Israel for its political purposes and paid for this by economic support. Oscar Gass, an American economist who at one time acted as an economic adviser to the Israeli government, recently wrote:

> What is unique in this development process . . . is the factor of capital inflow. . . . During the 17 years 1949–65 Israel received $6 billion more of imports of goods and services than she exported. For the 21 years 1948–68, the import surplus would be in excess of 7½ billion dollars. This means an excess of some $2650 per person during the 21 years for every person who lived in Israel (within the pre-June 1967 borders) at the end of 1968. And of this supply from abroad . . . only about 30 percent came to Israel under conditions that call for a return outflow of dividends, interest or capital. This is a circumstance without parallel elsewhere, and it severely limits the significance of Israel's economic development as an example to other countries.[5]

Seventy percent of this $6 billion deficit was covered by "net unilateral capital transfers," which were not subject to conditions governing returns on capital or payment of dividends. They consisted of donations raised by the United Jewish Appeal, reparations from the German government, and grants by the US government. Thirty percent came from "long-term capital transfers"—Israeli government bonds, loans by foreign governments, and capitalist investment. The latter benefits in Israel from tax exemptions and guaranteed profits by virtue of a "Law for the Encouragement of Capital Investments";[6] nevertheless, this quasi-capitalist source of investment came far behind the unilateral donations and long-term loans. In the entire period from 1949 to 1965, capital transfers (both forms taken together) came from the following sources: 60 percent from world Jewry, 28 percent from the German government, and 12 percent from the US government. Of the "unilateral capital transfers," 51.5 percent came from world Jewry, 41 percent from the German government, and 7.4 percent from the US government. Of the "long-term capital transfers," 68.7 percent came from world Jewry, 20.5 percent from the US government, and 11 percent from other sources. During the 1949–65 period the net saving of the Israeli economy averaged zero, being sometimes +1 percent and sometimes –1 percent. Yet the rate of investment over the same period was around 20 percent of the GNP. This could not have come from within because there was no internal saving within the Israeli economy; it came entirely from abroad in the form of unilateral and long-term capital investments. In other words the growth of the Israeli economy was based entirely on the inflow of capital from outside.[7]

Since 1967 this dependence on foreign capital has increased. As a result of the changed Middle Eastern situation, military expenditure has risen. According to the Israeli minister of the Treasury, in January 1970 military expenditure was estimated as 24 percent of GNP for 1970, which was twice the US ratio in 1966, three times the British ratio, and four times that of France.[8] This has placed an additional strain both on internal sources of investment money and on the balance of payments, and has had to be met by a commensurate rise in capital inflow. In 1967–68 three "millionaires' conferences" were called in Israel; foreign capitalists were invited to join in increasing the inflow of capital and foreign participation in industrial and agricultural projects. In September 1970, the Israeli minister of the treasury, Pinchas Sapir, returned from a three-week fund-raising tour in the United States and summed up the situation at that time:

> We set ourselves the aim of raising $1,000 million from world Jewry in the coming year, by means of the United Jewish Appeal and the Israel Development Bonds campaign sponsored by the Jewish Agency. This sum is $400 million higher than that raised in the record year of 1967. . . . During the recent visit to Israel of the US financial research team we explained to them that even if we succeed in raising all that we expect from the United Jewish Appeal and the Israel Development Bonds campaign we shall still be millions of dollars short of our requirements. After summing up our requirements in arms we informed the US that we shall need $400–$500 million per year.[9]

It thus appears that the dependence of Israel on the United States has changed significantly since the 1967 war. Fund-raising among Jews all over the world (by cashing in on their sentiments and fears) no longer suffices to support the enormously increased military budget. The rough average of $500 million from fund-raising has now doubled, and on top of this the US government has been asked to provide directly an additional $500 million. It is obvious that the readiness of the US government to forward these sums depends on what it gets in return. In the particular case of Israel this return is not economic profit.[10]

British capital has also been developing close ties with Israel.[11] Twenty percent of Israel's imports come from Britain, and trade has nearly doubled since the 1967 June war. British Leyland participate with the Histadrut (who have a 34 percent holding) in bus production, and with private Israeli capital in car and jeep production. Marks and Spencer buy £2–3 million a year of goods from Israel, one-third being textiles and the rest oranges, vegetables, and fruit juices. British financial interests, led by Sir Isaac Wolfson and Charles Clore, are also major participants.

Wolfson is the chairman of Great Universal Stores in Britain, which has a 30 percent share of GUS Industries (Israel). Wolfson and Clore cooperate with Israel's largest domestic capitalist group, the Mayer brothers, in real estate in Israel and Africa, and built the only skyscraper in the country, the Shalom tower in Tel Aviv. Wolfson also controls 30 percent of the major petroleum chain, Paz, which was sold off by Shell under Arab pressure in 1959. Wolfson is also one of the backers of the Israel Corporation, a $30 million company with a minimum subscription of $100,000, which was set up after the June war to finance industrial development in Israel.

The increased participation of foreign capital in Israel has led to certain changes within the economy itself, which have also been carried out under the increased pressures set off directly by the level of military expenditure. The economy has been made more "efficient" by American capitalist standards: taxes have been reformed, investment conditions "liberalized," and army generals sent to US business schools and then put in charge of industrial enterprises. In the period 1968–69 there was a compulsory wage freeze, and some public enterprises were even sold off to private capital—for instance, the 26 percent state share in the Haifa oil refinery.

This influx of resources from abroad does not include the property that the Zionist establishment in Israel took over from refugee Palestinians as "abandoned property." This includes land, both cultivated and uncultivated; only 10 percent of the land held by Zionist bodies in pre-1967 Israel had been bought before 1948. It also includes many houses, and entire deserted cities such as Jaffa, Lydda, and Ramleh, where much property was confiscated after the 1948 war.

The Distribution of Foreign Funds

The enormous influx of capital did not come into the hands of the small Israeli bourgeoisie, but into the hands of the state, of the Zionist establishment,[12] and this establishment has been under the control of the bureaucracies of the Zionist workers' parties since the 1920s. This has determined the way in which all inflowing capital, as well as conquered property, has been put to use. Funds collected abroad are channeled through the Jewish Agency, which, with the Histadrut and the Israeli government, forms part of the triangle of governing institutions. All the Zionist parties, from Mapam to Herut, are represented in the Jewish Agency. It finances sections of the Israeli economy, in particular the nonprofitable parts of agriculture like the kibbutzim, and it also distributes funds to the Zionist parties, enabling them to run their newspapers and economic enterprises. The funds are divided according to the votes cast for the parties at the previous election, and this system of subsidies enables the Zionist parties to survive long after the social forces that created them have disappeared.[13]

Historically the purpose of this system was the strengthening of the colonization process, in accordance with the ideas of the Zionist workers' parties, and the strengthening of the grip that the bureaucracy itself had over Israeli society. This has proved successful, since not only is the Israeli working class organizationally and economically under the complete control of the labor bureaucracy but so too is the Israeli bourgeoisie. Historically the bureaucracy has shaped most of the institutions, values, and practices of Israeli society without any successful opposition from within, and subject only to the external constraints imposed by imperialism and the resistance of the Arabs. Most of this enormous inflow of resources went into immigration projects and the housing and employment necessary to cope with the inflow that raised the Jewish population from 0.6 million in 1948 to 2.4 million in 1968.

This process was accompanied by relatively little personal corruption, but by a lot of political and social corruption. The influx of resources had a decisive effect on the dynamics of Israeli society, for the Israeli working class shared, directly and indirectly, in this transfusion of capital. Israel is not a country where foreign aid flows entirely into private pockets; it is a country where this aid subsidizes the whole of society. The Jewish worker in Israel does not get his share in cash, but he gets it in terms of new and relatively inexpensive housing, which could not have been constructed by raising capital locally; he gets it in industrial employment, which could not have been started or kept going without external subsidies; and he gets it in terms of a general standard of living, which does not correspond to the output of that society. The same obviously applies to the profits of the Israeli bourgeoisie whose economic activity and profit-making is regulated by the bureaucracy through subsidies, import licenses, and tax exemptions. In this way the struggle between the Israeli working class and its employers, both bureaucrats and capitalists, is fought not only over the surplus value produced by the worker but also over the share each group receives from this external source of subsidies.

Israel and Imperialism

What political circumstances enabled Israel to receive external aid in such quantities and under such unparalleled conditions? This question was answered as early as 1951 by a senior op-ed writer of the daily paper, *Ha'aretz*: "Israel has been given a role not unlike that of a watchdog. One need not fear that it would exercise an aggressive policy toward the Arab states if this would contradict the interests of the USA and Britain. But should the West prefer for one reason or another to close its eyes, one can rely on Israel to punish severely those of the neighbouring states whose lack of manners toward the West has exceeded the proper limits."[14] This evaluation of Israel's role in the Middle East has been confirmed many times, and it is clear that Israel's foreign and military policies cannot be deduced from the dynamics of the internal social conflicts alone. The entire Israeli economy is founded on the special political and military role that Zionism, and the settlers' society, fulfills in the Middle East as a whole. If Israel is viewed in isolation from the rest of the Middle East, there is no explanation for the fact that 70 percent of the capital inflow is not intended for economic gain and is not subject to considerations of profitability. But the problem is immediately solved when Israel is considered as a component of the Middle East.

The fact that a considerable part of this money comes from donations raised by Zionists among Jews all over the world does not alter its being a subsidy by imperialism. What matters is rather the fact that the US Treasury is willing to consider these funds, raised in the United States for transfer to another country, as "charity donations" qualifying for income-tax exemptions. These donations depend on the goodwill of the US Treasury and it is only reasonable to assume that this goodwill would not continue were Israel to conduct a principled anti-imperialist policy.

This means that although class conflicts do exist in Israeli society they are constrained by the fact that the society as a whole is subsidized from the outside. This privileged status is related to Israel's role in the region, and as long as this role continues there is little prospect of the internal social conflicts acquiring a revolutionary character. On the other hand, a revolutionary breakthrough in the Arab world would change this situation. By releasing the activity of the masses throughout the Arab world it could change the balance of power; this would make Israel's traditional politico-military role obsolete, and would thus reduce its usefulness for imperialism. At first Israel would probably be used in an attempt to crush such a revolutionary breakthrough in the Arab world; yet once this attempt had failed Israel's politico-military role vis-à-vis the Arab world would be finished. Once this role and its associated privileges had been ended, the Zionist regime, depending as it does on these privileges, would be open to a mass challenge from within Israel itself.

This does not mean that there is nothing for revolutionaries inside Israel to do except sit and wait for the emergence of objective external conditions on which they have no influence. It only means that they must base their activity on a strategy that acknowledges the unique features of Israeli society, rather than on one that reproduces the generalizations of analysis of classic capitalism. The main task for revolutionaries who accept this assessment is to direct their work toward those strata of the Israeli population who are immediately affected by the political results of Zionism and who have to pay for it. These strata include Israeli youth, who are called on to wage "an eternal war imposed by destiny," and the Palestinian Arabs who live under Israeli rule.[15] These strata share an anti-Zionist tendency that makes them potential allies in the revolutionary struggle inside Israel and the revolutionary struggle throughout the Middle East. Anyone who follows closely the revolutionary struggles within the Arab world becomes aware of the dialectical relationship between the struggle against Zionism within Israel and the struggle for social revolution within the Arab world. Such a strategy does not imply that activity within the Israeli working class should be neglected; it only implies that this activity too must be subordinated to the general strategy of the struggle against Zionism.

Israel's Role in Africa and Asia

Israel's primary relationship with imperialism is as a watchdog in the Middle East, funded and privileged for serving this purpose. But it has a secondary relationship, that of serving as a channel through which money and ideology can be routed to neocolonial countries in Asia and Africa. It is obviously in Israel's own interest to build economic and political ties with non-Arab Afro-Asian states and to strengthen pro-Israeli influence there; and at the same time US imperialism often finds it more convenient to funnel its aid through a third country, rather than to expose itself by organizing the aid directly. This project is realized in three different ways: 1) highly trained Israeli "experts" are placed at the disposal of African states, often in strategically important positions; 2) various categories of African personnel, including students, civil servants, labor leaders, and military cadres are given specialized training in Israel itself (this training is usually provided quickly and efficiently); and 3) Israeli businessmen and their government have set up joint economic enterprises with African states and private business.[16]

Since the 1950s, Israel's aid program to Africa has been growing, and as it grows it serves both Israel's specific interests and the broader interests of world imperialism. Various sections of the Israeli state were mobilized to implement this policy, two of which were the trade union organization, Histadrut, and the army, Tzahal (Israel Defense Force). The specific nature of the Histadrut, being both boss and domestic trade union at the same time, facilitates Israeli penetration into the third world, where one often finds a governmental one-party, one-union structure. This penetration takes place as a function of Israel's own interests and to further a collusion of interests between Israel and imperialism. "The Israeli model might well prove to be a sort of economic 'third force'—an alternative differing from the Western pattern, but certainly far more compatible with free-world interests than any communist model," wrote Arnold Rivkin in the US journal *Foreign Affairs* in 1959 (vol. 37, p. 494). The author of the article was director of the Africa Research Project at the Center for International Studies organized by the CIA at the Massachusetts Institute of Technology. Later, in a book published in 1962, Rivkin was more precise about the role Israel plays in Western penetration in Africa: "Israel's role as a third force could also be reinforced by imaginative use of the Third Country Technique. A Free World state wishing to enlarge its assistance flow to Africa might channel some part of it through Israel because of Israel's special qualifications and demonstrated acceptability to many African nations."[17]

Little is known in Israel about this aspect of the Histadrut's activity. While keeping this activity discreet, the Histadrut prefers to publicize its Afro-Asian Institute. The head of the political department of the Histadrut (the Histadrut's "foreign minister" who works in close collaboration with the real minister) recently summarized the activities of the Afro-Asian Institute:

> The Institute, which was created by the Histadrut in 1960 . . . is an important link in its international activity especially in the under-developed countries of Africa and Asia. But its activity and its world-wide renown contribute to reinforcing the Histadrut's links with other countries and organisations. To date, the Institute has trained 1,848 delegates from trade unions and co-operatives, from Institutes of Fur-

ther Education, as well as high officials from 85 African, Asian and Latin American countries. . . . The Institute has been called upon to organize seminars in various African and Asian countries. . . . It was former students of the Institute, now occupying high positions in their respective countries and organizations, who took the initiative for such seminars. Up to the present the Institute has organized such seminars in the following countries: Nigeria (twice), Dahomey, Togo, the Ivory Coast, Liberia, Singapore, Korea (twice), Ceylon, India, and Nepal. About 500 people participated in these activities. Next month three short seminars will be organized for the militants from Cypriot trade union organizations, and the 1970 programme includes the following countries: Swaziland, Lesotho, Botswana, Zambia, Singapore, Hong Kong, Korea ... others will follow.[18]

George Meany, president of the AFL-CIO, which finances the Afro-Asian Institute, stated clearly: "The Histadrut is a national center which has worked for the cause of democracy and liberty in the free world, particularly in Asia and Africa, through the intermediary of its Afro-Asian Institute."[19]

Israel's direct military assistance to African states began in 1960 and includes both general assistance to neocolonial governments and aid to forces on the southern periphery of the Arab world who might further imperialist interests. The latter category has included provision of military advisers to the Chad government's anti-guerrilla campaign, and aid to the guerrilla movement in Southern Sudan. Israel has also given military assistance to Ethiopia's campaign against the Eritrean liberation movement. In other countries, including Tanzania and the Congo, Israel has trained air force, navy, and army personnel and has supplied arms and advice for the establishment of paramilitary agricultural settlements modeled on pioneering settlements in Israel itself. Many of these projects have been carried out in cooperation with US foreign aid programs or with funds funneled through Israel from the United States.[20]

In Asia Israel has been less successful in carrying out such a program, with the notable exception of Singapore where it is helping to sustain Britain's East of Suez strategy. Since 1966 Israeli experts, originally described as "Mexican agricultural experts," have been training the Singapore army, and have supplied it with tanks and electronic equipment.[21]

Which Is the Ruling Class?

The subordination of the entire economy to political considerations has characterized Zionist colonization from the very beginning and is the key to decoding the unique nature of the Israeli ruling class. Zionist colonization did not proceed as an ordinary capitalist colonizing process motivated by considerations of profitability. The bourgeois elements in this colonization always preferred to employ Arab labor, but the bureaucracy of the Zionist labor movement struggled against this and demanded a policy of "Jewish labor only." A bitter struggle was waged throughout the 1920s and 1930s and formed the main conflict within the Zionist community in Palestine. It was finally won by the labor bureaucracy, to a considerable extent due to the support it received from the world Zionist movement. That support was based on political considerations, for the aim of political Zionism was, from the very beginning, to establish a purely Jewish nation-state in Palestine and to displace the indigenous population. As early as June 1895, Theodor Herzl wrote in his diary:

> The private lands in the territories granted us we must gradually take out of the hands of the owners. The poorer amongst the population we try to transfer quietly outside our borders by providing them with work in the transit countries, but in our country we deny them all work. Those with property will join us. The transfer of land and the displacement of the poor must be done gently and carefully. Let the landowners believe they are exploiting us by getting overvalued prices. But no lands shall be sold back to their owners.[22]

It was this consideration, embraced by the world Zionist movement, that tipped the scales in favor of the Zionist labor bureaucracy in Palestine and its policy of "Jewish labor only." The defeat of the bourgeois elements established a pattern of joint rule in which the labor bureaucracy played the senior role and the bourgeoisie the junior one, combining to form a new embryonic ruling class. This specific combination within the ruling establishment has remained unchanged from the 1940s to this day and constitutes a unique feature of Israeli society. If the dominant ideology in any given society is the ideology of the dominant class, and if the identity of the dominant class is rather blurred, then one can try to analyze the dominant ideology itself and deduce from it the identity of the ruling class. In Israel the dominant ideology was never a capitalist one; it was a blend of bourgeois elements combined with dominant themes and ideas typical of the Zionist labor movement, ideas derived from the socialist movement in Eastern Europe but transformed to express the aims of political Zionism.

This balance between the different sections of the ruling class is not static, and recently the balance has been shifting in favor of the bourgeois partner. One of the symptoms of this is the division between Golda Meir and David Ben-Gurion on the one hand and their disciple Moshe Dayan on the other. The issue was the old one of whether to employ Palestinians from the Occupied Territories for work within the Israeli economy. Golda Meir was strongly opposed to this policy, whereas Dayan supported it and the bourgeois paper *Ha'aretz* supported Dayan. But whatever the different tendencies at any one moment the labor bureaucracy still dominates through its three centers of power: the government, the Jewish Agency, and the Histadrut. Wielding the tremendous apparatus of the state and the unions it dominates Israeli society and most of the economy. In 1960 the privately owned sector produced only 58.5 percent of the total net product of the Israeli economy[23] and it is doubtful if this proportion has changed much in the subsequent decade.

But the economic power of the Zionist labor bureaucracy is far greater than this figure suggests. Apart from its direct control of the state and the Histadrut it has indirect bureaucratic control over the private sector. This control goes far beyond ordinary intervention of the state in the economy of the kind that occurs in most capitalist countries. The entire Israeli economy, including the private sector, depends on subsidies from abroad that flow mostly through state-controlled channels. By controlling the flow of subsidies through the policies of the Treasury and the Jewish Agency, the labor bureaucracy directs and regulates this flow. This also gives it a useful grip on its capitalist partner. Israel has a unique form of capitalism, ruled by a unique class partnership. The control of the bureaucracy over the flow of funds from abroad enables it to exercise a far-reaching control over the broad masses of the population, not only in political and economic matters but even in aspects of everyday life. The majority of the Israeli population depend directly, and daily, on the goodwill of this bureaucracy for their jobs, housing, and health insurance. Some of the workers who have rebelled against the bureaucracy, such as the seamen in the great strike of December 1951, were denied employment, and some who refused to surrender were forced in the end to emigrate. At the same time there is no national health service in Israel, only that of the Histadrut, so those who refuse to join or who fight it are deprived of health insurance. Indeed the key to the hold of the bureaucracy over the proletariat is the trade union federation, the Histadrut.

The Histadrut: National Interest before Class Interest

Israeli workers might seem to be in an enviable situation, since the Trade Union Federation, known simply as the "Federation" (Histadrut) gives the impression of being an advanced and powerful workers' union. From a certain viewpoint the Histadrut and its facilities are indeed quite exceptional: it has 1.1 million members out of a total population of nearly 3 million; a quarter of Israeli wage-earners work in concerns belonging to the Histadrut; and the Histadrut has for years accounted for around 22–25 percent of the Israeli net national product.

The Histadrut was founded in 1920 during a General Congress of Jewish workers and until 1966 it was known as the "General Confederation of Hebrew Workers in the Land of Israel." The number of Jewish workers in Palestine in 1920 was some five thousand, while there were around fifty thousand Arab workers, according to the estimate of a Zionist historian.[24]

The founders of this "General" Federation, who were all inspired by Zionist ideology, and most of whom were members of Jewish petty-bourgeois parties, limited membership of the Histadrut exclusively to Jews, and to Jews "living on the fruits of their labor"—workers, artisans, tradesmen, and self-employed workers. When the basic principles of the Histadrut were being laid down, the founders made it clear that "national interest" took priority over "economic interest" and "cultural interests." The internationalist approach to the class nature of society was never brought up at the Histadrut's founding congress, not even by a minority group. A year after its foundation, the Histadrut created its first enterprises. These were a large company dealing with public works—Solel Boneh—and Bank Hapo'alim (the "Workers' Bank") the latter in association with the World Zionist Organization. Solel Boneh has been engaged on a variety of construction work over the past few years, in several parts of the world; for example, it has built luxury hotels in certain African countries, and has constructed roads and various military installations in several Asian countries, including US air bases in Turkey. The fact that from the start, the Histadrut made Zionist interests its primary concern, at the expense of its trade union role, has led to an extremely hierarchic organizational structure. A bureaucratic machinery was set up such that the entire organization of the trade union was subordinated to the management and to the political "bosses"—who were always from Zionist parties. There has never been the least trade union independence in the Histadrut.[25]

The Histadrut was not merely concerned with its role of maintaining Jews in national isolation while they were living in an essentially Arab milieu. Since its creation it has been at the spearhead of Zionist colonization in Palestine. Its choice position among the country's Zionist colonizers, and its extremely strong organization, made it a pioneer in the process of agricultural colonization and in winning places of work for Jewish workers by evicting Arab peasants and workers. The Zionist slogans of the 1920s and '30s—"the conquest of work" and "the conquest of the soil"—found their principal militants in the Histadrut. Its leader, Berl Katznelson, explained: "Our Histadrut is unique among trade unions, for it is a union which both plans and executes. This is not due to our wisdom or perspicacity. This was always our vision, in all our actions. From the moment that the young immigrant reaches the shores of Palestine and looks for work in the plantations, he finds himself up against hard reality, and, at the same time, in our world of vision."[26] More recently, the then general secretary of the Histadrut, Pinchas Lavon, summed up the historical role of the Federation: "The General Federation of Workers was founded forty years ago by several thousand young people wanting to work in an under-developed country where labor was cheap, a country which rejected its inhabitants and which was inhospitable to newcomers. Under these conditions, the foundation of the Histadrut was a central event in the process of the rebirth of the Hebrew people in its fatherland. Our Histadrut is a general organization to its core. It is not a workers' trade union, although it copes perfectly well with the real needs of the worker."[27] Being "general to its core," the Histadrut has effectively become the central force of the Jewish community in its many aspects. It organized the Zionist armed forces, sometimes in collusion with the British occupation, and sometimes secretly against its wishes; it created a system of social security, the only one in existence in Israel, which has become an important weapon in the domination of the Jewish masses and the organization of the workers under the authority of the Histadrut; it has opened recruitment offices everywhere, thus reinforcing its domination, whilst at the same time regulating the right to work; it possesses its own school network, its own promotion societies, and its own production and service cooperatives; as an organization it completely dominates all the kibbutzim and collective farms of the whole country. It is not for nothing that the Histadrut was considered the central pillar of the Zionist project from its beginning, or as the Zionists say, "the state in embryo."

The Histadrut leadership decided the political line of the Jewish community, both in matters of "Jewish interest" and in its relations with the British occupiers and the Arab masses. The political leaders of the State of Israel—David Ben-Gurion, Levi Eshkol, Golda Meir—have all come from the ranks of the Histadrut.

It was only in 1943, at the end of the period of the British mandate, that the Histadrut created a special department for Arab workers; its aim was to organize them within a paternalistic framework, so as to divert them from the political struggle—that is, from the anti-imperialist and anti-Zionist struggle. The experiment was summed up at the time by a Zionist historian—a specialist in Arab issues and a Histadrut member:

> As a national feeling develops among the [Arab] workers, their opposition to those who want to organize them from the outside is becoming stronger. The most intelligent and dynamic among them never have an opportunity to show their talent and initiative. A pamphlet in Arabic (published by the Histadrut) explains that one should only be concerned with the economic interests of the Arab workers, and that one should exclude all political activity. This condition is difficult for people who are aware and close to public life to accept. The conception of work and the conquest of work held by the majority of the Histadrut is equally an obstacle, since it is difficult to explain things convincingly to an Arab worker. The discrimination in salaries between Jewish workers and Arab workers exasperates the Arabs, particularly since work conditions and price-levels tend to be equal. In these circumstances it was easy for Arab organizations to send us their members to ask "naive questions" at the time of the May Day demonstration—"Is proletarian solidarity compatible with a call for the conquest of labor, and for the creation of the Jewish State?"[28]

No Zionist has ever been able to answer that question; they cannot answer it today, any more than they could yesterday.

A Crisis of Confidence in the Histadrut

With the creation of the State of Israel in 1948, the integration of the Histadrut into the ruling Zionist system became more evident. The economic sector of the Histadrut, with its business concerns and its immense wealth, forms part of the public sector, whose development had to accelerate with the arrival of new immigrants, at the same time as capital was flowing into the new state. The Histadrut made it possible to form a nationalized economy. The theory propagated for years by Histadrut leaders, according to which the economic sector of the Histadrut constitutes the basis for the construction of socialism, collapsed with independence. Another often-stated argument, that the economic sector of the Histadrut belongs to the workers, was also invalidated. The minister of agriculture, Haim Gvati, who is one of the principal leaders of the Histadrut, had to admit during the Histadrut conference in 1964: "We have not succeeded in transforming these immense riches into socialist economic cells. We have not succeeded in maintaining the working-class nature of our economic sector. Actually there are no characteristics to differentiate it from the rest of the public sector, and sometimes even from the private sector. The atmosphere, work relations and human relations of our economic sector are in no way different from any other industrial enterprise."[29]

A complement and illustration to these remarks is to be found in the attitude of the Israeli workers toward the Histadrut. Among all the evidence on this point it is most interesting to quote some from the Histadrut itself, published in its *1966 Year Book*. "A very considerable number of workers hardly notice the Histadrut's trade union activities, and they consider that their situation would not have been modified if there had been no trade union." According to an enquiry undertaken for the Histadrut, the results of which are in the *Year Book*, a growing number of workers believe that the local trade union branches in their places of work (called "workers' committees" in Israel) should be independent of the Histadrut. Twenty percent of all wage-earners indicated that strikes have broken out in their enterprises against the advice of the Histadrut; 47 percent thought that in certain cases it was desirable for the workers to embark on a strike without Histadrut authorization. The *Year Book* continues: "The conclusions of the enquiry into the action committees are even more serious." (These are committees formed against the authorization of the Histadrut and aimed at, or on the occasion of, wildcat strikes or wildcat action.) "Against 8 percent of wage-earners who stated that strikes that had broken out were contrary to the advice of the local trade union branch, 29 percent were of the opinion that such strikes are justified in certain cases. *In short, the tendency to break with the established order is getting stronger,* in so far as work relations go" (our emphasis). The same publication shows that a majority of Histadrut members consider that the trade union conference has no influence on the functioning of the central body. Among the minority who do believe that ordinary members can exercise some influence, there is still a major number who estimate this influence to be insufficient. In reply to the question "Why are you a member of the Histadrut?" the official source says that about 70 percent replied that it was an "automatic thing," or "because they made us" or "because it was the done thing" or "because of the social security." A minority (16 percent) stated that they belonged for ideological reasons, whereas 15 percent said they were members because the Histadrut defended the interest of the workers.

The *Year Book* concludes that "a majority of Histadrut members, in other words, 55 percent, joined of their own free will, a third (24 percent) joined automatically on immigrating to Israel, and a fifth (20 percent) found they had become members automatically because they had been registered as such in their employment." Histadrut leaders, industrial circles, and government members are now openly expressing their concern at what they call the workers' "crisis of confidence" toward the Histadrut. This crisis is getting worse from year to year. It is, in fact, the reason for the change in the Histadrut top leadership in 1969, when the former secretary general, Aharon Becker, was replaced by Itzhak Ben-Aharon, known for his vigorous rhetorical style and the working-class phraseology he customarily uses. The former secretary general and the new one are both members of the ruling Labor Party.*

Wildcat Strikes and Action Committees

Certain important strikes have occurred in the short history of the workers' struggle in Israel. The first took place in 1951, relatively soon after the creation of the State of Israel, with the famous seamen's strike; next came a series of wildcat strikes in 1962, after the devaluation of the Israeli currency; the third wave took place in 1969, with the postal workers' and the Ashdod port workers' strike.

The seamen's strike was the most violent in the history of strikes in Israel. The battlefield was the port of Haifa, and on Israeli ships there, and in foreign ports. It was special because it was a strike led by young seamen without a trade union tradition, and because the conflict was about the means of electing trade union delegates by the mass of seamen. For those who know the nature of the Histadrut it is not surprising that it immediately mobilized all the forces at its disposal against the strikers. The strike leaders were dragged before an "internal tribunal" of the Histadrut and drafted into the army. Vast police forces engaged in violent battles against the strikers. The 1962 wave of strikes for the first time gave rise extensively to a kind of organization now known as an "action committee." The two fronts were once more clearly defined: the Histadrut on one side of the barricade, the workers on the other. It was during this period that the first steps to group the action committees on a national, or at least a regional basis, were taken—but this attempt was not successful. The 1969 strikes were a warning to the government and to the employers that strikes were possible despite the situation of war and of "national unity." The postal workers' strike saw the Israeli government once again issue mobilization orders, with the Histadrut's agreement, against the strikers, to force them back to work, as the existing laws allow. The strikers defied the law and were brought before the courts, but the trial was never concluded. Another factor characterized the Ashdod port workers' struggle. The Histadrut threatened to bring the local trade union militants before an "internal tribunal," but the local militants, with the support of the workers, held their ground. The trial opened in the presence of television cameras and was covered widely across the country. The workers were denounced as Al-Fatah agents and as "saboteurs." The threats of the Histadrut leadership were:

---

* Since this article was written, especially after the 1977 elections when the Zionist labor movement suffered defeat, its power and influence has declined. By 2009 it had dwindled to a minor force. In the elections that year, it won 11 out of 120 Knesset seats (8 were won by the centrist Labor Party, and 3 by the left-of-center Meretz). By then, almost all nationalized and Histadrut enterprises, as well as most kibbutzim, had been privatized. The Israeli economy is dominated by highly globalized, privately owned capital.

Strikes in Israel

Year	Strikers in thousands	Strike days in thousands	Number of Strikes
1949	5	57	53
1950	9	55	72
1951	10	114	76
1952	14	58	94
1953	9	35	84
1954	12	72	82
1955	10	54	87
1956	11	114	74
1957	4	116	59
1958	6	83	48
1959	6	31	51
1960	14	49	135
1961	27	141	128
1962	38	243	146
1963	87	129	127
1964	48	102	138
1965	90	208	288
1966	87	156	282
1967	25	58	142
1968	42	72	100

Sources: Israel Government *Statistical Year Books*, 1965; *Annual Report* of the Bank of Israel.

Note: Until 1959, only strikes lasting more than one day were included. Since 1960, strikes lasting more than two hours were also included. The figures also include lockouts, but these are rare and do not affect the yearly comparisons.

"If you are found guilty, the maximum sanctions will be applied, which means you will be excluded from the Histadrut, thus losing all the advantages of social security for you and your families." The workers continued their struggle and turned from accused to accusers. The Histadrut leadership suffered from bad publicity, and hastened to end the spectacle without pronouncing a verdict.

The Parties of the Zionist Right

If the Histadrut is controlled by the parties of the Zionist left, the other two main centers of power, government and the Jewish Agency, reflect a wider spectrum of

Zionist opinion. The electoral system is a proportional one, with each party presenting a nationwide list at the elections and the 120 seats in the Knesset being allocated accordingly, to parties obtaining more than 1 percent of the votes.

From the 1930s to the 1960s the Zionist right consisted of two parties, the "General Zionists" and Herut (Freedom). The General Zionists represented Zionist private capital in Palestine—the citrus grove owners, other landowners, and the industrialists. It was a typical capitalist party with the same slogans as in the West, except that it called for limiting Histadrut powers, rather than for turning the economy into a fully private one. Herut was not based on economic interests in the way the General Zionists were, but rather on militant and extremist Zionism. Its mottoes were (from the 1930s onward): "Two banks has the Jordan; one is ours, the other is ours too," and "In blood and fire Judaea fell, in blood and fire Judaea will rise." They demanded a policy of military conquest rather than one of colonizing settlement, which was the policy of the Zionist left. Herut employed fascist tactics in the 1930s, including brown shirts and armed terror, and it draws most of its adherents from Mizrahim attracted by its crude nationalistic slogans. In the mid-1960s these two parties merged under the leadership of Herut's leader, Begin, and formed the Herut-Liberal Bloc—known by its acronym "Gahal." (In Israel "Liberal" means "Conservative.") For the first time in Israeli history Herut was accepted into the cabinet on the eve of the June war to form part of the so-called National Unity cabinet; but they left Golda Meir's cabinet in August 1970 because of her acceptance of the Rogers plan, which called for an Israeli withdrawal from the 1967 cease-fire lines. Like the Zionist left, Gahal receives most of its financial support from the Jewish Agency.

The Dilemmas of the Zionist Left

From the early 1900s to this very day the backbone of the Zionist project in Palestine has been the Zionist left, and in particular those émigrés who came from Eastern Europe in the years between 1904 and 1914. This left has always been reformist and nationalist, but even as such it has split again and again as a result of the inherent conflicts between its Zionism and its socialism. The conflicts it has experienced can be grouped under three headings:

1. Foreign Policy: What position to adopt on imperialism in the Middle East and elsewhere, and on the socialist movement throughout the world, especially when the struggle against imperialism or cooperation with socialist movements conflicts with Zionist aspirations.
2. Class Struggle: What policy to have toward Jewish employers in Palestine and toward the capitalist sector within Zionism.
3. Socialist Internationalism: Whether to have a joint or separate struggle with the Palestinian peasants and workers against capitalism in Palestine, and whether to support other revolutionary movements.

All those who differed on these issues were still Zionists, that is, they considered their main goal to be the establishment and maintainence of an exclusively Jewish nation-state and of Jewish immigration from all over the world. Outside the Zionist left there were always a few groups making up the anti-Zionist left; they did not face the political dilemmas outlined here; their differences with each other were on issues of the strategy and tactics of the struggle against Zionism and for socialism in Palestine. They will be examined later. Of the Zionist parties by far the most important is Mapai (Israeli Labor Party), founded in 1930 through the merger of two smaller parties and the dominant party in all coalition governments in Israel since 1948. Originally the two components of Mapai agreed that Jewish exclusiveness must take precedence over cooperation with Arab workers and peasants in Palestine. However, they differed on the degree of class collaboration with Zionist employers, and only when agreement was reached did they decide to merge. The policy they agreed on was one of subordinating class interests to Zionist interests within the Jewish community itself, and Mapai became the main protagonist of the "Jewish labor only" policy. This policy meant that Jewish employers were pressured to employ only Jewish workers, and both Arab workers and Jewish employers were terrorized, often by violence, into enforcing this policy. This was the main internal issue within the Jewish community in the 1930s and it was finally won by Mapai, thus ensuring its dominant role.

Leaders such as Ben-Gurion, Eshkol, and Meir have remained dedicated to this policy to this day and are still dominant within Israel. Mapai has never considered itself Marxist or revolutionary, but socialist-reformist; yet although Meir spoke in 1950 of "socialism in our time," the party no longer claims any allegiance to socialism. In all the conflicts between imperialist and anti-imperialist forces in the Middle East this party had consciously collaborated and even plotted secretly (as in the Suez war) with imperialism. It has a clear stake in the continuation of imperialist influence in the area and considers any victory for anti-imperialist forces as a threat to Israel itself.

After twenty-two years in power certain changes have occurred in the party, the most important of which has been the emergence of a technocracy consisting of army officers who have entered the economy as administrators and specialists;[30] this group is in conflict with the old guard, and represents the growing influence of the army on Israeli politics as a whole, both because of the technical skills it contains and because of the increased weight of the military in the period after the June war. When Ben-Gurion was ousted from power in 1965 many of this group joined him to form Rafi (List of Israel's Workers), but when these technocrats realized that Ben-Gurion could no longer return to power they hastened to rejoin the ruling party. The newly reunited party is now called Avodah (Labor), and it can be expected that when the old guard disappears over the next few years it will be this new group that will be the dominant force in Israeli politics.*

---

* This prediction was not borne out: Avodah has declined and lost its dominant position.

The second largest Zionist left party is Mapam (United Workers' Party), formed in the late 1940s; its main component is Hashomer Hatza'ir (The Young Guard). Mapam originally considered itself to be both Marxist and revolutionary and proposed a binational state in Palestine; however, there had to be a Jewish majority guaranteed by the constitution, and until such a majority was achieved—through immigration—Palestine was to remain under "international trusteeship." The idea of a binational state was dropped in 1947 when the United Nations and the Soviet Union accepted the partition of Palestine. Mapam was always a little to the left of Mapai on many trade union issues in Israel and—at least verbally—in matters of foreign policy as well. But it has always remained loyal to Zionism and this has led it into collaboration with imperialism, as over Suez. In Israeli politics Mapam always trails, under protest, behind Mapai but it is the main instrument for defending Zionism against criticism by socialists, Marxists, and revolutionaries at home and abroad, and it still plays this role, although somewhat less so since 1967. Mapam always points to its kibbutzim as a new mode of communal life; but it never mentions that many of them are on lands from which the Arab peasants were driven off, that there is not a single Jewish-Arab kibbutz, and that all are subsidized by Zionist funds.[31] Mapam talks of the "right of the Jews to self-determination in Palestine," but by this it does not mean the rights of the Jewish population now living in Israel. Rather, it means the political rights of world Jewry in Palestine. Like all Zionists, Mapam insists on maintaining the Israeli immigration law that grants automatic immigration rights to Jews while denying them to anyone else. Like all other Zionist parties Mapam is financed by the Jewish Agency, and this enables it to maintain a party apparatus, daily papers, and a publicity network abroad.

The permanent conflict with the Arab world, and with anti-imperialist trends within it, forces Zionism to depend increasingly on imperialism, and this creates a permanent pressure shifting the Zionist left to the right. On its long road from its origins in the Russia of 1905 the Zionist left has one by one shed its slogans of revolution, socialism, and anti-imperialism. Each shift to the right leaves behind it a splinter group loyal to the abandoned slogan.

The latest offspring of this kind is Siah (Israeli New Left). It was formed after the 1967 war by members of Mapam who were opposed to their party's collaboration with the Dayan-Eshkol-Begin bloc, and their main emphasis is on the lack of a peace initiative in Israeli policy. Yet although they consider themselves Marxists and revolutionaries they pledge allegiance to Zionism. The editor of one of their publications recently stated: "Our struggle to change the image of Israeli society and to consolidate a peace policy must be based, whatever happens, on principled and consistent affirmation of the State of Israel and of the Zionist principles on which it is founded. Any departure from this will lead Siah astray from the aims it set itself when it was founded."[32] At the same time Siah has been able to attract support from young Israelis hostile to the official line; its second congress held in Tel-Aviv in November 1970 was attended by 350 people—mainly ex-Mapam and ex-Maki—and passed resolutions calling for peace without annexations of Arab territory, recognition of the right of the Palestinian people to self-determination, unconditional talks with the Arabs and Palestinians, and Israeli acceptance of the Jarring mission.

The Non-Zionist Left

Outside the Zionist camp there exist two forces: the Israeli Communist Party—Rakah—and the Matzpen group. The Israeli CP was founded in the late 1920s and was, almost from the beginning, a Stalinist party. It has remained so to this day. In its history the party has undergone many splits, most of them over the question of what policy to adopt toward Arab nationalism; and in general the party has always followed the foreign policy of the Soviet Union. The most recent of the many absurd positions that such a policy leads to is the support of the party for the US Rogers peace plan.* The aim of this plan is to stabilize the political setup in the region and to consolidate both the Zionist regime and the reactionary Arab regimes. Rakah originally defined this plan as an attempt by the United States "to save its tottering influence in the Arab world";[33] it subsequently called for a joint struggle of all peace-loving forces in Israel to implement it. The key to this absurd position is the policy of the Soviet Union, since the Rogers plan is the result of an agreement between the United States and the Soviet Union.

In 1965 there was a split in the party, when the Mikunis-Sneh leadership, which had always leaned toward Zionism, demanded a "more constructive" policy toward Zionism. This group supported the June 1967 war and applied for membership in the Zionist Congress. Although it has usurped the official daily paper of the party and its name, Maki, it hardly has any influence in Israel. The other faction, led by Meir Wilner and Tawfik Toubi, is the same old Stalinist party; it has an equal number of Jewish and Arab members, and appears under the name of New Communist List, also known by its acronym, Rakah. Actually, there is nothing new about it. The CP has always defended the rights of the Palestinian Arabs, and not only their right to self-determination but many of their individual rights in Israel. It has waged a courageous, day-to-day struggle to defend the rights of the Palestinians, but it abandoned the theory and practice of revolution a long time ago. It is now dedicated to the slogan of "the peaceful road to socialism," and considers its main goal to be "peace and democracy."

It was this absence of revolutionary politics that compelled a group of members to leave Maki in 1962 and to form the Israeli Socialist Organization, better known by the name of its magazine, *Matzpen* (compass). The Matzpen group accepted the Maki positions on the right of the Palestinian people as well as the Israeli people to self-determination. It gives primacy to the anti-Zionist struggle and subordinates

---

* William P. Rogers was secretary of state in the Nixon administration.

all other issues, such as the economic struggle of the working class, to this struggle. It considers the overthrow of Zionism as the first task confronting revolutionaries in Israel. At the same time it believes that Israeli society, unlike white society in South Africa, can be revolutionized from within, provided that such a development is subordinated to revolutionary developments in the Arab world. Despite its small size Matzpen has gained influence among the youth in Israel, especially after the 1967 June war, which it opposed. Matzpen has carried out an open dialogue with left tendencies within the Palestinian resistance movement, and throughout the Arab world. It supports anti-imperialist struggles and the Palestinian struggle against Israeli domination. However, it does not support Arab nationalism, or Nasserism. Recently two tendencies split off from Matzpen on these issues. One considers the struggle against Zionism irrelevant, and is calling for ordinary "working-class struggle against bourgeois policies." The other regards Arab nationalism as a revolutionary force. Such a split was expected, but the majority of Matzpen members have chosen to reject these two lines. Matzpen believes that revolutionaries in Israel have a significant role to play in contributing to the overthrow of Zionism within Israeli society; and in this Matzpen differs not only from Siah and the Communist Party but also from the groups that have split from them.

This analysis has illustrated the specific class structure of Israeli society and the particular structure of the ruling class. It is a society formed through immigration and the colonization of an already populated land, a society whose internal unity is maintained through conflict with an external enemy. In this society the ruling class is allied to imperialism and depends on it, but does not itself serve imperialism by economic exploitation of the Israeli people. This class rules through a set of bureaucratic institutions that were developed during the colonization process (Histadrut, Jewish Agency), and only a subordinate section of it operates through private ownership of the means of production. These features cannot be explained as products of the internal dynamic of Israeli society; yet they are easily understood as products of the dynamic of the Zionist project as a whole.

Both the experience of political activity in Israel and the theoretical conclusions presented here lead to a conclusion about the strategy of the revolutionary struggle in Israel: in the immediate future political struggle against the Zionist nature of the regime must take precedence over everything else. This struggle must be directed to win the support of all those who directly suffer from Zionism. This includes all those who, like Israeli youth or the Israeli Arabs, are brought in their daily experience into conflict with the regime itself. It is a strategy that points to the shattering of the Zionist character of the regime.

14

Zionism and "Oriental" Jews: A Dialectic of Exploitation and Co-optation

Ehud Ein-Gil and Moshé Machover

In recent years, the complex relationship of the Mizrahim[1] to Zionism has been presented in an oversimplified way by some Israeli anti-Zionist Mizrahi activists and ideologues—including notably some social-science academics—as well as by some Palestinian leftists. It has been claimed that Zionism is essentially a project of the Ashkenazim.[2] The implication is that the Mizrahim in Israel, far from sharing the blame for the iniquities of Zionism, are in fact its victims alongside the Palestinian Arabs. The main dividing line in Israel/Palestine is accordingly that between Ashkenazi-Zionist "Orientalist" oppressors and "Oriental" oppressed, the latter comprising both Mizrahi Jews and Palestinian Arabs.[3]

In this article, we argue for a far more nuanced view. The Zionist project was indeed initiated by Ashkenazim who were mostly infected by racist European Orientalist attitudes and applied them to the Mizrahim, whom they treated with contempt, as mere instruments. However, the *response* to Zionism among Mizrahi communities before 1948 was not very different from that of Ashkenazi communities before the Second World War. Mizrahi immigrants were imported to Israel as colonization fodder. However, despite the subjective Orientalist racism of most veteran Zionist leaders, the objective logic of the Zionist project has eventually led to the co-optation of a substantial Mizrahi elite. Moreover, with the passage of time, the ethno-cultural aspect of the oppression of the Mizrahim—stressed by the Mizrahi identity ideologues—has gradually receded in importance, as compared with the socioeconomic disadvantage of the Mizrahi masses.

This article was written in June 2008. It was published in *Race & Class* 50, no. 3, March–January 2009.

"Human Dust"

In some sense, the claim that "Zionism is Ashkenazi" is obviously correct: the Zionist project was initiated by Ashkenazim and the Zionist movement has been led predominantly—and, for quite a long time, almost exclusively—by Ashkenazim.[4] It is also true that the attitude of the Zionist leaders to the Mizrahim tended to be overtly racist and instrumental. We need not expand on this here, but instead refer the reader to the masterly materialist account by Raphael Shapiro.[5] Let us just recapitulate briefly part of his account.

From its very early days, the Zionist project—aiming to displace the indigenous Palestinians—needed an alternative *Jewish* labor force. In a report commissioned by the Palestine Office of the Zionist movement (1908), one of its experts, Dr. Jacob Thon, stated that "it is hardly in need of pointing out that the question of employing Jewish instead of Arab agricultural workers is one of the most important problems of the colonization of Palestine." This was to come from two sources: first, "from the Zionist youth in the Diaspora, especially from Russia"; second, "from among the [indigent] Oriental Jews, who are still on the same cultural level as the [Arab] fellahin." Those few thousand Mizrahim already living in Palestine at the time, "especially the Yemenis and Persians," are suited for agricultural work. "Since they are frugal, these Jews can be compared to the Arabs, and from this point of view they can compete with them."[6] In view of this report, the Palestine Office decided to import new Jewish immigrants from Yemen. These efforts were quite successful, in fact, all too successful: by 1912, the supply of Yemenite immigrants exceeded demand.[7] However, eventually the expanding Zionist colonization of Palestine, especially following the First World War and the Balfour Declaration (1917), created a constant need for importing a Jewish labor force.

Following the creation of Israel (1948) and the massive ethnic cleansing of the Palestinian population from the areas it occupied in the 1947–49 war, the Zionist project's hunger for Jewish immigration intensified immeasurably. It was now driven not only by the political-*economic* aim of replacing Palestinian workers with Jews in preexisting or projected jobs. A large number of new Jewish immigrants were needed urgently for political-*demographic* purposes: repopulating the newly occupied areas from which the Palestinian Arabs had been driven out, especially near the 1949 Armistice Lines ("the Green Line"), and thereby staking a de facto claim to these areas, establishing a Jewish majority in Palestine and supplying conscripts for the growing needs of the army. Europe provided one source: following the Nazi genocide, there were not only many Jewish refugees seeking permanent settlement but also other Jews who were not refugees, but were traumatized by recent horrors and wished to leave Europe. But this reserve of immigrants was insufficient. Mizrahi Jews—mainly from Yemen, Iraq, and North Africa—were seduced and encouraged to immigrate to Israel. In some cases, provocations (such as simulated anti-Semitic outrages) were allegedly staged in order to stimulate a mass Mizrahi exodus from Arab countries. These new immigrants were more or less dumped where political-demographic considerations dictated, without any real economic planning or productive employment. Mizrahi immigrants were subjected to racist treatment by the Zionist establishment (then dominated by "labor" Zionism), many of whose members regarded them as mere "human material," faceless "human dust," who ought to be grateful for being saved from Oriental backwardness. The next, Israel-born generation was to be molded in the image of the "Sabra" model.

An interesting observation made by Shapiro is that the Zionist definition of Israel as a state of all the world's Jews (rather than of its own citizens) makes it automatically an Ashkenazi state: the Ashkenazim are an overwhelming majority of world Jewry, although in Israel they are a minority of the population and barely a majority among its Jewish inhabitants.[8]

Mizrahi Zionism

In view of the facts described above, it may at first sight seem surprising that there has been little hostility or opposition to Zionism among Mizrahim, either in their countries of origin or following their mass migration to Israel. Before 1948, there were a few anti-Zionist voices raised in Mizrahi communities outside Palestine: those came mostly either from religious leaders or from members and supporters of communist parties. Many were not so much opposed to Zionism but resented it for putting them in a compromising position, suspected of dual loyalty. A small minority responded positively to Zionism, including some who actually migrated to Palestine quite voluntarily. But the great majority were simply indifferent.

Thus the Mizrahi response was not substantially different from that of the Ashkenazi communities before the 1940s. True, Zionism was initiated and led by Ashkenazim, but before the Nazi genocide it remained very much a minority movement in the Ashkenazi communities. There, too, it was actively condemned by most Orthodox and Reformist religious authorities, by supporters of the Jewish Socialist Bund, and the communist parties, as well as by secular Jews who favored assimilation. The majority there too were simply uninterested. The overwhelming majority of those east European Jews who wished to emigrate chose to go to the Americas, Australia, South Africa, and Western Europe rather than to Palestine.

According to official Israeli statistics, between 1919 and May 14, 1948, when the State of Israel was declared, over 420,000 Jews arrived in mandatory Palestine: 44,809 (10.4 percent) came from Asia and Africa and 385,066 (89.6 percent) came from Europe and the United States.[9] Now, 10.4 percent seems a rather small proportion of Jewish immigration to Palestine. But note that, before the Nazi genocide, the Mizrahim constituted roughly 7.5 percent—considerably less than 10.4 percent—of world Jewry.[10] So, as far as immigration was concerned, Zionism in fact elicited a *proportionately greater* positive response among Mizrahi communities than among other Jews.[11]

Mizrahim also played a considerable part in voluntary militant Zionist activism in pre-1948 Palestine. Precise data are hard to come by, but the general picture that emerges from various sources (personal reminiscences, examination of name lists of persons involved in various activities) is fairly clear. In organizations affiliated to Labor ("socialist") Zionism, including the underground armed Palmah,[12] Mizrahim were underrepresented compared to their proportion in the Jewish population. Consequently, there were relatively few Mizrahim in the co-operative and collective agricultural settlements established by these movements. In the mainstream Zionist clandestine militia, the Haganah (precursor of the Israeli armed forces), the proportion of Mizrahim was roughly the same as in the Jewish population as a whole.[13] On the other hand, Mizrahim were overrepresented in right-wing—and more extreme—Zionist organizations, including notably the clandestine armed Etzel and Lehi.[14] Of the twelve members of these two groups executed for terrorist acts during the British Mandate, only five were Ashkenazim.[15]

The Mizrahi Attitude to Zionism in Israel

After 1948, the mass immigration of Mizrahim to Israel was, for the main part, not motivated by Zionist commitment on the part of the immigrants; rather, it was a response to real or perceived menace in the countries of origin. In some Arab countries, notably Iraq, a feeling of panic was encouraged, if not actually created, by Zionist propaganda and the actions of Zionist agents.[16]

Yet Mizrahim in Israel have not shown any marked tendency to join or form anti-Zionist political groups. Among the small minority of Israeli Jews who are openly anti-Zionist, Mizrahim are not proportionately overrepresented. In fact, the only numerically significant group of Mizrahim in anti-Zionist ranks were some immigrants from Iraq who had been members or supporters of the Iraqi Communist Party and who, upon arrival in Israel, transferred their allegiance to the Israeli CP. But this had little to do specifically with their being Mizrahim: a similar pattern existed also among new immigrants from Eastern Europe who had supported the CPs in their countries of origin.

The discrimination and humiliation experienced by the Mizrahim in Israel led to disaffection, including occasional militant eruptions, beginning with widespread violent demonstrations of Yemenite immigrants in 1950, which, though widely reported at the time, are now almost forgotten.[17] Better remembered are the Wadi Salib riots (July 1959), involving mostly North African immigrants.[18] There were sporadic outbreaks in later decades.

Yet in all these Mizrahi social protests there was little or no attempt to connect the struggle of the Mizrahim for social equality with that of the Palestinian Arab citizens of Israel. The only partial exception was the Israeli Black Panther movement, which erupted in 1971 and whose initial slogans protested on behalf of "all the downtrodden"—a coded reference to solidarity with the Palestinians. This stance—all the more remarkable for being exceptional—was no doubt largely due to the involvement of leftist militants, mainly members of the socialist anti-Zionist organization Matzpen, who gave the Israeli Black Panthers some logistic and political support.[19]

On the whole, opposition to Zionism and solidarity with the Palestinian Arabs found little support among the Mizrahim: certainly no more than among other Israeli Jews. Meanwhile, the disaffection of the Mizrahim has been exploited by right-wing and religious Zionist parties that are noted for their extreme anti-Arab ideology and which have won a great deal of Mizrahi electoral support.

"Arab Jews"?

The weakness of specifically Mizrahi opposition to Zionism and, especially, the almost total absence of solidarity with the Palestinian Arabs may seem strange in view of the fact that the Mizrahim are often labeled as "Arab Jews." This terminology has been used especially by a few Mizrahi exponents of identity ideology but also in some Palestinian nationalist discourse.[20] The ideological motivation behind this is quite obvious. For the Mizrahi identity ideologues, this labeling helps to depict Palestinian Arabs and Mizrahi Jews as joint victims, counterposed to their Ashkenazi Zionist oppressors. For Palestinian nationalist supporters of the unitary "one-state solution," it serves to avoid the problem posed by the existence of a new Hebrew (Israeli-Jewish) nation and depicts the national character of the future unitary Palestine as predominantly Arab. Thus, in an authoritative programmatic article, "Toward the Democratic Palestine," published by Fatah in 1970, the author points out that "the call for a non-sectarian Palestine should not be confused with . . . a bi-national state."[21] He goes on to claim that in the reality of Palestine "the term bi-national and the Arab-Jewish dichotomy [are] meaningless, or at best quite dubious." This is so because "the majority of Jews in Palestine today are Arab Jews—euphemistically called Oriental Jews by the Zionists. Therefore Palestine combines Jewish, Christian and Moslem Arabs as well as non-Arab Jews (Western Jews)."[22]

However, this labeling of Mizrahim as "Arab Jews" is quite wrong. Of course, we are not questioning the right of any individual to *self*-identify as an Arab Jew if s/he feels inclined to do so. But there is no justification for thrusting this label upon the mass of Mizrahim, who do not choose to identify themselves as "Arab" and who would, at best, regard this label as alien to their self-identity. For a start, the label "Arab" makes no sense at all as far as some Mizrahi communities are concerned: for example, Iranian, Kurdish, South Indian, and Bukharan Jews. These communities had little or nothing to do with the Arabic language and culture. But the label is also inappropriate for describing members of Jewish communities who lived in Arab countries, most (though not all) of whom did speak some Arabic dialect. These may be described as *culturally* Arabized but not as "Arab" in any *national* or *ethnic* sense.[23]

In Israel, the overwhelming majority of Arabic-speaking immigrants had an obvious reason to avoid being labeled as "Arabs" and thus being automatically classified as part of the subordinate national group, hostile to the Jewish state. In struggling to improve their social status and economic conditions, Mizrahi immigrants were able to achieve some results by invoking Jewish solidarity and the Zionist claim that all Jews, wherever they are, constitute a single nation. In a colonizing settler state, affinity with the indigenous people is quite undesirable.

But our main point has nothing to do with the racism of the Zionist state. The label "Arab" is a grave anachronistic error when applied to the mass of the Jews living in Arab countries *before* their emigration. The point is that "Arab" as a national category, a label of national identity (as distinct from the Arab*ic* language), is a relatively recent construct.[24] Most if not all Jews living, say, in Baghdad would describe themselves as "Baghdadi" or perhaps "Iraqi" Jews, or—stressing the antiquity of their community—as "Babylonian" Jews. Similarly, members of the Jewish community in Fez would normally refer to themselves as "Moroccan" or "Mughrabi" Jews. It would simply not occur to them (with the possible exception of a very small number of individuals) to label themselves as "Arab" Jews.[25] Indeed, it would have been bizarre for them to self-identify in that way, given that the majority of their *non-Jewish* compatriots did not normally apply the label "Arab" to themselves at that time.

Arab national identity, first urged by a few intellectuals and political activists, was not widely adopted in the Arabic-speaking countries until well into the twentieth century. Toward the middle of the century, with the rise of secular Arab nationalism, it was gaining currency—alongside more local national identities, such as Iraqi, Egyptian, Algerian, etc.[26] However, the Jewish minorities in these countries did not participate in this process and kept, or were kept, outside the Arab nationalist movement.[27] To some extent, this was due to the lack of any serious attempt by the nationalist movement to attract Jews to its ranks. Zionist colonization had led to an acute conflict in Palestine and most Arab nationalists eventually fell for Zionism's claim that it spoke and acted for all Jews. The Jewish minorities were thus regarded with suspicion as pro-Zionist and therefore disloyal.[28] This suspicion was compounded by the fact that the majority of the Mizrahi intelligentsia and the Jewish secular leadership in their countries of origin adopted Western culture, usually that of the colonial power ruling their country. Thus, Jews living in the Arab world neither shared, nor were they encouraged to share, the newly constructed Arab identity. By the time Arab national consciousness reached its high-water mark and achieved mass popularity, there were very few Jews left in the Arab countries.

In any case, there is no evidence that, when there were still large Jewish communities in the Arab countries, they generally regarded themselves, or were regarded by their non-Jewish compatriots, as Arabs. The label "Arab Jews," as a *generally applicable* category, must therefore be dismissed as an anachronistic and purely ideological construct. Moreover, it is useless as an "objective" sociological term because Mizrahi immigrants to Israel who had no Arabic cultural background have shared a similar social status with Arabic-speaking immigrants. In other words, there is no *sociologically meaningful* category in Israel that includes all Jews from Arabic-speaking communities but excludes all other Mizrahim, such as those of Kurdish or Iranian origin.

Partial Integration

More than half a century has elapsed since the mass Mizrahi immigration to Israel. During that time, the situation of the Mizrahim in Israel has changed to a considerable extent. According to some social, cultural, and political criteria, their position has significantly improved compared to the early decades—although they have by no means achieved equality with the Ashkenazim in these respects.

The Zionist promise to make Israel a Jewish "melting pot," in which "blending of exiled communities" (*mizzug galuyyiot*) would take place, has not proved to be an utterly empty slogan. Here it is very important to note that, while racist attitudes toward the Mizrahim have been widespread and endemic among the Ashkenazi elite (especially among the "left wing" or "labor" Zionist leadership), there is nothing structurally inherent in the Zionist project itself that dictates or legitimizes such attitudes. On the contrary: the logic of Zionist colonization requires minimizing internal ethnic antagonisms and maximizing unity and solidarity within the settler nation—against the indigenous Palestinian victims of Zionist colonization and the surrounding Arab world. It is in the interest of Zionism that Jewish racist attitudes and resentments—in so far as they exist and seek an outlet—be directed exclusively against Arabs, not against fellow Jews.

True, members of the racist Ashkenazi elite have found this ideal psychologically difficult to achieve due to the many elements of resemblance between Mizrahi culture (in the widest sense of this term) and that of the hated and despised Arabs. And this resemblance seemed even greater than it really was when viewed from a great cultural distance and from the height of social arrogance. However, the more astute members of the elite eventually realized that it was politically expedient to try to overcome this psychological difficulty. Moreover, as we shall see, the difficulty itself has tended to diminish with the passage of time.

Arguably the greatest integrationist success has been the cooptation of Mizrahim into the military and political ruling Israeli elite. (In Israel, high military rank is quite often a stepping-stone to a political career.) This process accelerated after 1977 (with the first Likud-led government) and especially after the rise of the religious SHAS party (founded in 1984), which has won large electoral support among Mizrahim. Thus, among chiefs of staff of the Israeli armed forces—the highest military position—were Moshe Levy (born in Israel, parents born in Iraq), Shaul Mofaz (born in Iran), and Dan Halutz (born in Israel, father born in Iran, mother in Iraq).

Mizrahim who have held prominent political positions include: Professor Shlomo Ben-Ami (formerly Shlomo Ben-Abu, born in Morocco; foreign minister, minister of internal security); General Binyamin (Fuad) Ben-Eli'ezer (born in Iraq; deputy prime minister, minister of defense, Labor Party chairman); Rabbi Aryeh

Der'i (born in Morocco; minister of internal affairs); Dalia Itzik (born in Israel, parents born in Iraq; speaker of the Knesset); General Avigdor Kahalani (born in Israel, of Yemeni origin; minister of internal security); Moshe Katsav (born in Iran; president of the State of Israel, deputy prime minister); David Levy (born in Morocco; deputy prime minister, foreign minister); General Shaul Mofaz (born in Iran; minister of defense), General Yitzhak Mordechai (born in Iraqi Kurdistan; deputy prime minister, minister of defense), Yitzhak Navon (born in Palestine, to Sephardi father and mother of Moroccan origin; president of the State of Israel, deputy prime minister); Amir (Armand) Peretz (born in Morocco; minister of defense, Labor Party chairman, chairman of the Histadrut); Silvan Shalom (born in Tunisia; deputy prime minister, foreign minister, minister of the treasury); Meir Shitrit (born in Morocco; deputy prime minister, minister of internal affairs, minister of the treasury).[29]

Israel has yet to elect a Mizrahi prime minister but, in recent years, the number of Mizrahi ministers in Israeli governments has tended to correspond roughly to the proportion of Mizrahim in the Jewish population. (This is true of Mizrahi *men:* Israeli women—Ashkenazi and Mizrahi alike—are still very seriously underrepresented at the top and may rightly envy the Mizrahi men's achievements in this respect.) There are also quite a few Mizrahi mayors of towns and cities, including some that were established long before 1948 and the wave of Mizrahi immigration.

A considerable degree of cultural integration has also taken place. As time goes on, the descendants of the original Mizrahi immigrants tend to lose touch with their ancestral language and culture. By the third generation (grandchildren of the immigrants, or children of those who immigrated when very young), that cultural heritage has largely faded away. Significantly, this is true also of Mizrahi immigrants who were settled in towns where a part of the former Palestinian Arab population remained after 1948 (when the majority of that population was ethnically cleansed). In these mixed towns—such as Jaffa, Acre, Ramleh, and Lydda—the proximity of indigenous Arabic speakers did little to preserve an Arabic culture among the immigrants.

This is not only due to imposition and pressure by the Ashkenazi elite. In fact, it is a normal process in most countries of immigration and a similar process has taken place also among the Israeli Ashkenazim (except the ultra-orthodox).[30] Few members of the third generation of any ethnic origin speak the language of their grandparents. They speak Hebrew and even the specific ethnic accents, which are still clearly discernible in the second generation, tend to fade away in the third. A new national Hebrew culture has emerged, partly a synthesis of the diverse immigrant ethnic cultures, partly homegrown, and partly imported from the global cultural marketplace. Intermarriage among the communities has also contributed to this blending.

If many aspects of Israeli culture are more "European" than "Oriental," this is largely due to global "Western" importation rather than to the input of the ancestral Ashkenazi cultures. The privileged political, commercial, and cultural relations that Israel has developed with the European Union (without any noticeable objection by Mizrahim) has surely affected this. Indeed, Israel has been granted the status of an "honorary" European country: for over thirty years, it has been welcome as a participant in European sports tournaments and championships, as well as in the annual Eurovision song contest, which it has won three times. As it happens, the three winners were Mizrahim (all three of Yemenite origin): Yizhar Cohen in 1978, Milk and Honey with Gali Atari as the lead singer in 1979, and the transsexual Dana International (born Yaron Cohen) in 1998. This illustrates the fact that, in some aspects of the new national culture, the Mizrahi contribution is more dominant than the Ashkenazi. This is true of popular music, a significant part of which has a Mediterranean character, and perhaps even more so of popular cuisine: Middle Eastern dishes are far more common than traditional Ashkenazi ones.

Some cultural differences have persisted but they have a less pronounced ethnic character and are attenuated in some respects. The most important cultural difference is perhaps in matters of religion: the Mizrahim are relatively underrepresented in the two extreme parts of the spectrum—secular and orthodox—and overrepresented in the moderately religious middle. The various communities have kept their separate synagogues and their variants of religious liturgies, practices, and customs. Israel has two chief rabbis: one for the Ashkenazim and one for the Sephardim and Mizrahim. The Mizrahim also have their own religious political party, SHAS, the only predominantly Mizrahi party to have won mass support.

Other cultural differences are associated with socioeconomic differences (discussed below): Mizrahi ingredients are more evident in the subculture of the poor and working class, whereas the middle-class subculture is more influenced by Western (though not specifically Ashkenazi) elements.

Socioeconomic Stratification

The foregoing is however only part of the story; the total picture is by no means as rosy as that account may have suggested. For a better balance, we must turn our attention to the class aspect of the position of Mizrahim in Israel. This subject deserves an article in its own right; here we can only touch on it very briefly.

While a sizeable proportion of the Israeli political elite are now Mizrahim, they constitute a very thin upper stratum of the Mizrahi population as a whole. According to social, educational, and economic criteria, this population is, on average, significantly disadvantaged compared to the Ashkenazim. True, the Mizrahim no longer provide the bulk of the very bottom of the labor market, as they did in the 1950s and 1960s. Following the 1967 war, during the 1970s and 1980s, they were replaced in the most menial and lowest-paid jobs by Palestinian workers. Since the late 1980s, following the first Palestinian intifada, the latter were largely excluded and have in turn been replaced by migrant foreign workers. During the 1990s, there was also an important demographic change in Israel's Jewish population: a large influx of immigrants from Russia and Ethiopia, who entered some of the lower ranks of the labor market (just above migrant foreign workers). This somewhat improved the relative position of the Mizrahim. By now, many of the Russian immigrants have leapfrogged the Mizrahim and enjoyed rapid upward mobility. However, not only most of the Ethiopian immigrants but also some of the Russians are still employed in semi-skilled low-paid jobs. Thus, the latter constitute a stratum of Ashkenazi workers who are socioeconomically disadvantaged.

A few Mizrahim—such as Sadiq Bino and Shlomo Eliahu (both from Iraq), Lev Leviev (from Bukhara), the Nimrodi family (originally from Iraq) and Itzhak Teshuvah (from Libya)—have joined the Israeli superrich. Many more have acquired small businesses or managed to enter various middle-class occupations. Nevertheless, the overall socioeconomic and educational gap between Mizrahi and Ashkenazi Jews has remained very wide and appears to be narrowing very slowly, if at all. The reasons for this are quite clear. They have less to do with present-day *active* discrimination—there is considerably less of this than in the early decades— and more to do with low transgenerational socioeconomic mobility (which is typical of many capitalist countries). In other words, it is mainly a persisting effect of the original active discrimination practiced in Israel's early decades: the initial advantages and disadvantages tend to be inherited by successive generations. Thus, with the passage of time, the balance of the grievance felt by the majority of ordinary Mizrahim has shifted. Cultural humiliation, a sense that they and their specific ethnic cultures are despised by an alien ruling political elite, does persist, but is of less central importance. Of relatively growing importance is a feeling of socioeconomic discrimination, of being stuck at the bottom of the (Jewish) heap as a consequence of being of the "wrong" ethnic origin.

Political Assessment

Mizrahi identity discourse, like that of other identity ideologies, raises very real and important issues. But these issues can be conceptualized and theorized in politically progressive or not-so-progressive ways—depending on how they are articulated with questions of class, on the one hand, and of colonizing national oppression on the other. Painting a picture that puts Ashkenazi Zionists on one side of the main dividing line and lumps together as co-victims Palestinian Arabs and Mizrahim on the other side, irrespective of class, is a travesty.

Reality is far more complex than this simplistic picture. A Mizrahi senior cabinet minister is not in the same boat as a Mizrahi worker living in a depressed "development township." Nor is the latter in the same position vis-à-vis the Zionist project as a Palestinian worker or peasant. The difference is not merely that of degree but a decisive qualitative one. Zionism excludes the Palestinian Arabs as the absolute "Other," some of whom may at best be tolerated as second-class citizens as long as they remain a docile minority, and all of whom are under the constant threat of being ethnically cleansed whenever the opportunity arises. The Mizrahim were recruited to replace the Palestinians, and are theoretically embraced by Zionism as brethren, although in practice most of them were placed in inferior positions.

The extent to which Mizrahim in present-day Israel can be regarded as victims of the Zionist regime is strongly class-dependent. Indeed, as we saw, a Mizrahi elite has been co-opted and successfully integrated into Israel's military and political leadership. For the mass of the Mizrahim, socioeconomic deprivation is increasingly the central issue. Issues of cultural discrimination, being subjected to contemptuous or patronizing Ashkenazi attitudes, while still very much alive, are gradually becoming less relevant as a distinct issue and tend to become an aspect of class-based cultural antagonism.

Moreover, even the most deprived Mizrahi is hugely privileged, as a member of the dominant oppressing nation, compared to a Palestinian Arab of similar socioeconomic status in Israel—let alone in the West Bank or Gaza. The Mizrahim in Israel are indeed an underprivileged group—but only in the sense of being a *relatively* underprivileged part of the oppressor settler nation. There is a qualitative difference between their position and that, say, of the descendants of the African slaves in the United States, who really had no share whatsoever in the responsibility for the settlers' oppression and genocide of the Native Americans.

The idea of basing an alliance between the Mizrahim and the Palestinians on the grounds of their being fellow "Orientals" or Arabs, as opposed to the Ashkenazim, who are to blame for Zionism, is a pure fantasy. It is not based on any reality that exists or is ever likely to exist even under greatly changed regional conditions. Rather, the struggle of the ordinary, socioeconomically disadvantaged Mizrahim for their rights and against the racism of which they are victims must be an explicit and distinct but integral component of a general struggle for equal rights and social justice for all: encompassing workers' industrial actions, social struggles for better housing, education and health, civil society's campaigns for human rights and against any discrimination of minorities, and even for a better environment. All these issues are in the interests of ordinary Mizrahim no less, and it seems even more, than pure cultural identity issues, let alone those based on a false analysis.

Part III
RACISM AND
THE NATIONAL QUESTION

15

The Case for Hebrew
Self-Determination

One of the central issues raised by people concerned with the future of Palestine is that of the status of the Israeli Jews (i.e., the Hebrew-speaking national community). The ISO (Matzpen) has argued that, despite the fact that it was created by Zionism, a Hebrew nation in the full sense of the term now exists in Palestine. And as such it has the right to self-determination, not certainly in the Zionist sense but within the context of a socialist federation of the Middle East. On the other hand, many revolutionaries, including the Democratic Popular Front for the Liberation of Palestine (DPFLP) favor "union of Jews and Arabs of Palestine as *one people* as the only possible basis for a socialist transformation." Obviously, nations and national communities cannot simply be wished out of, or into, existence. If this were possible, the only truly socialist "wish" would be for the whole human race to form a union "as one people." This is also the condition that one hopes to achieve in the long run under communism—the withering away of all national differences, and therefore of nations as such. But for the present, nations and national problems do exist and socialists must formulate a correct policy on the national question.

By "correct" we mean in greatest accordance with the interests of the struggle for socialism. The policy adopted by many socialists (including the ISO) is to recognize the right of all nations to self-determination. The purpose of this is not to encourage separatism and national particularism. On the contrary, it is designed

---

This piece was written in response to an article by Bill Hillier, "Revival of the Palestinians," which appeared in *Peace News*, June 6, 1969. Hillier raised some pertinent questions, a central one being the right of Israeli Jews to self-determination. He also demanded a prompt reply from the Israeli revolutionary left. In point of fact, the ISO (Matzpen) stated its views on these issues in an article by A. Sa'id and Moshé Machover, "Palestinian Struggle and Middle-East Revolution" (chapter 4 in this book). The present article further elucidates Matzpen's position concerning self-determination. This article is based on chapter 12 of *The Other Israel: The Case Against Zionism* (Doubleday, 1972).

to minimize them and to create, wherever possible, a basis for voluntary convergence, unification, and integration.

A question that remains to be answered is whether the Hebrew-speaking community does, in fact, constitute a nationality. But this is not just a matter of historical analysis; it is, to a great extent, an empirical question. Our answer—based both on historical analysis and on the direct and close familiarity with the relevant empirical facts—is that, according to any reasonable definition of "nation" or "national community," the Israeli Jews do constitute such a group.

Those who oppose recognition of the principle of self-determination of the Israeli Jews assert that merging of Arabs and Jews in Palestine into a single Palestinian national entity is the only basis for a socialist transformation. Let us analyze this assertion. No true socialist would deny that in order to achieve a socialist revolution in a country inhabited by two peoples, they should join together in a common struggle—this is elementary. But it by no means implies that they must merge into one people. Moreover, an analysis of the Middle East shows that a socialist revolution is extremely unlikely to occur within the framework of Palestine alone; it can be thought of only as a process embracing the whole Arab East.

This thesis, that revolution cannot be localized in Palestine, but must encompass the entire Middle East, is accepted not only by the ISO but by all Arab revolutionary socialists. Why then should the Israeli Jews merge only with the Palestinian Arabs rather than with the entire Arab nation? If one claims that the creation of a single nation is the prerequisite for the revolution, and if one also accepts the concept of a total Middle Eastern revolution, then one must advocate the view that the Israeli Jews should be regarded as part of a "Middle Eastern" people.

Those who support the idea of one Palestinian people consisting of Palestinian Jews and Arabs do so because they believe that the entire territory of Palestine should be constituted as one new Palestinian state. On the other hand, it is generally agreed that such a new state can be created only by a socialist revolution victorious throughout a much wider region, and that one of the aims and results of such a revolution would be the creation of a united, socialist Arab East. It follows, therefore, that the new Palestinian state must be conceived only as a relatively separate constituent of a larger socialist union. And to follow this one step further, the raison d'être of such a new Palestinian state can only be to furnish a national home for the new Palestinian nation. This definitely begs the question: We come back to the starting point. The view of the ISO is more coherent; it views the solution of the Palestine problem as one of the tasks of a socialist revolution throughout the entire region. The main obstacles that must be overcome in order to achieve this revolution are direct imperialist intervention, neocolonialist domination, and imperialism's two partners, Zionism and Arab reaction.

The struggle of the Palestinian Arabs, carried out directly against Zionism and resulting from the fact that they are the direct and chief victims of Zionism, must be regarded in light of the wider revolutionary struggle. A victorious revolution will have to solve (among other things) the national problems bequeathed to it by imperialism. The following three points must be considered if the real problems existing in the Middle East today are to be solved.

1. *Arab national unification.* The Arabs of the Middle East are a nation in the process of crystallization (roughly comparable to the Italians in the late nineteenth century on the eve of the political unification of Italy). The balkanization of the Arab East imposed by British and French imperialism after 1918 does not make sense in terms of past history and—more important—would block any kind of serious socioeconomic reconstruction and development. Within the Arab nation—as within most big nations, especially in their formative period—there exist numerous subgroups with their own local or regional particularities. It follows, therefore, that a united socialist Arab East would be likely to have some sort of federal structure.

2. *The Palestinian Arabs,* who are a component part of the Arab nation, are victims of a specific and acute form of national oppression. The revolution will overthrow Zionism and arrange the repatriation of all the refugees who choose to be repatriated, as well as the full compensation and rehabilitation of all those who suffered in any way as a result of Zionism. Territorial arrangements can be made for the establishment of a Palestinian (plus Jordanian) Arab constituent, part of the united socialist state.

3. *The non-Arab nationalities* living within the Arab world (Israeli Jews, Kurds, South Sudanese) will be recognized and granted their national rights—in other words, self-determination. This is not only correct in principle but is also the only conceivable basis for attracting the masses of these nationalities to a joint struggle with the Arab masses.

This third point has been a source of anxiety to some: It raises the question of how the concept of self-determination ties in with the full restitution of Palestinian rights lost since 1948. For the geographical reintegration that would ensue would not necessarily be reconcilable with a separate Hebrew state, particularly if given territory and boundaries are involved. Some people argue that the concept of a separate state for Jews leads inexorably back to the contradiction inherent in Zionism and represents essentially a compromise with the Zionist idea.

This line of thinking, however, is based on false assumptions. First, the ISO does not advocate a *separate* Jewish state. An official statement published in May 1967* reads:

> Self-determination does not necessarily mean separation. On the contrary, we hold
> that a small country which is poor in natural resources such as Israel cannot exist as

---

* Chapter 3 in this book.

a separate entity. It is faced with two alternatives only—to continue to depend on foreign powers or to integrate itself in a regional union.

It follows that the only solution consistent with the interests of both Arab and Israeli masses is the integration of Israel as a unit in an economic and political union of the Middle East, on the basis of socialism.

The restitution of Palestinian rights lost since 1948 would not make self-determination for the Jews geographically impossible. Even in 1947, when Arabs outnumbered Jews by about two to one, the Jews remained numerically predominant in continuous portions of Palestine. At present, the ratio is about five Israeli Jews to three or four Palestinian Arabs. Consequently, even if all Arabs that were displaced in and after 1948 (together with their descendants) were to return to their precise original homes, Jewish self-determination still would not be geographically unfeasible.

Actually, the repatriation and rehabilitation of the Palestinian refugees must involve mainly industrial and urban projects, the construction of new towns and industries, et cetera. Before 1948, most Palestinians were peasants with rather small holdings, but in the context of an integrated socialist economy in the Middle East, the geographical area of Palestine will certainly not be devoted primarily to agriculture—other areas are much more suited to this. The region of Palestine will play an increasingly industrial and urban role, with relatively few people employed in agriculture. Thus the idea of resettling the refugees in their exact original location—and as peasants—is scarcely progressive.

Finally, the ISO's concept of self-determination, far from compromising with Zionism (which insists on an exclusively Jewish state that is supposed to "belong" to all the Jews in the world), actually assumes the *overthrow* of Zionism. The formula inherent in self-determination is part of a program for a victorious socialist revolution—it has no meaning in any other context. The program must be declared immediately in order to mobilize the people struggling for it; but it will be effected only after the overthrow of imperialism and its allies—Zionism and Arab reaction—in the Middle East. Of course, if one thinks in terms of an independent Palestinian state, then Jewish self-determination within it may lead to a phenomenon that is now part of Zionism but is conceivable without it—namely, domination of Jews over Arabs. And given existing numerical and socioeconomic facts, this would be quite likely even within an independent Palestinian state. Rather than proving the danger of self-determination, however, it shows that the concept of an independent or separate Palestine is dangerous. Conversely, the ISO concept of self-determination, in the context of a united socialist Middle East, does not contain any such danger.

16

Zionism, National Oppression, and Racism

The public controversy that has followed the UN resolution condemning Zionism as a form of racism* provides us with a convenient and desirable opportunity to expound once again our view on Zionism and particularly on its racist aspects. But it seems to me that discussion of this topic is often marred by a conceptual lack of clarity—not only in the Zionist camp but also in the anti-Zionist left—about racist phenomena and by a tendency to confuse them with phenomena of national oppression. I would therefore like to devote this article to clarifying these concepts. Such clarification is also needed in a somewhat different context: the very same confusion sometimes creeps into the discussion in the Israeli left about the national problem.

I do not intend here to delve deep into this issue and go into a social-class analysis of the roots and causes of racism. Nor do I intend to discuss racist *ideology*. In posing the question "What is racism?" I am referring right now simply to the typical form in which racism appears *in practice*, in social reality.

One common mistaken idea is that "racism" refers solely to phenomena of discrimination by one *racial* group against another *racial* group. Thus, for example, some Zionist apologists have attempted the following line of defense: "When Zionism is accused of being racist, what is meant is mainly its attitude to Arabs; but Arabs and Jews belong to the same race, so Zionism cannot be racist in relation to Arabs." According to this argument, even if Zionism does discriminate against Arabs and in favor of Jews, this cannot be a matter of racism.

This article was published in *Matzpen* 76, March 1976. Translated by the author.

* Resolution 3379 of the UN General Assembly (November 10, 1975) asserted that "Zionism is a form of racism and racial discrimination." It was revoked on December 16, 1991—the only UN resolution ever to have been revoked.

This is of course an inane argument. By the same logic one could claim that in South Africa the discrimination practiced against persons of African origin is indeed racist, but the discrimination against members of the *Indian* minority is supposedly not racist, because in the latter case the discriminated and discriminators belong to the same Indo-European race. And similarly in each case of discrimination we would supposedly have to check whether the discriminated do indeed belong to a race different from that of the discriminators, and only if this is the case would we be able to pronounce that racism is involved.

But in fact this kind of pedantry is beside the point. In order to tell whether a given case involves racism we don't need to go into all that palaver about the division of the human species into races—which is in any case quite dubious, and is certainly irrelevant to the political categories we are dealing with here. Because the term "racism" refers to discrimination of persons due to their origin—be it "racial," or ethnic, or tribal, or even national.

It is important to stress another basic aspect that all cases of racism have in common: racist discrimination always pertains to individual rights. The rights denied are not the collective rights of an entire group, but the individual rights of every person belonging by origin to a given group.

Let me illustrate the difference with a few cases in which a given group is subjected to collective oppression, but there is no individual discrimination against individuals belonging by descent to that group. For example, in fascist Spain the Basque people has been severely oppressed; this went so far as extreme bans against teaching and using the Basque language. However, a person of Basque origin who lives, say, in Madrid and is happy to use the Castilian language and assimilate into the Castilian culture has not been subjected to any special discrimination compared to any other citizen of Spain. A similar situation exists in relation to the Kurds in Iraq, and even more so in Turkey. (In Turkey, not only is the Kurdish language banned, but even use of the term "Kurd" is illegal; the Kurds are officially referred to as "mountain Turks.") As a final example of this kind, let me mention Britain: many Scottish and Welsh people claim that they are discriminated against as nations. Arguably, Scotland and Wales are relatively neglected and exploited within Britain; and their languages and cultures are not encouraged and have inferior status compared to English. But no one in Britain is individually discriminated against because of being of Scottish or Welsh origin. In all these cases we can talk of national oppression, but not of racism.

Of course, there are many cases (including Israel, as we shall see) in which a group is subjected to national oppression, in other words collective discrimination, and at the same time members of this group are subjected to individual racist discrimination. We shall discuss this below. For the time being let us just state that these two phenomena are different and distinct, at least in principle.

Racism in Israel

In the State of Israel there is severe and conspicuous discrimination in favor of Jews and against non-Jews—especially Arabs—in many varied areas of *individual rights:* for example, immigration and citizenship, the right to choose one's place of residence and workplace, in land ownership, in various benefits granted or withheld by the authorities, and in a thousand and one aspects of everyday life.

Some of these facets of discrimination are inscribed explicitly in the state's laws, such as the Law of Return and other laws governing citizenship. Other facets, of greater importance, are not stated directly in laws but are part of the constitution or charter of the Jewish Agency and the Jewish National Fund (JNF), which have official status in Israel. According to these regulations—which are explicit—an Arab is barred not only from buying land belonging to the JNF but even from getting a lease or being employed on it as a wage worker. But the greatest and most important part of the discrimination suffered by Arabs in Israel is not inscribed in the state's laws or anywhere else but operate as unwritten practices. For example, there is no written law or regulation according to which land must always be expropriated from Arabs for settling or housing Jews, rather than the other way around; but in practice it never happens that land expropriated from Jews is given over to Arabs, whereas the reverse is an everyday occurrence. Hundreds of examples of this sort could be cited from all spheres of life, but I will confine myself to just one more example, which is not especially important in itself but is very interesting because of its pettiness.

As is well known, an Israeli resident returning to the country after a long stay abroad is entitled to various concessions and grants. Well, the following story appeared in the evening paper *Yedi'ot Aharonot* on August 30, 1970:

> The personnel of the Ministry of [Immigrant] Absorption in the Haifa district have recently been faced with an embarrassing problem: a resident of the village of Ar'ara in Wadi Ara applied to them demanding to receive all the benefits and concessions due to a returning Israel resident. "How come?" asked the surprised officials. The Arab replied: "Soon after the establishment of Israel I emigrated and went abroad. Now I have come back, and found out that as a returning Israeli resident I am entitled to many benefits, including a housing loan and the right to buy a car free of duty." The officials explained to the man that only Jews are entitled to the benefits of a returning resident, and the Arab went back to his village, disappointed.

Since then, the Israeli authorities have learned their lesson. Recently Israel's newspapers printed new advertisements about various concessions and benefits for returning residents; but this time these advertisements were not sponsored by the government alone but jointly with the World Zionist Organization (WZO) and the Jewish Agency. The reason is that the government has no convenient legal way to deny benefits and grants to a returning Arab resident, but the WZO and the Jewish Agency are "private" bodies, which are allowed to be openly racist. In order to make doubly sure and bar all unintended applications, these advertisements advise "Israelis living abroad who wish to return to Israel" to apply for information not to the nearest Israeli embassy but "to the nearest office of the Department of Aliya* and Absorption of the Jewish Agency/World Zionist Organization." Moreover, whereas in the past the benefits were granted according to fixed published rules, which is how that naïve Arab of Ar'ara found out about them, this time our cunning Zionists announce that "grants will be decided individually, according to the situation and needs of each applicant." So now even if an Arab Israeli citizen staying abroad would be so naïve as to imagine that the advertisement applies also to him, and will turn up at the nearest office of the WZO, they can always explain to him "individually" that according to his "situation" as an Arab he is not going to get a single worn penny.

I have expanded on this example just in order to illustrate the nauseating pettiness to which racist baseness descends. (It is worth mentioning other examples: an Arab wishing to convert to Judaism is first subjected to investigation by the security services; and a mixed young couple who meet, fall in love with each other, and live together are often subjected to intervention of the police, who respond in such cases to requests by the Jewish family to separate the couple.)

Let me stress that for the moment we are not discussing the restrictions imposed on the Arab community in Israel as a *community*, which prevent it from freely expressing its national existence and *collective* identity. That is another story. For the moment we are dealing with discrimination that victimizes each and every Arab person as an individual, solely due to their origin. These forms of discrimination apply also to an Arab who speaks fluent Hebrew, lives among Jews (there are still a few places in this country where this is possible!), and takes no interest in politics or Arab nationalism, and is even prepared to wear a *kippah* and adopt a Hebrew name. On the contrary, such an Arab is at an additional risk of being harassed by the Israeli police and accused of "impersonating a Jew." Such things have actually happened.

This heinous crime of "impersonating a Jew" is the sort of crime that exists only in the most racist countries. In South Africa too it is a crime for a person of African origin to pretend to be a White, and in Nazi Germany it was a crime for a Jew to pretend to be "Aryan." But as far as we know no one in Britain has been accused of the "crime" of pretending to be English. . . .

The point is that in the State of Israel being a Jew means enjoying a privileged status both in customary practice and in law. Therefore a Gentile who pretends to be a Jew thereby violates the law by claiming an "undeserved" legal status.

This explains the importance of the question "Who is a Jew?" that every year or two arouses controversies and scandals in Israel. These are not merely academic debates about the historical essence of Jewishness. These controversies have in Israel an utmost practical and *legal* importance: the answer to the question "Who

---

* Aliya is by definition a racist term: literally meaning ascent, it refers exclusively to Jewish immigration to Israel.

is a Jew?" determines who is or is not entitled to the range of legal and customary privileges conferred exclusively on Jews—from acquiring automatic citizenship according to the Law of Return to the duty-free import of a car by a Jewish resident returning from a stay abroad. By the way, it is interesting to note that in the twentieth century there was yet another country in which the question "Who is a Jew?" had legal importance: Nazi Germany. The reason there was somewhat similar, but opposite.

In enlightened countries—*including many bourgeois ones*—this kind of legal question cannot arise. For example, in France the question "Who is a French citizen?" has legal importance, but all French citizens are considered equal under the law (this is one of the achievements of the French Revolution; the fact that equality under the law is a *bourgeois* right should not make us, as socialists, despise it, although we cannot regard it as sufficient). Therefore, the question "Who is French by descent?" has no legal importance and does not preoccupy the French public.

Before we go on to another topic, we must deal with another argument that is sometimes voiced by Zionist apologists. It is claimed that the forms of discrimination practiced in Israel cannot be regarded as racist because the term "Jewish" is defined according to the Jewish religion; therefore persons who are of non-Jewish descent can also enjoy all the privileges of a Jew, provided they convert to Judaism. However, this claim only proves that the racism practiced in Israel is not mere racism, but racism mixed with clericalism. It is indeed true that the legal definition of "Jew" follows, at least in part, the religious prescriptions of Judaism. But these religious prescriptions themselves depend critically on descent rather than on faith. Thus, an atheist who is not of Jewish descent cannot convert to Judaism; but a person whose mother is Jewish may be an atheist, and even stew pork in milk publicly on Yom Kippur that falls on the Sabbath—and would still count as a Jew.

So the conclusion is inescapable: the State of Israel is racist, since it has—both in written law and in unwritten customary practice—an extensive system of discrimination that applies to persons according to their *descent* and in the sphere of their *individual* rights.

Racist Discrimination and National Oppression

Where [official] racist discrimination is practiced, the oppressors endeavor to institutionalize and consolidate the distinctness of those belonging to the oppressed group, to emphasize differences and prevent assimilation. Clear distinctions are needed by the oppressors in order to make it clear who is to be discriminated against and who "deserves" to enjoy privileges. In such places there are laws or regulations forcing the victims of racism to bear certain external identifying marks or carry special documents showing their "inferior" origin, they are prevented (legally or in practice) from marrying members of the dominant group, and they are subjected to various other restrictions of this kind.

In contrast, where there is national oppression, the situation in this respect seems almost the opposite: it is the oppressed people that strives to institutionalize its national distinctness, to get recognized status for its distinct national language, to win cultural autonomy, self rule, and in many cases it demands full political separation and establishing its own state. On the other hand, the oppressors refuse to recognize the national identity and distinctness of the oppressed people, they try to prevent it from freely expressing its separate national culture, and they deny it the right to exercise self-rule or establish its own state. In most cases, where it is a matter of "ordinary" national oppression, without an admixture of racism, the oppressors even try to force the oppressed people to assimilate.

This contrast follows from the fundamental difference between these two forms of oppression. Whereas racism denies *individual rights* of members of the oppressed group, national oppression consists in denying the oppressed people's *collective* rights. The national problem is not a matter of individual discrimination against members of the oppressed people but denial of the collective right of the oppressed people to institutionalize its national identity. This (analytic) distinction must always be made, even when the two forms of oppression occur together, because the national problem calls for different solutions from that of racist discrimination.

The socialist movement is not, and cannot be, in a dilemma regarding problems of racial discrimination. The ideas and aims of the socialist movement prescribe resolute opposition to discrimination, to denial of individual rights of members of one group and privileging members of another group based on different origins. Socialists are therefore committed to struggle against institutionalization of differences of origins, and for equal rights to all, both in law and in practice.

The position regarding national questions is more complicated. Socialists do not stand for raising barriers between peoples but for removing them; they do not wish to encourage any form of national separatism. On the other hand, opposing the aspiration of an oppressed people to institutionalize its nationhood amounts to supporting national oppression. For example, in Spain the Basque people demands recognition of its right to its own national existence, whereas it is the Spanish oppressor that denies this right, claiming that there does not exist a distinct Basque entity, and the Basques are part of the Spanish nation—similarly in all cases of national oppression. If socialists were to deny the right of each people to its own national existence, they would thereby find themselves siding with oppression. Socialists have been, and still are, divided regarding the national question; but what they differ on is not *whether* but *how far* to support a people's right to institutionalize its nationhood. On this there are two views held by socialists. One view, probably that of a majority, advocates support for the right of peoples to full self-determination, including the right to establish an independent national state. The other view advocates supporting the right of each people to linguistic-cultural autonomy, but not to full political separation. I do not wish to enter here into this debate; let us leave it for another occasion. I would only like to make here three comments, for the sake of clarification.

First, both sides in this debate agree that every people has the right to give an institutionalized expression to its nationhood and distinctiveness: for national autonomy also institutionalizes nationhood.

Second, even those who support the formula of "the right to self-determination, including the right to political separation" agree that in general political separation should not be *encouraged.* Support for the right to self-determination does not imply such encouragement; it only means opposing the forcible imposition of a common political framework by one people on another. For example, the Kurds in Iraq do not demand a separate state but only a certain measure of autonomy within the Iraqi state. If we support their right to self-determination, it does not mean that we ought to encourage them to up the ante and insist on establishing a separate state. But if in the future the Kurds themselves raise such a demand, and the Iraqi government tries by force to prevent them achieving it (and this can only be done by force), then we would have to oppose this attempted coercion. Those who support the right to self-determination maintain that only in specific cases, where special reasons exist, should a people be *encouraged* to establish a separate state. Briefly, then: support for the *right* to separate does not mean blanket *encouragement* to separate—just as support for free speech obliges us to support the right of people even to talk rubbish (and to oppose any attempt at gagging them), but it does not imply encouraging anyone to talk rubbish.

Third, this debate, which is long-standing in the socialist movement, applies only to the national question, that is, to cases of national oppression. National oppression consists in denying a people's collective right. This debate has no bearing whatsoever on racist discrimination; the attitude to the latter is not, and cannot be, a matter for debate among socialists worthy of this name.

What Kind of State Is Israel?

Zionism used to declare that it aimed to establish a Jewish nation-state in this country. However, the State of Israel, established by Zionism, is undoubtedly a Jewish state, but not a *nation*-state—at least, not in the usual sense of this term.

I cannot enter here into a discussion of the social-class roots of modern nationalism and of the idea of the nation-state as they evolved since the French Revolution. But one thing is clear even without such a thorough discussion: in normal nation-states, established by the bourgeois classes (mainly in Europe), the "nationality" of the state is not regarded as justifying racist discrimination. For example, France is a French nation-state. Its "Frenchness" consists in the fact that its territory coincides (more or less) with the geographic area in which members of the French nation are a majority of the population, as well as in the fact that France's language and culture are French. Inside France there are also other national or quasi-national groups: Basques, Bretons, Corsicans. In the name of France's French uniformity, these groups are denied the right to a distinct national existence; but, as explained above, this is not a matter of racist discrimination, but, at most, a national problem. Of course, there is hardly a bourgeois state in which there are no manifestations of racism, and France is no exception. Racist discrimination does exist there—albeit not by law but "only" in practice—for example, against persons of Arab-Algerian origin; but this is not directly connected with the "Frenchness" of France. At any rate, it cannot be argued that whoever recognizes the right of France to exist as a French nation-state thereby consents to racist discrimination against persons of Arab or any other descent. This is also the case with any other normal nation-states.

But the situation in Israel is entirely different. The majority of Israel's inhabitants do constitute a national entity—the Israeli-Jewish nation—which has a language of its own and something resembling a national culture; but the "Jewishness" of the State of Israel does not consist in giving national expression to this national entity. According to the dominant Zionist ideology, as well as by law and to some extent also in practice, Israel is "the state of world Jewry," in other words, a state of a group defined by descent. Moreover, in the name of Israel's "Jewishness" its non-Jewish—and in particular Arab—citizens are denied individual rights. It must be stressed that all Zionist currents, including the most "left-wing" and "dovish," accept this racist discrimination against Arabs. (In this regard, see articles in the previous and present issues of *Matzpen*.)

So the "Jewishness" of Israel is unlike the "Frenchness" of France or the "Spanishness" of Spain. Because Israel is not a nation-state in the usual sense but embodies a special combination of nationalism, racism, and clericalism.

Of course, the Palestinian Arabs living in Israel are not only subjected to racist discrimination; they are denied not only individual rights but also collective national rights—the right to institutionalize their distinct national identity as part of the Palestinian Arab people and the entire Arab nation. They are therefore placed between the hammer and the anvil: they are not permitted to merge their identity with the Jews (even if they wished to do so) and on the other hand are not allowed to express their distinct national identity.

Such a fiendish combination of racist discrimination and national oppression against the very same group does not exist (as far as I know) in any normal nation-state. But it does occur often in states of another kind: settler states.

This largely explains the special nature of the Zionist State of Israel: it is a colonizing state, product of Zionist colonization and an instrument for extending and expanding this colonization. The point is not that many Zionist leaders and their followers have held and continue to hold racist *views*. The truth is that among the Zionists there were and are also many who do not believe that the Jews are a superior people and the Arabs are an inferior rabble. Zionist racism is principally a matter of *practice*, due to the fact that Zionist colonization could only be implemented at the expense of the Palestinian Arabs' rights—both their national and individual rights. The Zionist project—past and present—is a project of colonization by Jews of territories inhabited by Arabs, turning an Arab country into a Jewish country. In order to implement such a project, it is necessary to discriminate in favor of Jews and against Arabs in matters of immigration, citizenship, land ownership, and so on—right down to discrimination regarding the rights of returning residents.

By the way, it seems that this combination of national oppression and racist discrimination is a function of the *generic* nature of the Zionist project as a project of colonization, rather than of the *specific* characteristics of this project, which distinguish it from other models of colonization. A similar combination also exists in Rhodesia and existed in Algeria during French rule, although the colonization of Rhodesia and Algeria do not belong to the same type as the Zionist project.

Some Political Conclusions

To conclude, I would like to point out the implication of the foregoing discussion for our political agenda.

First, since the Arabs living under Israel's rule are victims of a twofold combination of national oppression and racist discrimination, we must address both components of this combination. It is not enough to struggle only against the discrimination of the Arab inhabitants, just as it is not enough to struggle only against the national oppression of the Palestinian Arab people. Therefore we generally use formulas such as "support for the struggle of the Palestinian Arab people for its human and national rights." Our support for the national rights of the Palestinian people manifests itself, for example, in struggle for its right to establish its own state and against any attempt by Israel's government to prevent it from doing so. But we do not regard this struggle as a substitute for the struggle against the racist discrimination of Arabs practiced in Israel.

Second, the right of the Palestinian people to self-determination—which we support—is the right of this people to institutionalize its national identity; it includes the right to establish its own state; but it does not imply a "right" to discriminate against Jews or any other group. The claim made by some people that if a Palestinian Arab state were established, it would necessarily practice discrimination against Jews is a falsehood based on a confusion between a nation-state and a racist state.

Third, we support the right to self-determination of the Israeli-Jewish people. This however does not mean that we are in favor of the continued existence of a separate Jewish state. Quite the contrary—we stand for integration of Israel in a regional socialist union of the entire Arab East. However, we insist that this integration should not be coerced but voluntary and freely chosen. If, when such a union is established, Israel's Jews would refuse to join it, we would regret this and do everything in our power to change their minds; but we shall oppose any attempt to impose it on them by force. So long as they refuse to join, we shall support their right to maintain a separate nation-state. True, such a state would be Jewish, but we shall in no way consent to a Jewish state in the Zionist sense of this term. We can never, under any circumstance and in any situation, present or future, support a "right" to discriminate against persons by reason of their origin. Again: the claim that in supporting the right of Israeli Jews to self-determination we thereby support discrimination against Arabs is a falsehood infected by the Zionist confusion between a nation-state and a racist state.

17

Summing Up Our Position
on the National Question

In order to reach a correct, clear, and consistent formulation of our position on the national question, we must first state correctly the question itself. We must distinguish between phenomena of national oppression and racist oppression. This distinction is particularly important when dealing with the Israel-Arab conflict, in which (as in other conflicts having a colonial aspect) phenomena of both kinds intersect each other, so that reality displays a complex combination of national oppression and racist discrimination. Theoretical analysis must unravel this tangled skein, and separate its various elements from one another. This is a precondition for arriving at a correct political position. Failing to distinguish between the two kinds of phenomena is dangerous because it may lead to taking a one-sided position: confronting only the aspect of national oppression while ignoring the problem of racist discrimination, or vice versa. However, elimination of national oppression does not automatically remove racist discrimination or the other way around.

In the article "Zionism, National Oppression, and Racism"* we explained in some detail the difference between national oppression and racist discrimination, and showed that they belong to two different levels of social reality.

Against Racism; for Total Individual Equality, Irrespective of Origin

In essence, racism violates personal human rights. These include the right to acquire citizenship and take part in political life; the right to immigrate to and emigrate

---

This article, dated January 1978, was included (unsigned) in a Matzpen pamphlet, *Our Position on the National Question* (1978). The pamphlet was issue number 4 in a series "Dappim Adumim" (Red Pages). Translated here by the author.

* Chapter 16 in this book.

from a country; the right to choose one's place of residence, occupation, and workplace; the right to education; and—in extreme cases—the right to life. If rights of this kind are granted to some persons and denied to others on grounds of their different origins—this constitutes racist discrimination. If persons of different origins are prevented (by law or by other constraints) from living together, working and enjoying recreation together, having sexual relations and marrying—this constitutes racist segregation, apartheid.

We socialists are implacably opposed to these phenomena and fight unrelentingly against them. We struggle uncompromisingly for abolition of all forms of apartheid and racist discrimination, and for total equality of rights for all human beings, irrespective of their racial, ethnic, or national origins.

All this is clear and obvious. But what seems not to be sufficiently clear is that the above demands for equal rights are applicable in the struggle against racism but do not address problems of national oppression. In this regard there is some confusion (unintentional or willful) among those who are incapable or unwilling to confront the national problem; they repeat over and over again formulas such as "equal rights," "one person, one vote," "living together," and pretend that by doing so they are addressing the problem of national oppression. But this is not the case.

It is quite possible to have a situation in which there is absolute equality of individual rights among all persons, irrespective of origin, while at the same time there is severe national oppression. Let us imagine the following situation: suppose that in Israel all the laws, regulations, and practices discriminating between Jews and non-Jews have been abolished; the religion and nationality of persons are no longer indicated on their ID cards; all citizens, regardless of their origin, enjoy fully equal rights in theory and practice. But suppose that at the same time Israel's Palestinian Arab citizens are not allowed to organize as a national community; Arabic is not recognized as an official language and its use is not admitted for public and official purposes; and the state does not fund educational and cultural institutions whose principal language is Arabic.

Such a situation, in which there is national oppression but no racist discrimination is possible, because national oppression does not consist in denying the *individual* rights of members of the oppressed people but their *collective* rights as a national group. Moreover, national oppression can coexist with "separation between nationality and state": the [Israeli] state could proclaim that it does not recognize any national grouping (neither the Hebrew nor the Palestinian) but only a single category: "citizen of the state"; but in practice, since the majority of the citizens are Hebrew, their language and culture would enjoy automatic privilege—precisely according to the principle of "one person, one vote."

The situation just described is imaginary in the context of Israel, because here, due to the colonizing nature of Zionism, there is both racist discrimination and national oppression. But there are countries in which such a situation (national oppression unaccompanied by racist discrimination) exists fully or approximately.

Moreover, even within the Zionist movement there were ideologies, and also organized groups, that recommended granting full equal rights to the country's indigenous non-Jewish people, but at the same time denied the national existence of the Arabs and advocated repressing their national identity—in order to encourage their assimilation by the Hebrew colonizers. True, these groups never gained real political leverage in the organized Zionist movement; but they did have some ideological influence in both the Zionist left and the Zionist right.

Thus, for example, B. Borochov—one of the ideologues of "socialist" Zionism*—claimed that "the natives of Palestine lack any economic or cultural character of their own"; in his view they were not one single nation, nor would they become one for a long time to come. At the same time, he opined, they are not part of the greater Arab nation: "except for language and religion, the fellaheen of Palestine have nothing in common with the Arabs"; therefore "the Arab national movement does not and cannot have any relation to Palestine." On the other hand, Borochov asserted that "the local population of Palestine is closer in its racial composition to the Jews more than any other people, including the Semitic peoples . . . the racial difference between the Jews of the Diaspora and the Palestinian fellaheen is not greater than that between Ashkenazi and Sephardi Jews." Consequently, Borochov expressed the hope that "the local population of Palestine will eventually be economically and culturally assimilated by the Jews." Clearly, in order to encourage this assimilation, of which Borochov approved, it would be necessary to avoid racist discrimination and an apartheid policy—because apartheid is designed to impose separation and prevent assimilation.[1]

In the 1940s, similar ideas were put forward by the Young Hebrews group, nicknamed "Canaanites." Despite their small numbers, the Canaanites had considerable cultural influence, although they never gained any real political importance. Contrary to widespread opinion, the Canaanites were not anti-Zionist, but flesh of Zionism's flesh, and of right-wing Zionism at that. They advocated national oppression not only against the Palestinian Arabs but also against substantial parts of the Arab nation beyond and called for the creation of a new Hebrew nation that would dominate the entire territory between the Mediterranean and the Euphrates. That nation, which would sever itself from the Jews of the Diaspora, would be formed through assimilation of the local population by the new colonizers, bearers of the Hebrew language and culture. Again, such assimilation would require granting full equal civil and individual rights.

Following the June 1967 war, the remaining standard-bearers of Canaanism became active in the Greater Israel movement but at the same time advocated a secular democratic state, all of whose citizens would enjoy full equal rights—a combination that can seem paradoxical only to those who refuse, or are unable, to understand the difference between racism and national oppression. Especially notable

---

* See chapter 22 in this book.

among the last preachers of the Canaanite message are the important poet Yonatan Ratosh, who has had an enormous influence on modern Hebrew poetry, and his brother the linguist and grammarian Uzzi Ornan. The latter is well known for his many public appearances and comments in the press against religious coercion and racism, and for full equality in individual and civil rights between the inhabitants of Israel and the Occupied Territories. At the same time he advocates the suppression of Palestinian nationality. (Of course he does not use the term "national oppression": he simply denies the very existence of a Palestinian nationality. But this is a transparent move, widespread all over the world: denying the very existence of a nation one wants to oppress. . . .)

As we mentioned, these ideas have never gained much political influence in the Zionist movement. On the other hand, on the opposite side, in the Palestinian national movement, a formula that ideologically is an almost exact mirror image of the Borochovist-Canaanite ideas has won decisive influence. We are referring of course to the formula "A unitary secular democratic Palestine, in which Christians, Jews, and Muslims will live in equality and without discrimination."

Here we must emphasize: *In no way should what we say be interpreted as though in our view there is political symmetry between Zionism, or any currents within Zionism, and the Palestinian national movement: the former is a movement of colonization and oppression, whereas the latter is a national liberation movement of an oppressed people. But this fact must not blind us to the ideological symmetry that we have pointed out here. Besides, as socialists we must not be lured by any national ideology, including that of a national liberation movement.*

That formula, "a unitary secular democratic Palestine . . . ," has received widespread international attention following Yasser Arafat's famous November 1974 speech at the UN Assembly. But in fact it appeared not long after the June 1967 war, and by 1969 it had become the official position of Fatah, and subsequently of the PLO as a whole. Its most detailed and authoritative elaboration and interpretation was given by Dr. Nabil Sha'th, who was then one of the chief ideologues of Fatah. From the wording of this formula, two things are immediately evident— and are confirmed by Arafat's speech and even more so by Dr. Sha'th's numerous detailed articles—namely:

1. In raising the secular democratic state formula, the Palestinian movement has abandoned the talk of "throwing the Jews into the sea," that is, expelling them from this country, which was current in the old Palestinian movement led by Ahmad Shuqeiri (and which may also be implied by the Palestinian Covenant, adopted as the founding document of the PLO in 1964 and amended in 1968). On the contrary, now the Palestinian movement was proposing to the Israeli Jews that they stay and be citizens with equal rights in the secular democratic Palestine. This is no doubt an important step forward in the Palestinian movement's view on the Israeli Jews and their common future with the Palestinians. Moreover,

there is no reason to doubt that those who adopted this formula, or at any rate most of them and the most influential ones, were fully sincere about it and did not regard it as a mere propaganda ploy.

2. The equality proposed by the PLO to Jews within the unitary secular democratic Palestine is only individual civil equality. In other words: in the unitary Palestine envisioned by the PLO, Jews would not be subjected to racist discrimination and would enjoy (along with all other citizens) equal individual rights (including freedom of religious worship, which is considered—since the French Revolution—as an individual right). But on the other hand this formula does not recognize the existence of the Hebrew (Israeli-Jewish) nation, and hence of course does not promise it national rights. Dr. Nabil Sha'th, who is, as we mentioned, an authoritative interpreter of the formula, expands on this. He makes it clear that the PLO formula must not be interpreted as binational, and goes on to say: "[R]eligious and ethnic lines clearly cross in Palestine so as to make the term bi-national and the Arab-Jewish dichotomy meaningless, or at best dubious. The majority of Jews in Palestine today are Arab Jews—euphemistically called Oriental Jews by the Zionists. Therefore Palestine combines Jewish, Christian and Moslem Arabs as well as non-Arab Jews (Western Jews)."[2]

In other words, in Palestine there exists one national entity, which is Arab and comprises the Mizrahim (who are Jews by *religion* but Arab by nationality) as well as the Muslim and Christian Palestinian Arabs. Apart from these there is also the Ashkenazi Jewish community, which (by implication) does not constitute a national entity, and in any case is not part of the same people as the Mizrahi Jews.

True, in the sequel the author draws back a little and agrees that the Jews would be granted, at least for a transitional period, "some collective or group privileges besides the pure individual privileges"; namely, "the right to . . . develop culturally and linguistically as a group." He also agrees that "it is quite logical . . . to have both Arabic and Hebrew as official languages taught in governmental schools to all Palestinians, Jews or non-Jews."

But he does not thereby withdraw from the denial of the existence of the Hebrew (Israeli-Jewish) people as a national group, and the refusal to grant that people real national rights. It appears that in his opinion the Israeli Jews constitute at most a linguistic-cultural-religious group, which deserves to enjoy collective rights appropriate for such a group but not national rights in the full sense. By the way, let us note that the linguistic rights offered here to the Jews living in the [proposed] secular democratic Palestine are roughly the same as those currently accorded to Arabs and the Arabic language in Israel: Arabic is (at least in theory) an official language and is taught in many (albeit not all) state Jewish schools. Nevertheless, there is no doubt that the Palestinian Arabs in Israel are subjected not only to racist discrimination but also to national oppression.

We can therefore see that the PLO's famous formula—literally and in its authoritative interpretation—offers to Israel's Jews a future in which they would enjoy full civil-individual equality but will not be recognized as a national group and would not be granted real national rights. As far as nationality is concerned, it will be an *Arab Palestine*,* because according to the PLO there exists in Palestine just one national group, which is Arab. However, denial of national rights constitutes national *oppression*.

Whoever accepts the PLO formula as a solution of *national equality* between Arabs and Jews reveals thereby inability or unwillingness to understand both that formula and the difference between racist discrimination and national oppression, between individual and national rights.[3]

Against National Oppression; for Self-Determination

As stated above, we struggle against all forms of discrimination and for full equality of rights for all human beings, irrespective of origin. But whereas this struggle and these slogans address racism, they do not provide an answer to the problem of national oppression.

What is national oppression?

As we have seen, national oppression—unlike racist discrimination—does not consist essentially in denial or infringement of the individual rights of members of the oppressed people. National oppression exists wherever one nation imposes on another a subordinate status, and denies the latter the right to exist as a nation, or any of the *collective* rights of free national existence.

If a national group is denied the freedom to use its language and develop it culture, and is coerced into linguistic and cultural assimilation—this is national oppression. Take for example the situation of the Kurds in Turkey.

If, in a country where there are several national groups, one of them aspires to autonomy (self-rule) within a multinational framework, and is denied this right—this is national oppression. Look at the situation of the Kurds in Iraq.

If a given people aspires to establish a sovereign state of its own in the areas it inhabits (where it constitutes a substantial majority of the population) and this right is denied to it by outside intervention, by another people—this is national oppression. See the situation of the Palestinians in Palestine.

What is common to all these and similar cases, where there is national oppression, is external coercion that denies the oppressed people the freedom to exist as a national group and to institutionalize this existence to the extent it prefers: whether (1) linguistic-cultural autonomy; or (2) self-administration; or (3) limited

---

* This is clearly implied by the authoritative article quoted above, which states: "The liberated Palestine will be part of the Arab homeland and will not be another alien state within it. The eventual unity of Palestine with *other Arab states* will make the boundary problems less relevant." [Emphasis added.]

political self-rule within a larger (multinational) framework; or (4) full political sovereignty. Briefly, national oppression is essentially denial of the right to national self-determination.

The right to self-determination is the principal national right, and includes or implies all other national rights. And since denial of the right to self-determination is what constitutes national oppression, support for the right to self-determination means neither more nor less than opposition to national oppression.

These are simply two ways of expressing the very same principle, differing only in that the former is phrased positively (*"support* for the right . . ."") and the latter negatively (*"opposition* to . . . oppression"). For various reasons, mainly educational and propagandist, the positive mode of expression tends to be preferred; but this is a secondary matter, one of style. In essence and principle there is no difference between the two formulations.

In order to forestall misunderstandings and fatuous objections, we note that the concept of the right to self-determination—like all social concepts and principles—did not fall "from heaven" but grew and evolved in definite historical circumstances. Before nations in the modern sense had come into existence, and when the very concept of nation had not reached its full development, the right to self-determination made no sense as a universal right; and the concept of national oppression as well did not exist as a separate concept, distinct from other forms of oppression, persecution and discrimination. (The same can be said about individual rights, such as freedom of speech. The very concept of a "free individual" possessing certain universal "rights" reached its full development only in the modern period, in definite historical circumstances.) If and when the socialist vision of the dissolution of national barriers will be realized, then the concept of nation will also be voided of its actual content, and thereby national rights will lose their meaning. However, in the present article we are not dealing with the historical dimension of nationhood and the national question but their current form in our present time.

The principle of the right to self-determination—in other words, opposition to all forms of national oppression—is the only general principle we, as socialists, have regarding the national question. Regarding this question we have no special ideal or detailed model that we wish to implement in every single case. For us nationality is not a separate value, let alone a supreme value. Our position on each given case is determined by the interest of the struggle for socialism. Therefore we do not have, and cannot accept, any additional general principles regarding the national question.

For example, we are not prepared to commit ourselves to recommending and encouraging each and every people to establish its own separate independent state; and on the other hand neither are we prepared to commit ourselves in advance to opposing in every case the establishment of separate national states and insisting on binational or multinational states. The only general thing we do insist on regarding this issue is that any waiving of national independence should be done freely and voluntarily, not under coercion by another people because any framework shared by several peoples that is based on coercion by one people against another is a framework of national oppression.

There are cases where the establishment of a separate sovereign nation-state is in our view desirable as such (for example, where the people in question is struggling against the rule of a foreign colonial power, as in the case of Mozambique, 1961–74); in such cases socialists ought to encourage aspirations for independence. Against this background, the reactionary nature of the ultra-leftist position calling for "separation of nationality from the state" is fully revealed.

On the other hand, there are cases in which we believe that the best solution is a multinational state; but even in such cases, if it transpires that the existence of this common framework involves coercion against one of the peoples concerned, within which an aspiration for separate national existence is widespread, then we must prefer separation to coercion. Because such coercion is a denial of the right to self-determination and as such constitutes national oppression.

Such is the case in which we are directly involved. We aim for the creation of a common socialist political framework for all the peoples living in the Arab East. Such a framework—which may, for example, have a federal structure—will incorporate several Arab peoples—among whom is the Palestinian people—which are component parts of the Arab nation; and also some non-Arab peoples, among whom is the Hebrew people. Establishment of such a framework means that each of the participant peoples will waive full sovereignty and settle for a suitable measure of autonomy. But we insist that this waiver must be based on the right to self-determination; in other words, it must not be imposed by one people on another. Otherwise, the common framework would be founded on national oppression, which is in total contradiction to socialism. This is of course a long-term program; but it guides our activity even at present.

Three Objections—and Our Responses

Various objections are occasionally voiced against Matzpen's position on the national question. To some extent, they are caused by confusion and lack of proper understanding of the subject. We shall deal here with three of these arguments.

(a) Our long-term program, which we have just sketched, includes among other things recognition of the right of the Hebrew people to self-determination. The following objection is put forward against this. "The Hebrew (Israeli-Jewish) people is not oppressed but an oppressor. What is the point of demanding the right of self-determination for an oppressor people? Clearly, the demand for self-determination is legitimate only with regard to an oppressed people!"

True, at present the Hebrew people is not oppressed but oppresses another people, the Palestinian Arab people. Therefore our demand for self-determination for the Hebrew people does not apply to the present; in other words, it is not an immediate demand. At present is has indeed no immediate sense. It is not the right of this people that is now at issue but that of the Palestinian people.

But the roles of oppressor and oppressed are not immutable. They may change, as has indeed happened more than once in history. An oppressor may become oppressed and vice versa. Our above-mentioned programmatic demand refers to a situation that would arise when a victorious socialist revolution in our region would overthrow the Arab regimes as well as Zionism. In that situation, the Hebrew people would no longer be an oppressor but may become oppressed: if it would be coerced against its will to join a regional political framework, that would constitute oppression. In that context we insist on the Hebrew people's right to self-determination, because denial of this right would necessarily constitute national oppression. We are not among those who propose to establish "justice" by turning the oppressor into a victim of oppression.

However, if our demand for self-determination of the Hebrew people does not apply to the present situation but to one that may arise in future, why do we insist on mentioning it now? Why not wait and cross that bridge when we come to it?

The reason is that in our opinion the revolutionary forces ought to mobilize for the struggle for their socialist program the largest possible numbers, not only among the Arab masses but also among the Hebrew masses. To this end, it is necessary to make it clear to the latter that the socialist program does not propose to deny their legitimate rights, including the right to self-determination—in other words, their right to freedom from national oppression. We do not delude ourselves. We know that our program can only be realized in the long term, and the road leading to it is long. But this road *begins* here and now; the struggle for it is not only a task for the future but also for the present. Therefore our aims must be made clear right now; we cannot put off their clarification to some future date.

(b) As explained above, the right to self-determination includes the right to establish a separate nation-state. Of course, *right* is not the same as *duty*, so we are not committed to supporting the establishment of a separate state in every case. But we are committed at least to consenting to the establishment of such a state if this can only be prevented by coercion and national oppression. So we are faced with the following objection. "What if there is a serious danger that the regime set up in the prospective new state is going to be reactionary? Does this not mean that your support for the right to self-determination commits you to consent to the establishment of a reactionary regime, if the people concerned would choose to do so?"

This objection is really beside the point. Consider an analogy. Suppose a slave-owner responds to the demand to free his slaves by saying that among his slaves there are some evil persons, utter villains, who no doubt would become murderers if set free.

These spurious objections (in both cases) are based on a sleight of hand of fabricating a package deal: the charge that by consenting to the establishment of an independent state we also commit ourselves in advance to consent to any regime that would be set up in it. We absolutely reject this fake package. Consent to independence is just this, and no more; it does not constitute advance approval of the regime that would be set up in the prospective state. Conversely, struggle against a state's reactionary regime is just this, and does not constitute struggle against the very existence of that state.

(c) We sometimes encounter the following objection: "How can you consent to the establishment of any nation-state whatsoever? In every nation-state, the nation to which the state 'belongs' has as a matter of course privileged status, which means that every citizen or resident who does not belong to that nation is underprivileged, oppressed, and discriminated against."

In responding to this objection, we must distinguish between two cases. If what is at issue is concern about curtailment of the *national rights* of a national minority within a state whose majority belongs to another nation, then the answer is that the right to self-determination applies also to the minority group. The need to protect the rights of national minorities is not an argument against the right of self-determination but for it.

Alternatively, if what is at issue is not concern for the collective rights of national minorities but for the *individual rights* of those who do not belong to the majority nation, then this argument is based on confusion between national rights and individual rights. The existence of a nation-state neither justifies nor entails any discrimination whatsoever against individuals who do not belong to the majority nation. In any case, whether in a nation-state or in a multinational state, socialists must struggle against all forms of discrimination, and for equality of rights for all persons, irrespective of their origin and national identity. This is what the struggle against racism is all about.

Clearly, support for national self-determination does not exempt us from the struggle against racist discrimination—just as the latter struggle is insufficient on its own, and does not exempt us from supporting the right to self-determination, or in other words: opposing national oppression. These two kinds of struggle do not contradict but complement each other.

Our Position on the Immediate Term

We have seen that within Zionism there were groups (albeit small and lacking political influence) that did not support anti-Arab racism on the one hand, but on the other hand advocated national oppression of the Palestinian Arab people.

Contrariwise, there is a Zionist current promoting the exact opposite line. We are referring to those hypocrites located on the "left" fringe of the Zionist camp, who are content to recognize the national rights of the Palestinian people, at least in part, but on the other hand are not averse to applying apartheid and racist discrimination against non-Jews. Of greatest concern to such people are Israel's Jewish "purity" and the perpetuation of the privileges of Jews in this country. In order to secure these, they are prepared to pay the price of recognizing the right of the Palestinian people to establish its own state "alongside Israel."[4]

But the great majority of Zionists—the decisive currents in the bourgeois-Zionist, clericalist-Zionist, and labor-movement-Zionist camps—support *both* racism and national oppression. The difference between the various current and groupings is only in the differing proportions of the ingredients in this nauseating brew: some give slightly more emphasis to racism and some prefer the ingredient of national oppression.

But we, as consistent socialists, oppose Zionism root and branch; we reject all its aspects and components. Thus we struggle both against Zionist racism, which discriminates against Palestinians as individual human beings, and against the Zionist oppression of the Palestinians as a people. Or, putting it in positive terms: *we support both the human and the national rights of the Palestinians.* This twofold principle guides us not only in our long-term program (discussed above) but also in our current struggle and immediate demands.

There is no need to expand on our demands and struggle for equality of individual rights, because this should be obvious not only to every socialist but also to every true liberal. But one point ought to be emphasized. As socialists, we are concerned in the first place with the rights of workers and all those who make a living by their own labor, the rights of the exploited, the poor who possess little or no property; we are not devotees of private property. However, we struggle uncompromisingly against any violation of private property due to racist discrimination. When the Zionist state confiscates land from private Arab owners, precisely because they are Arabs, in order to establish on that land cooperative villages or "socialist" kibbutzim exclusively for Jews—then we take the side of the private owners against the hypocritical racist "socialism" of Zionist colonization. We reject "socialist" justifications of racism.

Similarly, we reject "socialist" justifications of national oppression. The Palestinian people's right to self-determination includes, among other things, the right of this people to determine its own political representation. We are not adherents of the PLO; on the contrary, we have detailed and principled criticism of its tactics and strategy, as well as of its political program (part of this criticism has been made clear in the present article, and other parts have been made clear in statements published by our organizations and in articles published in *Matzpen*). We do not regard the PLO as a socialist organization. But we take a stand against any attempt by Israel (or the United States, or the Arab states) to disqualify the PLO as the legitimate representative of the Palestinian people. Any external attempt to dictate to the Palestinian people who is entitled to represent it constitutes national oppression. This is the case whether or not the PLO is a "good" or "bad" organization.

Similar things may be said regarding the establishment of a Palestinian state in the West Bank and Gaza Strip. We do not delude ourselves that the establishment of such a state would be a real solution to the Palestinian problem. We are also aware of the possibility that if such a state were established, it may be ruled by non-progressive forces. But we take a stand against any attempt to deny the right of the Palestinian people to establish its own state. No other nation has the right to dictate to the Palestinian people and deny its right to self-determination.

Therefore we struggle:

For full, immediate and unconditional Israeli withdrawal from all the conquered territories.

Against any Israeli attempt to dictate to the Palestinian masses who should represent them.

Against any Israeli attempt to dictate the future status of the territories from which Israel will withdraw.

Part IV
POLEMICS AGAINST ZIONISM

18

New Premises
for a False Conclusion

Z ionism has two aspects, and it cannot be analyzed or combated without addressing both of them. Politically and from a Middle East viewpoint, it is very important to analyze and understand the essence and history of the *Zionist project*—the colonization of Palestine by Jewish immigrants, led and guided by Zionism. Without such analysis it is impossible to understand Israeli political reality, because the State of Israel of today is a *product*—as well as an *extension*—of the Zionist project.

But from a theoretical and more general viewpoint it is also necessary to understand Zionism as an *ideology*, a specific system of concepts, premises, views, and conclusions regarding the so-called Jewish problem.

The present economic recession has led to a general feeling that the Zionist project is in deep crisis and has reached an impasse. In the Zionist camp, the former naïve optimism has vanished and given way to a feeling of unease, skepticism, and anxiety. Given this prevailing atmosphere, it is no wonder that some doubts have arisen in that camp regarding the *theoretical* foundations of Zionism.

A striking illustration of this skepticism can be found in the official organ of the Alignment.* In the latest issue of *Ot* (no. 2, Winter 1967) there are two articles addressing this topic. Yitzhak Ben-Aharon's[†] article, entitled "Toward Re-evaluation of Relations between Israel and the Diaspora," voices his feelings of unease and doubts following his visit to the United States and his meetings with American

---

This article was published under the pen name Z. Pe'er in *Matzpen* 35, May 1967. Translated by the author.

* The Alignment was a bloc of two "left"-Zionist parties: Mapai and Ahdut Ha'avodah, established in 1965. In 1968 it merged with another faction to form the Labor Party. Mapai, together with its close allies, dominated Israeli politics and led all government coalitions from 1948 to 1977.

† Yitzhak Ben-Aharon (1906–2006) was a leading "left"-Zionist politician.

Jews. Yig'al Elam,* an editor of the journal, examines in his article "New Premises for the Same Zionism" some basic premises of Zionism in the light of reality. These two articles complement each other: Ben-Aharon provides illustrations to Elam's theoretical generalizations.

Zionism and Anti-Semitism

There are two attitudes to the problem of anti-Jewish persecution and discrimination. One is that the Jews should pin their hopes on the general movement for social progress, which would bring about the eradication of all existing reactionary phenomena, including oppression of Jews. The underlying assumption of this view is that anti-Semitism is not essentially different from other reactionary social phenomena: it too is a product of mutable conditions. This implies that the struggle against anti-Semitism is part of the general struggle for social progress: Jews, like other groups subjected to special oppression, must—even from the viewpoint of their specific problem—take part in this general struggle. Zionism is based on the opposite view. Its underlying assumption is that anti-Semitism is an eternal and "normal" phenomenon, and the Jewish problem cannot be remedied except by separating the Jews from general society and gathering them in a separate state of their own. In this connection Elam quotes Theodor Herzl's *Der Judenstaat:* "The Jewish question persists wherever Jews live in significant numbers. . . . We are naturally drawn into those places where we are not persecuted, and our appearance there gives rise to persecution. This is the case, and will inevitably be so . . . I believe that I understand anti-Semitism, which is really a highly complex movement. I consider it from a Jewish standpoint, yet without fear or hatred."

Clearly, from this viewpoint Jews have no special reason to take part in the general movement for social progress. Moreover, there is not much point even in a particular struggle against anti-Semitism, because it is caused by the very presence of Jews as a minority among other peoples. Indeed, Zionism and anti-Semitism share a *common* basic premise: Jews are, and must be, out of place as a minority in a non-Jewish society. Yig'al Elam admits: "To this day we [Zionists] carry with us this feeling of unease, especially when we realize that anti-Semites almost always like to give a friendly slap on the Zionist shoulder." For this very reason Zionism aroused from the start opposition in many Jewish circles. Yig'al Elam quotes Lucien Wolf, a leader of British Jews, who wrote in a letter to Lord James de Rothschild (August 31, 1916):

> I understand . . . that the Zionists do not merely propose to form and establish a Jewish nationality in Palestine, but that they claim all the Jews as forming at the present moment a separate and dispossessed nationality, for which it is necessary to

---

* Yig'al Elam is a historian and Zionist ideologue.

find an organic political centre, because they are and must always be aliens in the lands in which they now dwell. . . . I have spent most of my life in combating these very doctrines, when presented to me in the form of anti-Semitism. . . . They constitute a capitulation to our enemies.*

Although Yig'al Elam does not mention this, it is known that in the Zionist movement there have always been groups that welcomed anti-Semitism and were pleased when it intensified. They believe that anti-Semitism is in any case inevitable, and the Zionist solution is ineluctable—but Jews are sometimes tempted to trust that they do after all have a future in the Diaspora. An intensification of anti-Semitism disabuses them of this "illusion"—so it must be welcomed, as it drives Jews toward the inevitable conclusion; the earlier, the better. This view has rightly been called "cruel Zionism."

But even putting "cruel Zionism" aside, it is clear that Zionism *as a whole* has lacked motivation for a real struggle against anti-Semitism. As Yig'al Elam puts it, Zionism was "ambivalent" about the struggle of Jews for emancipation or even for national minority rights in the inter-war period. He goes on to comment:

> For this reason, in the 1930s, as the struggle against the anti-Semitism and the dispossession policy of the Polish authorities intensified, Zionism lost its strong positions in the Jewish community in Poland in favor of the Bund. The Polish authorities did not hesitate to use "Zionist" arguments and exploit the embarrassment of the Zionist leaders for their own purpose.
>
> Moreover, even when it came to rescuing Jews, Zionism was uninterested except inasmuch as the rescue would follow the Zionist prescription: immigration to Palestine.

Yig'al Elam quotes the following interesting passage from Ben-Gurion's letter, dated December 17, 1938, to the Zionist Executive Committee just before the London Conference on Palestine:

> Millions of Jews are now facing physical extermination. The refugee problem has now become an urgent worldwide issue and England, assisted by anti-Zionist Jews, is trying to separate the refugee problem from the Palestine problem. The horrible extent of the refugee problem requires a speedy territorial solution and if Palestine won't absorb any Jews, one would have to look for another territory. Zionism is endangered. All other territorial experiments, which are doomed to failure, will require huge amounts of capital, and if the Jews are faced with a choice between the refugee problem and rescuing Jews from concentration camps on the one hand, and aid for the national museum in Palestine on the other, the Jewish sense of pity will prevail and our people's entire strength will be directed toward aid for the refugees in the various countries. Zionism will vanish from the agenda and indeed not only from world public opinion in England and America but also from Jewish public opinion. We are risking Zionism's very existence if we allow the refugee problem to be separated from the Palestine problem.

---

* Original letter reproduced in B. Destani, ed., *The Zionist Movement and the Foundation of Israel 1839–1972* (10 vols.), *Political Diaries 1918–1965*, vol. 1 (Cambridge: Archive Editions, 2004), 727.

What Did the Holocaust Prove?

The Zionist assumption that anti-Semitism and the plight of Jews are normal phenomena that would persist so long as Jews live as dispersed minorities, arose in the situation of extreme distress of the Jews in the disintegrating semi-feudal society of the tsarist empire and the aggressive nationalism prevalent in Central Europe at the end of the nineteenth century. How should this assumption be assessed in light of present-day reality?

Zionists often claim that the calamity that befell Europe's Jews in the Second World War confirms the Zionist thesis. It has been "proved" that an inevitable catastrophe awaits the Jews of the Diaspora; whereas those Jews who managed to immigrate to Palestine were saved from extermination.

Yig'al Elam notes, quite correctly, that this claim is unfounded. He points out that "the bottom line is that the rescue of the Jewish people depended on one factor: the combat capacity of the Allies that waged war against Hitler." Indeed, the Jews of Palestine were spared extermination not because of the Zionist colonization process that was then taking place here, but simply because the advance of the Nazis was halted just before they managed to conquer this country—which had nothing to do with Zionism. Similarly, most Jews of the Soviet Union (as well as those who escaped there from Poland) survived because the Red Army managed to repel the Hitlerite attack. Moreover, those Jews who immigrated to the United States were in *lesser* danger than their fellow Jews who opted for the Zionist solution. Nor did the Holocaust prove that persecution of Jews is "normal," and that extermination awaits Jews wherever they live as a minority. On the contrary, the Holocaust proved that anti-Semitism is—to use Elam's apt expression—"a pathological symptom of a society in crisis." Persecution of Jews never occurs in isolation, but always as part of an entire gamut of pathological and reactionary phenomena rooted in the crisis of capitalist society (or, in the case of the Soviet Union, in deformations and distortions of socialism). It follows that what can ensure against repetition of the holocaust is not migration of Jews to some other place but struggle against reaction generally. As Yig'al Elam rightly states: "The one thing that the Holocaust proved, as far as the Jewish people is concerned, is that the fate of the Jewish people is connected and intertwined with the fate of the world surrounding us, and with what happens in it, for good or ill."

Failure of Zionist Propaganda

For years the Zionists have been longing in vain for mass Jewish immigration from the "prosperous countries." The reason for its absence is simple: the Jewish masses do not accept the usual Zionist message about the calamity awaiting them; their own experience shows clearly that the Zionist thesis is incorrect. Yig'al Elam asserts: "Zionism offered a solution that assumed anti-Semitism to be a universal, natural and permanent given; but Zionism in this aspect is not credible to Jews living in a world in which anti-Semitism is not a natural and permanent given—a world that wishes to get rid of anti-Semitism, which it regards as a pest." Yitzhak Ben-Aharon writes on the same subject: "Zionist ideology (as propounded by Borochov or Herzl, [Nahman] Sirkin or Berl [Katznelson]), whose point of departure is the catastrophe awaiting the [Jewish] Diaspora, has no hold on the consciousness of the coming young generations in America. It is a fact that we are identified with the generation that is on its way out . . . Any attempt to reproduce these theories in American reality is doomed to failure."

Hence he concludes: "From the moment I no longer brandish the dread of Hitler in their faces, from the moment I no longer envision a catastrophe for them—from that moment it is as though I admit that they can be good and loyal Jews even if they go on building their lives in America."

A paradoxical situation has arisen, which Elam points out very disapprovingly: formerly, Zionism appealed to the Jews of the Diaspora to immigrate to Palestine in order to rescue themselves; now, when this argument is completely groundless, they are being asked to come in order to rescue the State of Israel.

> An inversion has occurred: the problem of existence of the Jewish people has been inverted into the problem of existence of the State of Israel; behind the demand addressed to the Jews of the Diaspora, that they immigrate to Israel . . . one detects fear, anxiety—lest we be left on our own, two or three million, in an area of twenty thousand square kilometers, in the midst of the Middle Eastern front, in the midst of the hostile Arab region, lonesome, weak, without a real long-term prospect. If the Jews would converge here, then we shall be sitting pretty, ten or fifteen million, great in number and strong.

By the way, Yig'al Elam rejects the idea that in the absence of Jewish immigration Israel's future as a Zionist state would be endangered. In his opinion, the existence of large Jewish communities in the United States and Soviet Union is actually a source of strength for Israel.

Shell and Kernel

What solution is proposed by the two Alignment spokesmen?

There is a difference between the approaches of Ben-Aharon and Elam. The former does not go far beyond the traditional Zionist conception, and is looking for new ways to persuade US Jews to immigrate to Israel. As a matter of fact, he himself evidently believes that in the long run the future of US Jews is in danger; but he has given up trying to make them realize it. So he proposes new methods for attracting Jews, mainly of the younger generation, to Israel. His proposed plan can be summarized in two points.

First, Israel should not concentrate on conducting among American Jewry "intensive" propaganda aimed merely at generating immigration but cooperate with the Jewish communities for a broader aim: to develop the Jewish identity of US Jews (even if they are not about to immigrate to Israel) and prevent their assimilation in the surrounding society. (It hardly needs to be added that, being a nationalist, he regards assimilation—even if it is completely free and voluntary—as a terrible disaster.)

Second, he proposes making Israel a focus of attraction for young Jews who would come here not necessarily out of specific Jewish motives but in response to universal cultural and moral challenges. He does not tell us how Israel would turn into a world cultural, scientific, and moral center that would be so attractive to the young generation; but he does remark that "when they come to us, we will gain the initiative." In other words, from the moment the young Jews step on Israel's soil, it would be possible to influence them and try to persuade some of them to stay and settle here. There is no need to discuss this childish idea in detail; it is not much more than a fatuous fantasy resulting from disappointment and despair.

In contrast, Elam takes a more radical position. "Certainly," he says, "Jewish immigration ought to be approved of, encouraged and welcomed"; but it is not vital. One should not be too concerned even if it is slow to arrive. "Under present world conditions we can achieve all that we wished to achieve in the State of Israel—with or without Jewish immigration." According to him Jewish immigration is only a *shell* of Zionism, a shell that must be discarded as outdated.

The *kernel* of Zionism is "the linkage of the State of Israel to the Jewish people . . . It is only this linkage that gives the State of Israel a sense and a *raison d'être*; it is only from this linkage that it developed, and only with this linkage can it exist and sustain itself in the world's consciousness." Israel is a Zionist state so long as it is not a political instrument of its inhabitants but of all the world's Jews; and the world's Jews must be harnessed for pro-Israel activity. As mentioned above, Elam remarks that from the viewpoint of pro-Israel activity there is some advantage in the fact that Jews do not immigrate to it but stay where they are in order to exert influence in "the global power centers—the US and the Soviet Union."

He therefore proposes that Israel's Zionist character be given an official, constitutional, and institutional expression:

> The State of Israel will be accepted as the *political project* of the Jewish people, in the *domain of responsibility* of the Jewish people *everywhere*. This means that responsibility for the State of Israel and for whatever happens in it will not be confined to the citizens living within its borders. The Israelis will have to assert this issue in their constitution and give it immediate institutional expression. [Emphasis in original.]

In order to secure the "permanent linkage between the Jewish people and the State of Israel" Elam proposes the following two institutions: (a) A written constitution that will proclaim the linkage between the State of Israel and the Jewish people. (b) A Senate, in which the Jews of the Diaspora will sit, and which will act alongside the Knesset and will be empowered to prevent or delay legislation that is contrary to the constitution of the State of Israel or to Jewish public opinion around the world.

To the objection that it is unacceptable for the destiny of a country to be decided by those living abroad, Elam has a ready response: this is nothing new; this is precisely what Zionism has always practiced. Indeed, the colonization of Palestine was carried out without consulting its inhabitants, so the very existence of the Zionist state is based from the start on the premise that the destiny of Palestine ought to be determined not by its inhabitants but by the entire Jewish people.

◆ ◆ ◆

We absolutely agree with Yig'al Elam's definitions: this is indeed the "kernel" of Zionism. It is exactly this kernel that must be struggled against. The choice is between an *Israeli and Middle Eastern* State of Israel, aiming to integrate in its environment—and a *Zionist* state, a foreign body in this region, a state that is subordinated to the Jewish communities around the world and to the global "power centers" (i.e., the foreign powers) where most Jews are located.

19

Resurrection of the Dead

History cannot bear being ignored, and whoever tries to ignore it ends up being hit by it in the face.

For years we, members of Matzpen, have insisted repeatedly that the State of Israel is a *Zionist state*—it came into being as a result of the Zionist project and is an instrument for extending and expanding it. We were not playing with words or trying to attach labels. Understanding the nature of Israel is a prerequisite for understanding the essence of the Israeli-Arab conflict. From the proposition that Israel is a Zionist state it follows that the Israeli-Arab conflict is not an ordinary conflict between nations but a direct extension of the conflict between *Zionism and the Arabs*—which is to say, an inevitable and unbridgeable conflict between a colonizing movement and the indigenous population living in and around the area in which the process of colonization is taking place.

From this we concluded that resolution of the conflict would be impossible without a profound revolution that would change the character of Israel and transform it from a Zionist state into a normal state, that would be solely a political expression of the Hebrew nation living in it and would cut itself off from Zionism and the "Zionist vision." *Such* a state would not be in essential and irreconcilable opposition to its Arab environment, and would eventually be able to integrate into a socialist union of this environment.

A Spurious Death Certificate

We therefore considered it very important to analyze the foundations of Zionism and to struggle against its ideology. We regarded this as laying the necessary theo-

This article was published under the pen name Israel Morr in *Matzpen* 38, October 1967. Translated by the author.

retical foundations for a revolutionary struggle against Zionism.

(Let us note here parenthetically: we rejected as superficial and inadequate the view of the Israeli Communist Party, which concentrates on attacking Zionism's ties to imperialism and its hostile attitude to the Soviet Union. Of course, we do not deny that Zionism has always collaborated with imperialism and was backed by it; this is a fact. But it is a grave error to concentrate on attacking a *phenomenon* without analyzing its roots. From such a conception of Zionism it would only be possible to draw one of two conclusions: either that Zionism is simply an "artifact" of imperialism, which supposedly created it at its own initiative, and that their relationship is confined to the former "obeying the orders" of the latter; or that Zionism is "generally OK," except that it ought to change its foreign policy, and then everything would be fine. The first of these conclusions leads to gross political errors caused by misunderstanding the nature of the adversary; the second leads to compromise with Zionism.)

There were those who accused us of tilting at windmills: "True," they said, "Zionism created the State of Israel, but this is past history; in what way is the Zionist nature of Israel pertinent *today*?" We pointed at the Law of Return as one example. But there were some who countered that in any case there was no mass Jewish immigration in recent years, and it was doubtful whether there would be such in the future—so the Law of Return is to a large extent a purely academic issue.

Indeed, the Law of Return is only an example. But, admittedly, in normal times, when in practice there were no decisively important issues on the agenda but only day-to-day ones, it was possible to be deluded into the belief that Zionism is no longer relevant, no more than a collection of dusty slogans without any connection to actual reality, which elderly leaders keep mouthing out of habit.

The truth is that Zionism was always *much more than that*; it was lying at the very foundations of the *whole* of Israel's policy, and in the final analysis it was the motive or justification for innumerable deeds of the authorities. But when these deeds are small and routine, their Zionist common denominator is not too apparent. This was used by those who, for various reasons, did not wish to appear *openly* as Zionists, and attempted to disguise the closeness or *rapprochement* between them and the Zionists camp. They simply declared Zionism to be irrelevant, and issued it with a spurious death certificate.

Debate among Zionists

Then came the Six-Day War [of June 1967] and resurrected the "dead." The debate taking place in Israel about the future of the Occupied Territories concerns inevitably the nature of Israel and the Zionist claim that the Jews have a "right" over the Palestinian territory. Thus the most fundamental principles of Zionism are back on the agenda.

For years the leaders of all the Zionist parties—*except Herut**—had been declaring that they were "satisfied" with the status quo created following the 1948 war; they asserted repeatedly that they had no further territorial claims. But the annexationist claims raised following the Suez-Sinai war [of 1956], and more insistently following the Six-Day War, prove that in fact none of the Zionist currents have ever abandoned in principle the claim to the "entire Land of Israel." The old disclaimers, repudiating any desire for territorial expansion, were motivated either by propagandist considerations (the wish to appear righteous in the eyes of the world) or by pragmatic readiness to accept the facts when there did not seem to be any practical prospect of gaining further territory. But when the prospect of annexations appears to be realistic, the fundamental, essential position of Zionism is exposed.

It is true that even now there are those in the Zionist camp who do not support annexations (except for the Arab part of Jerusalem, which no one in the Zionist camp argues against). In most cases, their argument for opposing annexation is also thoroughly Zionist: they refer to the "demographic peril," the danger that extensive annexations would cause the State of Israel to lose its exclusively Jewish character. Those who use this argument would surely be happy to annex *all* the Occupied Territories, if there were some reasonable means for getting rid of the inhabitants of these territories.

But there are some Zionists who also put forward principled and ethical arguments against annexation. Amos Oz, in an article entitled "The Minister of Defence and the Lebensraum" (*Davar*, August 22, 1967), comes out against the horrifying overtones accompanying the annexationist orgy. The arguments citing Jewish "historical" rights over the "entire Land of Israel" are described by him as "hallucinations of a myth." He asserts that territorial rights and political borders can only be based on the *demographic principle*: every people has a right over the territory it inhabits and in which it constitutes a majority. Any other principle is baseless.

Yitzhak Auerbach-Orpaz comes out vehemently (*Ha'aretz* literary section, September 8, 1967) against those intellectuals who encourage and whip up the nationalistic frenzy engulfing the multitude, instead of standing up *against* it. He condemns the immorality of annexing a territory against the wishes of its inhabitants, and points out the damage it would cause to the spiritual complexion of Israel itself: "So long as there exists one slave, I am not free; much less so when I am his master."

Of course, these positions of Amos Oz, Yitzhak Orpaz, and others like them must be welcomed. It is encouraging to see that there are still some people not

---

* Herut, led by Menachem Begin, was the major right-wing political party in Israel from the 1940s until its formal merger with other parties to form the Likud in 1988. Its ideology was "Revisionist" (right-wing) Zionism.

swept off their feet by the general murky tide. But the truth of the matter is that the arguments put forward by them can in no way stand up in the debate—so long as it is conducted on a *Zionist basis*. Because these arguments are valid not only against the annexations proposed at present but also against those implemented during and in consequence of the 1948 war, as well as against the initial Zionist claim over Palestine. Here are a few quotes from the polemics of supporters of annexation against the arguments of Oz and Orpaz (all emphases in the original):

> This criterion, "who inhabits this piece of land *today*," can in no way be the sole criterion. Because if Amos Oz would apply it, and it alone, *Zionism has no justification at all.*
>
> If Amos Oz approves of the borders within which we existed so far because they have a demographic rationale, he should ask himself whether that demographic situation that determined the borders had always existed or was created in a colonizing process. Indeed, according to a demographic criterion we did not have, at the start of the realization of Zionism, any right over this country! The entire right followed from hallucinations of a myth. This is what the anti-Zionists have always claimed. Nevertheless we were not prepared to accept a given demographic situation as the sole criterion. We did everything to alter the demographic situation. Is it permissible to do this? If it is not—there is no justification to our very existence here. If it is—there is nothing sacred about the borders determined by one specific military confrontation, and it is permissible to alter the demographic reality in other zones as well. (Ariel Renan, *Davar*, September 14, 1967)

> There arises a question: do these words [of Yitzhak Orpaz] not apply to the conquests of Israel in the War of Independence? Is the annexation of Jaffa or Nazareth permissible, and that of Nablus and Jenin forbidden? Why? Is the Old City [of Jerusalem] less Arab [sic] than Ramleh in 1948? Was Nazareth more Jewish in 1948 than Nablus is in 1967? What is the difference in the degree of Arabness between Tulkarm and Umm al-Fahm? Is the date of their conquest the only thing that matters? (Avraham Kena'ani, *Ha'aretz*, 15 September 1967)

> By the way, the fact that the Occupied Territories are inhabited by Arabs who are not delighted with Israeli rule is emphasized and stressed so assertively by the remonstrators that one wishes to ask them first of all whether they have noticed that within Israel's former borders there have lived, and are living, Arabs for whom the Jewish state was not an outcome of free choice; and whether it is not right that the same moral principle of taking their view into consideration ought to apply to the whole of the State of Israel.
>
> I do not ask this for the sake of mere polemics. From the whole substance of these remonstrators' words and the tone of their arguments one can well perceive also the shaky foundation of our very right to be in this country, even in its former borders. I do not say that it is forbidden to discuss this right. No topic is taboo. But in this case, as in other cases, it ought to be clear what the discussion is about. (Nathan Alterman, *Ma'ariv*, September 15, 1967)

Who Is Right?

On this point, Nathan Alterman is right: it ought to be clear what the discussion is about. A consistent person can hold only one of the following two positions.

1. *Accepting the Zionist argumentation.* According to this argumentation, the whole of the Land of Israel, not only Palestine of the British Mandate, but much beyond its borders, belongs to the entire Jewish people by virtue of a divine promise. There are, it is true, some Zionists who put forward other arguments, such as the fact that about two thousand years ago there existed in this country a Jewish state; but no sane person—except for a few Zionists—would take seriously this kind of argument as a basis for political and territorial rights. Likewise, there are those who put forward as an argument the age-old yearnings of Jews for the Land of Israel. This too is a ridiculous argument: the spiritual attachment of Jews to the Holy Land is undeniable—but yearnings are not grounds for ownership rights. The only non-ridiculous basis for the Zionist position is the promise of God to Abraham in the midst of the divided carcasses (Genesis, ch. xv), and other such revelations. The advantage of this basis is that it does not require recognition by other peoples of the alleged right. Divine right is in no need for human recognition.

2. *Rejecting absolutely the hallucinations of the Zionist myth.* In this case the inescapable conclusion is that the entire Zionist project from the start (including the conquests of the 1948 war) was not based on any right.

We hold the latter position. In our opinion, the Jews as such have no special political right over Palestine. What we do recognize—*and demand that the Arabs also recognize*—is the right to self-determination of the Hebrew people (i.e., the Jews living in Israel).

Insofar as the debate revolves around "morality," "justice," and "historical rights," the inescapable fact is that the Arab case is irrefutable: the Zionist colonization in Palestine was unjust and was not based on any true right.

Our criticism of Arab nationalism is that it gets stuck at the level of debate about justice and rights concerning a process that has taken place in the past, and is unable to provide a *political* solution to an existing problem.

A political solution requires recognition of the right of the Hebrew people to self-determination—not because this people has an alleged "ownership rights" over Palestine but because it exists here and cannot be extirpated. So long as the Arabs do not realize this, the problem will remain unsolved.

At the same time, it must be asserted that so long as the Hebrew people puts forward claims based on the Zionist argumentation, it will not be able to reach a settlement with the Arabs. The Zionist argumentation demands recognition *de jure* of the "rights" of colonization, which is unacceptable.

So long as Israel is a Zionist state, its conflict with the Arabs contains an outstanding element of a colonial conflict, which cannot be resolved except by a total and absolute defeat of one of the two sides, which means—in the present case—that it cannot be resolved at all.

Resolution of the conflict would only be made possible by a total break with Zionism. This cannot be achieved by ignoring the past and refusing to confront it but only by a full and frank settling of accounts, in a revolutionary way.

As for the question of the borders, it must be stressed that a complete resolution of the conflict will come about through integration of Israel in the Arab world, in the framework of a socialist union. In such a union the question of borders loses much of its sting, and becomes a secondary matter. Within a socialist union or federation, borders will not be determined by myths nor by merely demographic considerations. Demography is only *one* factor among others, such as economic efficiency, administrative convenience, and so on.

In any case, as far as we—as socialists and enemies of nationalism—are concerned, there is nothing sacred about any border: neither the borders of the [1947 UN] Partition Plan nor the [post-1949] Armistice lines; neither whatever border would be determined as a consequence of the Six-Day War nor any border that would result from a future war.

20
Liars

A few weeks ago I received a letter from a personal friend of mine in Israel. "Lately," he writes,

> the press is full of attacks against you people. The style of the stories is very infuriating. In none of them, for example, have they seen fit to quote a single sentence from you. And without describing what you actually do the reports make it "clear" that you are traitors. Today, for example, *Ma'ariv* printed a report headed "Jews in the service of Fatah in London," in which it is said, "Dr. Machover will surely be very angered by me calling him a Jew." You know that in substance I do not share your views, but I am infuriated by the inflammatory tone of the stories; especially because after reading them you would either like to tear Dr. Machover to pieces or shrug your shoulders, but in either case you don't really know what he is supposed to have done.

The *Ma'ariv* story mentioned in the letter—which is one of many in the same vein—was written by Gabriel Strassman, *Ma'ariv*'s London correspondent, and was published on May 6, 1969. And, true enough, whoever read that story carefully and critically, as did my friend, realized at once that it contained absolutely nothing about the substance of what "Dr. Machover and his friends of the Matzpen group" say in London. Indeed, the factual content of that story—as of all others of the same kind—is very meager. (And here I must add something that my friend could not have inferred from reading that material: even the few "facts" that Mr. Strassman's story cites are distorted. For example, he mentions a meeting organized by the Arab students in London, and implies that I was one of the platform speakers there. Yet the truth is that I made no speech from the platform but took part in the discussion that followed the speeches, in which also other Israelis participated from

---

This article was written in London, where the author has been living since September 1968. It was published in *Matzpen* 50, August 1969. Translated from Hebrew by the author.

the floor, like me. The only difference was that I did not defend the official Israeli position but utterly dissociated myself from it.)

I am unable—even had I been so inclined—to enter into a debate with Mr. Strassman and the other authors of the inflammatory stories. There is simply nothing to debate about. At most, it would be possible to list several dozen more or less blatant factual distortions. But that would bore both the reader and me; and in any case it is unimportant. Because, in the best demagogic tradition, the facts (even the distorted ones) do not constitute the substance of the incitement, but only an embellishment designed to mislead the unguarded reader and lend the defamatory articles a credible air of "factuality." As my friend discovered on careful and critical reading, the main incitement is in the form of very general evaluations and allegations such as: what is said by the members of Matzpen abroad is "poisonous" and "serves the seditionists of al-Fatah."

So a debate is not called for. Neither is it necessary to give a detailed account of what we do say, because what we say abroad is exactly the same as what our comrades say in Israel, with which readers of *Matzpen* are in any case familiar through reading this paper.

Instead, it is much more interesting to consider the following question: Why is the Israeli press so enraged? Why is the Israeli establishment so indignant? What has caused this furious campaign of baiting, libel, and incitement?

The answer is quite simple. The incitement campaign is a symptom, a cry of pain. The Israeli establishment has been wounded in a sensitive weak spot.

Israel is not the only state that practices oppression and denial of rights of members of "inferior" peoples (or races); neither is it the only state located geographically in the midst of the third world and serving there as a partner and buttress of global imperialist powers. There are many examples of such states, some less bad, some worse: for example, South Africa. But South Africa does not expect to have the sympathy of world public opinion (let alone that of the international left). The rulers of South Africa have long been accustomed to the world's condemnation; and they can also afford to thumb their noses at it. They rule over a rich industrialized country that does not depend on charitable funds or American subsidy. On the contrary, the present regime of South Africa enables the huge American and British capital invested there to extract fat profits. Therefore those racists are not too bothered by the world's antipathy. And the rest of the world for its part has long been used to seeing South Africa in its true light. For the South African press is printed in European languages that can be widely read abroad, and the whole world can easily read it and witness the depth of moral and political vileness of its dominant ideology.

Israel has no rich natural resources. The Israeli establishment does not rely on exploiting diamond and iron mines but on exploiting the sympathy of world public opinion. (To be precise, this is its second most important mainstay; the first one is the common interest of imperialism and Zionism, but this lies outside the topic under discussion here.)

The State of Israel holds the world record in balance-of-trade deficit. The deficit is covered by an enormous flow—unparalleled in size and the length of time during which it has kept flowing—of money from outside. A major part of this money comes in the form of tax-free donations. This is how it works. A Jew in New York, for example, donates $1,000 to the United Jewish Appeal. The US Treasury recognizes this as a "charitable" donation, free of income tax. Had that $1,000 not been paid to the UJA, most of it (say $770)* would have had to be paid to the Treasury. It follows that in reality only $230 are donated by the donor, while $770 are donated by the US government.

This arrangement—which exists also in other Western countries—depends on two conditions. First, the treasury department of the country in question must recognize the donation as "charitable"; second, the Jewish donor must prefer the UJA to other appeals for charity. If local public opinion will turn its back to Israel, both of these conditions would be put in doubt. The treasury department would find it difficult to resist public pressure and continue recognizing donations to Israel as "charity"; and many Jewish donors—who also form part of public opinion, and influence it as well as being influenced by it—would prefer donating their money to other causes, such as animal welfare.

Now since the June war the true face of the Israeli authorities has been uncovered, and the world's sympathy is progressively vanishing. Of course, the main cause for this is not the "failures of Israeli *hasbarah* [propaganda]" or the "hate propaganda of the al-Fatah inciters and their Matzpen helpers"—but simply the facts themselves. For example, the fact that Israel plays thoroughly the role of occupier—the whole world smiles ruefully at the pious "liberal" pretensions of various occupiers—and shows very clear signs of having an appetite for annexations.

How far has this gone? Take one example. Piet Naak is a Dutch docker, an ordinary person, but a very brave one, as well as what is known in Israel as "Righteous among the Nations." During the Nazi occupation he organized a movement of strikes and demonstrations against the deportation of Jews to extermination camps. At present he is the secretary of the Dutch Palestine Committee, devoted to mobilizing support for the Palestinian struggle; and he makes public appearances and declares that a few years ago, when he agreed to accept an honorary citizenship of Israel, he was still unaware of the true nature of its policy, whereas now he thinks that Moshe Dayan is Nazi-like.

Should we then be surprised by the furious rage of the Israeli establishment?

As I pointed out, the change in public opinion is not mainly due to some kind of deliberate propaganda. It is stupid to believe that a tiny handful of dissident Israelis staying abroad is able—even with the greatest effort—to cause such a great change of public mood. But we, this handful, can easily do something quite simple: we can

* In 1969 the top rate of US federal income tax was 77 percent.

translate into European languages the thoughts of the Israeli establishment, as they are published in Hebrew, in the Israeli press. In doing this we topple one of the natural defensive walls behind which the establishment used to hide from the world's scrutiny. Who, in the great wide world, can read Hebrew? Which important international paper would bother publishing a detailed survey of what is printed in the Israeli press?

It seems that up till now Israel has been able to indulge in a luxury that is not available to other states of its kind: it could manage a domestic public opinion inflamed by nationalist and militarist preaching, by a chauvinist press that utters in a nonchalant tone stuff that would horrify every decent person around the world—and at the same time conduct abroad pious propaganda wrapped in a cloak of humanist values. These two propaganda worlds are separated by the natural barrier of language. And the Israeli correspondents of the world press—the great majority of whom are Zionist Jews—do little to breach this barrier. But now this handful of Israelis turn up and publish translations of what is printed in the Israeli press. This too causes the establishment great pain, and it reacts hysterically.

We do not wish to exaggerate the importance of our public educational work, but we are convinced that it is not only absolutely legitimate but also good for the hygiene of Israel's internal political life: let those who conduct racist and chauvinist propaganda in Israel know that what they say is being heard abroad. We shall go on translating.

Especially hysterical is the incitement and haranguing issued by those Israeli journalists who are in the habit of wrapping themselves in a cloak of "decency" and even "progressiveness," and who like to pretend that they are not quite happy about the Israeli establishment.

- *Amos Kenan* has gone very far in publishing in *Yedi'ot Aharonot* a series of incitement articles against the whole of the international left, and in particular against Matzpen. I recall that when Mr. Kenan started to work for Dr. Herzl Rosenblum's paper, I wondered how a person who wishes to be regarded as a progressive can write regularly for a clearly reactionary evening paper. Some people then told me, with a knowing wink, that the editor of *Yedi'ot Aharonot* is an elderly person, whose views do not carry much weight, and so Amos Kenan can fool him and smuggle some progressive views into that bastion of reaction. Why not use that forum? But now it has become clear who is using whom. Amos Kenan has become the paper's expert in unbridled attacks against the left.
- *Boaz Evron* is also one of those "progressive" journalists who work on Dr. Rosenblum's paper and who "fool" him by smuggling into the weekend issue of that esteemed evening paper attacks on the international and Israeli left. This fastidious professional intelligentual* does not shrink from telling outright lies. In his article entitled "Neo Anti-Semitism"

---

* This untranslatable dismissive made-up word is in the original Hebrew text.

(April 25, 1969) he tries to prove that the left is and has always been anti-Semitic. And in the final part of that profound article he authoritatively reports that "the Israeli, Moshé Machover, member of the Israeli Matzpen group, published in [the French daily] *Le Monde* an article in which he praised, among other things, the attack by members of the Popular Front for the Liberation of Palestine on an El-Al plane in Athens." Mr. Evron knows very well that this is a lie (in my article I pointedly and explicitly refrained from going into the question as to whether the Athens attack was morally or pragmatically justifiable), but he assumes that ordinary readers would not bother to verify his allegation and just take his word for it.

- *Knesset member Uri Avnery* goes so far as to make himself ridiculous. In the June 4, 1969, issue of *Ha'olam Hazeh* he published an article in which he accuses *ISRAC* (a pamphlet published in London by the Israeli Revolutionary Action Committee abroad) of spreading anti-Semitic propaganda. The principal "proof" of this is a cartoon that appeared in *ISRAC*, showing a nasty-looking man standing in a field strewn with corpses; a balloon coming out of the man's mouth contains the words "say it with flowers." Mr. Avnery avers: "This is, literally, an anti-Semitic cartoon. Anyone who has any knowledge at all of the history of anti-Semitic psychopathology will recognize it." Why? Because the image of the man in the cartoon is very familiar to the English reader as being anti-Semitic—so the cartoon expert Mr. Avnery asserts categorically. Of course, an expert like him does not notice small details, such as the fact that the cartoon in question—except for the "say it with flowers" balloon—is a well-known lithograph by the French artist Honoré Daumier (whose signature appears in the bottom left-hand corner). It was originally published about a hundred years ago, and had nothing at all to do with Jews or anti-Semitism. Describing the man in the lithograph as "the stereotypical image of the Jew in British anti-Semitic drawings" is due to astonishing ignorance combined with a sick and malevolent imagination.*

By the way, in the same article Mr. Avnery casts a personal complaint against us. The *ISRAC* pamphlet included a translation of an article by him about the situation in the Gaza Strip. In one part of the article, in which Mr. Avnery spoke about the annexationist tendencies of all the parties in the Israeli government coalition, there was a note added by the *ISRAC* translator, reminding the non-Israeli reader that Mr. Avnery himself had voted in the Knesset for the annexation of

---

* The ISRAC pamphlet in question can be viewed and downloaded: www.israelimperialnews.org/iin07.htm. Daumier's antiwar cartoon is on p. 4.

eastern Jerusalem.* Now Mr. Avnery complains that we did not bother to add that at the time of that vote, and many times thereafter, he declared that he was "for making the united city of Jerusalem the joint capital of the State of Israel and the State of Palestine." We would like to take this opportunity of apologizing to Mr. Avnery. He is right; we ought to have explained to the non-Israeli reader that Mr. Avnery's support for the annexation of eastern Jerusalem is part of his scheme for an "Israel-Palestine" federation. This would have shown the reader what a lovely "federation" it is supposed to be: in order to establish it, its intended capital must first be annexed by Israel.

Again, also in the case of people such as Kenan, Evron, or Avnery, there is not much point in detailing the many falsehoods, both large and small, that they spread about us. The really interesting question is why it is they who lead this campaign of incitement against the international and Israeli left.

Here too, it is not hard to guess the real reason. These people would very much like to keep normal relations both with the Israeli establishment and with progressive public opinion. To criticize the government a little, to play at being a parliamentary opposition—why not? This is very nice and very satisfying. But to get into total conflict with the establishment and uphold openly views that are absolutely rejected by an inflamed public opinion—no, not that. That is not so amusing; it is even a bit unwise from a journalistic viewpoint.

When a war breaks out, our cute heroes start swimming very vigorously . . . no, not *against* the current. Thus, following the 1956 Suez-Sinai war Uri Avnery called for the annexation of the Gaza Strip; and during the June 1967 days he published a short-lived evening paper called *Daf* (page) that excelled in its extreme militaristic and nationalistic tone; and following that he voted for the annexation to Israel of eastern Jerusalem (as part of the scheme for . . . an "Israel-Palestine federation"). But all this does not prevent him from posing in the great outside world as a courageous combatant for peace. Very impressive!

The only trouble with this is that those Matzpen rascals spoil this lovely game. They reveal to the outside world the true face of the peace heroes that swim with the current, the annexers of Jerusalem "for the sake of the federation," the writers of intellegentual articles in Dr. Herzl Rosenblum's newspaper. Even worse: those Matzpen guttersnipes occasionally tingle the conscience that has been anesthetized and wrapped in thick layers of opportunism.

Therefore it is necessary to incite and taunt, to spread fantastic lies about Matzpen and its supporters abroad. Therefore Avnery has to call [our comrade] Dinah Hecht "the al-Fatah girl" and spread the deliberate lie that the [Palestinian solidarity] demonstration at which she made a speech (in London's Trafalgar Square on May 11, 1969) was an "al-Fatah demonstration"; therefore it is necessary to de-

---

* Avnery's article is at pp.12–13 of the pamphlet. The translator's parenthetical note is at p. 13.

scribe the works of Honoré Daumier that are reproduced in *ISRAC* as "anti-Semitic cartoons in British style"; therefore Evron and Kenan must write lengthy articles against the new left and Matzpen.

For our part, we are not too upset by the campaign of incitement waged by the Strassmans and by Avnery-Kenan-Evron. On the contrary, we see it as proof that we have managed to hit their weak spot. This is why the liars rage.

21

The Zionist Left and
the Palestinian Resistance

The official Mapam* publication, *Al Hammishmar*, has been forced into the position of having to engage in a rearguard battle of ideas against the ISO.† Mapam's traditional role has been to "sell" Zionism to left-wing circles around the world. Having lost the last vestiges of its ideological individuality and having finally capitulated to the chauvinist policy of its senior partners in power, Mapam now is quickly losing its ability to conduct a dialogue with those left-wing circles. Under these circumstances Mapam is irritated more than ever by Matzpen's existence and by the support that Matzpen has won among the revolutionary left throughout the world.

At first Mapam tried to ignore Matzpen; then it joined the national orchestra of anti-Matzpen calumnies and vilifications. Now it has been compelled to try to contend with Matzpen by using arguments that are almost to the point.

Both the title and contents of Peretz Merhav's article, "Fighters for Peace or Warmongers?"[1] reflect this new development. Merhav is head of Mapam's international department (the department that deals with Mapam's foreign contacts), and according to an editorial comment in *Al Hammishmar*, his article illustrates Mapam's propaganda abroad. As for the title (in which Merhav implies that the ISO's members are warmongers), we are not going to repay Mapam members with

---

This article, cowritten with Akiva Orr, was originally written in Hebrew (under the title "Against the Zionist Left") at the end of 1969 for publication in *Matzpen* 51. It was banned by the Israeli military censor, along with several other items from that issue of *Matzpen*. It was then published (along with some other banned material) as a leaflet, in defiance of the censor. The present version is based on an edited translation in the collection *The Other Israel*, ed. A. Bober (New York: Doubleday, 1972).

* Hebrew acronym of the party's full name, "United Workers' Party."

† Israeli Socialist Organization—official name of Matzpen. Subsequently changed to Socialist Organization in Israel (SOI).

their own coin and claim that we think they are warmongers. They do, however, have a tradition of trailing after their senior partners in the Zionist camp whenever the latter decide to make war, and thus might be said to bear a large part of the responsibility not only for the decision to start the 1967 war but also for the decision made in 1956 to start the Suez war. (In both cases Mapam was part of the Cabinet.) They have no right, therefore, to call Matzpen members warmongers. He who has partaken of a feast in which the dove of peace was served roasted must not be allowed to sport her white feathers!

Mr. Merhav begins his article with a "factual survey" on Matzpen and its history. Many of his "facts" are inaccurate, and the rest are completely misrepresented—intentionally, it seems. The ideological-polemical part of the article also suffers from serious inaccuracies. Merhav does not quote from the original ISO article, which he condemns. He attempts to paraphrase our position in his own words, and the result is necessarily quite bungled.

An example: Merhav writes that Matzpen demands "withdrawal from all the territories populated by Arabs and now held by the Israel Defense Force, without exception." This is a translation of our principled position into the devious language typical of Mapam. We raise a demand for the short-term *immediate and unconditioned withdrawal from all the Occupied Territories*. In order to dodge the term "Occupied Territories," Merhav is compelled to wriggle with "populated by Arabs and now held by the IDF."

Another example: Our demand for the de-Zionization of Israel is interpreted by Merhav as calling for "severing it from the Jewish people and turning it into an exclusive 'local state,' without aspirations and ties overseas." Wherever did he get such a strange definition? Certainly not from Matzpen. According to our position, the question is not whether Israel should have no "aspirations and ties overseas," but *what kind* of aspirations, and ties *with whom*? Ties with Cohn-Bendit or with Rothschild? Affinity with Karl Marx or Marks and Spencer? In our revolutionary spirit, Matzpen's affinities are quite clear.

We are not against ties overseas. We are only against certain ties such as those of the Mapam coalition government with American imperialism, which are merely a continuation of the traditional and natural ties of Zionism with imperialism.

De-Zionization means the abolition of Jewish exclusiveness (which is inherent, e.g., in the Law of Return) whereby a Jew living in Brooklyn gets more civil and political rights in Israel than a Palestinian Arab who was born there (whether he is now a refugee or an Israeli citizen). In our view, the fact that the Brooklyn Jew feels an emotional tie to the Holy Land does not entitle him to have any political rights in the country, whereas the Palestinian Arab is entitled to full civil and political rights.

The aim of Zionism—to use Mapam's own formulation—is "to concentrate the majority of the Jewish people in a whole and undivided Palestine." This aim provides the guide according to which the Zionist establishment in Israel decides on each political, economic, social, or cultural step. Even today the State of Israel is, from Zionism's viewpoint, not a finished product but only an intermediate stage and an instrument in achieving the full aim of Zionism.

The Zionist aim puts those who uphold its doctrine into an inevitable and inescapable conflict with the Arab world, in whose midst—and at whose expense—this aim is realized. The fundamental essence of the conflict has not changed from the beginning of Zionist colonization to the present. This is no ordinary national-territorial conflict of the kind that sometimes breaks out between nations existing in a historically stable proximity. It is a conflict between a movement of colonization—which according to its own declarations has not yet achieved its full aim—and the indigenous population of the area that is being colonized.

Merhav prefers not to enter into a discussion of the roots of the Israeli-Arab conflict. He merely alleges that Zionism is not to blame for "the extension of the borders of Israel and the tragedy of the wandering and suffering of Arab refugees." The blame, in his opinion, is that of "the blind, violent and military resistance to Zionism from the time of the Mufti Hajj Amin al-Husseini to the June 1967 war and his disciples in Al-Fatah." This was exactly the claim of hypocritical colonizers everywhere: "It is not our fault, but that of the natives, who refuse to accept our colonization with love." This kind of hypocrisy is typical of Zionism's left wing, torn in an attempt to find a compromise between Zionist practice and socialist conscience. Dayan, in contrast, is not afraid to admit openly that the Arabs' resistance is a natural and necessary result of Zionist colonization.

As mentioned above, Merhav avoids serious discussion of the origins of the conflict. His main argument is that the de-Zionization formula is simply not realistic because it is "the idea least acceptable to the Israelis . . . since de-Zionization and severance from the Jewish people is in the eyes of every Israeli giving up the very *raison d'être* of the State of Israel."

This, too, is a typical Mapam argument. They are not looking for a way to end the conflict but for a formula that would be acceptable to the majority of the Israeli public. In our view this kind of realpolitik suffers not only from opportunism but from short-sightedness and a misunderstanding of basic reality. For any arrangement that does not include de-Zionization will be only imaginary and temporary: the basic problem will continue to exist.

Let us illustrate this by an extreme example—that of South Africa.[2] At present no military clash exists between South Africa and the neighboring African states; nevertheless, there is a historic conflict between a settlers' society and the African population. There is only one solution: to abolish the racist nature of the Republic of South Africa, which is not only the historical source of the conflict but also the cause that re-creates it at present. It is well known that this solution is categorically rejected by the majority of the white population who regard it as abandoning the raison d'être of their state. Does the revolutionary movement in South Africa therefore have to seek other solutions?

When Merhav turns to discuss Matzpen's attitude to Fatah, he again carefully refrains from directly quoting us. He paraphrases our position in his own words—and, as usual, it does not come out well. It is characteristic of those who cannot present a principled position in an argument to put their opponents' ideas into their own words in a bungled form. They then find it quite easy to fight the scarecrow they have set up.

Let us repeat Matzpen's position. We distinguish between the resistance to occupation of the Palestinian Arabs as a group and the specific policy of this or that organization within the resistance movement. We recognize the right and the duty of every conquered and oppressed people to resist occupation and to struggle for freedom. Our position concerning various organizations within the resistance movement is determined primarily according to their respective political programs. In this we differ from those who reject these organizations because of the very fact that they are struggling against occupation or because of the means that they use in the struggle.

Our position—*we repeat*—is determined by a political program. Our political criticism of the dominant currents of the Palestinian resistance movement is based on two main points. First, they do not regard social and political revolution throughout the region as a condition and framework for the solution of the Palestinian problem, but rather they defer all struggles within the Arab world and subordinate them to the Palestinian cause. They believe in a national unity that is "above classes"—and therefore false. The solution they propose refers to an artificial political entity—Palestine within the borders of the British Mandate—instead of the region as a whole.

Second, they do not accept the principle that the victorious revolution in the region, which will defeat the existing regimes, including the Zionist regime in Israel, will grant the right of self-determination to the non-Arab national entities living inside the Arab world, including the Israeli people.

In our view there is only one struggle—the revolutionary struggle for a new society in the Middle East, including Israel. Only within the framework of such a revolution will it be possible to solve the problems of the region, including the Israeli-Arab problem.

Merhav summarizes his own position as follows:

> The problem is how to reach an understanding, agreement, and peace between the two neighboring and rival national collectives (or between the decisive majority of each of them), that is, between the Arab countries and the Palestinians who inscribe on their flag the idea of Arab nationalism, revival, and unity, and the State of Israel that inscribes on her flag the idea of nationalism, revival, unity of the Jewish people and the gathering of its exiles in the historic homeland. To the challenge of creating contacts and an atmosphere favorable to conducting a friendly, purposive, and constructive dialogue between these two real national collectives as they are now—our efforts are dedicated.

This is a classic formulation of the nationalist trend in the socialist movement: It kneels down before "the national collective as it is now." Merhav is seeking understanding, agreement, and peace between the Arab world and Arab nationalism as they are now, and Israel and Zionism as they are now.

In our opinion, this approach must be discarded as a matter of principle. But the experience of the last seventy years of Middle East history also shows that what Merhav says he is seeking cannot be achieved. Even if the Israeli-Arab conflict did not exist, we would oppose the regimes that now exist in Israel and the Arab countries. All the more reason for this, since we know that the conflict cannot be solved while they remain "as they are now."

In fact, those who claim that the solution should be found through agreement between "the two national collectives as they are now" make no contribution to solving the problem but only seal their own fate: perpetually to tail behind the forces that dominate their national collective.

Mr. Merhav states, quite correctly, that we regard the struggle for a new society as the central and dominant issue, to which all other matters are subordinate and from which they are derived. He, in contrast, puts forward a different principle: activity for peace—between Israel as it is now and the Arab world as it is now. This, he asserts, is of paramount importance, and all other matters must be subordinate to it.

This is typical Zionist thinking. Zionism does not speak of the solution of the Israeli-Arab *problem*, because as far as it is concerned no such problem exists; it does not even like to speak of solving the Israeli-Arab *conflict*. As far as Zionism is concerned, everything can be summed up in one word: peace. It is not difficult to understand why. Zionism is engaged in a process of creating facts that are favorable to it and of realizing its goals. At each stage of partial realization, it wants only one thing: that the Arabs acquiesce in the facts that it has created. From the point of view of Zionism no political or social problem exists, only the problem of Arab psychology. Therefore the Zionist demand is "peace," not "a solution to the problem."

Of course, this does not mean that Zionism is particularly peace-loving; it is not prepared to have peace at any price but only on its own terms. Even Merhav writes that "we are prepared, in the event of peace, to return most of the territories now held by" the Israeli Army. *Most of the territories*, not all of them. To return all the Occupied Territories would be too high a price to pay for peace, even for the "socialist" Merhav. If all the territories were to be returned, it would seem that Zionism did not really advance, as a result of the June 1967 war, to the full realization of its aim. This would not be a worthwhile price for peace. In Zionist terminology, "peace" does not necessarily mean the opposite of war. When the Zionists demand peace, what they really mean is that the Arabs should peacefully accept the accomplished facts that Zionism has created at their expense, that they should peacefully accept Zionism.

A public discussion is currently taking place in Israel on the relation between "peace" and "security." It is a debate between those—like Mapam—who think that the Arab world may ultimately accept Zionism and those who have inferred from the historical experience of Zionism that it would never be accepted by the Arabs and

The Zionist Left and the Palestinian Resistance 163

must therefore impose itself by military superiority alone. Merhav states, quite correctly, that Matzpen is taking no part whatever in this national discussion on peace versus security. For it is a sterile discussion that we totally reject. *A Zionist Israel can never achieve peace and can never achieve security.* In this sense it will share the fate of all other settler regimes that are trying to exist in the midst of the third world—regimes that are based on discrimination against the indigenous population, on its exploitation or expulsion, and that are tied by an umbilical cord to the global imperialist alignment. In this respect Israel does not differ from South Africa or Rhodesia.

The only path to take is that of the struggle to abolish the Zionist nature of Israel, to set up a new society through active collaboration with revolutionary forces throughout the region. Whoever refuses to recognize this thereby sentences himself to a future of permanent warfare, of permanent militarization in all fields of social life and in all aspects of culture, morals, and science. Whoever adheres to Zionism sentences himself to perpetual war against the Arab world and to perpetual dependence on the suppliers of Phantom jets. This is absolutely inescapable.

Up to this point we have been discussing principles. But we cannot end the discussion without stressing that Mapam members themselves do not take their own principles seriously; in fact, the whole history of Mapam is the history of surrendering one principle after another. Let us mention their kibbutzim—for one example, Bar'am—which are founded on lands confiscated from Arab peasants, Israeli citizens who nevertheless were dispossessed to make room for these Zionist settlements. Let us recall Mapam's participation in the coalition government that decided to start the Suez war of 1956; let us recall that in 1957 Mapam helped to organize mass demonstrations against Israeli withdrawal from Sinai. Let us remember that they are part of the Dayan-Begin government, that they voted for the annexation of East Jerusalem to Israel (what has this got to do with peace or security?) and continue to support further annexations.

In short, Mapam's "principles" exist only for the sake of "the propaganda activity of our party abroad." In Israel there has never been a single instance of Mapam voting against a decision taken by its senior partners on matters of Zionist policy or on military questions.

The latest item on the list of surrenders exposes once more Mapam's role in the Zionist camp. The Israeli daily *Ha'aretz* of September 12, 1969, reports that the Alignment (a bloc of all Zionist workers' parties led by the Labor Party—formerly called Mapai—and including Mapam) adopted a platform for the general elections, which were to be held in the following month. One of the points in this platform was support for Zionist colonization in the Occupied Territories. *Ha'aretz* goes on to state that Mapam was against this point and at first insisted that its objection be mentioned in the platform itself; but Moshe Dayan announced that he would not allow such a thing. Finally, there was found what *Ha'aretz* rather amusingly calls "an honorable way out": The point in support of colonization would be included in the platform without any reservation and all partners in the Alignment—including

Mapam—would be bound by it. However, Mapam, while being bound by the platform, was given permission (with the consent of Mr. Dayan) to speak in public against that particular point.

The division of labor is quite clear. Mapam will continue to participate in the ruling alignment that supports and actually carries out the colonization of the Occupied Territories; at the same time, this policy contradicts Mapam's declared principles, and Mapam will go on declaring those principles. So Mapam will in fact support the colonization policy but—with the consent of Dayan—will continue to make noises against that policy, in particular when speaking to the left abroad.

22

Borochovist "Revival"

Preface

Borochovist ideology is at present being exhumed by the Zionist propaganda machine. A whole network of Zionist emissaries and functionaries are busy printing Ber Borochov's works in several European languages, writing their own exegeses on these works and diligently spreading the rehashed gospel among young Jews throughout West Europe and the Americas.

At first sight, this is rather strange; for, after a long period of stagnation, decline, and decay, Borochovism years ago ceased to exist as a living political force in the Zionist movement. In Israel, the Borochovist party Po'alei Zion Smol (Workers of Zion, Left Wing) ended its existence in 1948, when it combined with two larger—and non-Borochovist—factions (Hashomer Hatza'ir and Ahdut Ha'avodah) to form a united left-Zionist party, Mapam.* For the Borochovists this meant complete capitulation in the field of theory, as well as total organizational liquidation. The program adopted by the newly formed Mapam was not based on a compromise between Borochovism and other left-Zionist ideologies but was simply non-Borochovist.[1]

Organizationally, Mapam was divided into factions. However, Po'alei Zion Smol did not even constitute a distinct faction but merged with Ahdut Ha'avodah in the party's right-wing faction, which was dominated by the latter. Toward the mid-1950s Mapam split; the right-wing faction—still dominated by Ahdut Ha'avodah, but including most of the ex–Po'alei Zion Smol elements—constituted itself as a party that existed semi-independently for a number of years until it was incorporated into the big right-wing social-democratic Mapai,† which was then renamed the "Israeli Labor Party."

ISRACA pamphlet no. 4, London, March 1971.

* Hebrew acronym of the party's full name, "United Workers' Party."

† Hebrew acronym of the party's full name, "Party of the Workers of the Land of Israel."

By then there was hardly a trace left of the Po'alei Zion Smol group; most of them had become rather elderly by 1948, and in the meantime many died. In the Zionist movement outside Israel the old Borochovist guard has similarly disappeared and has not been replaced by a new generation.

The recent attempts to exhume Borochovism and revive interest in it therefore raise a *twofold* question: where does the new audience for Borochovism come from? And why are Zionist emissaries and functionaries so eager to "sell" to this new clientele an ideology that has long ago ceased to exist inside the Zionist movement itself?

It seems that the answer to the first part of the question lies in the fact that there is a rough analogy between the present political and intellectual atmosphere in the West, and that which existed at the place and time in which Borochovism originally came into being—Eastern Europe at the beginning of this century.

True, the general social and economic conditions that prevailed in Eastern Europe sixty years ago bear little similarity to the present socioeconomic reality in the West; and in particular the position of the Jews in the last period of the Russian empire was—as we shall try to show—very different from their position now anywhere in the world. The analogy that we want to draw is therefore confined mainly to the political and intellectual spheres.

It consists in this: in both cases we have a major upsurge of revolutionary socialist consciousness, mostly among the young. A state of excitement and turbulence, typical mainly of periods preceding great revolutions, spreads first of all among students and other young intellectuals; a new awareness of political questions; apathy and cynicism give way to feelings of involvement and urgency; formation of a host of circles and groups; heated debates; direct action. No alert and self-respecting young intellectual can remain indifferent to all this; he is drawn in and must take a stand, make a choice.

Also, in both cases, Jews are very prominent in this process. As an ethno-cultural minority group haunted by a collective memory of persecutions ancient and recent, they are especially sensitive to social questions. As a group with a high proportion of intellectuals, it is not surprising that they are very much in evidence in the revolutionary movement.

So a whole new generation of young Jews is becoming politicized in West Europe and the Americas, as another generation was politicized in the tsarist empire. And now, as then, when they come to make their choice they find themselves between two roads leading in opposite directions: socialism or Zionism. In practical terms, this is a choice between joining the revolutionary struggle where they are, or opting out of it in order to take part in the Zionist colonization of Palestine. In theoretical terms, the choice is between Marxism and a peculiar kind of nationalism.

For many the decision is a very difficult one. The attraction of socialism is counteracted by the weight of a petty-bourgeois class origin and a specifically alienated social psychology created by the circumstances of Jewish history. They try to

compromise: choose Zionism without turning completely away from socialism—
"socialist Zionism."

This compromise has had many variants, of which Borochovism was only one—
and, as we have seen, one which was in practice much less successful than others
and became a dead branch of the Zionist movement. But as an ideology there is
something special about Borochovism.

The other brands of "socialist Zionism" consisted simply in eclectically mixing
together these two heterogeneous ingredients. At most, some of them spoke about
a *synthesis* between Zionism and socialism, but by this they only emphasized the
fact that their theory is derived and composed from two completely different elements and premises.

Borochov, on the contrary, attempted to *deduce* Zionism from Marxism. He
claimed to start from a *purely* Marxist position and to arrive at Zionist conclusions
without making any extraneous additional assumptions.

This makes Borochovism as a theory much more attractive for a young person
who wants to be a Zionist but has already had a taste of Marxism. Because Marxism
is by its very nature a monist theory that does not mix well in a hotchpotch with
alien ingredients. In particular, a "synthesis" between Marxism and any kind of nationalism is quite unacceptable—and this is perhaps more true today than it was
in the beginning of the century, because in the meantime nationalism became more
completely discredited and is now out of fashion even in non-Marxist circles.

Socialists today—more than ever before—are unready to support nationalist
causes, unless this can be justified *without making any theoretical concessions* to nationalism but purely on *socialist* grounds, for example, wars of national liberation
against imperialism.

All this explains the new *demand* for Borochovist theory: it is the only existing
brand of Zionist ideology that suits the tastes of young Jews in the West who have
become politicized, radicalized, and exposed to present-day socialist currents and
the tradition of Marxist thought, but are still seeking a compromise between joining
the revolutionary struggle and opting out of it.

But we also have to say a few words about the *supply* of Borochovist literature
and propaganda. We would like to point out that the present purveyors of this ideology, the emissaries and functionaries of the Zionist machine, are not Borochovists;
they do not belong to a Borochovist party in Israel or to a Borochovist group in
the Zionist movement.

Such a party or group does not exist[2] and the professional Borochov wholesalers
and peddlers do not have the slightest intention of creating one. In fact, they do
not believe a word of the gospel they are preaching.

During 1968 the present author established close relations with a group of young
people who had just arrived in Israel from several Latin American countries. They
were experiencing a very painful disillusionment at finding Israeli realities so different
from the image that had been painted for them by the Israeli emissaries in their

countries of origin. One of the things that bewildered them was that they could find in Israel hardly a trace of the Borochovism that had been fed to them in Latin America. One day a member of that group happened to meet in Jerusalem the emissary who had indoctrinated him with Borochovism. (That emissary had in the meantime finished his stint in Latin America and was transferred back to Israel.) In the course of their conversation, my friend—who was delighted to find at last a true Borochovist with whom he could have an interesting discussion—eagerly raised the subject. "Oh, Borochov," responded the emissary, "he was just a third-rate sociologist whom we merely use in Latin America to attract the Jewish youth away from Castroism!" To which my friend could only reply sadly: "And I was one of them. . . ."

The Zionist propaganda machine is prepared to use all sorts of methods in order to attract the Jewish youth in the West away from Castroism, Trotskyism, and various other harmful ideas and movements. And if one of the ways is to indoctrinate young people with a doctrine in which the propagandists themselves do not believe, the latter console themselves that this is only a temporary measure, because "when they (i.e., the young Jews) come to us, we shall regain the initiative."[3]

◆ ◆ ◆

The purpose of this article is to examine two questions concerning Borochovist Zionism.

1. In what respects does it differ from other brands of "socialist Zionism," which, unlike it, did not die out but became dominant?
2. How far do the implicit and explicit assumptions that Borochov made regarding social facts and dynamics (especially in Jewish society, but also in the world as a whole) correspond to present-day reality?

However, we shall not attempt a thorough discussion of how far Borochovism fitted the realities of the beginning of the [twentieth] century.

We do not aim to convince those who use Borochovism merely as an excuse. We are addressing only those who have come to Borochovism in the course of a *genuine* search for solutions to problems that trouble their minds, and who are therefore prepared to think critically and non-dogmatically even about the *present* position into which their search has so far carried them. The present author does not feel entitled to sneer or laugh at such people; he too, in his own struggle to liberate himself from Zionist ideology, passed first through a Borochovist phase.

◆ ◆ ◆

All page numbers cited below refer to the Hebrew edition of Borochov's works, published by Hakibbutz Hame'uchad and Siffriath Po'alim in Israel in 1955. We use the following abbreviations of the titles of Borochov's works:

ZT—*On the Question of Zion and a Territory* (originally published in Russian in 1905)

PL—*Our Platform* (originally published in Russian in 1906)

RP—*The Role of the Proletariat in the Realization of Territorialism* (originally published in Yiddish as a sequel to PL, 1907)

Basic Premises

According to Borochov, the Jews all over the world constitute a nation. In his article "The Class Struggle and the National Question," in which he discusses the national question *in general*, he defines *nation* as "a social group that has developed on the basis of common conditions of production and . . . which is, moreover, united by a consciousness of affinity based on a common historical past." Although we think this general definition is not satisfactory, and the claim that the Jews constitute a nation is false, we do not propose to argue this point here. What interests us here is neither the terminology nor the general concept *as such* but the *factual* and *concrete* assumptions that Borochov makes concerning the Jewish people.[4] Let us therefore return to his own line of argument.

"The most general condition of production, which is also the receptacle and basis for all the internal conditions as well as the channel of external influences" is the national territory (PL, p. 193). The national territory is therefore "the *positive* foundation" upon which a nation leads a national life of its own (ibid.).

The Jews, lacking this positive foundation, are (according to Borochov) an *anomalous, extraterritorial* nation. Their national existence is determined by a purely *negative* factor. Living in a foreign national environment of another normal nation, they tend to adapt to it and to assume the character of the surrounding society; but this tendency is checked and counteracted by the economic competition that exists between the Jews and the host nation.

Because "national competition is always about the material possession of nations," mainly about territory, and the Jews have no territory, they are always defeated in the national competition (PL, p. 195). This tends to separate and isolate them from the host nation. First they are pushed into economic sectors that have not yet been occupied by the host nation—generally speaking these are not the primary sectors (agriculture, production of means of production) but the secondary sectors (the final stages of production, commerce). This is *incomplete* isolation. Then the host nation enters into competition with the Jews even in the sectors that the latter were earlier allowed to occupy. The Jews then become *totally* isolated (PL, p. 197).

Up to this point, Borochov has not told us anything original. A similar analysis was expounded not only by other "socialist Zionists" but also by bourgeois Zionists, including Herzl.

Without going into the question as to how far this analysis corresponds to the facts of Jewish history *in general*, we can say that on the whole it seems to give a plausible (although perhaps inaccurate) picture of the position of the Jews *at the time and place* at which Borochov was writing.

But if we compare that analysis to the condition of the Jews *today* (especially in countries where Borochovist ideas are at present actively disseminated—United States, Latin America, Germany, France, England, etc.), then Borochov's analysis is much less plausible. While it is quite true that Jews do concentrate in certain sectors of the economy (although not to the same extent as in Russia at the beginning of the twentieth century), they are not on the whole *isolated* or *separated* from the host nations by an economic competition. Of course, capitalist competition does exist, but it is not usually a "national" competition between members of the host nation on the one hand and Jews on the other, in which, moreover, the latter as a group are the constant losers.

The Jews in tsarist Russia were confined—by law—to a certain area, the Pale; the proportion of Jewish students in universities was limited by *numerous clausus* laws; they were not allowed to enter various occupations and professions, and so on. As a result, the Jewish masses, who were losing their traditional economic role, were being to some extent isolated from society, pushed out of it and forced to emigrate.

No such process exists in, say, the United States (where the Jewish community is the largest in the world). The forces of integration are certainly stronger than those of isolation.

Of course, one can *claim* that this process of integration will one day be reversed, but this is no more than a mere claim so long as one does not point at a plausible socioeconomic cause for such a reversal. However, the causes that operated in tsarist Russia are completely lacking in the United States. In Russia, the Jews at first fulfilled certain economic functions (in some crafts and in commerce) that Russian society required but could not itself fulfill because it was still feudal or semifeudal. In such a society there is a "natural" place for relative strangers who perform tasks that are useful to society but do not form an organic part of it. Later, when capitalism developed in Russia, the traditional occupations of the Jews either became unnecessary or were taken over by non-Jews. Moreover, in Russia—as Borochov himself states—the upper echelon of the Jewish bourgeoisie was hardly affected by that process and adapted rather well to the new conditions. The true victims were the great mass of petty middlemen and craftsmen, the poorer sections of the lower middle class. But in what way is all this relevant to any big Jewish community today? In no way at all. *All these communities either do not live in precapitalist countries or do not have a social composition that would make them particularly vulnerable to capitalist development.*

We want to make it clear that we are not claiming here that a Jewish problem no longer exists. But this is not the question we are discussing. The question is to what extent Borochov's analysis of that problem reflects the realities of Jewish life today. And our conclusion is that the relevance of that part of his analysis that we have followed so far is extremely doubtful.

But let us follow his analysis still further.

The Jewish Proletariat

One of the central points in which Borochovism differs from other brands of "socialist Zionism" is that it claims to deduce Zionism not from the dynamics and interests of the Jewish people "in general," or even from those of the Jewish lower middle classes, but, very specifically, *from the interests of the Jewish proletariat.* From Borochov's point of view, it was *not correct* to talk of a Jewish problem in a general way, without making any class distinction. And it was not enough to show that the spontaneous dynamics and real interest of the largest Jewish class of his time (i.e., the lower middle class) lead to Zionism. In PL (p. 264) he writes: "The anomalies of the Jewish people *as a whole* interest us only as an objective explanation for the causes of contradictions in the life of the working class; but *the subjective argumentation of our program follows only from the class interests of the militant Jewish proletariat.*" And even more specifically (p. 240):

> If it were found that in fact the interests of the Jewish bourgeoisie and of the masses that are about to become proletarianized [i.e., the lower middle class] lead them to territorialism [i.e., to a territorial solution of the Jewish question] but that the interests of the Jewish proletariat are not connected with territorialism—then there would not be any grounds for saying that the future of the whole Jewish people is also the future of the Jewish proletariat. One should not take as a *starting point* the general national future and deduce the future of the proletariat from it. On the contrary, one should take as a starting point the interests of the proletariat, and from this arrive at the future of the whole nation. . . . From the starting point of the interests of the militant Jewish proletariat and from our view of it as the *vanguard* of the Jewish future, we *deduce* territorialism for the whole of the Jewish people.

It must be stressed that when Borochov claimed that his Zionism expresses the objective movement and interests of the Jewish working class, he was not speaking about a *potential future class* but about a class in *actual existence.* He makes this absolutely clear not only in the remarks quoted above but over and over again, in many places. In particular, the beginning of the fifth chapter of PL consists of a sharp and detailed polemic against rival left-Zionist theories precisely on this point.

This occupies such a central position in Borochovist theory that without it the theory loses even its *formal* claim to be regarded as proletarian Zionism, and becomes "*ordinary*" (i.e., "classless" or *bourgeois*) Zionism.

Po'alei Zion Smol was the only Zionist group to hold this view with any degree of consistency. All other Zionist groups and parties—including other factions of Po'alei Zion, and all the parties and factions that at present exist as organized forces in the Zionist movement—reject this central Borochovist idea. They present Zionism as a Jewish national movement without any particular reference to class, or justify Zionism as necessary for *creating* a Jewish proletariat—a justification that Borochov did *not* accept. This is one of the reasons why all these parties and factions cannot be regarded as Borochovist; and the claims to the contrary that are made from time to time are based on theoretical confusion or intellectual dishonesty or both.

It is not difficult to understand why Borochov *had* to insist so much on the proletarian nature of his approach and make it a central pillar of his theoretical edifice.
As mentioned in our preface, the real choice for him, and for all politically conscious
young Jews of his generation in Russia, was between the Russian revolutionary movement and Zionism. To choose the Russian revolutionary movement meant working
for the interest of the Russian *and international* working class, for its emancipation,
which would bring about the emancipation of the whole of mankind. But what did
Zionism mean? If it meant working for the interest of a "Jewish nation" in general,
without any reference to class, or for the interest of the Jewish middle classes—then
anyone who had been seriously influenced by internationalist-socialist ideas would
have to reject Zionism as an illegitimate diversion. If he wanted to be a Zionist, he
had to legitimize and rationalize Zionism as an expression of the interests of the Jewish proletariat; and then he could tell himself that, after all, struggling for the Jewish
proletariat is not less important than struggling for the Russian proletariat, and for
a Jewish revolutionary his own working class should naturally come first.

Let us now see how Borochov develops his analysis of the specific conditions
and interests of the Jewish working class.

To begin with he points out that "national competition" tends to isolate the
Jewish worker and to restrict his field of employment. "Because of national competition among the masses that are becoming proletarianized and are seeking employment, Jewish labor is employed only by middle Jewish capital; the
anti-Semitism of the non-Jewish employers and non-Jewish workers does not allow
Jewish labor to penetrate into workshops owned by non-Jews" (PL, p. 202). The
Jewish worker, he observes, suffers from certain handicaps in this competition, such
as his weaker physique and higher demands (compared to peasants who come to
the towns to seek work), his lack of technical skills, and his observance of Saturday
as a day of rest. "But all these special and internal characteristics are significant
merely as marginal or temporary factors, while the most important and constant
factor is the national competition. The latter operates also when the Jewish masses
that are being proletarianized migrate to other countries, the countries of big capital,
in search of employment" (ibid.).

The effect of all this is not merely a *quantitative* restriction of employment.

> Since almost the whole of Jewish capital is invested in production of consumer
> goods, in which labor is always more or less seasonal, which is dominated by hand-
> icraft with its high rate of exploitation, without mechanized production, in which
> the functions of the producer differ little from those of the tradesman-middleman,
> and in which piecework is more usual than time work—it is easy to see that quali-
> tatively too, Jewish proletarianization is on a level lower than required. The exclusion
> of Jewish toilers from heavy industry and from machines is so widespread and con-
> spicuous that the Christian workers have adopted the view that operating a machine
> is their own special prerogative and privilege, and they systematically forbid Jews to
> operate machines even when the machine replaces handicraft in a branch of pro-
> duction where Jews are employed (PL, p. 203).

Thus the employment of Jewish labor is numerically restricted, confined to branches where Jewish capital is invested—that is, to nonbasic branches of industry—and even within these branches it is confined to nonbasic jobs. This restriction and isolation has an organizational consequence: "The Jewish proletariat spontaneously organizes itself during the process of development of capitalist economy; and in doing so it unites separately from the workers of other nations, in special national organizations. The reason for the special organization of the Jewish working class is the fact that its national existence is economically special, isolated. Since the economic isolation of Jewish life is growing, there is also a growing need for a special political organization" (RP, p. 324).

On the other hand, because of the branches and jobs to which Jewish labor is confined, the Jewish proletariat does not have a proper "strategic base" in its economic and political struggle against capital.

> The economic struggle of the Jewish worker is most successful in the busy season, when the employers have to make concessions in order not to waste time. But the employers regain in the slack season what they had lost, and by next season the fruits of the economic struggle vanish, and the Jewish worker is compelled to engage in the very same struggle to regain the same unstable results as before. But the strategic base of the Jewish proletariat is even less satisfactory from the political point of view. Since the Jewish proletariat is almost entirely employed in producing consumer goods, and is not active in any primary stage of the economic processes, it does not hold any lifelines of the economy of the country where it lives; hence its influence on the general trend of life is necessarily quite restricted. It cannot paralyze at once the whole economic machine, as can the railway workers and other workers whose conditions are more favorable. It is exploited not by big capital but only by middle capital, whose own role in production is also small. While the Jewish proletariat can paralyze by militant struggle that capital that it produces, it cannot shake the country to any considerable extent. Even in its most just demands it is powerless to defend itself if other, more fortunate, workers of the surrounding people do not support it. It cannot achieve even the slightest improvement when this concerns its special national needs that are not shared by others. (PL, pp. 219–20).

In a later article ("The Economic Development of the Jewish People," 1911) Borochov elaborates this point further. "The dry, numerical data imply that the Jews are separated just from the most important and influential branches of production, from the branches that are the hub of the wheel of history. . . . These numbers mean that Jewish socialism, Jewish class struggle, Jewish revolution will also play an insignificant role in socialism, class struggle, and revolution of the surrounding peoples, just as the Jewish needle, the Jewish flat iron, are insignificant compared to the non-Jewish plough, non-Jewish steam engine and shipping company."

From this Borochov deduces that a territorial solution to the Jewish problem is in the interests of the Jewish proletariat:

> All these national anomalies will disappear only after the conditions of production of Jewish life will undergo a fundamental change, after the Jewish people will no

longer be extraterritorial. When the Jews will be employed in the primary, most important branches of production, when the Jews will produce not only consumer goods but also means of production—then the Jewish proletariat will hold the lifelines of the country's economy . . . then the class struggle of the Jewish proletariat will be directed not against an impotent bourgeoisie in the Jewish economy, as it is today, but against a strong bourgeoisie that organizes production in a whole country: then the class struggle of the Jewish worker will achieve the necessary political, economic and social impact" (PL, p. 264).

It is not our purpose here to make a theoretical assessment of Borochov's *general* conceptions of the class struggle and of the national problem. We merely want to point out, in passing, that the idea that the Jewish proletariat in prerevolutionary Russia needed an independent "strategic base" for "its own" class struggle was quite wrong and harmful.

The proletarian class struggle *begins* as a confrontation between the worker and "his own" capitalist, his direct employer; it is *at first* conducted in relative isolation within a given industry, given branch, given locality, and (in a multinational country) given national or ethnic group. But the struggle assumes its true social and political significance only by overcoming these backward and narrow limitations. The task of a revolutionary working-class movement is therefore not to take the isolated struggles separately and look for a separate "strategic base" for each separate struggle, but on the contrary—to coordinate and *unite* them all on the basis of the *whole* country (and then in the international arena).

The answer given by Borochov to the question of the "Jewish strategic base" was wrong, because *the question itself* was posed in a narrow, nationalistic—and therefore wrong—manner.

The struggle of the Jewish workers *began* in the ghetto, in the Pale, *within* the Jewish community. In this struggle the strategic position of the Jewish workers was certainly quite weak, *so long* as it remained isolated.

Borochov *assumed* that the struggle must *remain* isolated, must remain a confrontation between Jewish worker and Jewish employer. And this assumption is embodied *in advance* in the way he posed the problem: the problem of finding a *separate* "strategic base" for the Jewish proletariat.

In fact, what the Jewish workers needed was not a separate "strategic base" but a *common struggle* together with *all* the workers in the country.

While true internationalist revolutionaries were busy building a united workers' movement that would transcend all backward divisions between branches, regions, and ethnic groups, Borochov was engaged in searching across the seas for a "strategic base" for the Jewish proletariat, for a place where it could fight against a strong *Jewish* bourgeoisie.

Borochov wrote that Jewish socialism and revolution could not—so long as the Jews were not concentrated in a country of their own—play a significant role in the socialism and revolution of the peoples among whom they lived. But only six years later, Russia was swept by a great revolution in which Jews such as Trotsky played an important role—precisely *because* they were not looking for a Jewish national socialism on a Jewish national "strategic base." And what was Borochov's own contribution to the history of world socialism and revolution? A truly insignificant, but negative, quantity. There is a lesson here that young Jewish socialists in Paris, London, Frankfurt, New York, Cordoba, and Montevideo should not ignore.

(To those who would point out that Jewish revolutionaries suffered a tragic fate when the Russian Revolution degenerated, we reply: The lesson to be learned from this is not that Jews should have nothing to do with "other peoples'" revolutions, but that they, together with all other revolutionaries, should guard the revolution against degeneration.)

Borochov's "proletarian Zionism" came to wrong and harmful theoretical conclusions. But many of the *factual* assumptions that he made were not imaginary; they were somehow based on an existing reality. The Jews were relatively isolated and they were being squeezed out of their traditional economic role. The Jewish masses were becoming proletarianized. Jewish workers did find it difficult to get employment in non-Jewish enterprises. Their first experiences of the class struggle were within the Jewish community, in confrontations with the mid-level Jewish bourgeoisie. They formed a relatively coherent and geographically concentrated social group. The term "Jewish proletariat" was therefore not empty; it denoted a definite, and to some extent distinct, social group. It was meaningful to talk of the class interest of the Jewish proletariat.

But let us now come to the *present*. What possible meaning can "proletarian Zionism" have in relation to the Jewish communities that now exist in Europe and the Americas?

As we saw, the whole point about Borochovism was its claim to express the class interests of the Jewish proletariat. But *a Jewish proletariat does not exist anywhere* (except, of course, in Israel—but this is irrelevant, because we are talking not about Israel, but about the Jewish "Diaspora"). We are not saying that there are no Jewish workers. There *are* Jewish workers (and although their proportion among the Jewish people is rather small, this is not important in the present context). What we are saying is that there is no Jewish proletariat *as a coherent social group*. The factors that tended to segregate the Jewish workers in prerevolutionary Russia and to form them into a relatively distinct social group do not now operate anywhere. A Jewish worker in Britain is—as a worker—a member of the working class in general, not of any "Jewish" class.

To talk about the class interests and needs of the "Jewish working class" is not merely wrong. It is completely meaningless.

But then we must conclude that Borochov's "proletarian Zionism" is today not merely wrong, but a meaningless, absurd, and irrelevant anachronistic fiction. This is perhaps the main reason why Borochovism became a dead branch in the Zionist movement: the social group on which it based itself and which it claimed to represent had ceased to exist.

Borochovism and Reality

There was another reason that led to the extinction of Borochovism as a tendency within Zionism. Borochov died at the end of 1917, just before Zionism began to colonize Palestine on a big scale. But during the actual process of colonization, many arguments and forecasts on which Borochov had repeatedly insisted turned out to be false. This, of course, weakened the position of his faithful followers. Since a detailed account of Borochov's prognosis and its divergence from reality would take us far too long, we confine ourselves to listing just a few points and making short comments.

1. Borochov claimed (see e.g., PL, chap. 2) that the petty-bourgeois Jewish masses that immigrated into the advanced capitalist countries (e.g., the United States) would soon become impoverished and proletarianized. A new Jewish proletariat would emerge in those countries, and it would be subject to the same process of national competition and isolation as in Russia. The Jewish masses in the advanced capitalist countries would therefore gravitate to "proletarian Zionism" and migrate to Palestine.

   In reality this did not take place. The Jewish immigrants in the advanced countries were not pauperized and proletarianized but, on the contrary, managed on the whole to improve their economic and social position.

2. Borochov insisted (see RP, p. 323) that there was no need to make propaganda among the Jewish workers to go to Palestine. He repeated many times that Jewish middle capital would gravitate to Palestine in a spontaneous way, and the Jewish workers would follow it—also in a purely spontaneous way.

   In fact, Jewish capital did go to Palestine (although not quite as spontaneously as he supposed), but the Jewish workers did not follow it. Among those who went to Palestine there were very few workers indeed. (Many people *became* workers in Palestine—but this is not the same thing.)

3. For Borochov, one of the main virtues of Palestine was that it was under Turkish rule. He repeatedly and emphatically rejected the idea of Jewish colonization in any country ruled by an advanced capitalist power. In particular, he bitterly opposed the idea of colonizing Palestine (or any other country) under a charter granted by an advanced capitalist power. (These matters are discussed in great detail in chapter 9 of ZT and, more briefly, also in chapter 9 of PL.)

   In practice, Zionist colonization started on a big scale only when Palestine came under British rule. And the only way in which such a colonization could ever be realized was precisely the way in which it *was* in fact realized: under British imperialist sponsorship, granted in a charter. (The Balfour declaration was issued a few days before Borochov died.)

4. In Borochov's view (see chapter 9 of ZT and especially chapter 8 of PL) the Palestinian Arabs (he does not call them "Arabs" but simply "natives of Palestine") lack any national culture of their own and do not have any other national characteristic. "They easily and quickly adopt any imported cultural character higher than their own; they cannot unite for an organized resistance against external influences, they are not capable of national competition"(PL, p. 282). He therefore deduced with great certainty and repeated several times that "the natives of Palestine will assimilate economically and culturally into whoever brings order into the country, into whoever undertakes the development of the forces of production of Palestine" (ibid.). As for the Arab national movement, Borochov was confident that "it does not have and cannot have any relation to Palestine" (PL 90, footnote).

Well, well, well . . .

Conclusion

We do not think there is a serious danger that Borochovism will become an important trend, with more than transient influence on young Jewish socialists in Europe and the Americas.

A person who has been convinced by Marxism but is still emotionally unready to dissociate himself from Zionism may first be attracted by this strange attempt to deduce the latter from the former. The very existence of such an attempt pleases him so much, that at first he is not aware that the deduction is not only based on a rather narrow and backward kind of "Marxism" but also relies on many "empirical" assumptions that have absolutely no connection with existing reality.

Later he will realize that this is just a compromise, and a compromise that cannot work. He will then have to make up his mind: socialism or Zionism, this time without compromise. If his socialist conviction is strong enough, he will dissociate himself completely from Zionism.

We hope that the present pamphlet will help to make this process a little less painful.

23

Reply to Sol Stern

srael seems to do all sorts of strange things to many Jewish-American intellectuals. Alex Portnoy is not the only one, but in the case of others it is their critical faculty that is unstiffened by the Holy Land. And so it happens that nice compassionate Jewish radicals, who react quite normally to any other colonial situation, suddenly sink into sweet self-pity when Israel is concerned. They simply refuse to believe that Jews can—like anybody else—play the role of baddies and aggressors; in their collective consciousness, tortured by the search for self-identity and haunted by memories of persecutions ancient and recent, the role of baddies is reserved exclusively for the Goyim.

This is a response to a "left" Zionist article by Sol Stern in August 1971 in the journal *Ramparts*. My response was published in January 1973, in bulletin no. 5 of *ISRACA* (Israeli Revolutionary Action Committee Abroad). I have changed little in that 1973 piece, except for minor stylistic corrections, adding some subheadings and deleting a couple of digressive paragraphs, in which I rebutted Sol Stern's slurs on my political group, the Socialist Organization in Israel (Matzpen).

Of course, the world has changed greatly since 1973. But, as the reader will discover, the essential nature of Israel and its conflict with the Palestinian people and the Arab world have remained unchanged. Some significant political changes have occurred on both the Palestinian and the Israeli side.

The PLO, dominated by Fatah, allowed itself to be trapped into capitulation at Oslo. Following this, it was systematically undermined and finally trashed by Israel—to be replaced as the leading Palestinian tendency by the Islamist organization Hamas.

In Israel, the long dominance of "labor" Zionism came to an end in 1977. Almost all Israeli prime ministers since then—Begin, Shamir, Netanyahu, Sharon, and Olmert—belong to the "fascistoid" Zionist tendency discussed toward the end of this reply. Shamir was a disciple and close associate of Abraham Stern, whose chilling racist program I quote. Meanwhile, the Israeli "Labor" Party has willingly colluded with this dominant tendency.

A Settler State

Incredible—but nevertheless true; in his long, rambling apology for "left-wing" Zionism ("My Jewish Problem—and Ours," *Ramparts*, August 1971) Sol Stern evades the central theoretical issue, without which one is inevitably left wading in shallow sloppy value judgments. He never tries to define and analyze the precise nature of the Zionist-Arab conflict. Most of the time his thesis on this cardinal question remains a concealed assumption, which only peeps out when he condemns the left for not "seeing the Palestine-Israel struggle as a tragic and destructive struggle between two nations fighting over the same turf, a collision that requires healing by compromise and mutual recognition."

Now, if someone were to hint that the battles between settlers and Native Americans in American history were just a case of nations "fighting over the same turf," or that what is happening in southern Africa (and, for that matter, in America) is merely a "tragic collision" between two races—then Sol Stern would probably be one of the first to dismiss such definitions with disgust as hypocritical cant. Why? Because those formulas try to dress up in symmetric language issues that are strongly asymmetric. They gloss over the question, who is the colonizer, the oppressor, and who is—in the given historical situation—the victim.

One must stress "in the given historical situation," for the fact that in other situations Jews were the victim must not be allowed to obscure our realization that in the Middle East their role has been reversed. Political Zionism is not just another "national movement." It is a colonizing project, intrinsically directed against the indigenous population (primarily and most directly against the Palestinian Arabs, but also against the whole of the Arab nation); inherently and necessarily aligned with world imperialism. The State of Israel in its present—Zionist—form is by its very nature a *settler state*: exclusivist, expansionist, and discriminatory.

"Continual Warfare"

Before *colonization* came to be regarded as a dirty word, the Zionist movement unabashedly used it to describe its own aims. Later, it preferred to use Hebrew equivalents: *hityashvut* or *hitnahalut*, but the meaning is precisely the same.

The major premise of political Zionism is that anti-Semitism and anti-Jewish persecution are inevitable so long as the Jews constitute minority groups among the Gentiles. No amount of social progress would solve the conflict between the majority and (ethnic, racial, or religious) minorities, which Zionism regards as *inherent in human nature*. The only solution for the Jewish problem is then to concentrate all, or at least most, of the Jews in a nation-state of their own, where they would be the dominant majority. Since there did not exist a country where the Jews already constituted a majority, the only way to create it would be by *colonizing* some country. For emotional and religious reasons the choice fell on Palestine. (But not without internal struggle; Herzl, the founder of political Zionism, strongly believed that East Africa was more suitable.* It is interesting to speculate what form the Zionist–Mau-Mau conflict would have taken had Herzl had his way.)

But Palestine was not empty. In 1891 Ahad-Ha'am (a prominent Jewish thinker, who believed in creating a Jewish *spiritual* center in Palestine, but opposed *political* Zionism) reports after his voyage to Palestine:

> We, abroad, are used to believing that Eretz Yisrael is now almost entirely desolate, an uncultivated desert, and whosoever wants to buy land there can come and do so at will. But this is not so. In the whole country it is difficult to find arable land that is not already cultivated . . .
>
> We, abroad, are used to believing that the Arabs are all savages of the desert, people that are like unto asses, and that they do not see or understand what is happening around them. But this is a big mistake . . . The Arabs, especially the town dwellers, see and understand what we are doing and what we are aiming at in that country, but they do not regard what we are doing as dangerous for their future. . . . But if the time comes when the life of our people in Palestine will develop so much that they will displace, to a lesser or greater extent, the indigenous people, then the latter will not give way easily . . . (*Collected Works*, Hebrew, 1947, pp. 23–24)

Prophetic words.

By 1895 Herzl had it all worked out. On June 12 he writes in his diary: "The poorer section of the (indigenous) population we shall try to transfer across the border, without raising a fuss, by giving them employment in the transit countries, but in our own country we shall deny them all work." (*The Diaries of Theordore Herzl*, Hebrew edition, p. 86)

He then goes on to describe how lands would be acquired through secret agents from the local landowners, but once a piece of land had been acquired by the Jewish settlers it would never, never be sold back to a native. Herzl was even very worried about his own dignity as a white colonizer. An entry of the same day (June 12, 1895) contains a reminder to prepare a "special helmet, like Stanley" for the inauguration ceremony of the colonization process.

Needless to say, when Zionist colonization really got under way, all these directives about not giving jobs to the natives, about acquiring land from the landowners by means fair or foul, about prohibiting resale of land to Arabs—all these became official rules of the Zionist movement, and were fanatically enforced. Only the white colonial helmet à la Stanley was missing; by that time it had gone out of fashion. The actual *halutzim* (pioneers) came dressed in embroidered Russian peasant-style shirts.

It isn't as if the Zionists were evil, wicked people. Many of them were sincerely worried about the obvious moral issue involved. But the logic of the situation was

---

* The colonization plan presented by Herzl to the Sixth Zionist Congress in 1903 is misleadingly known as the "Uganda Plan." In fact, the territory offered to Herzl by Britain's colonial secretary Joseph Chamberlain was in present-day Kenya.

inexorable: if you want to colonize Palestine and transform it into a Jewish nation-state, with a predominant Jewish majority, then the indigenous people will simply have to go. (This is what Stern chooses to euphemize as "two nations fighting over the same turf.")

Among the nicest Zionists who were worried about all this was Dr. Arthur Ruppin, one of the architects of the Zionist venture, who was in charge of Zionist colonization during the 1920s and 1930s. He really tried to face the issue, and not just gloss it over in the manner of latter-day apologists. But by 1928, "it became clear how difficult it is to realize Zionism and still bring it continually into line with the demands of general ethics." And in 1936 he had to admit that it was not only "difficult" but simply impossible: "On every site where we purchase land and where we settle people, the present cultivators will inevitably be dispossessed."

And he concluded: "The Arabs do not agree to our venture. If we want to continue our work in Eretz Yisrael against their desires, there is no alternative but that lives should be lost. It is our destiny to be in a state of continual warfare with the Arabs. This situation may well be undesirable, but such is the reality." (For the quotations from Ruppin, see *The Jerusalem Post Weekly*, September 30, 1968.)

Ethnic Cleansing

Ruppin saw clearly that there could be no compromise between Zionist colonization and its victims. The choice—then, as now—was between Zionism and "general ethics." Being an ardent Zionist, he chose Zionism and the "continual warfare" that it implied and still implies. Every decent Zionist—from Ruppin to the members of the Siah group who like to regard themselves as oh-so revolutionary—is sooner or later impaled on the horns of the same dilemma and becomes anti-Zionist or a cynic.

Some Zionists of course *start off* being cynics. No moral self-torment for them. Ruppin's successor as the man in charge of Zionist colonization, Joseph Weitz, reports (in the official Histadrut daily *Davar*, September 29, 1967) that in 1940 he and other Zionist leaders (including Ber Katzenelson, who was Ben-Gurion's predecessor as leader of the main Zionist "workers' party" and of the Zionist settlers' community as a whole) had come to the conclusion that

> [A]mong ourselves it should be clear that in this country there is no room for both peoples together. . . . With the Arabs we shall not achieve our aim to be an independent nation in this small country. . . . The only solution is Palestine, or at least Western Palestine [i.e., the territory west of the river Jordan], without Arabs . . . and there is no other way but to transfer all the Arabs from here to the neighboring countries. To transfer all of them; not one village, not one tribe should be left behind. . . . For this purpose money, plenty of money, can be found. And only after such transfer will the country be able to absorb millions of our brethren.

At that time (1940) the Arabs still constituted the overwhelming majority (over two-thirds) of the population of western Palestine. This is the Zionist concept of self-determination. But as Sol Stern rightly remarks, "If the Jews had been willing to accept minority status, there could have been a settlement with the Arabs 30 years ago. But then what was the point of going to Palestine in the first place?" What indeed! However, let us return to Weitz's reminiscences:

> Years later, when the UN resolved to partition Palestine into two states the War of Independence [of 1948–49] broke out, to our great good fortune [*sic*] and in it there came to pass a double miracle: a territorial victory and the flight of the Arabs. In the Six-Day War [of 1967] there came to pass one great miracle, a tremendous territorial victory, but the majority of the inhabitants of the liberated [*sic*] territories remained "stuck" to their places—a fact that may undermine the very foundation of our state.

Mind you, Comrade Weitz is not a member of some lunatic fascist fringe but a venerated "left" Zionist.

And General Moshe Dayan (that half-blind who is leading the blind) summed it all up as follows: "During the last hundred years our people have been undergoing a process of building up the country and the nation, of expansion, of getting more Jews and settlements and of colonization [*hitnahalut*] in order to expand the borders here. Let there be no Jew who says that this is the end of the process. Let there be no Jew who says that we are near the end of the road" (quoted by the Israeli evening paper *Ma'ariv*, July 7, 1968).

Ominous words, especially when uttered in a mass youth rally on the "liberated" Syrian Golan Heights. But let there be no mistake about it: this is the only kind of Zionism there is. There has never been and there cannot be any other kind. What we have plenty of, though, is self-pitying hypocrisy that tries to plaster over the ugly facts with talk about "tragic collision," by talking about a war of colonization as if it was a "civil war" for which "the Arabs at least bear a share of the responsibility."

There can be no "compromise and mutual recognition" that does not presuppose a *total* rejection of Zionism. Zionism must be overthrown because it is an absolute negation of self-determination. The only kind of "self-determination" consistent with Zionism is that according to which the Zionists, all by themselves, determine the fate of the Palestinian Arabs. Even those "left-wing" Zionists who in 1946 proposed a "binational" solution were careful to include the proviso that there would first have to be a period of twenty-five years of "international trusteeship" over Palestine, during which time Jewish immigration would be encouraged so that the Jews would become the absolute majority. Then, the preservation of the Jews as the majority would be built into the constitution of the "binational" state. If this seems an odd sort of binationalism, we only have to remember Sol Stern's comment that otherwise "what was the point of coming to Palestine in the first place?" At which unanswerable rhetorical question the Arabs presumably have to shut up and be happy with whatever Zionism is pleased to offer them.

It is by no means an accident that Israel is governed by the principle of Jewish supremacy. It is no accident that any Jew—no matter where he is, or where he was born—is automatically entitled to Israeli citizenship, which is denied to most Arabs who were born there and whose fathers and forefathers had lived there for generations. It is not (as Sol Stern seems to suppose) just the stupidity of Israeli bureaucrats that is responsible for the project according to which Arabs are to be brutally evicted from parts of Jerusalem to make room for architectural monstrosities where Jews are to be housed. It is not just the wickedness of this or that Israeli government that is responsible for the oppression of the Israeli Arabs during the twenty-three years of Israel's existence and for the cynical methods of legal robbery by which most of their lands were taken away from them and given to Jews (including, of course, the oh-so-socialist kibbutzim). Israel's refusal during twenty years to repatriate "substantial numbers of refugees" is not (as Sol Stern would have us think) just "one of the most serious blights on Israel's record." From the viewpoint of Zionism all these things are inevitable and absolutely necessary.

The Zionist state was never meant to belong to its inhabitants whoever they may be. Zionism did not base its claim over Palestine on the right of self-determination—and it could hardly do so, because during most of the period when it was colonizing the country the Arabs were the majority. Its claim is based on the Divine Right of the whole of the Jewish people over the Promised Land to which they should eventually immigrate. This, from the Zionist standpoint, is necessary in order to solve the Jewish problem of Sol Stern and others. As for the Arabs, they may at best be tolerated, and even then only in small numbers. Otherwise, who knows if they might not one day become the majority—the Zionists are terrified by the Arabs' relatively high rate of natural population growth—and then "what was the point of coming to Palestine in the first place?"

To justify the State of Israel in its present (Zionist) form in terms of self-determination is a cynical mockery. The only context in which self-determination for the Hebrew-speaking nation makes any sense is that of a socialist revolutionary Mashreq—which presupposes the overthrow of Zionism as well as that of Arab reaction.

Now, it is quite true that the biggest Palestinian guerrilla organization, Fatah, does not accept the idea of Hebrew self-determination even in that context. Much worse, the Palestinian movement is dominated not by socialists but by lower-middle-class nationalists. True, their propaganda is often very crude and sometimes chauvinistic. Sol Stern goes at length into all this. But before we let ourselves be hoodwinked by this way of justifying Zionism, let us pause to realize that we are in effect asked to take the inadequacies of the victim as an excuse for his oppressor. The most misguided dispossessed Palestinian Arab is many times better than a nice progressive and cultured colonizer who merely defends his Divine Right to maintain his "socialist" settlers' state.

We in Matzpen have often criticized the political positions of the leadership of the Palestinian movement. We believe we have won the right to do so by our total and uncompromising opposition to Zionism, by being internationalist socialists.

In return for which we get—and expect nothing better—repressions from the Israeli authorities (directed particularly against our Arab members) and supercilious derision from the likes of Sol Stern.

"A New Attachment: America-Zion"

When you colonize a country, the indigenous people may not like this at all (they usually don't, though Sol Stern may think it terribly mean of them). Even if you try to show them that the Bible says the country was actually promised to you by God, you will probably not get very far; for one thing, they are likely to be illiterate, or to believe in a different religion, or both. Eventually, they will turn nasty—ignorant savages that they are—and even use violence against you. Your obviously superior moral stature is not enough; you need some real force as well. If you are an Englishman or a Frenchman, for instance, then you don't have much to worry about, because the Old Country will naturally send a few gunboats to defend you against the vicious attacks of those bloody-minded savages. But if you yourself are a member of a hitherto persecuted race—a Black or a Jew say—then you are in a fix. The only way for you to be a colonizer is to become a subcontractor to one of the Big Boys. You make a deal with a Big Power; you get a charter entitling you to colonize the place under the Big Power's protection, and in return promise to help maintain order in that part of the world. Marcus Garvey tried to do it on behalf of the American Blacks, but failed to get a commission from the Big Boys—they didn't like his black face and suspected that instead of keeping the African natives down he might actually have the wrong kind of influences on them. (Thereby the Black movement was saved from the terrible fate of an oppressed turned oppressor.) The Zionists also tried it, and succeeded—for one thing, they were reasonably white and besides they seemed to be much better at this game.

Sol Stern admits that "Israel has often made unscrupulous alliances with imperialist powers like the US when it has been in her interest," but then Israel is not the only country to have done this, so what is so special about Israel?

What he refuses to see is that in the case of Zionism and the Zionist state this kind of alliance is not a matter of a policy of this or that wicked government, but is in the *very nature* of things. Zionism *always* "found it in its interest" to make "unscrupulous alliances" with imperialist powers, because this followed inexorably from the very essence of the Zionist venture.

In his programmatic book, *The Jewish State* (1896), Herzl promises that "for Europe we shall serve there as part of the rampart against Asia, and function as the vanguard of civilization against the Barbarians. As a neutral state we shall keep our ties with all the European nations, who will guarantee our existence there." (Hebrew Edition, 1944, p. 30)

It was left to his successors in the Zionist leadership to obtain the longed-for charter from British imperialism. The marriage between the imperialist bridegroom and the Zionist bride, consummated in 1917 in the Balfour declaration, was a marriage of convenience. Sir Ronald Storrs, who was instrumental in the arrangement of it all and became the first British governor of Jerusalem, explains that the Zionist project was to be "one that blessed him that gave as well as him that took by forming for England 'a little loyal Jewish Ulster' in a sea of hostile Arabism." (*Orientations*, definitive edition, Nicholson & Watson, London, 1943, p. 345)

After about thirty years, the partners began to quarrel. One of the reasons was that the Zionist settlers' community had in the meantime expanded and grown in bulk and confidence, and felt that it needed more sovereignty. Besides, by the end of the Second World War Britain had lost its dominant position (in the Middle East as elsewhere) and was yielding its place to the United States. But from the Zionist viewpoint it only makes sense to be aligned with the real Big Boss, not with a has-been. So, as a "socialist" Zionist political pundit approvingly says, "In those very years of struggle [between Zionism and British imperialism] there took place a process of a beginning of a new attachment: instead of England-Zion, America-Zion—a process that relied on the fact that the US was penetrating the Middle East as a decisive world power." (Michael Assaf, in the Histadrut daily, *Davar*, May 2, 1952)

To talk of this, as does Sol Stern, as if it was an "anti-imperialist" struggle is nearly as farcical and as mystifying as to depict the differences that Rhodesia's Ian Smith has with Her Majesty's [British] government as an "anti-imperialist" struggle. A settler state remains a settler state even when it wants more sovereignty or a new boss, or both.

Sol Stern really gets carried away. He grows eloquent telling us that "Israel was, after all, made of a revolution in the streets against a colonial occupying power." The fight "against imperialism" was, according to him, waged mainly "by two underground military organizations, the Irgun, and its smaller offshoot, the Stern Group."

In actual fact, these two groups were on the extreme right wing. What they demanded was immediate *Jewish minority rule over Palestine*, while the official Zionist leadership was a bit more cautious. The Irgun later transformed itself into the fascistoid party Herut, noteworthy for its extreme expansionism and militarism. The Stern Group had no continuation after the State of Israel came into existence. But in the pre-state years it was, if anything, more right wing. True, some rank-and-file Sternists did believe their fight to be against "imperialism" and hoped to get some Arab support. But one must surely distinguish between such vague sentiments and the program of the group.

Now, Abraham Stern, the founder and first leader of that group was a real right-wing fanatic. In 1940 he split from the Irgun (which was too soft for his taste) and published a program consisting of eighteen points. (This document has recently been published by his nephew in the Jerusalem student paper *Pi-Ha'aton*, February 24, 1971.) The first three points are:

1. The People of Israel is a Chosen People, creator of monotheism, legislator of the ethics of the Prophets, founder of the world's culture, great

in tradition and dedication, having the will to live and the strength to suffer, in this lies its confidence in salvation.

2. The fatherland is Eretz-Yisrael within the boundaries stated in the Bible—"Unto thy seed have I given this land, from the river of Egypt unto the great river, the river Euphrates" (Gen. 15:20). In this country of life the entire Hebrew People will dwell securely.

3. Eretz-Yisrael was acquired by the Israelites by the sword, in it they fought and in it alone the People of Israel will be resurrected. Therefore the People of Israel alone has exclusive right of property over Eretz-Yisrael. This right is unalienable for ever.

Now, between the river of Egypt and the Euphrates there are of course a lot of Arabs. What do we do with them? In the fourteenth point it is revealed that their "problem will be solved by means of population exchange." The sixteenth point demands: "Aggrandizement of the Hebrew People so that it becomes a first-rate military, political and economic factor in the East and on the Mediterranean shores."

That's quite a bit of Zionism, but no *anti*-imperialism. Quite the contrary.

By the way, has Sol Stern asked his friend Amos Kenan, the Sternist veteran (who we are told is "Israel's most widely read left-wing journalist") to tell him about the Deir-Yassin massacre, where in 1948 the Irgun and the Sternists applied their anti-imperialist theories by butchering an entire Arab village, including old people, women, and children? No? What a pity! The story is very interesting, if a bit gory.

So much for anti-imperialism.

"A Kind of Watchdog"

Sol Stern is right in saying that Israel is no "imperialist power" and "has no access to the oil and raw material in the Arab world." Except, of course, for the mini-empire which it has recently set up and for the Arab oil that it cheerfully pumps out of the Sinai. But this is really just peanuts in comparison to the Big Boys.

Israel is not an imperialist power in its own right; it is just the local caretaker for the real imperialists: the Americans, mainly. Or, as an op-ed in Israel's most respectable daily, *Ha'aretz*, put it as long ago as September 30, 1951:

> Israel has been assigned the role of a kind of watchdog. It is not to be feared that she would apply an aggressive policy toward the Arab states if this would be clearly against the wishes of America and Britain. But if the Western Powers will at some time prefer, for one reason or another, to close their eyes, Israel can be relied upon to punish properly one or several of her Arab neighboring states whose lack of manners toward the West has exceeded permissible limits.

In return for this, Israel is economically (as well as politically) maintained by imperialism. The internal saving of the Israeli economy is zero, or even slightly negative. Yet, it is one of the fastest growing in the world. Israel's balance of payments deficit, which was about $500 million per year before 1967—an astronomic figure for such a small country—has now quintupled. This means that every Israeli man, woman, or child needs a daily external subsidy of two to three bucks. This is covered by a huge flow of money from the West, mainly from the United States, which Oscar Gass has rightly described as "a circumstance without parallel elsewhere." (*Journal of Economic Literature*, December 1969, p. 1177). For additional detailed data see "The Class Nature of Israeli Society," Hanegbi, Machover, and Orr in *New Left Review*, 65, January–February 1971.)*

What do you think, Mr. Stern, maybe American imperialism gives all this money just for the sake of Golda Meir's beautiful eyes? And don't come telling us that a lot of this money is privately donated by American Jews. Because we all know that the American administration agrees (and if it had not wanted to, it would disagree) to regard this *schnorr* as "charitable donations," which makes them income-tax deductable; so that the American Jews don't mind giving so much, since a large part of it is at Uncle Sam's expense anyway.

Now how about Sol Stern's opinion that Israel is "dependent ultimately not on big-power support, but on its own willingness to fight for its survival"? And what should the Israelis *eat* while "fighting for their survival"? Maybe sand?

No Mr. Stern; sand is not edible. The only use you can make of it is to throw it in our eyes—which you are trying very hard to do. But it isn't so easy, because facts are tougher than *schmaltz*.

---

* Chapter 13 in this book.

24

Zionism and Its Scarecrows

Moshé Machover and Mario Offenberg

More than ten years have passed since the beginning of the occupation of the areas conquered by Israel in the June war of 1967. The Palestinian liberation movement has become a factor that can no longer be disregarded in any discussion on the perspectives of the Palestinian question and the Middle East conflict. The relative victories of the Arab armies over Israel in the October war of 1973, the economic and ideological fragility of the Israeli state, and finally the new attitude of the United States and the West European states toward the Arab states—along with the resulting inevitable readjustment of the nuances regarding the question of Israel-Arab confrontation—these things reveal all too clearly the political weakening of Israel's position both at home and abroad. Viewed internationally, the isolation of Israel occurred not only in the countries of the third world and Eastern Europe but to a certain extent also in the West.

While the bourgeois mass media in the West express "solidarity" and "anxiety" for "threatened" Israel but also for the first time report—cautiously and distortedly—on the Palestinians' struggle for national self-determination, the Western left assesses the Middle East conflict in terms of its anti-imperialist policy. The left attributes the causes of the Middle East conflict to the fact that Zionism—a reactionary, colonizing movement associated with imperialism—realized its intention of creating the Zionist State of Israel at the expense of another people. After its establishment, Israel assumed the role of "watchdog" for imperialist interests in the Arab East.

This article, cowritten with Mario Offenberg, was published in *Khamsin* 6, 1978, 33–59. It is a translation of an article entitled "Der Zionismus und sein Popanz: Eine Antwort an die 'linken' Zionisten," published in the German journal *Probleme des Klassenkampfs*, vol. 19/20/21, 1975, 299–327. A *Khamsin* editorial note says: "In the present translation we have omitted a passage dealing with the current Zionist propaganda concerning Soviet Jews, since this topic is covered in greater detail in an article by one of the two authors in *Critique* 9." This refers to Moshé Machover's article "Zionism or Human Rights?," *Critique* 9, 1978, 121–25.

However, it is clear that Zionism and its propagandists abroad, using both "historically based" accounts and appeals to the emotions, do their utmost to prevent and reverse the discrediting of Zionist policy and positions. These propagandists no longer project the traditional image of the "brave little pioneer who is 150 percent right," nor do they come out openly with crude, arrogant nationalism in support of Greater Israel and the expulsion of the Arabs. It's all handled more subtly and modestly today—and for good reason: whenever the Zionist nature of the Israeli state is seriously challenged—whether by actual political and military developments, or by ideas calling for a multinational Palestine or a supranational socialist union of the whole region, the pro-Zionist side tries to present the Palestine conflict in terms of a "tragic confrontation between two equally justified national aspirations," which can be settled on the basis of freezing the Zionist acquisitions of 1949 (with "corrections").

This article aims to show how the objective and subjective henchmen of Zionism in the West, in their attempt to fluster the critics of Zionism, present "leftist"-tinged arguments in support of the Israeli state, especially directed *against* its Jewish opponents of the anti-Zionist socialist movement inside Israel.

Some time ago the West German magazine *links* published in serialized form the article "The Class Nature of Israeli Society," which was written in 1970 by Haim Hanegbi, Moshé Machover, and Akiva Orr, members of the Israeli Socialist Organization Matzpen.* A reader of *links*, Alfred Moos, in a critique, objected both to the Matzpen article and the anti-Zionist position in general.[1]

We consider Alfred Moos's article typical of the arguments of the so-called left-wing Zionists. Therefore, besides dealing with the central points of the argument in his article, we also want to try to use this example to explain the position of "left-wing" Zionists generally, to criticize it and to show how this position is very similar to that of the official Zionist propaganda, albeit with different nuances.

First, however, a preliminary remark: The attack on the Matzpen article takes advantage of the fact that it does not contain a historical analysis of Zionism: neither as to the relation of Zionism to the Jewish question in Europe nor as to the relation of the Zionist project to the majority of the indigenous population of Palestine (the Palestinian Arab people) and to the various imperialist powers that have dominated the region since the beginning of the Zionist colonization to this day.

The reason why there is no such historical analysis in that article is simple: the article did not intend to present a comprehensive historical reckoning with Zionism but more particularly to point out the basic structure of Israeli class society today.[2]

Zionism and Anti-Semitism

Typically, "left-wing Zionists" always start their attacks on Israeli anti-Zionists with the remark that the Jewish immigrants to Palestine—who provided the human raw

---

* Chapter 13 in this book.

material for the Zionist project—"fled all too frequently from physical extermination and from anti-Semitic humiliation and the loss of their means of livelihood at the very least." Behind this introduction there is a concealed threat that the propagandists of Zionism like so much to use: whoever denounces Zionism, whoever rejects the Israeli state, whoever puts up a fight against the Zionist nature of Israel and Zionist policy—is an ally of anti-Semitism.

The threat is expressed even more bluntly: for example, that the present struggle against Zionism "is garnished with crumbs from the Nazi kitchen." Still more: "Sometimes one almost has the impression that Zionists are the newly costumed 'Elders of Zion' for many leftists." Words of warning and threats are also aimed directly at anti-Zionist Israelis: "Young Israelis, who are calling upon people to participate in the struggle against Zionism, shouldn't forget that their parents or grandparents in most cases were persecuted people for whom Palestine/Israel was the only refuge and that they would hardly have the right today to close Israel's borders if sometime in the future Jews should be forced to flee to Israel in the face of anti-Semitic persecution. The old Jewish self-hatred sometimes gives rise to strange practices."

Such calumnies are not new. They were already directed against the Jewish communists in Russia who denounced Zionism at the second World Congress of the Communist International:

> We are referring to the Zionists in Palestine, who, under the pretext of founding an independent Jewish state, oppress the working population and force the Arabs living in Palestine under the yoke of the English, whereas the Jews are only a minority there. This matchless lie must be stamped out and indeed most vigorously, as the Zionists are working in every country, approaching all the backward Jewish working masses and trying to create groups of workers with Zionist tendencies (Poalei Zion), who have recently been endeavoring to adopt a communist phraseology. . . . The Communist International must oppose this movement most vehemently.[3]

One of the most well-known protagonists of Zionism made no secret of his opinion of the anti-Zionist communists: "These psychopaths and sadists, full of hatred for everything Jewish, shall rot in their own depravity and hideousness and suffocate in their own filth."[4] The way the Zionists treat their (Jewish) critics, who oppose them on the basis of the principles of internationalism, has not changed. A cofounder of the precommunist group in Palestine was labeled a "traitor" and "enemy of the Jewish people" in 1920,[5] because he dared to say abroad that the expulsion of the Arab fellahin by the Zionist movement provoked the entire Arab world to make a stand against the Jews of Palestine.[6] Even the "doves" of Zionism show no mercy; for them, the anti-Zionists from the "Holy Land" are suffering from a "pathological feeling of enmity toward the Jewish national creation," as they are propagating the "belief in inciting a war of genocide against the Jewish community of the country."[7]

Israeli revolutionary socialists have long been accustomed to the reproach of "self-hatred" and have been well armed against it. However, from their own experience they know that the defamatory scarecrow of equating anti-Zionism with anti-Semitism still succeeds in intimidating a considerable part of the left (not to mention democratic non-leftists) outside Israel. It is therefore essential that the left in Western Europe also learn to see through this false and defamatory equation and to recognize it as a propagandist scarecrow on the part of Zionist policy.

There is no doubt that the modern Zionist movement arose as a reaction to anti-Semitism and the plight of the Jews in Eastern and Central Europe at the end of the nineteenth century and the beginning of this [twentieth] century. But it is not enough merely to point out that Zionism constitutes a reaction to anti-Semitism; we must determine *what kind* of reaction it is. In principle there can be two opposing attitudes toward anti-Semitism as toward other similar phenomena of discrimination and oppression on racial, ethnic, religious, and similar grounds.

The first attitude is common not only to socialists but also to all those who have a progressive outlook (radical liberals, radical democrats, etc.). The way they see things, discrimination and oppression of minorities are not inherent in human nature but are rather the result of certain conditions—namely, social, economic, and political conditions, which are *historical* and consequently *mutable*.

According to this view, only the struggle to change the prevailing social, economic, and political conditions is the politically correct reaction to anti-Semitism and other similar phenomena, this change being an organic component part of the general struggle for "a better world." Of course the various progressive tendencies (revolutionary socialists, social reformists, radicals) differ considerably from one another both in their conceptions of the new world they are striving for and also in the means necessary to wage the struggle. All, however, share one common assumption: the struggle against the roots of anti-Semitism and similar phenomena is not futile and (as a part of the general struggle for a better society) is the only correct political answer.

In the case of those who hold reactionary and racist views, we generally find an opposing attitude: antagonism and conflict between the majority of a population and racial, ethnic, and religious minorities are rooted in "human nature" itself; a struggle against anti-Semitism (or against similar phenomena) is pointless because anti-Semitism is a necessary, normal, indeed even healthy phenomenon. The only way to solve the problem once and for all is to eradicate its alleged roots: it is imperative to change the situation where Jews live as a minority among non-Jews. It will not be difficult for the reader to see that this latter attitude is the one characteristic of anti-Semites. However, the truth is that this attitude is the basic premise and the point of departure for *both anti-Semitism and Zionism*. The only difference is that Zionism appeals to the Jews to leave the "non-Jewish" peoples *of their own free will*, whereas anti-Semitism simply demands that *they be thrown out*.

One can show that many anti-Semites are aware of the elements that anti-Semitism and Zionism have in common. For example, the British colonel R. Meinertzhagen (who was political officer on the staff of the conqueror of Palestine in the First World War, General Allenby) confides to us: "My inclination toward Jews in general is governed by an anti-Semitic instinct which is invariably modified by personal contact. My views on Zionism are those of an ardent Zionist."[8]

To the anti-Semite's friendly wave the Zionist responds with an elegant bow. In his diary, the founder of Zionism, Theodor Herzl, reports how he was influenced by the Dreyfus trial, on which he, Herzl, reported for a Vienna newspaper: "In Paris . . . I achieved a freer attitude toward anti-Semitism, which I now began to understand historically and to pardon. Above all, I recognized the emptiness and futility of trying to 'combat' anti-Semitism."[9]

The ideology of Zionism, as conceived by its founder, Theodor Herzl, is based on earlier essays by other "race theoreticians." For one of them, anti-Semitism is founded on a biological law: "Jew-baiting is a kind of demonopathy with a difference: it is not a quality of a particular race but common to all mankind. . . . Like a psychic affliction, it is hereditary, and as a disease it has been incurable for two thousand years." Another "theoretician on things Jewish" opines: "Jewish noses can't be reshaped and black, curly Jewish hair can't be changed into blond hair or combed straight by christening. The Jewish race is a basic one and reproduces itself in its integrity despite climatic influences. The Jewish type has itself always remained the same throughout the course of the centuries. . . . It's no use Jews and Jewesses denying their origin by being christened and disappearing into the great sea of Indo-Germanic and Mongol tribes. The Jewish type cannot be erased."

These statements read as though they were mirror images of ravings of the Alfred Rosenberg Nazi school of racism. But we must name the actual authors: the first is the Zionist thinker Leo Pinsker, the second is Moses Hess.[10]

It is not difficult to cite many further quotations from Zionist sources, from the beginnings of Zionism to the present day, that show the common theoretical point of departure of Zionism and anti-Semitism. We shall spare the reader these quotes and make do with the analysis of a young contemporary Israeli historian, Yig'al Elam:

> Zionism assumed anti-Semitism to be a natural state of affairs as far as the attitude of the world toward the Jews was concerned. . . . Zionism did not consider anti-Semitism an abnormal, absurd, perverse, or marginal phenomenon. Zionism considered anti-Semitism a fact of nature, a standard constant, the norm in the relationship of the non-Jews to the presence of Jews in their midst. . . . Zionism considered anti-Semitism a normal, almost rational reaction of the gentiles to the abnormal, absurd, and perverse situation of the Jewish people in the Diaspora.[11]

Revealing and illuminating is the almost apologetic understanding a prominent Zionist leader shows for Nazism in 1934:

> (The Jews) have been pulled out of the last secret recesses of christening and mixed marriages. We are not unhappy about it. In their being forced to declare themselves, to show real determined courage, to stand by their community, we see at the same time the fulfilment of our desires. . . . The theory of assimilation has collapsed. We

are no longer hidden in secret recesses. We want to replace assimilation by something new: *the declaration of belonging to the Jewish nation and the Jewish race.* A state, built according to the principle of purity of the nation and race [i.e., the Third Reich], can only be honored and respected by a Jew who *declares* his belonging to his own kind.[12]

The far-reaching harmony between Zionism and anti-Semitism, caused by their common ideological point of departure, goes even further than could be assumed. . . .

The introduction to an official edition of the infamous racist Nuremberg Laws of September 15, 1935, states among other things: "If the Jews had a state of their own in which the bulk of their people were at home, the Jewish question could already be considered solved today, even for the Jews themselves. *The ardent Zionists of all people have objected least of all to the basic ideas of the Nuremberg Laws,* because they know that these laws are the only correct solution for the Jewish people as well."[13]

Such implicit harmony between Zionism and anti-Semitism certainly came as a dreadful blow to those Jews and non-Jews who saw the solution of the issue in waging a political struggle to "democratize" their societies. Isaac Deutscher reports that in Eastern Europe, and especially in Poland, the Yiddish-speaking workers who considered themselves Jews without reservation were the most resolute enemies of Zionism. They were determined opponents of emigration to Palestine. These anti-Zionists thought the idea of an evacuation, an exodus from the countries they called home, where their ancestors had lived for centuries, amounted to abdicating their rights, yielding to hostile pressure, betraying their struggle, and surrendering to anti-Semitism. For them, Zionism seemed to be the triumph of anti-Semitism, legitimizing and validating the old cry "Jews out." The Zionists accepted it, they wanted "out."[14]

Zionism was indeed *a reaction* to anti-Semitism; however, the *basic assumption* on which Zionist ideology is based *agrees with that of anti-Semitism.*

Zionism and the Rights of the Jews

From what has been explained above, it becomes clear why Zionism was so often indifferent to the struggle against anti-Semitism and for equality for the Jews; because it denies from the very outset the possibility and usefulness of a struggle against anti-Semitism. The situation of Jews living outside Palestine interests Zionism only in so far as they are moved by their situation to emigrate to Palestine or at least to support Zionism. This is expressed by the Israeli historian Y. Elam, whom we have quoted above, as follows: "From the very first moment it [Zionism] gave up all considerations relating to the situation of the Jewish people in the Diaspora, except in so far as they contributed to the Zionist project." And so it came about that following the Nazi takeover in Germany, "when the demonstrations and protest actions against the Nazi regime of terror reached their climax, the voice of Zionism was not to be heard."[15]

The Zionists in their entirety rejected the continued existence of the "Diaspora." According to this view, the life of Jews outside Palestine/Israel is reprehensible, whereas only emigration to Palestine, active participation in the Zionist project, is considered desirable. Regarding the attitude of Zionists toward Jews living in the Diaspora, the Israeli professor of history and veteran Zionist functionary, Arieh Tartakower, says: "They [the majority of Zionists] considered every attempt to protect Jewish rights in the Diaspora to be a complete waste of energy."[16] Even if Zionism's contempt for the Diaspora was an apparent contradiction—for selfish reasons Zionism could not be indifferent to what befell the reservoir of immigrants—it seems that the Zionists (like Herzl originally) considered anti-Semitic intrigues, which might drive the Jews to Palestine, to be more important, up to a certain point, than the struggle against anti-Semitism. Without doubt, this way of reasoning implies to a degree an element of discipline, but also self-justification and most certainly a deep contempt for humanity, as well as infinite hypocrisy.

Before and during the Second World War, individual Zionists such as Nahum Goldmann and Yitzhak Grienbaum demanded participation in the struggle for the rights of the Jews. However, all major trends and all important leaders of Zionism refused this demand. In 1935 the board of the Jewish Agency, the institution that ran Zionist activities in Palestine, appointed a special commission to look into the problems of the Jews in Germany. So it came about that during the board meeting of the Jewish Agency on December 31, 1935, David Ben-Gurion, in answer to the demand of Y. Grienbaum that the Zionist movement should take part in the struggle for the rights of the Jews in Germany, stated that:

> Even according to Grienbaum, the job of the commission appointed by the board was not to deal with the rights of the Jews in Germany. This commission's job was to discuss the question of the Jews in Germany only from the aspect of their immigration to Palestine, and its report is not at all inconsistent with any measures which might be taken in support of the rights of the Jews in Germany. The commission's job was to discuss the Zionist aspect of the question and not to deliberate on measures to be taken in support of the rights of the Jews in the Diaspora.[17]

Even if we accept the idea that the report of this commission was "*not inconsistent*" with the struggle for the rights of the German Jews (and this is by no means sure!), the fact still remains that the commission was quite unwilling to pay any attention to this struggle. Indeed, it was the main job of this commission to organize the famous "transfer" deal, the trade contract between the Zionist movement and the Hitler government, according to which the money and property of German Jews were transferred to Palestine in the form of German goods, thus breaking an anti-Nazi economic boycott organized by antifascist forces. Here too (as Y. Elam rightly points out) it was "not the attempt to save Jewish property in the Diaspora which was behind the deal, but the attempt to increase the economic strength of the Jewish 'Yishuv' in Palestine."[18]

This indifference of Zionism toward the struggle for the rights of the Jews has existed all along. It continues even today, for example, in the case of the Soviet Jews. It must be pointed out that the vociferous campaign of the Zionist movement in this matter does not aim to help the Jews in the Soviet Union as such but is only directed at securing *one single privilege*—namely, the right to emigrate to Israel. The struggle for the rights of the Jews, which, like any other struggle to secure equal rights for a national or ethnic minority, deserves the support of every progressive person, is hardly of interest to Zionism. Moreover, as we shall see later, it is certain that if, for whatever reason, there is a decline in the propensity of Soviet Jews to emigrate, this will cause many Zionist leaders disappointment and regret. This has become especially evident since 1967.

Any attempt to present the "Jewish problem" in the Soviet Union in an ahistorical "eternal dimension"—which is typical of idealism generally and Zionism in particular—is from the outset manipulative and misleading, and mainly based on exploiting the emotions and the ignorance of the observer. The "Jewish problem" in the Soviet Union is *one* of the national problems there—not the only one, not even the most important one; it does not exist "autonomously" (according to the false slogan: "even socialism can't solve the problem of the Jews"), separately or independently of the other inner social processes of the Soviet Union.

It would definitely be very presumptuous to attribute the Soviet Jews' willingness to emigrate only to their desire to satsify Jewish religious and cultural needs to a greater extent than is possible in the Soviet Union, or to their wish to strengthen Zionism politically, economically, and militarily in Israel. For some of them that may be true. For many, however, the simple wish to live outside the Soviet Union is the main drive. Over half of the Jews allowed out of the Soviet Union, ostensibly on their way to Israel, never arrive there. They "drop out" during the stopover in Vienna or Rome and that's the end of their "journey to Jerusalem."[19] The Russian Zionist activist, Dr. Viktor Polski, who left Moscow in 1974 and emigrated to Israel, laments: "Should exit conditions be relaxed and fewer refusals be issued by the Soviet government, I have no doubt that the emigration flow will increase considerably. However, I greatly fear that the flow of those arriving in Israel will not increase proportionately. If the Soviet Jews' image of Israel and the actual conditions behind it don't change, the proportion of those who drop out in transit will be greater than those arriving in Israel.[20]

Many of the Soviet Jewish emigrants have fallen victim to Israeli propaganda, which by radio and much more subtle and seemingly "unofficial" means, penetrates into the interior of the Soviet Union. Recently the situation has begun to change: relatives and friends already emigrated report in detail on the rude awakening they have undergone in the Zionist state. Instead of a completely harmonious, affluent society without any friction, they found a class society in which they are exposed to the same exploitation, unemployment, inflation, bureaucracy, alienation that make up the day-to-day life of the rest of the working population of Israel—in spite of the great financial benefits they enjoy as privileged immigrants. In addition, there is the constant deadly peril of confrontation with the Palestinians and neighboring Arab states. In 1974 half as many Jews emigrated from the Soviet Union to Israel as in the previous years 1973 and 1972 respectively.[21]

With the worsening of the economic crisis in Israel and increasing inflation and unemployment rates, the resentment of the Israeli population against the Soviet Jews, with their special prerogatives as regards housing and jobs and their special tax reductions, is becoming more marked. Any member of the working population can easily realize that the national income cake, in any case inadequate, and the capital collected abroad by the Zionist organization are being distributed most unfairly.

In the past, grievances were voiced quietly and confidentially about the preferential treatment of the immigrants; but they were "needed." Today, however, many in Israel express their annoyance openly. Israeli Jews and more specifically the Jewish underprivileged social strata, such as the Mizrahim, sections of the youth and the working class, are venting their protests more blatantly and explicitly against immigration at their own expense. For the most part they are reacting quite spontaneously, generally without realizing that thereby they are assailing one of the basic principles of Zionism. "Ingathering" of the Jews in Palestine/Israel, demographically outnumbering the Arabs, feeding the insatiable—and in the long run, inadequate—Israeli military machine with human raw material for its fight to the bitter end: this is Zionism, among other things. All immigration to Israel is—today as in the past—directed, controlled, and run by Zionism. The objective contradiction between Zionist immigration and the interests of the working population of Israel cannot be solved. It is an additional source of internal Israeli class conflicts.[22]

But what becomes of the Soviet Jewish "dropouts"? The Israeli journalist Abraham Tirosh reports on Jewish immigrants from the Soviet Union, who either arrived in Israel and then left the country, or who managed to "beat it" in Vienna, in transit from Moscow to Tel-Aviv, despite constant Israeli surveillance.[23] These Jews, who are in a terrible predicament and urgently need help, are as a rule turned away by the Zionist Jewish Agency, which has offices in all major cities in Western Europe. The European office of the only allegedly independent Jewish refugee organization, the HIAS, is in Rome. Tirosh continues: Penniless and disoriented, these Jewish refugees trudge to Vienna and Rome. "The HIAS organization refuses to take care of the Soviet emigrants who arrive at their offices in Vienna, Rome, or in Israel, unless they have received the confirmation and permission of the Jewish Agency, which looks into each case thoroughly. The acting director of the immigration department of the Jewish Agency, Yehuda Dominitz, and leading circles of the HIAS have strongly denied recent news, according to which, contravening the agreement, HIAS has begun to handle Soviet emigrants from Israel to Europe and the USA."

The issue of the Soviet Jews can be summed up as follows: The Zionist movement is not struggling for the recognition of the right of *every person* to be able to emigrate from one country to another—in itself a progressive demand that every socialist should support—but it demands this right as a special privilege *only for Jews*, and then only on the condition that they immigrate to Israel and to no other country.

The basis of the Zionist campaign on Soviet Jews is not the general idea of universal human rights but the Zionist thesis according to which every Jew everywhere in the world has a special right to Palestine. And in the same breath, Zionism denies the political and national rights of the Arabs of Palestine to their homeland.

Indeed, this same Zionist government and this same Zionist view demand the automatic right of a Jew born in Moscow to emigrate from the Soviet Union to Israel and automatically grant him Israeli citizenship. At the same time, the same view and the same government deny the right of an Arab born in Haifa, who today for example is living in the Gaza Strip or in a camp on the outskirts of Beirut, to return to his home town and to get his civil rights there. Human rights in general and even the rights of the Jews as a whole interest Zionism only in as far as they help to promote Jewish immigration to Israel.

"Cruel Zionism"

We have already mentioned the "transfer," that morally dubious business deal between the Zionist movement and the Hitler government. When this deal was criticized—at the time progressive forces were calling for an economic boycott of the Third Reich—Moshe Shertok (later known as M. Sharett, a well-known Zionist leader and Israel's first foreign minister) answered as follows: "Here there is a conflict between the Diaspora and Eretz-Yisrael [i.e., the Zionist project in Palestine]. . . . It is Zionism's lot to have to be cruel to the Diaspora at times, when the development of this country demands it."[24]

This cruelty of Zionism toward the Jews of the world is sometimes especially cynical. It often happens that people who belong to an oppressed group, but who nevertheless do not want or are unable to participate in the struggle against the cause of their oppression, prefer an individual solution—emigration to another country. Socialists do not propose to rob them of this option; on the contrary, they insist on the right of every individual to emigrate freely. They object most strongly, however, to emigration being presented as a collective political solution, as a substitute for the struggle against oppression. It must be mentioned at this point that in the 1920s, 1930s, and also later, many of the East European Jews did in fact choose this individual solution of emigration. Many millions emigrated from countries where they had suffered great hardship to the United States and other countries, and thus found their own satisfactory solution to their problem. Zionist emigration to Palestine was negligible in comparison with the flow of Jewish non-Zionist emigration to other countries. The difference, however, lay in the fact that Zionist propaganda was directed at the more active and also more conscious elements, who were looking for a political and not simply an individual solution; and it offered them the wrong political solution. Moreover, it tried stubbornly to prevent these Jews from joining in the revolutionary struggle in their own countries—this was to a certain extent both the requirement and aim of the Zionist campaign.

There are also exceptional situations in which there is no possibility at all of a struggle on the part of the oppressed minority, and this minority is particularly exposed to extreme danger. In such cases the only humane solution is the prompt organization of emigration for those in immediate danger to any countries ready to grant them asylum. (A fairly recent example is that of people of Indian origin in Uganda in 1972.) Such was the situation of the Jews in Germany and other European countries at the end of the 1930s. It was clear that to save the Jews from the danger of extermination, it was necessary to enable them to emigrate to any safe place.

At that historical moment truly cruel Zionism (without quotation marks) showed its absolutely cynical attitude toward the problem of saving the Jews. The leaders of Zionism reacted with indifference and even hostility toward the emigration of Jews from the countries where they were in danger to places other than Palestine. Zionism clearly showed that in principle it is not interested in saving the Jews *per se*, but only in saving them by emigration to Palestine. The leader of the Zionist movement, Chaim Weizmann, said: "Zionism is eternal life and, compared with that, saving thousands of Jews is merely extending their lives on borrowed time."[25]

David Ben-Gurion's letter of December 17, 1938, to his colleagues in the Zionist Executive is particularly shocking. In reaction to attempts by the Western powers—under pressure of public opinion—to find various expedients for the problem of the Jews in Germany, Ben-Gurion writes:

> The Jewish problem now is not what it used to be. What is now happening to the Jews in Germany is not the end but the beginning. Other anti-Semitic states will learn from Hitler's deed. . . . Millions of Jews are now faced with physical extermination. The refugee problem has now become an urgent worldwide issue and England, assisted by anti-Zionist Jews, is trying to separate the refugee problem from the Palestine problem. The frightful extent of the refugee problem requires a speedy territorial solution and if Palestine won't absorb any Jews, one would have to look for another territory. Zionism is endangered. All other territorial experiments, which are doomed to failure, will require huge amounts of capital, and if the Jews are faced with a choice between the refugee problem and rescuing Jews from concentration camps on the one hand, and aid for the national museum in Palestine on the other, the Jewish sense of pity will prevail and our people's entire strength will be directed at aid for the refugees in the various countries. Zionism will vanish from the agenda and indeed not only from world public opinion in England and America but also from Jewish public opinion. We are risking Zionism's very existence if we allow the refugee problem to be separated from the Palestine problem.[26]

It is not just that Zionism and saving Jews in danger of extermination are not one and the same thing; at a critical historical moment, Zionism took a stand *against* saving the Jews. Here we must add: it is true that those Jews who before the Second World War had participated in the Zionist emigration from Central and Eastern Europe thereby escaped annihilation by fascism. The attempt, however, to use this as a "socialist" justification of Zionism is nothing but demagogy and moral blackmail.

First, many more Jews managed to save themselves without Zionism, indeed contrary to Zionism, either by emigrating to America or by fleeing to the interior of the Soviet Union. Secondly, the deliverance of the Jews in Palestine was due to the fact that the German army in Africa under Rommel got no further than El-

Alamein, and did not conquer Palestine. Palestine was also on the planned route of the fascist conquerors. If Rommel's army had conquered Palestine and had got as far as Syria, the fate of the Jews in Palestine would undoubtedly have been the same as of those in Poland. No "magic-mystical" power of Zionism would have protected the Jews of the Zionist community from the Nazis then.

Few Zionists were ready to recognize the untenability of the Zionist axiom, according to which Jews could "escape" world history through Zionism and consequently be outside the fascist/antifascist process. This is what the Zionist leader Ya'akov Zrubavel said in January 1945 during the congress of the World Organization of Poalei Zion and thereby gave rise to violent disagreement:

> Is it admissible to build everything on this catastrophe [the annihilation of the European Jews]? And isn't it pure chance that we have survived in Palestine? Wasn't Hitler at the gates of the country? What would have been our situation and fate here then? Large sections of the population here and certainly those present here could have defended themselves, just as the Jews in Warsaw defended themselves. Hitler didn't only plan to annihilate the Diaspora but *Jewry*, all Jews everywhere. We have saved ourselves *by pure chance*.[27]

Those who consider the extermination of the Jews by German fascism to be a "refutation" of the Marxist view of the Jewish problem and its solution by social struggle and social change, and who invoke this as proof of the "necessity" of Zionism, should be answered in the words of Isaac Deutscher:

> To my mind the tragic events of the Nazi era neither invalidate the classical Marxist analysis of the Jewish question nor call for its revision. . . . Classical Marxism reckoned with a healthier and more normal development of our civilisation in general, with a timely transformation of the capitalist into a socialist society. It did not reckon with the persistent survival of capitalism and its degenerative effects on our civilisation at large. Nevertheless Marx, Engels, Rosa Luxemburg, and Trotsky repeatedly said that mankind was confronted with the alternative of either international socialism or barbarism—*tertium non datur*. . . . European Jewry has paid the price for the survival of capitalism, for the success of capitalism in defending itself against a socialist revolution. This fact surely does not call for a revision of the classical Marxist analysis—it rather confirms it.[28]

Indeed there was no essential connection between survival of Jews in the Second World War and Zionism. What brought about the survival of the Jews in Palestine was the fact that Hitler's war machine had been brought to a halt. The Jews were saved wherever Nazism could not reach. The historical conclusion to be drawn from this is that only the worldwide struggle against fascism and reaction is an effective answer to anti-Semitism. This conclusion is exactly opposed to the one drawn by the "left-wing" Zionists.

Israeli anti-Zionists are accused of ignoring the alleged fact that the immigrants to Palestine/Israel from Eastern and Western Europe and recently from the Arab countries came because of anti-Semitism and lack of a means of livelihood: "Zionist ideology played in most cases no role at all or at the most a secondary one. . . .

These people did not need any pressure or Zionist propaganda to decide to emigrate to Palestine."[29]

The answer to that is: first, no one is trying to deny that Zionism used countless thousands of people as human raw material for its own project, people looking for an escape from destitution and oppression—although many of them were not particularly enthusiastic Zionists to begin with. However, the assertion that Zionism did not have to exert any particular pressure on these people to get them to immigrate to Palestine/Israel is very far from the truth. Let us recall as an example the emigration of the Jews from Iraq at the beginning of the 1950s. Here is a brief outline of the affair: in 1950 the Zionist movement concluded a secret deal with the reactionary government of Iraq, according to which the emigration of the Jews of that country to Israel was to be encouraged. The Iraqi government concluded this deal in part because it had a financial interest in it: the property of emigrant Jews was to be confiscated and handed over to the government. Both the Zionists and the Iraqi government were completely satisfied with this arrangement. The only problem was that the Iraqi Jews themselves did not want to play along. The way they saw things, they had absolutely no reason to emigrate from Iraq to Israel. Their relations with the Islamic and Christian sections of the Iraqi population were in general quite good.

Then something strange happened: bombs exploded in various Jewish establishments and meeting places. Some Jews were killed by the bombs. As a result, the Iraqi Jews panicked and within a short time most of them applied to emigrate to Israel. Some time later it turned out that those who had planted the bombs were without any doubt agents of the Zionist movement who were following their movement's instructions. So the leaders of cruel Zionism had decided that wherever there is not enough anti-Semitism, it must be intentionally created or simulated in order to frighten the Jews and motivate them to implement the Zionist solution. All the details of this affair, based on the statements of Iraqi Jews and some of the "heroes," and the names of the bomb-planters were published only fifteen years later in Israel. Many Jews from Iraq living in Israel today, when asked who planted the bombs, admit in private conversations: "Hatnu'ah"—"the Movement," which in Hebrew usage means the *Zionist movement*. This is not the only affair of its kind. In this case, however, many of the details have come to light.[30]

Land and Expulsion

We have seen that Zionism is not quite the same as rescuing Jews from danger and anti-Semitism. Moreover, the main point about Zionism is not that it wants to solve the problem of the Jews by emigration generally. The main point is Zionism's insistence that Jewish emigration be directed exclusively at a systematic colonization of Palestine with the aim of establishing an exclusivist Jewish nation-state. The character traits of the Zionist project in Palestine are the inevitable result of this aim.

"Left-wing" Zionists often argue that "the land they immigrated into was already populated by Arabs—that is the tragedy of the Jewish immigration to Palestine, which doubtlessly is frequently unrecognized or suppressed; but then, who can expect an ethnic group—whatever it is and whenever it was—to be prepared to commit collective suicide, when there is the possibility of migrating, even if the country in question is already populated by other people?"[31]

There was nothing tragic about the fact that the United States was already populated, for those Jews who chose to escape danger and persecution by migrating as individuals to the United States—and there were many, many more of them than those who chose the Zionist solution. It did not even enter their heads that in order to escape "collective suicide" they should expel the non-Jews from the United States. The "tragedy" only began when the Zionist settlers aimed not only to settle in Palestine but to change it from an Arab country into an exclusivist Jewish nation-state. We put the word "tragedy" in quotation marks because the "left-wing" apologists of Zionism use it to create the impression that it was a matter of some cruel play of blind fate, not the result of intentional and planned actions on the part of the leaders of the Zionist colonizers. Chaim Weizmann, president of the Zionist Organization, explained the Zionists' aim before the Paris Peace Congress in March 1919 as follows: "With the establishment of a Jewish national home we intend to create such conditions in Palestine that would enable us to transport 50,000 to 60,000 Jews yearly, to develop our language, establish our schools, universities, and other national institutions and to continue to work in this direction until Palestine is finally just as Jewish as America is American and England is English."[32]

And what was to become of the existing population of Palestine, which was predominantly Arab? Some prominent Zionists are much more honest on this question than many of their apologists; Menachem Ussishkin, member of the Zionist Executive, reports on the Zionist solution planned for what was called in the Zionist parlance the "Arab question": "We are condemned to remain a small island in the Arabian ocean forever; but that does not mean that we should allow ourselves to be humiliated or subjugated. We have to keep silent and go to Palestine. Hard times are ahead. *But if we go to Palestine ten by ten, hundred by hundred, thousand by thousand, hundreds of thousands, the Arab question is solved.*"[33] The "Arab question" was "solved" satisfactorily for Zionism: the Arab people of Palestine were made foreigners in their own country. "Tragedy"?

The territorial expansion of Zionism, which can be traced exactly from the famous maps of Israel (1947, 1949, 1967, 1973), is no coincidence, no historical mishap. It arose from the global matter-of-factness of the Zionist movement, which on the one hand lays exclusive Zionist claim to the whole of Palestine—naturally, only for Jews—while on the other hand believes it can counter the objective incompatibility of the Zionist entity with its Arab environment by means of the military, strategic, and demographic advantages gained by expanding its borders. The annexation of Arab territories under Zionist rule has both history and method. In

1918 the population of Palestine consisted of 599,000 Arabs and 67,000 Jews, who owned two million hectares and 65,000 hectares of land, respectively. By 1970 only 86,000 hectares of Israeli land (i.e., approximately 4 percent) were still in Arab hands.[34] Until 1948 Zionism had to take over and colonize land "step by step"; but after achieving state sovereignty, it was able to take over both the lands and the villages of the Palestinian refugees (in Israeli legal terminology "abandoned property") as well as substantial parts of the lands of those Arabs who stayed in Israel, by their administrative transformation into "closed military areas" and their consequent confiscation. For example, this was how the "Judaization" of the Galilee was engineered and imposed from the 1950s.[35]

The Zionist policy on land left nothing to chance. The fact that it involved iniquities, expulsions, and great suffering for the Arabs of Palestine was not a "mistake" but a logical consequence of the policy that Zionism pursued consciously and systematically. Before the terms "colonization" and "colonialism" generally came to be regarded throughout the world as dirty words, the Zionist movement used them to describe its own pursuits in Palestine. It spoke of "*Kolonizatzia.*" The nasty connotation of the word later led them to use the Hebrew terms for the same concept. At its founding congress in Petah-Tikva in 1919, Ben-Gurion's party, Ahdut Ha'avodah, (which was to be the leading "left-wing" party in the Zionist movement ever since) proclaimed the aim of the "Zionist Workers' Movement in Palestine": "The transfer of the land of Palestine, its rivers and its natural resources to the possession of the entire Jewish people."[36] A definite aim without doubt, but the Zionists knew very well that "our country (is) not only small but for the most part in the possession of others."[37]

A complicated and fateful project in the opinion of both its supporters and opponents who knew one thing very well: *Palestine was already populated, its transformation into a "Jewish" country would have to be at the expense of the indigenous population!* The Zionist economist Alfred Bonné says:

> The problem of land is one of the questions that has become particularly acute and politically significant with the expansion of Jewish colonization in recent years. If Palestine had been an unpopulated country or if conditions there had been the same as in the colonial territories of Australia, Africa, or South America, which are hardly populated [*sic!*], the significance of the question would not have gone beyond the bounds of pure economics. *But Palestine was a populated country when the Jewish colonization movement began and it was even more densely populated on average than the neighbouring countries.*[38]

Yaakow Meiersohn, whom we have quoted above, says in 1920: "In Palestine there is no unsettled land at all; the land of Palestine is settled, but not intensively cultivated. I am stating quite frankly and clearly that up till now not one piece of land has been bought in Palestine which had not been cultivated before by Arabs."[39] The Palestine Communist Party states regarding this: "The Zionist movement does not like to buy lands which have to be drained before construction can begin. It prefers land which has been worked for years by the fellahin. . . . First, it is more economical and in the public good to build kibbutzim on land that has already been cultivated than on uncultivated land; and secondly by doing this one fulfills a (Zionist) duty: the Arabs, the 'goyim,' are expelled from the 'Holy' Land, now 'redeemed' by the hands of Jewish workers."[40]

Today it can no longer be denied that the Zionist movement in Palestine, which was under the leadership of Ben-Gurion from *1920 until the mid-1960s*, intended to have the biggest possible Jewish majority in the largest possible territory—and for the most part "free of Arabs" . . . Ben-Gurion writes: "First and foremost I am a Zionist and strive for the concentration of the Jewish people in its own country. Only after that do I see the Arab question arising." And further: "If the Zionist idea has any true content, it is the content of the state. Zionism is the desire for a state of the Jews, the yearning for the country of Palestine and for the establishment of a government." Four years later, in 1928 he wrote: "Palestine for the Jewish people and Palestine for the Arab people is not one and the same thing. . . . We would be deceiving ourselves if we said that it were one and the same. . . . Palestine is destined for the Jewish people and the Arabs who live there."[41] It must be noted here that Ben-Gurion means *all the Jews in the world* and refers to them as a *people*, whereas in Palestine there was not even an Arab people, just "the Arabs who live there." In 1931 he writes: "I have always only viewed the Arab problem from the Zionist point of view, that is, I wanted to solve the problem of the Jewish people in Palestine, concentrate them in this country in order to make them a free people living in their own country. There isn't an Arab problem in Palestine, only a Jewish one— like everywhere else, by the way."[42]

That the very vociferous Zionist "workers' movement" practices colonialism under the cloak of socialism may be confusing, but the facts speak for themselves. For those who could not understand how socialism could be consistent with colonialism, internationalism with nationalism, workers' solidarity with expropriation and repression, the "left-wing" Zionists proclaimed in 1912: "Whenever we come across a contradiction between national and socialist principles, the contradiction should be resolved by abandoning the socialist principle in favor of the national activity. We shall not accept the contrary attempt to solve the contradiction by dispensing with the national interests in favor of the socialist idea."[43] If one sees through the "socialist" claim of Zionism, its contradictory nature and untenability, the Zionist movement loses one of its most important propagandistic hobby horses that has helped it to rope in and delude socialists, who are subjectively all too sincere but nevertheless confused, in support of an objectively iniquitous colonial and repressive project.

Indeed, that is what happens, whether it is a "bourgeois" or "left-wing" Zionism. As far as the practical implementation of the Zionist project in Palestine is concerned, the consequences for the Arabs of Palestine, the objective consequence of the Zionist project for the country in general are the same, no matter how one subjectively would like "one's own" Zionist activity to be understood—as opposed to that of "the others."

This is quite clearly a matter of deliberate policy. The founder of Zionism, Theodor Herzl, writes in his diary on June 12, 1895:

> By buying land we are immediately giving material advantages to the country that takes us in. By and by, we have to get the private land in the areas given to us out of the hands of its owners. We want to get the poor inhabitants across the borders without making a fuss, by giving them work in the transit countries. But in our country we won't give them any work at all. . . . It's good for the landowners to believe they are exploiting us and getting excessive prices for their land. But no land will be sold back to them.[44]

This was and still is even today Zionism's conscious and planned policy: the "poor population," in other words, the majority of the Arabs in the Promised Land, should be excluded from the country by every possible means. In 1940 Joseph Weitz, head of the Colonization Department of the Jewish National Fund in Palestine at the time, and therefore responsible for the practical implementation of Zionist colonization, wrote in his diary:

> Among ourselves it should be clear that in this country there isn't room for both peoples together. With the Arabs we won't achieve our aim of being an independent nation in this small country. The only solution is Palestine, at least a West Palestine [i.e., the entire area west of the Jordan, as distinct from "Eastern Palestine," which refers to Transjordan] without Arabs . . . and there's no other way but to transfer the Arabs from here to the neighboring countries; to transfer all of them. Not a single village, not one tribe should be left behind. . . . For this purpose money, plenty of money will be found. Only after this transfer will this country be able to absorb millions of our brethren.[45]

In his article in the daily newspaper *Davar* (officially the organ of the Histadrut but actually the mouthpiece of the Mapai/Labor party) of September 29, 1967, Joseph Weitz himself tells us that this excellent plan, which he had entered into his diary twenty-seven years previously, was not just his own idea. The most important Zionist leaders in Palestine supported this plan, and they started to put out feelers to see how it could be implemented. Indeed, a large part of the program was realized eight years later in 1947 when "the UN passed a resolution to partition the country into two states and *to our great good fortune* [our italics] the War of Independence broke out and in it there came to pass a double miracle: a territorial victory and the flight of the Arabs."

There can be no doubt that the expulsion of the Palestinians from their country was not a "tragic blow" of blind fate but the result of consciously planned Zionist policy. Under these circumstances the question posed naïvely by "left-wing" Zionists sounds really amazing: "In the years of the Mandate 1920–1947/48, before the Arabs offered violent resistance to the UN resolution to partition the country, how many Arab peasants actually lost their land, despite the legislation of the Mandate protecting the Arab peasants, and could no longer work in agriculture, and how many Arabs immigrated in this period from the neighboring countries to Palestine?"[46]

Some typical characteristics of this argument can be deduced from these questions. First, it is implied that the expulsion of the Arab fellahin was warranted after the Arabs had "offered violent resistance to the UN Partition Resolution." Such views should be met with silent scorn. We should remember that in all the hypocritical apologies of colonialism throughout the world it is usual to call mass expulsions of the colonial peoples a just punishment for the fact that these wicked natives dare to offer violent resistance to their mass expulsion. Secondly, it appears that we are supposed to ignore the known intentions of Zionism, as expressed in the above quotations and in many other documents and the known historical facts. Instead one should tell the story that Zionism did not expel the Arab fellahin on a large scale until 1948. The truth, however, is quite different.

Examples of mass expulsions of Arab fellahin as a result of Zionist colonization can be cited very easily. Many expulsions took place before the establishment of the Zionist state and continued during the entire period of the British Mandate, that is, till 1948.

Such questions from "left-wing" Zionists are also intended to lead one to believe that British imperialism—with the Mandatory government—offered some effective protection against expulsion. This is not true either. In this context let us refer to the memoirs of a Jewish English Zionist, Albert Montefiore Hyamson, who in the first half of the Mandate period was a high-ranking government official in Palestine. Hyamson reports on the first attempt, which was made at the beginning of the 1920s, to protect Arab tenants from expulsion:

> The need [for these regulations] became urgent because Jewish agencies bought relatively large amounts of land from [Arab] landowners who lived in Paris, Beirut, or Cairo, whereby the moral—if not the legal—rights of the tenants, who had been resident on that land all along, were ignored. According to the new legislation the transfer of lands was forbidden if the tenant's interests were not ensured by leaving him enough land to guarantee his own and his family's livelihood. This, however, was contrary to the interests of both sellers and buyers. The buyers were willing to pay prices higher than usual but demanded that the land be available for settlement. The sellers, who had no local interests at all, were of course keen to sell at as high a price as possible. They very quickly found a way to dodge the law by means of a small payment. They found allies in the moneylenders to whom most of the tenants were deeply in debt. In order to get the tenants to abandon the land before it was transferred, they paid them small sums of money with which they could settle some of their debts to the moneylenders. Then, when the transfer came, there were no more tenants there to take care of. So everyone was completely satisfied: the sellers, the buyers and understandably the moneylenders, but of course the tenants only for a limited time.

The tenants were only satisfied for a short time because the "damages" they received from the landowner amounted to very little. It was hardly enough to repay their debts to the moneylenders. Moreover, Hyamson says the fellahin and tenants who were forced to leave their lands "could not obtain employment in most of the newly developed manufacturing plants in the country." These manufacturing plants were Zionist, and Zionism refused in principle to employ Arab workers. Hyamson goes on to say that "in 1929 a new regulation was passed which gave the tenants still less protection . . . it virtually legalized the established practice."

Two years later the purchase of land began once more on a large scale and the expected problem of the landless Arabs was again at the top of the agenda. This problem caused unrest and forced the Mandatory government to enact new regulations. However the new regulations of 1931 did not offer the tenants any effective protection either, for "those landowners who wanted to sell their land at 'acceptable' prices could still dodge the objectives of the law." This state of affairs continued until the end of the Mandate.[47]

We have summarized only a small part of Hyamson's interesting chapter on this topic. It clearly follows from the extracts above and from the entire chapter that the problem of those tenants who lost the basis of their livelihoods (i.e., the land that they and their forebears had cultivated for generations) because of Zionist colonization was an extremely serious one and involved a great number of people. Similarly it is clear that the decrees of the Mandatory government could not protect the tenants effectively against the collusion between the Zionist institutions, landowners, and moneylenders, serving their common interests. Here is only one example: The eight thousand fellahin from twenty-two villages who had lost their land at the beginning of the 1920s, when the great Lebanese landowner family Sursock sold land to the Zionists, received exactly ten shillings per capita from the Zionist Organization.[48]

To make Zionist colonization seem harmless, Zionists often point out that at that time "a total of only 664 claims for damages" were placed by Arab peasants. Here, besides the fact that the availability of so-called (and relatively low) damages was publicized as little as possible, nothing is said about the number of dispossessed peasants who from the outset were excluded from the possibility of claiming "damages":

- Peasants who were expelled after their land was sold to non-Jews. (There were many sales to Arab agents and profiteers who then resold the land to the Acquisition of Land Department of the Zionist Organization.)
- Peasants who were not classified as tenants; agricultural workers and peasants who only sold part of their land.
- Peasants who had no documentary proof of their tenancy rights (very many!).
- Peasants who after the sale were allocated other land, even if it could not be cultivated.
- Peasants who had found other employment after being expelled.

That is how, in the interests of Zionism, Zionists managed to limit the classification "landless Arab" to a small group.[49]

In the period 1920–36, the time when the foundations of the Zionist project in Palestine were being laid both in the towns and in rural areas, there was an increased exodus of peasants from the rural areas—an exodus that must be understood correctly: not out of the country but a migration as a result of the peasants' losing their land. The Arab urban population of Palestine increased from 194,000 in 1922 to 298,000 in 1936.

The landless Arabs met with increasing unemployment in the Zionist-dominated urban economy, caused by the Zionist insistence on "Hebrew labor" and boycott of Arab labor. But let us get back to the fact that the fellahin were mostly expelled by the sellers before the sale (by prior agreement with the buyers). This fact enabled Zionism, like Pontius Pilate, to protest its innocence and to maintain it was not responsible for the expulsion of the fellahin. However, there are also enough examples of cases in which the Zionist colonizers, in collaboration with the British police, actively participated in the expulsion of the indigenous fellahin as in Al Fuk (today Afulah) at the end of 1924, or Wadi al-Hawarith (today Emeq Hefer) in 1933.

Still, today the propagandists of Zionism spread the claim that the Zionist institutions (at least until 1948) in most cases received "deserted lands" so that Zionism is not responsible for the expulsion of the masses of fellahin. From a technical point of view and applied to the appropriate cases that is not a lie but actually a half-truth—which is worse than a lie. For the Zionist propagandists conceal the fact that, to dodge the laws enacted to protect the fellahin, the Zionist institutions demanded that the sellers expel their tenants themselves, before going through with the sale.

By the way, we can see here how far from the truth is yet another claim of the "left-wing" Zionists, namely that "it was not the poor fellahin but the great landowners who, for reasons of class consciousness, rejected Jewish immigration and they consequently feared 'infection' of their fellahin with social ideas imported from Europe." In the first place, the "social ideas" Zionism brought from Europe were intended for exclusively Jewish use. All the institutions of organized work and community life were in no way intended for Arabs. Zionism never propagated any progressive social ideas among the fellahin. On the contrary: Zionism was, as we saw above, an objective ally of the great landowners. This was the only social class in Arab society that benefited from Zionist colonization—they received for their lands prices that were higher than before colonization. The fellahin were in fact the victims of an alliance between Zionism, the great landowners and the moneylenders. It is true that to veil their real interests and intentions, the great landowners sometimes launched vigorous verbal campaigns against Zionism. But it was all talk.

Here we must mention that the method of expulsion (which was usually concealed, to evade the law) and the lack of any reliable registration of proprietary and usufructuary rights are the reasons why it is still impossible today to supply exact details as to the extent of the expulsions. There is no doubt that there must have been many thousands. The exact figure, however, would have to be determined through painstaking detailed research. The question how many fellahin lost their land because of Zionist colonization can at present only be answered generally.

In this context, here is an extract from a speech of Moshe Dayan at a meeting of the students of the Haifa Technical University (Technion) as quoted by the Israeli daily *Ha'aretz* of April 4, 1968:

> We came to this country, which was already inhabited by Arabs, and established here a Hebrew, that is, a Jewish state. In large areas we bought lands from the Arabs. Jewish villages arose in place of Arab villages. You don't even know the names of these villages and I'm not reproaching you for that, as those geography books no longer exist. Not only do the books no longer exist but the villages do not exist anymore either. Nahalal arose in place of Mahlul, Gevat in place of Jibta, Sarid in place of Haneifs, and Kefar Yehoshu'a in place of Tel-Shaman. Not one place in this country was built where there hadn't formerly been an Arab population.

Indeed the professional generals of Zionism often speak more clearly and more frankly than many of their "left-wing" apologists. The colonization of a country and the resulting expulsion and oppression of its indigenous inhabitants, and all this with the propagandistic aim of a "progressive" society in Palestine, as the Zionists, disguised as socialists, saw it, is not only pure hypocrisy but also the theoretical and practical prostitution of revolutionary theory—a theory advocated only verbally.

The first systematic research into the extent of the destruction which Zionism and Zionist colonization caused to the original Palestinian society, compiled by the Palestinian historian Aref al-Aref and presented on February 15, 1973, by the chairman of the Israeli League for Human Rights, Professor Israel Shahak, contains a complete list of those Arab villages in Palestine which existed until 1948 and which today would be sought in vain. They no longer exist. In figures: 385—in words: three hundred and eighty-five.

It follows from some of the quotations above that it was part of the Zionist expulsion policy to exert pressure continually on the Arabs by not employing them. "Left-wing" Zionists feel slightly uncomfortable about this point . . . but only for a moment. They concede that the displacement of Arab workers from their jobs is one of those things that has "a repulsive effect on us Europeans." However, in the same breath they call on their readers to free themselves from such merciful, weak, apparently specifically European "prejudices." You must understand, the Arab workers had to go, "to protect these (Jewish) workers from starvation, as it was just impossible for Jewish workers to live on the same wages as Arab workers." So, one has to excuse them: the Jewish workers had a European stomach, which was bigger than that of the Arab members of the same class.

After such a brilliant argument, however, they apparently get an uneasy feeling once more and admit, as Alfred Moos puts it, that perhaps "some kind of solution more favorable to the Arabs could have been found. For example, one need only have somehow institutionalized the actual circumstances—the Arab peasants sold their products unhindered at lower prices even in Jewish towns—and a lot of dirty linen would have been avoided."

This apologetics, however, is a twofold failure: an untruth and an absurdity at one and the same time. It is untrue that the Zionist institutions did not systematically interfere with and hinder the sale of products by the Arab fellahin: this was done not only with propaganda but also with the aid of more effective means of "persuasion." (The Zionist leader David Hakohen reports for example in the supplement of the newspaper *Ha'aretz* of November 15, 1968, how he and his colleagues poured kerosene over tomatoes being sold by Arabs and broke their eggs.) The attempt at an excuse is fundamentally absurd because the only way of solving the problem that would have avoided "a lot of dirty linen" would have been for Zionism to abandon its main aim.

From the standpoint of the Zionist aim—the transformation of Palestine, which was an Arab country, into a "Jewish" nation-state—the presence of the Arabs was an obstacle that had to be removed. The way to achieve this goal was to deny the Arabs work, as all Zionists since Herzl have realized.

The policy of "Zionizing" and at the same time "de-Arabizing" Palestine has not changed fundamentally. On the contrary: the Arab areas conquered in the 1967 June war gave Israel the opportunity to erect more than eighty additional civilian and military settlements there and to expel many thousands of Arabs, some for the second time in twenty years. The guiding words of Moshe Dayan say it quite clearly: "In the course of the last hundred years, our people have been undergoing a process of building up the country and the nation, of expansion, by increasing the number of Jews and settlements and of colonization in order to expand the borders. Let there be no Jew who says that this is the end of the process. Let there be no Jew who says that we are near the end of the road."[50]

Israel as a state is a huge fait accompli. However, it is not likely that Israel, even within the borders of June 4, 1967, "plus corrections," can look forward to peaceful and harmonious coexistence with its Arab neighbors in the long term. The Middle East conflict is not simply a "border conflict." The cause of the historical conflict between the State of Israel in its present Zionist form on the one hand and the Arabs on the other is the existence and the effects of Zionism. Whoever is sincerely interested in the future of Israelis and Arabs in the Middle East should seriously reflect on this.

25

Abominable Warmongering on the Left

In the cacophonous chorus of warmongers—among shrieks of hawks, howls of jackals, and foul laughter of hyenas—the attentive ear discerns a distinctive discordant sound coming from the far left: it is the hoot of the AWL. The misleader of the Alliance for Workers' Liberty, Sean Matgamna, has published an article ("What if Israel Bombs Iran?," *Solidarity and Workers' Liberty* 3, no. 136, July 2008) in which he argues that while an attack on Iran "will most likely lead to great carnage in the Middle East, and beyond," it would be wrong to object to it if it is undertaken by Israel.

He is not actually *advocating* or *endorsing* such an attack; oh, no! Nor does he "take political responsibility for it"—as if it would occur to anyone to hold SM or his little flock responsible for starting a major Middle Eastern conflagration. No, no, no! He only refuses to say anything against Israeli aggression. Go ahead, Israel, bomb away, feel free to cause "large-scale Iranian civilian 'collateral' casualties"! SM will look the other way.

Here is why SM thinks "that there is good reason for Israel to make a precipitate strike at Iranian nuclear capacity. . . . Yet the plain fact is that nuclear bombs in the hands of a regime which openly declares its desire to destroy Israel are not something Israel will peacefully tolerate. They will act to stop it while it can still be stopped without the risk of a nuclear strike against Israel. Unless work on an Iranian nuclear bomb has definitively ended Israel will bomb Iran, with or without the agreement of the USA and NATO."

This statement of alleged "plain fact" contains two assertions which, far from being factual, are sheer flights of fantasy.

This and the next chapter are a polemic against Sean Matgamna, leader of the Alliance for Workers' Liberty, which is the only radical-left group in the UK that sympathizes with Zionism, tends to Islamophobia, and does not resolutely oppose imperialist intervention. This piece was published in *Weekly Worker* 734, August 28, 2008.

First, SM repeats the fabrication of the warmongering propagandists that the Iranian regime "openly declares its desire to destroy Israel." This is simply untrue: no such declaration is on record. Indeed, SM knows very well that it is a lie, because the only Iranian "declaration" he himself dredges up is President Ahmedinejad's wishful statement: "Thanks to people's wishes and God's will, the trend for the existence of the Zionist regime is [going] downwards and this is what God has promised and what all nations want. Just as the Soviet Union was wiped out and today does not exist, so will the Zionist regime soon be wiped out."

There is nothing here about an Iranian "desire to destroy Israel"; nor even a wish to see that country destroyed by others. What is plainly expressed here is a wish for the disappearance of the Zionist regime. (On another occasion Ahmedinejad spoke about the "regime that is occupying the Holy City [of Jerusalem].") This is made abundantly clear by the explicit analogy with the demise of the Soviet Union. Even SM must know the difference between destruction of a country and demise of a regime. And as even he must be aware, the Soviet Union was not destroyed as a *country*; rather, the Soviet regime imploded and collapsed under its internal contradictions.

Other warmongers have mistranslated Ahmedinejad's statements and misquoted him as saying that he advocates "wiping Israel off the map." SM chooses a different tack, of warmongering lite: he simply endorses a blatant inflammatory misinterpretation of the Iranian president's words, so as to justify his own failure to condemn Israeli aggression.

Let me make it clear: the reactionary theocracy of Iran is detestable. But this does not give anyone license to distort what its leaders actually say—especially when the distortion is designed to excuse an aggressive war.

The second fanciful idea contained in SM's "plain fact" is that Israel might "bomb Iran, with or without the agreement of the USA and NATO."

Now, this is very strange indeed. It is universally acknowledged by Israeli politicians and commentators—both those who support an attack on Iran and those who oppose it—that Israel cannot possibly take such a step without an American "green light." This is also quite rightly taken for granted by all serious commentators outside Israel.[1]

Of course, as SM rightly remarks, "Israel is no state's puppet." Only a simpleton would claim this. In fact, it is a junior partner, regional subcontractor, and the most intimate ally of US imperialism. And precisely because of this it cannot undertake a major military move without US approval.

Indeed, of all Israel's many wars of colonial aggression, the only one in which it did not seek or get an American green light was the infamous Suez war of 1956. But in that case Israel conspired with Britain and France, the latter being at that time Israel's main imperialist ally and senior partner.

While the Suez aggression was exceptional in this one sense, it is an instructive model in another sense: the scenario in which an initial Israeli attack serves as a prearranged pretext for the intervention of its imperialist senior partner(s). If Israel will indeed attack Iran, we shall witness a broadly similar scenario.

So why does SM go out of his way to cast doubt on what is so obvious to every person familiar with the facts? Is it ignorance, or is there another reason?

I think there is another reason: it is his unique position *on the radical left* as cheerleader for Zionism and the Israeli settler state. Unlike bourgeois warmongers, he has a need to deny the umbilical ties of Zionism and Israel to imperialism; he does not wish to be seen winking indulgently at an imperialist intrigue. So he prefers to appear ignorant.

Sean Matgamna's Straw Men

Instead of straightforwardly producing further arguments for his refusal-in-advance to condemn a future Israeli attack on Iran, SM has hit on a diabolically clever and startlingly original stratagem—he erects a set of straw men: counterarguments as to why an Israeli attack supposedly *ought* to be condemned. As these arguments are all patently absurd, SM wins the debate with his straw alter ego by easy *reductio*: there is no need for him to contest the counterarguments, as they are self-refuting. He evidently expects his readers not to notice that this glorious victory is achieved by a sleight of hand: the arguments he sets up against Israeli aggression are all *deliberately* dodgy.

Let us have a look at these counterarguments, which are set up as a series of rhetorical questions. "In the name of what alternative," asks SM rhetorically, "should we condemn Israel [if it bombs Iran]? [Is it t]he inalienable right of every state to have nuclear weapons—and here a state whose clerical fascist rulers might see a nuclear Armageddon, involving a retaliatory Israeli nuclear strike against Iran in the way a God-crazed suicide bomber sees blowing himself to pieces?"

Apparently SM believes that Israel, a non-expansionist and non-aggressive state, is not sufficiently God-crazed to forfeit its inalienable right to monopoly of nuclear weapons in the Middle East.

Actually, the historical record shows that Israel has consistently acted in a much more ruthlessly aggressive and destructive way than Iran. The image of Iran's rulers as God-crazed fanatics who would not mind incinerating their own country for the satisfaction of destroying Israel is a pure invention of Western and Israeli warmongering propaganda, here recycled by SM. The truth is that these clerical leaders are clever, cautious, calculating bastards. Sadly, Western and Western-inspired adventurist aggression has repeatedly played into their hands.

And, just by the way, let me note that so far there is no evidence that Iran is about to develop nuclear weapons. We don't need to trust in the Iranian rulers' assurances that they are not planning to produce nuclear bombs; but neither should we believe the Western and Israeli warmongers' claim that Iran is engaged in such a project.

SM's next rhetorical question is: "[Should we condemn an Israeli attack] because Israel has nuclear weapons, and therefore the Arab and Islamic states should have them too?" Here again SM implies that Israel has some God-given right to monopoly of nuclear weapons. Moreover, he maligns the leftist opponents of aggression by attributing to them the absurd idea that Arab and Islamic states "should" possess nuclear weapons because Israel does. He slyly avoids turning the argument around: surely, no country should have nuclear weapons. And the only basis on which we can justly demand that Iran be forbidden to have them is to make the entire region free of nuclear weapons. This is the demand we must raise. Of course, Iran should not have nuclear weapons, but neither should Israel. And certainly we must condemn Israeli aggression designed to preserve its nuclear monopoly.

Next: "[Should we condemn an Israeli attack] because we are unconditional pacifists? We think military action is never justified, and therefore Israel has no right to attack Iran, not even to stop it acquiring the nuclear means to mount the ultimate suicide bomb attack on Israel." This is a deliberately silly question. But again we must turn it around. Iran has no nuclear weapons; and it has never threatened to attack Israel by nuclear or conventional means. On the other hand, Israel has a large nuclear arsenal, and it is known to have seriously considered using it against its Arab neighbors in 1967[2] and 1973[3] and—as has been widely reported in the press—recently against Iran. So should we condone a preemptive bombing attack on Israel's Dimona nuclear installation?[4]

And another silly rhetorical question: "[Should we condemn an Israeli attack] because we would prefer to live in a world where such choices would not be posed, where relations between states and peoples are governed by reason, and strictly peaceful means?" Well, yes, of course we would prefer to live in a world where such choices would not be posed. But so long as we live in today's world, where they are posed, we should make the *right* choice: oppose imperialist attacks—whether direct or by proxy—even when mounted against a detestable regime. Because today US imperialism is humanity's worst enemy, and its global hegemony poses the greatest danger to humanity's future.

And yet another one: "[Should we condemn an Israeli attack] because for choice we would live in a world where the workers of Israel, Iran, Iraq were united in opposition to all their rulers, and strong enough to get rid of them and bring to the region an era of socialist and democratic peace and understanding?" Ditto; see above. Now he slightly changes tack; his next rhetorical question is: "[Should we condemn an Israeli attack] because Israel would in attacking Iran be only an American imperialist tool, against a mere regional power; and that cancels out the genuine self-defence element in pre-emptive Israeli military action against Iranian nuclear weapons?"

As I have pointed out, the idea that Israel is "only an American imperialist tool" is a red herring. On the contrary, the fact that Israel will *not* be acting as a mere American imperialist tool makes it even worse, and is *all the more reason* for condemning and opposing its aggression. Because in addition to acting for its imperialist sponsor,

Israel will at the same time be acting to defend its own regional hegemony, nuclear monopoly, and freedom to oppress the Palestinian people and colonize their lands.

In this connection let me again recall the Suez war of 1956. It would have been bad enough if Israel had acted as a mere tool of French and British imperialism. But it was actually worse than that: Israel had its own special agenda of annexation and expansion. I am old enough to remember hearing Ben-Gurion's chilling (November 6, 1956) message to the Israeli forces in Sharm al-Sheikh, at the tip of occupied Sinai, in which he proclaimed the creation of the new and much expanded Third Kingdom of Israel. (He was obviously oblivious to the sinister Second-World-War connotation of this term.) Needless to say, on that occasion too the Israeli pretext was "self-defense." Israel's 1956 attempt at expansion was short-lived—only because the United States, which had not been consulted and had not given the tripartite aggression a green light, compelled the three unruly conspirators to withdraw, just to show them who is boss.

We have a few more clever rhetorical questions to get through. Here is the next one: "[Should we condemn an Israeli attack] because Israel has no right to exist anyway, and therefore no right to defend itself? (This will in fact be the underlying attitude of most of the kitsch left.)" Dear SM, please pull the other one. As we have just seen, the pretext of "self-defense" has a very long white beard. I have already pointed out that what Israel would be "defending" are its indefensible privileges and interests as colonial settler state and imperialist subcontractor.

One more thing. I suppose I must belong to what SM so cutely calls "the kitsch left," because I do think that Israel has no right to exist *as presently constituted or in anything like its present form*: a colonial expansionist ethnocratic-racist settler state, a junior partner of imperialism, to which it is structurally and inseparably allied. And I also think that those on the left who advocate that so-called "right" are in fact fake leftists.

The reader may be losing patience with SM's ever-so-clever rhetorical questions. Please bear with me: there are just three left. Here is the next one: "[Should we condemn an Israeli attack] because the Iranian government, Islamic clerical fascist though it is, is an 'anti-imperialist' power and must be unconditionally supported against the US, NATO, Israel?" This is a transparent pretext. SM himself knows very well that opposition to US/Israeli aggression against Iran in no way implies "unconditional support" for the Iranian regime. In fact, he himself has told us at the very beginning of his article that "[a]n attack would strengthen the Iranian regime and license a smash-down on its critics, including working class critics, inside Iran." Quite right! But since an attack on Iran is going to strengthen the Iranian regime, this is all the more reason why leftist opponents of that regime ought resolutely to condemn such an attack.

Incidentally, this rhetorical gem reveals what really goes on in SM's mind. As the reader may have noticed, in all SM's previous excuses for an attack on Iran he assumed explicitly or implicitly that the attacker would be Israel, acting in "self-defense." But this latest rhetorical question provides an argument for not opposing an attack by the United States or NATO. Inadvertently, SM has given us an illustration of the fact that you cannot consistently be soft on the Israeli state without being also soft on its imperialist sponsor and close senior partner.

Let me also note in passing that SM is doing here what no serious Marxist should do: for the second time in this article he is using "fascist" as a mere invective rather than as a precise political term. He should know better.

SM's penultimate pretext is a real beauty: "[Should we condemn an Israeli attack] because Israel refuses to dismantle the Jewish national state peacefully and agree to an Arab Palestinian state in which Jews would have religious but not Israeli national rights, and therefore socialists, 'anti-racists,' and anti-imperialists must be on the side of those who would conquer and destroy it, even, in this case, with nuclear weapons?"

The oh-so subtle rhetorical legerdemain here is to smuggle past the reader a false alternative: *either* you accept Israel as "the Jewish national state" *or else* you must accept an "Arab Palestinian state in which Jews would have religious but not Israeli national rights." SM implies that there is no other choice. And, moreover, he threatens his reader: if you reject the former, "the Jewish national state," then ("and therefore . . .") you must resign yourself to Israel's destruction "even with nuclear weapons."

I have already dealt with the hogwash of the threat of nuclear destruction of Israel. It is the old whine about "poor little Samson." In fact it is Israel that is the threatening regional nuclear superpower. The threat that it faces is not destruction but the possible loss of its regional hegemony.

But let us unpack this "national Jewish state," which is what SM wants us to accept. According to Zionist doctrine—which is the official ruling ideology of Israel—Israel is not the state of its actual inhabitants, irrespective of ethnicity. Rather, it is supposed to be the homeland of all Jews wherever they are. For, according to this ideology, all the Jews around the world constitute a single nation. The true homeland of every Jew is not the country in which s/he may have been born and in which his or her family may have resided for generations. The homeland of this alleged nation is the biblical Land of Israel, over which it has an ancient inalienable—indeed God-given—national right. Non-Jews living in the Jewish homeland are mere foreign interlopers. Past, present, and future Zionist colonization is justified as "return to the homeland"—a right possessed by Jews but denied to those foreign interlopers, the Palestinian refugees, who have been legitimately evicted from the Jewish homeland.

Socialists must surely reject this supremacist ethnocratic-racist colonizing ideology. Israel as a "national Jewish state"—in the actual sense, which I have just explicated—is unacceptable.

But the alternative to this is not an "Arab Palestinian state in which Jews would have religious but not Israeli national rights" as some bourgeois Palestinian Arab nationalists have proposed. Why should socialists confine themselves to the false choice offered to us by SM between Zionism and bourgeois Palestinian nationalism? Rather, the alternative supported by true socialists is a settlement based on equal rights: not only equal *individual* rights for all but also equal *national* rights for the two actual national groups of Palestine/Israel. Who are these two groups? First, the indigenous people, the Palestinian Arabs, including the refugees ethnically cleansed by Zionist colonization, who surely must have the right to return to their homeland. Second, the Hebrew-speaking settler nation that has come into existence in that country. (They are often referred to as "Israeli Jews"; but this real national group must be distinguished from the alleged worldwide Jewish "nation.")

No other kind of settlement is acceptable to socialists. But this clearly means rejection of the "national Jewish state" in the present Zionist sense; and indeed it requires the overthrow of Zionism.

We are coming to SM's final rhetorical question: "[Should we condemn an Israeli attack] because we don't deal in vulgar practical choices but in pure historical essences such as 'anti-imperialism'?"

It seems that SM has run out of pretexts, because here he is clearly repeating himself. So I can pass on this last one.

In conclusion, let me make an observation. From its very beginning, the Zionist project of colonization was based on a Faustian deal with whatever imperialist power was dominant in the Middle East. The Israeli settler state—which is both the product of that colonizing project and an instrument for its ongoing metastatic expansion—is structurally allied to imperialist domination of the region—not as a mere tool but as a regional colonial power with a malignant agenda of its own.[5]

For this reason, let me repeat, you cannot consistently be soft on the Israeli state without being also soft on its imperialist sponsor and close senior partner. Indeed, we have seen that SM himself, in at least one of his fake rhetorical questions, inadvertently provides an argument for acquiescing not only in an Israeli attack on Iran but also in one by the United States and NATO.

Those on the left who persist in supporting Zionism and its settler state end up as shamelessly open outright social-imperialists.

Comrades of AWL should wake up to the peril of the slippery slope down which SM is misleading them.

26

Zionism: Propaganda and Reality

In the July 24 issue of *Solidarity*, organ of the AWL, Sean Matgamna published an article "What if Israel Bombs Iran?" in which he argued against an outright condemnation of Israel in case it launches an attack on Iran. I responded with a brief polemic against him in the August 28 issue of *Weekly Worker*: "Abominable Warmongering on the Left." SM has now come back in *Solidarity* of September 11 with a tediously lengthy response, written as a personal letter to me: "Israel, Iran, and Socialism."

I shall not follow SM in using the form of a personal letter: I do not believe in personalizing political polemics. Nor do I intend to write a long reply: that would tax the reader's patience and in any case is quite unnecessary. Instead of refuting each and every allegation that SM makes in his "letter," I refer the reader to his original article and to my August 28 reply to it. The reader will find that SM's allegations and excuses are far-fetched or self-refuting. Here is just one example of many.

Matgamna's Mild "Objection"

In his "letter" he protests: "I did and do 'object' to [an Israeli attack on Iran], and said so a number of times in the short article!" This seems clear enough. But then it transpires that his "objection" is not really that much of an objection:

> My language expressed my determination not to join in with, or peacefully to tolerate, the outright condemnation of Israel that will most likely follow an Israeli attack, condemnation rooted in the "demon-Zionism" prejudice of the kitsch-left and in the view that Israel has no right to defend itself . . .
>
> I will not, in response to an Israeli strike at Iranian nuclear installations, adopt the viewpoint that there is something so incomprehensible in such a strike that Israel as such must be condemned outright.

This continues the debate of the previous chapter. It was published in *Weekly Worker* 737, September 18, 2008.

So he will "object," but will not "condemn outright." Weasel words. I suppose his "objection" will take the form of a gentle wistful shaking of his head.

In order to explain away this "objection" that is short of "outright condemnation," he now tells us: "I bracketed the possible 'strike' I was discussing with the September 2007 Israeli attack on nuclear facilities in Syria, and the June 1981 [attack] on an Iraqi nuclear installation; there is therefore no reasonable ground for you or anyone else not understanding what sort of attack I was talking about."

No reasonable ground? The 1981 Israeli bombing of Osirak and the 2007 bombing of the Syrian "facilities"[1] were directed against single vulnerable and isolated targets, and the countries attacked were not in a position to retaliate. None of this is true of the intended attack on Iran: its nuclear installations—so far consistent with nonmilitary use—are widely dispersed and dug deep underground, probably inaccessible to conventional (nonnuclear) bombs.[2] And Iran is well capable of massive retaliation, which means that the bombing will only be the start of a prolonged bloody conflict.

In fact, SM knows this very well, because at the very opening of his original article he told us exactly about what sort of attack he was talking: "An attack on Iran will most likely lead to great carnage in the Middle East, and beyond, as supporters of Iran resort to suicide bombings in retaliation. There might well be large scale Iranian civilian 'collateral' casualties. An attack would strengthen the Iranian regime and license a smash down on its critics, including working class critics, inside Iran. It would throw Iraq back into the worst chaos."

So we have every reason to conclude, despite SM's protestations, that it is this kind of attack for which he refuses to condemn Israel outright.

And so it goes. SM's ramblings are full of such inconsistencies and absurdities. It would take far too long and would be far too boring to list them here. I leave it to the reader to discover other gems of this sort, if s/he feels so inclined.

I prefer to concentrate here on the core issue: SM's appalling apologetic position on Zionism.

The Dream of "Demon-Zionism"

The fundamental fallacy in SM's lengthy "letter" is his failure to come to grips with the nature of Zionism. In the whole of that tedious tract, the word "Zionism" always appears in scare quotes, or in the dismissive-derisive combination "demon-Zionism." Anti-Zionism is referred to exclusively by the derogatory term "*absolute* anti-Zionism," as though opposition to Zionism were *per se* something distastefully fanatical.

This issue is fundamental because his basic argument is that if Israel attacks Iran, that would have nothing much to do with Zionism. Rather, it would be an act of preemptive self-defense, aimed at preventing the destruction of Israel by a future and hypothetical Iranian nuclear weapon. Here is a sample of his argument:

In the case at hand, none of the demon-Zionism stuff is necessary to explain Israel's likely action; there is good reason, from an Israeli point of view, to refuse to stand by and let people who have said that they want to destroy Israel acquire the weapons with which they just might try to do that.

. . . Some of what I wrote was explicitly an account of how Israelis would see nuclear-armed Islamist fanatics in Iran and clearly labeled as that. I used the tone and manner proper to one who thinks that Israel has a right to defend itself, against people on the would-be left whose starting point is that it doesn't, and, because of its origins, never could. To counter the demon-Zionism "explanations," I described how most Israelis see the prospect of an Iranian nuclear bomb.

. . . My language expressed my determination not to join in with, or peacefully to tolerate, the outright condemnation of Israel that will most likely follow an Israeli attack, condemnation rooted in the "demon-Zionism" prejudice of the kitsch-left and in the view that Israel has no right to defend itself.

This is perhaps how "*most* Israelis" see it. *Most* Israelis are brainwashed by Israeli propaganda—which SM himself has swallowed whole and regurgitates to his readers.

But when members of the Israeli "defense" establishment are engaged in serious discussion—rather than propaganda for the consumption of the deluded masses and willing dupes—they say something quite different. On September 9, 2008, the *Jerusalem Post* reported on a conference held at Israel's Institute for National Security Studies. Here is an excerpt from the report:

Iranian Nukes Mean End of Zionism

Iran's success in obtaining a nuclear capability will deter Jews from immigrating to Israel, cause many Israelis to leave and will be the end of the "Zionist dream," former deputy defense minister Ephraim Sneh said Tuesday.

"A nuclear weapon in Iranian hands will be an intolerable reality for Israel," Sneh said during a conference on Iran's nuclear program at the Institute for National Security Studies (INSS) in Tel Aviv.

"The decision-making process in Israel will be under constant [Iranian] influence—this will be the end of the Zionist dream."

Former Mossad chief Ephraim Halevy slammed Israeli political leaders for calling Iran's nuclear threat "an existential threat."

"There is something wrong with informing our enemy that they can bring about our demise," Halevy said. "It is also wrong that we inform the world that the moment the Iranians have a nuclear capability there is a countdown to the destruction of the State of Israel."

"We are the superpower in the Middle East and it is time that we began behaving like [a] superpower," he said.

Iran's real goal, Halevy said, was to turn itself into a regional superpower and reach a "state of equality" with the United States in their diplomatic dealings.

Sneh said that while the military option was not preferred, Israel needed to keep it on the table since such a possibility was the motivation for the international community's efforts to use diplomacy to stop Iran. Sneh added that he was confident that the IDF was capable of successfully carrying out a military strike against Iran.

"We grew up in a place that when the political echelon wanted something, the professional echelon knew how to do it," he said. "I believe this has not changed in 2008."[3]

We have just seen that SM attempts to explain—and excuse—an Israeli attack on Iran as a defensive measure in the face of an existential threat, rather than as motivated by "the demon-Zionism stuff." Next time the INSS holds a conference, they ought perhaps to invite SM to lecture to the Israeli "defense community" and tell them how wrong they are.

The two Israeli security bigwigs quoted above do not exactly see eye to eye with each other, but neither of them shares the view of the AWL expert on Israel's motives. Both Ephraims evidently agree that the issue is not the survival of Israel. Unlike SM, they do not believe Israel faces a real threat of physical destruction. Halevy, former head of Mossad (Israel's counterpart to the CIA or Britain's MI6) does not seem too worried. General Sneh, who is a "defense" politician and a bit of an ideologue, *is* worried; however, unlike SM, what he is worried about is not Israel's existence, but the fate of the "Zionist dream"—that very *"demon-Zionism stuff, none [of which] is necessary to explain Israel's likely action,"* according to SM.

Ephraim Sneh's worry may be excessive, but it is not irrational. Unlike SM, he knows very well that Zionism is an ongoing expansionist colonizing project. It requires an ever-growing Jewish population in order to colonize more and more Arab land and to neutralize the "demographic threat" of being "swamped" by the Palestinian Arab population. He is afraid that if Israel is deprived of its exclusive hegemonic position in the Middle East, then it may lose some of its appeal to Jewish immigrants and induce some of its existing Jewish population to leave. Moreover, a nuclear Iran may well impose constraints on Israel's political options: its "decision-making process . . . will be under constant [Iranian] influence [and] this will be the end of the Zionist dream."

In fact, if you read the *Jerusalem Post* report carefully, you will realize that Iran's nuclear program (whose military purpose is as yet purely hypothetical) is from Israel's point of view only part of a larger issue. What Israeli leaders and planners find "intolerable" is *any* threat to Israel's regional hegemony and its privileged status as "the superpower in the Middle East": because it is this status that allows it to proceed with the Zionist project of colonization without serious let or hindrance.

Let me make myself very clear. Socialists everywhere, and the Iranian working class, have very good reasons to oppose the theocratic repressive regime of Iran, and to condemn any plans it may have for acquiring nuclear weapons (if it transpires that it has such plans). But concern for the "Zionist dream"—let alone the spurious existential threat to Israel—are *not* among these good reasons.

Recycling Israeli Propaganda

This is just one of several instances of SM gullibly lapping up and recycling the crassest Israeli propaganda, while ignoring what Israeli political analysts and military chiefs say when they are not in propaganda mode.

Here is another example. In my August 28 article I pointed out that in 1967 and 1973 Israel seriously considered using nuclear weapons against neighboring Arab countries. In his "letter" SM retorts:

> It is not good that Israel has nuclear weapons; but the idea that Israel would use nu-clear bombs in any situation other than a perceived immediate threat of being over-whelmed by Arab or Islamist forces is, I suggest, on the same plane as what the *Weekly Worker*'s front-page text and picture attributed to me.
>
> Your own cited cases when Israeli leaders supposedly discussed using nuclear weapons, or the threat of nuclear weapons—"it is known to have seriously consid-ered using it against its Arab neighbors in 1967 and 1973"—were situations of such perceived immediate threat.

Perceived by whom? Admittedly, this was the perception spread about by the Is-raeli propaganda machine. But the reality was quite different. Both 1967 and 1973 wars were fought entirely outside the Green Line (Israel's de facto border from 1949 to 1967). It is true that in 1967 the task of Israel's disinformation campaign was made easy by Gamal Abdul Nasser's foolish saber rattling. But the Israeli leadership knew very well that this was mere posturing. General Ezer Weizman, member of the inner circle of the Israeli military and political establishment, who served as de-fense minister and eventually became president of Israel, affirmed that in 1967 "there was never any danger of extermination."[4] And the respected Israeli soldier and scholar General Matityahu Peled put it even more strongly: "To pretend that the Egyptian forces massed on our frontiers were in a position to threaten the ex-istence of Israel constitutes an insult not only to the intelligence of anyone capable of analysing this sort of situation, but above all an insult to the IDF [the Israeli armed forces]."[5]

I wonder what the late General Peled would have said about the intelligence and analytic capability of Sean Matgamna.

All serious historical research published since then—much of it by Israeli his-torians—confirms the assessment of Generals Weizman and Peled.

The situation in 1973 was actually more transparent: it was an attempt by Egypt and Syria to regain the parts of their national territories occupied by Israel in 1967. Israel within the Green Line was not even remotely threatened.

What was really threatened was not Israel's existence but its position of absolute regional military supremacy. This was felt by the Zionist leaders of Israel to be "in-tolerable," as it would have jeopardized the "Zionist dream" of ongoing coloniza-tion. This is why they seriously considered using nuclear weapons: in order to prevent Egypt and Syria regaining their occupied lands *by military means*. In the event, this proved unnecessary, as Israel was able—thanks to a massive airlift of conventional weapons from the United States—to push back both Arab armies, and even occupy briefly additional Egyptian territory, in Africa itself, west of the Suez Canal.

Is Zionism a Kind of Nationalism?

Underlying SM's blundering assessment of the true motives of Israel's past and present policy, which may drive its leaders to attack Iran, is his abysmal failure or deliberate refusal to recognize what Zionism is all about. I have heard SM accused of actually being a Zionist. I don't think this is quite true; but he has gulped a great deal of Zionist propaganda, of the kind concocted specifically for the Western left. A key element of this propaganda is the plea: *"Don't demonize Israel and Zionism; Israel is just a normal nation-state, and Zionism is a common or garden-variety of nationalism."* SM parrots this propaganda, including the use of the scare term "demon."

SM repeatedly characterizes Zionism as "nationalism," which according to him socialists should repudiate no less, but also no more, than they repudiate any other bourgeois nationalism.

But here he gets a little confused: he is unable to decide which *nation* it is that Zionism is supposed to be the *nation*-alism *of.* Sometimes he speaks of Zionism as synonymous with *"Israeli* nationalism"; for example: "Israeli nationalism is like any other nationalism, concerned with those it considers its own and downgrading and dismissive of others. . . . Israeli nationalism, 'Zionism'—as I'm sure you know far better than I do—faced tremendous opposition."

But almost immediately he changes his mind and refers to Zionism repeatedly as *"Jewish* nationalism."

These two descriptions of Zionism cannot both be correct: not all Israelis are Jews, and only about one-third of all Jews are Israelis. I will now show that *both* descriptions are in fact *incorrect.*

"Israel" is the name of a state, not of a nation; strictly and legally speaking— that is, according to Israeli law—"Israeli" denotes citizenship, not national affiliation. However, the majority community of Israel, the *Hebrews* (aka the "Israeli Jews") do indeed possess all the *objective* attributes of a nation, in the modern sense of this word: territorial contiguity; a complete class structure (similar to that of other modern capitalist nations); a common language of everyday discourse (modern Hebrew, which is unique to them); and a secular culture, both highbrow and pop.

Most Hebrews do subscribe to Zionist ideology, which is relentlessly inculcated into them by the Israeli state. So can Zionism be described as Hebrew (or "Israeli-Jewish") nationalism? Not really. Because the last thing that a nationalist ideology (as normally understood) can ever do is deny the very existence of the nation of which it is the nation-alism. But Zionism does adamantly deny the existence of a distinct Hebrew nation—that settler nation that has in reality come into being as a result of the Zionist colonization of Palestine! As a consequence, the Hebrew nation is but dimly self-aware of its being a distinct nation.

For according to Zionist ideology, all the Jews around the world constitute a single nation. The homeland of this alleged nation is the biblical "Land of Israel," which is considerably larger than Palestine of the British Mandate.[6] According to Zionist ideology there is no Hebrew nation but merely members of the worldwide Jewish nation who have already "returned" to their homeland, an advance guard of their brethren in the Diaspora, who have a right—indeed a sacred duty—to follow the vanguard and be "ingathered" in the Land of Israel.

Zionism portrays itself as the national movement of this worldwide alleged nation. But this self-description cannot seriously be taken at face value. Zionism cannot really be regarded as "Jewish nationalism," except in a very far-fetched and highly paradoxical sense, for the simple reason that world Jewry is not a nation in any recognizable modern sense of the term: it lacks *all* the objective attributes of a nation. A British Jew living in London and, say, an Iranian Jew living in Tehran have nothing in common except religion: the religion practiced by themselves; or (if they are "secular" Jews) residual memories of the religion practiced by their parents or grandparents. Needless to say: *nationhood* in the modern sense (at least since the French Revolution) is a secular concept, unrelated to religion.

So Zionism is not the nationalism of the real Hebrew ("Israeli-Jewish") nation, because Zionist ideology denies the existence of this nation. And it cannot rightly be the nationalism of the alleged worldwide Jewish nation, because such a nation does not really exist.

For the same reason Israel, as presently constituted, is not a nation-state. It is certainly not *a state of all its citizens*—which is the demand raised by the Arab and Hebrew democratic forces in that country, and should be supported by all progressive people everywhere. But it is not even the state of its real majority nation, the Hebrew nation. It is officially the self-declared state of a *non-nation:* world Jewry. This is enshrined in Israeli legislation, most prominently in the Law of Return, which grants every Jewish immigrant automatic Israeli citizenship. These immigrants are encouraged to colonize lands expropriated from Palestinian Arabs. At the same time, Israel denies the right of Palestinian Arab refugees to return to their homeland, from which they have been ethnically cleansed.

This is why the call for the overthrow, the *de-Zionization,* of the deeply discriminatory Israeli state is an elementary democratic demand.

What Is Zionism?

The above discussion is not a mere formal quibble; rather, it was a needed clarification, before I go on to explain what Zionism is in fact all about.

I will do so in bare brief outline. The reader can find a fuller analysis, with supporting quotes from Zionist documents, in the transcript of my lecture "Israelis and Palestinians: Conflict and Resolution."* (I referred to that lecture also in my August 28 article, but SM evidently didn't bother to look it up, for in his "letter" he poses to me questions that I addressed there in some detail.)

Zionism arose in the latter part of the nineteenth century as a false response to the so-called Jewish problem: the persecution of Jews in many European (mainly Eastern and Central European) countries. A minority of European Jews, predominantly bourgeois and petty bourgeois, came to believe that it is pointless to combat anti-Semitism, because it is inherent in the gentile (i.e., non-Jewish) psyche. In fact, these founders of Zionism accepted the main premise of anti-Semitism: that Jews ought not to live among gentiles but should go away and live among their own kind.†

That was the era of surging Central European nationalism and the heyday of imperialist colonialism. So the Zionist ideologues declared that the Jews were a nation, albeit a dispersed one; and concluded that "going away to live among their own kind" meant in practice colonizing some dependent territory in what was later called the "third world" and transforming it into a Jewish nation-state. The indigenous population was to be ethnically cleansed, as indeed was standard practice in many settler states. This would ensure that the Jewish colonizers would form a decisive majority in their projected nation-state. All this is very clearly stated in seminal Zionist writings.

After some hesitation in deciding the best territory to be colonized,[7] the Holy Land was chosen because of its powerful emotional appeal as the cradle and spiritual focus of Judaism.

That left only one problem: in order to colonize Palestine, the Zionist project needed the protection and sponsorship of whichever imperial power was dominant in the region. In Zionist parlance, what was needed was an imperial "charter" for colonizing Palestine. The Zionists understood perfectly well that in exchange for imperial sponsorship, the future settler state would have to serve as a Western bastion in the face of the "Asiatic barbarism" of the entire region. This too is stated clearly and explicitly in seminal Zionist writings.

Toward the end of the First World War, the British government issued the longed-for charter, known as the Balfour Declaration. The idea was that the Zionist settlers would serve Britain by "forming for England a little loyal Jewish Ulster in a sea of potentially hostile Arabism."‡

The rest is really and truly history. The Faustian pact between the Zionist colonizing project and Britain worked well, until the former expanded and outgrew

---

* Chapter 33 in this book.

† For a discussion of the affinity, and occasional collaboration, of Zionism with anti-Semitism, see chapter 24 of this book.

‡ Ronald Storrs, *Orientations*, 345. See chapter 23 of this book.

its utility to British imperialism by clashing with other British designs and interests in the region.

By that time British global power was declining in any case. So Zionism—true to its long-term strategy—found a new patron: the United States, which replaced Britain as the new global superpower and overlord of the oil-rich Middle East.

Now let us get back to the position put forward by SM. His claim that Zionism is simply a regular kind of nationalism is untenable not only because, as I have shown, there is no real nation of which Zionism is the nation-alism, but because it ignores and suppresses the very essence of what Zionism is in actual reality: a colonizing project, structurally and inseparably allied to imperialism.

Ridiculous Errors

Failure—or refusal—to grasp the essence of Zionism leads SM to all sorts of ridiculous and dangerous errors. Some of these I have pointed out above: his childishly naive recitation of the crassest claims of Israeli propaganda, in total disregard even of serious analysis by high-ranking members of the Israeli establishment.

His original article and subsequent "letter" are replete with such nonsense. For example, he assures us: "I would agree that Israel has no 'right' to continue occupying the West Bank and building Jewish-colonist settlements there. By that I mean: I don't want Israel to go on doing that, and I'm on the side of the Palestinians in the post-1967 Occupied Territories and of those Israelis, Jewish and Arab, who want that to stop and fight to stop it."

Implicit in this generous "agreement" is the absurd idea that Zionist colonization began in 1967. It ignores and suppresses the ethnic cleansing of 1947–9 and the right of the refugees of that war to return to their homeland. It also ignores the racist settler-state character of Israel *within* the Green Line, whose Palestinian Arab minority (those who escaped the ethnic cleansing of the majority in 1947–49) have been deprived of most of their lands (which were expropriated and given over to Jewish settlers), and denied equal civil rights, let alone rights as a national minority.

All that SM wants Israel to do is to stop building new settlements in the West Bank—which by now is already heavily colonized and torn into small fragments that are worse than bantustans: more like Indian reservations.

He only has to look at an up-to-date map of Israeli colonization of the West Bank to realize that the "AWL demand of Israel that it should vacate the 1967-occupied territories and agree to an independent Palestinian state" is not remotely realistic without removal of the "facts on the ground" created by Israel, including some half a million settlers. None of this can happen without a fundamental change within Israel, amounting to the overthrow of its Zionist regime. But SM does not seem to be interested in maps or facts on the ground. He is quite happy just repeating the inanities of "left-wing" Zionist mantras.

Another astoundingly ridiculous claim made by SM is that Israel might "bomb Iran, with or without the agreement of the USA and NATO." I am not sure what NATO—which is itself a largely American instrument—has to do with all this, but the very idea that Israel might bomb Iran without US consent is patently absurd.

As readers may recall, in 1982, when Britain wanted to regain the Falklands—which (moral considerations aside) were in international law sovereign British territory—it needed the consent of the United States. How can SM possibly imagine that Israel would take a step that would surely have a profound effect on US interests without an American green light? Besides, in order to reach Iran, Israeli bombers will need to overfly Iraq, which is under US occupation. If the overflight is not pre-arranged, the bombers may well be shot down. Israel will also need a fresh supply of appropriate weapons from the United States.[8]

SM commits such a silly error because he fails—or refuses—to grasp the true nature of the tie between the Zionist settler state and its imperial senior partner.

In his "letter" he compounds this absurdity by claiming that if Israel does attack Iran then "[w]e can be sure that everyone within earshot of us, including the British government, will oppose an Israeli strike."

He is sure, is he? What grounds does he have for such certainty? In 2006, when Israel invaded and bombed Lebanon, murdering over a thousand Lebanese civilians, and leaving behind a million cluster bomblets, Britain's poodle government followed the US lead in studiously refraining from even calling for a halt to hostilities, let alone condemning Israel. And now he believes that Britain would oppose an Israeli attack—an attack that, I repeat, will be unthinkable without overt or tacit US approval!

Enough! Let me conclude with Heywood's famous couplet, taken from his 1546 "Dialogue of Proverbs":

Who is so deafe, or so blynde, as is hee,
That wilfully will nother here nor see?

Part V
REVIEWS

27

Things Bad Begun . . .

B y far the best part of this book is its epilogue, in which Avishai berates American Jews for their uncritical adulation and idolization of Israel and its policies, to the point that "Israeli politicians, including the guilty General Sharon, [are] received in American synagogues with a reverence justly denied them at home" (p. 353). Among non-Orthodox American Jews, this subservience has replaced the Jewish religion as the basis for Jewish identity and institutional life. Avishai—a Jew who tried to make his home in Israel but returned to Canada when, after three years, he and his wife felt they "were living among foreigners"—believes in the possibility and desirability of developing a modern secular Jewish identity in America, but feels that it must not be based on servility to Israeli policies and the new post-1967 Zionism.

Avishai is by no means anti-Zionist. In the rest of the book, he argues that while pre-1948 Labor Zionism was "a good revolution" (p. 10), admirable in every way, it became outdated with the founding of Israel. This old Zionism, incapable of serving as the guiding ideology of a democratic state, ought to have been discarded. Instead, it was maintained but became increasingly ossified, holding on to power by means of anachronistic bureaucracies such as the Histadrut and the Jewish Agency. Since 1967, this atrophied Labor Zionism has been increasingly displaced by something much worse: the new Zionism of the right wing and the religious movements—expansionist, fundamentalist, chauvinist, and therefore inconsistent with democracy. This, post-1948 process is what he regards as the "tragedy" of Zionism.

Avishai's main thesis cannot be dismissed out of hand, even if it must ultimately be rejected. Nor should he be condemned for writing, in effect, a propaganda tract

---

Review of *The Tragedy of Zionism—Revolution and Democracy in the Land of Israel* by Bernard Avishai (New York: Farrar, Straus and Giroux, 1985), 389 pages. Published in *MERIP Bulletin*, November/December 1987.

rather than a dispassionate account. What does condemn this book is its cavalier treatment of the truth, its sheer lack of veracity.

I need not dwell here on numerous factual inaccuracies resulting from simple ignorance but otherwise quite harmless.[1] Much more serious are the numerous misstatements consistently biased in favor of Zionism. Significantly, these abound even in the second half of the book, which is ostensibly devoted to exposing the ugly face of the "new" Zionism.

A typical example, one of dozens: on page 276 he mentions the policy of collective punishment, instituted by Dayan, "by which the security forces routinely destroyed the homes of relatives and neighbors of convicted terrorists." The use of the past tense here is misleading, because (as Avishai, who can read Hebrew, must know) this same punishment is still in use. He must surely also be aware that this punishment is meted out not only to convicted "terrorists," but, much more frequently, to Palestinians who are merely accused or suspected of "terrorism," without any juridical process.

A more serious example is his report of the notorious events at Kafr Qasim: "During the Sinai War in 1956, Israeli soldiers shot forty-three people for breaking the curfew at Kfar Kassem.[2] (The Israeli commanders were court-martialed, and pardoned after a number of years)" (p. 317). There are several prevarications here. First, Avishai simply "forgets" to mention that the forty-three were not merely shot, but shot *dead* at point-blank range. In fact, most of these unfortunate Arabs were taken off trucks on which they were traveling, and then mowed down. Second, this massacre took place not merely "during" the Suez war, but on its very first day. While the victims were technically in breach of the curfew, they could not have known this, because they were returning home from their day's toil in the fields; on this first day of the war the curfew was announced in the village after they had left for work. The fact that the victims were unaware of the curfew was perfectly clear to the murderers, as transpired in their trial. Third, Avishai reports that the "commanders" were pardoned after a "number" of years. He omits to mention how small that number was: most of the murderers were out after less than two years; one or two served a bit longer. (By the way, one of the worst murderers was appointed, soon after his release, as adviser for Arab affairs in a mixed Arab-Jewish town.)

Now reread Avishai's two-sentence report and see how a gruesome massacre has been deodorized into a relatively commonplace, if regrettable, incident. The most charitable reading of this text would lead us to suppose that Avishai is merely guilty of a careless choice of words, perhaps subconsciously influenced by his basic political sympathy for Israel. However, the blurb on the dust jacket tells us that the author is "professor of writing at MIT." He is thus a professional in the art of deliberate use of the written word. And so it goes, page after page. Avishai is not the kind of person from whom you should buy a secondhand history.

Matters are, if anything, worse in the first half of the book, devoted to washing the older, pre-1948 Labor Zionism whiter than white. Writing about the eve of the

1948 war, Avishai tells us that "Ben-Gurion began to devote himself to organizing Labor Zionist settlements according to Haganah's military strategy, embodied in its detailed 'Plan D,' to drive out the Palestinian Arab *forces* that had been operating there *since the Second World War*" (p. 175, my emphases). Anyone who has even a slight knowledge of Palestine's history must be aware that after the British crushed the Palestinian Revolt in the late 1930s and until the beginning of the 1948 war, there were no Palestinian armed "forces" in the country. Certainly this was true of the time when Plan D was drawn up. Of course, many individual Palestinian peasants had arms, usually antiques, but this can hardly be described as "forces." So what was Plan D for? Its goal was to expel the Palestinian civilian population. Israeli military historian Colonel Meir Pa'il writes that it was a plan "for creating a Jewish territorial continuity from Metullah to Revivim" (that is, from north to south) and that in implementing it the Haganah "conquered tens of hostile Arab villages while expelling their population."[3] Avishai's prevarication conceals the fact that the Palestinian exodus of 1948 did not happen by chance, but according to a detailed plan, drawn up a considerable time in advance.

Avishai is keen to magnify and exaggerate the differences between Labor Zionism and the Jabotinsky-Begin school of political Zionism, both at present and in the past. He even goes so far as to claim that before the 1940s "statehood was not a critical element in labor Zionist ideology" (p. 12; see also pp. 136 and 157). This is patently false.[4] There was never such a disparity of aims between the two Zionist camps. Both wanted to convert Palestine into a Jewish state. A careful reading of the sources—even of the mostly biased sources used by Avishai—will reveal what the main dispute was really about. Before 1940, Labor Zionists argued that it was too soon to reveal the political aims of Zionism publicly, before the whole world, because this would needlessly arouse the hostility of the Arabs and the rest of the world; better to appear more modest. The Jabotinsky camp disagreed, claiming that a candid statement of the aim was necessary in order to maximize mass Jewish enthusiasm and mobilization.

Avishai simply refuses to accept the colonizing nature of Zionism, particularly Labor Zionism, which from the very start aimed not at exploiting the labor of the indigenous Palestinian Arabs but at their total expulsion and elimination. He actually claims that Labor Zionism was "humane" toward the Arab majority in prewar Palestine (p. 12), and was veritably imbued with "anti-colonialist ethos" (p. 147). Four pages later he forgets this, and speaks about "Labor Zionist colonial strategy." This passage, which borders on self-parody, deserves to be quoted: "If Labor Zionist colonial strategy is to be faulted for the injury it caused to Arab parents and grandparents, must it not also be credited with creating the conditions for partitioning the land fairly, i.e., between the two nations which grew up in essentially distinct economic systems? Such a partition was never feasible between the propertied *Pieds-Noirs* and the Algerian Arabs who worked for them" (p. 151).

So the Palestinians should be grateful to their colonizers for creating, by 1948, a situation in which what used to be the Palestinians' country could be "fairly" partitioned between themselves and the colonizers, who (even according to the 1947 UN Partition Plan) got more than half the cake. Such privilege was denied to the Algerian Arabs (as well as the Blacks of Zimbabwe, and others), who had to make do with retrieving their whole country.

Avishai is unable or unwilling to understand that Labor Zionism was a colonizing movement that created a settler state subject to an inexorable dynamic. Such a state has a frontier, across which the previously dispossessed "natives," resentful of their dispossession, mount desperate attacks. The frontier is always precarious and the colonizers feel insecure. The only way they can deal with this insecurity is to push the frontier still further. This is their manifest destiny. The process must go on to the bitter end, unless it is stopped by an insurmountable external resistance, or by internal revolutionary collapse, or by a combination of both. Israel could no more simply switch off Zionism than the expanding United States could stop itself short of the Pacific.

The "new" Zionism, which Avishai so dislikes, is the true and legitimate heir of the old Labor Zionism that he so adores. If there is a tragedy of Zionism, it is not a tragedy of something progressive and positive that has outlived its usefulness and become detestable. Rather, it is a Macbethian tragedy:

> *Thou marvell'st at my words; but hold thee still:*
> *Things bad begun make strong themselves by ill.*

28

Exploded Myths

Both books, very different in intention and style but closely related in subject matter, were written by Israelis belonging to the left fringe of Zionism. Both contain a wealth of hitherto little-known factual material, much of it recently declassified, whose combined effect is to overturn the Zionist propaganda version of events surrounding the 1947–49 Arab-Israeli war—a version that has largely been accepted as fact throughout the West.

Flapan, a veteran functionary of the leftish Zionist party Mapam, devoted many years of activity to promoting a dialogue and reconciliation between Israelis and Arabs. *The Birth of Israel*, completed shortly before he died at the age of seventy-six, is the culmination of his work. It is directed mainly at his own side: "Israelis interested in peace and . . . Americans and American Jews who have Israel's fundamental interests at heart" (p. 7). Frankly polemical, its declared aim is to destroy prevalent Zionist propaganda myths that have served to brainwash the Israeli (and Western) public and thus constitute an obstacle to a just peace.

This highly readable and well-researched book is divided into seven chapters, each devoted to one particular myth, which is stated at the beginning of the chapter:

> Myth One: Zionist acceptance of the United Nations Partition Resolution of November 29, 1947, was a far-reaching compromise by which the Jewish community abandoned the concept of a Jewish state in the whole of Palestine and recognized the right of the Palestinians to their own state. Israel accepted this sacrifice because it anticipated the implementation of the resolution in peace and cooperation with the Palestinians. . . .

Review of *The Birth of Israel: Myths and Realities* by Simha Flapan (London: Croom Helm, 1987), 277 pages; and *The Birth of the Palestinian Refugee Problem, 1947–1949* by Benny Morris (Cambridge: Cambridge Middle East Library, Cambridge University Press, 1987), 380 pages. This review was published in *Race & Class* 30, no. 4 (1989): 87–93. See update added at the end of the review in 2010.

Myth Two: The Palestinian Arabs totally rejected partition and responded
    to the call of the mufti of Jerusalem to launch an all-out war on the Jew-
    ish state, forcing the Jews to depend on a military solution. . . .

Myth Three: The flight of the Palestinians from the country, both before
    and after the establishment of the State of Israel, came in response to a
    call by the Arab leadership to leave temporarily, in order to return with
    the victorious Arab armies. They fled despite the efforts of the Jewish
    leadership to persuade them to stay. . . .

Myth Four: All of the Arab states, unified in their determination to destroy
    the newborn Jewish state, joined together on May 15, 1948, to invade
    Palestine and expel its Jewish inhabitants. . . .

Myth Five: The Arab invasion of Palestine on May 15, in contravention of
    the UN Partition Resolution, made the 1948 war inevitable. . . .

Myth Six: The tiny, newborn State of Israel faced the onslaught of the Arab
    armies as David faced Goliath: a numerically inferior, poorly armed peo-
    ple in danger of being overrun by a military giant. . . .

Myth Seven: Israel's hand has always been extended in peace, but since no
    Arab leaders have ever recognized Israel's right to exist, there has never
    been anyone to talk to.

Each of these myths is then effectively demolished, using the most reliable
source material and recent research.

If the main aim of studying history is to gain a better understanding of the present, then perhaps the most important illumination that emerges from Flapan's dem-
olition job is the absolutely central role played by the Zionist leadership's implacable
hostility to the creation of a sovereign Palestinian Arab state in any part of Palestine.
Flapan shows quite convincingly that it was this Zionist position (not, as propaganda
would have us believe, the Arab states' wish to prevent the creation of a Jewish state)
that foiled any chance of averting the 1948 war between Israel and the Arab states.

How did this come about? It has long been known that in a series of secret talks
during 1947–48 the Zionist leadership reached an understanding with Abdullah,
the emir of Transjordan (and grandfather of the present Jordanian king [Husain]),
whereby in case a war broke out he would be allowed to seize and annex the territory
that the UN Partition Resolution had allocated for a Palestinian Arab state. The war
between Israel and Transjordan was therefore largely phoney. (Abdullah stuck meticulously to his side of the bargain. The real battles between these two parties took
place almost exclusively in places where Israel grabbed parts of that territory.) For
Abdullah, the annexation of the West Bank was but a first step toward the realization
of his lifelong ambition: the creation of a Hashemite empire of Greater Syria, encompassing—in addition to Transjordan and Iraq, which were already ruled by the
Hashemite dynasty—also part of Palestine and the whole of Syria and Lebanon.

Recent research (mainly by Flapan's fellow Mapamnik, the historian Yoram
Nimrod) has brought to light documents showing that in the months following

November 1947 the other neighboring Arab states, Egypt and Syria, were trying behind the scenes to reach a peaceful settlement with the Zionist leadership. Despite their extreme warlike rhetoric—for the consumption of the Arab masses—they had no wish to fight against the emergent Zionist state, and little faith in their ability to win such a war. Moreover, what worried them was not so much the creation of a Jewish state but Abdullah's schemes for a Greater Syria. They therefore sought a peaceful settlement with the Zionist leadership, based on the creation of an independent Palestinian state, as provided by the UN Partition Resolution. On the other hand, they made it clear that if a war were to break out, they would have to step in, if only in order not to leave the field entirely to Abdullah.

David Ben-Gurion and the rest of the Zionist leadership were faced with a choice between the possibility of a peaceful settlement based on accepting the creation of a Palestinian Arab state, and a war in which, as prearranged with Abdullah, the creation of a Palestinian state would be prevented. Ben-Gurion showed no hesitation in choosing the latter option.

Why were Zionist leaders ready to go to such great lengths to prevent the establishment of a Palestinian Arab state and to promote the alternative Hashemite option? Surely, the fact that Abdullah was actually in their pay—recently declassified documents show that he was receiving a small "subsidy" from the Jewish Agency (Flapan mentions this, in passing, on p. 128)—is not sufficient to explain their apparently bizarre choice.

This question is all the more important, because implacable opposition to the creation of a sovereign Palestinian state—in any piece of land west of the Jordan River—is one of the fundamental constants in mainstream Zionist politics. It is just as much a cornerstone of Israeli policy today as it was more than forty years ago.

Since Flapan never quite spells out a clear-cut answer to this important question, I feel duty-bound to do it for him. Zionist opposition to the creation of a sovereign Palestinian Arab state, however small and emasculated, is not based on short-term military considerations but on long-term historical ones, which concern the very nature of the Zionist claim over Eretz Yisrael (the Land of Israel, aka Palestine). This claim is absolutely exclusive and cannot be reconciled with the recognition of Palestinian Arab national rights over, or even in, the Holy Land. For unavoidable reasons of realpolitik Zionists may agree to concede sovereignty over some part of Palestine to an external power, such as Jordan. Such a concession is, however, purely pragmatic and temporary, and therefore in principle reversible. Israel always reserves the right to "liberate" such conceded territories as the need or the ability to do so arises. But to allow the establishment within Palestine of a sovereign national entity of the indigenous people—that would undermine the whole self-justification and legitimation of the Zionist enterprise. A concession of this kind would be historically irreversible. Moreover, though a Palestinian state may initially be small and weak, there is no telling what changes might take place in the more distant future. The balance of forces, and hence the borders, between that state and Israel—like any balance of forces and any border—will be subject to the vicissitudes of future history. After all, had Israel itself not started from small and modest beginnings, only to expand over the whole of Cisjordanian Palestine and the Syrian Golan Heights?

It is of course not surprising that Flapan never completely exposes the deep roots of Zionist policy. After all, he remained a Zionist—albeit a heterodox one, tormented by doubts—to his dying day. Rather, what demands explanation is why a Zionist such as Flapan should be so keen to demolish the myths of Zionism and expose its historical culpability.

The answer is that Flapan (like the historian Yoram Nimrod and the late Arabist, Aharon Cohen) belongs to a small group of Zionists—a minority even within his own party, Mapam—who genuinely believe that it was possible to achieve the aims of Zionism without provoking irreconcilable conflict with the indigenous Palestinian Arab people, but rather with their consent and cooperation. In order to establish this thesis, he is motivated to expose the lies of the mainstream Zionist leaders, who hypocritically claim that they acted as they did because the wicked aggressiveness of the Palestinians (and the rest of the Arabs) never left them any choice. He must show that, on the contrary, momentous policy decisions of the Zionist leadership were not imposed from the outside, by the other side's actions, but were a matter of choice.

Personally, I think that Flapan's basic thesis is untenable. I cannot see how Zionism, a colonizing project, could possibly achieve its aims without violating the individual and national rights of the indigenous people of Palestine. I do not believe in the possibility of benign colonialism. True, Ben-Gurion and the other mainstream Zionist leaders often did have a choice. But in choosing as they did they acted under the inner compulsion of the logic of Zionism.

But whatever Flapan's motivation, and irrespective of what one may think of his underlying thesis, he deserves our deep gratitude for exposing so much of the truth, with very few and relatively trivial deviations from absolute honesty.[1]

The readability of the narrative and the generally high technical standard of the book's presentation[2] make it highly recommendable—indeed, required reading—to anyone seriously interested in the Middle East.

◆ ◆ ◆

Benny Morris is a historian (as well as being diplomatic correspondent for the *Jerusalem Post*) and his book is a scholarly work. Eschewing polemics, it comes close to being exhaustive as a factual account of the creation of the Palestinian refugee problem. On the whole, Morris's research confirms the less detailed account presented in the third chapter of Flapan's book.

The claim, often made by Zionist propaganda, that the Palestinian refugees fled at the instigation of the Arab leadership, which therefore bears the responsibility for their flight and plight, has long been dismissed by all serious scholars, simply because there is not a shred of evidence for it. What about the counterclaim of anti-Zionist propaganda, that the refugees were expelled by the Israelis according to a previously worked-out plan? Well, the picture that emerges from both books—there is no major factual disagreement between them—can be stated briefly as follows.

During the 1930s and 1940s, the mainstream Zionist leadership reached a virtual consensus in favor of "transferring" the bulk of the Palestinian Arab people away from their homeland. Various projects for achieving this were formulated and discussed in secret. It was hoped that the "transfer" might be achieved through political agreement with the Arab states and Britain. (Indeed, the British Labour Party, which came to office in 1945, actually adopted in its conference of that year a resolution in favor of the "transfer" idea!)

However, at the end of November 1947, when hostilities started between the Arab and Jewish populations of Palestine, the Zionist leadership did not have anything that might be called an actual plan for exploiting the specific conditions of war for the implementation of the "transfer." The reason for this seems to be that it simply did not occur to the Zionist leaders that such a thing was technically or politically feasible.

During the early months of the war, the growing feeling of insecurity, and the virtual collapse of proper administration in the Arab urban centers along the coastal plain, led to the spontaneous flight of middle-class urban Arab families, who sought shelter in parts of Palestine that were allocated to the proposed Palestinian Arab state, or in neighboring Arab countries. Gradually, this developed into something of a stampede, involving part of the rural population as well.

By the spring of 1948, it had dawned on the political and military leaders of the nascent Zionist state that a demographically "pure" Jewish state was a realistic possibility, if only the Palestinians' flight, which had began spontaneously, would be positively "encouraged" and the refugees prevented from returning to their homes. This is what these leaders proceeded to do. The shark had smelled blood in the water.

Even then, no formal resolution to expel the Palestinians was adopted by the official Zionist decision-making bodies, nor is there evidence of a detailed overall plan for the implementation of the forced transfer of population. Indeed, such a resolution and detailed plan were hardly necessary. It was enough that the small circle of military and political leaders around Ben-Gurion, "the real decision-makers," had a general "design . . . to reduce the number of Arabs in the Jewish state to a minimum, and to make use of their lands, properties and habitats to absorb the masses of Jewish immigrants" (Flapan, pp. 88–89). Local military commanders were not given specific orders in writing but were made aware of the general design, and were relied upon to do their bit in implementing it. For the most part (with few exceptions) they were willing to do what was expected of them. The majority of Palestinians in areas under Israeli control were terrorized into flight, and in many cases physically driven across the lines.

Benny Morris is not exactly a conformist. In fact, last year he spent some time in prison for refusing to do his military reserve service in the Occupied Territories. But, unlike Flapan, he does not express great moral outrage at the grand crimes of Zionism. He is sparing in expressions of value judgments; and when he does make such a judgment, he bends over backward to argue in mitigation of those crimes. Unlike Flapan, he does not seem to believe that Zionism could have acted in an essentially different way, and as a Zionist he feels obliged to plead that external circumstances left no other choice.[3] Also, the narrow scope of his book, dealing with the refugee question alone, allows him to accept at face value most of the myths demolished by Flapan's book.

Despite this grave shortcoming, Morris's book is an invaluable compilation of factual material on the creation of the Palestinian refugee problem.

Update (2010)

Since Morris's book was published, much new material has come to light that makes it very clear that the ethnic cleansing of the Palestinians in 1947–49 was considerably more planned and less spontaneous than Morris claims. In this respect see, for example, Ilan Pappé's book *The Ethnic Cleansing of Palestine* (2007), as well as two books by Nur Masalha, *Expulsion of the Palestinians: The Concept of "Transfer" in Zionist Political Thought, 1882–1948* (1992) and *The Politics of Denial: Israel and the Palestinian Refugee Problem* (2003).

Since 2000, Morris himself has voiced increasingly chauvinistic and war-mongering views. He has expressed regret—not for the ethnic cleansing of the Palestinians in the 1947–49 war, but for the fact that it did not go as far as it could have gone.

29

Lost in Translation

Z e'ev Schiff, military editor of the prestigious daily *Ha'aretz*, is widely regarded as Israel's most experienced and best-informed correspondent on military and security affairs. Ehud Ya'ari, Middle East affairs correspondent for Israel TV, is an expert on the Arab world. Together they possess a formidable network of contacts and sources of information—mainly in the Israeli army and intelligence community but also in some Arab countries and certain Palestinian circles.

Their previous collaborative effort, *Israel's Lebanon War* (in Hebrew *Milhemet Sholal*, literally "A War of Deception"), a condemnation of Israel's 1982 Lebanese war, contained many sensational revelations on the preparation for and conduct of that war by Ariel Sharon and his circle. It became a bestseller in Israel.

The present book contains few major revelations not already known to those who have followed the coverage of the intifada in the media—not least in the Israeli press. In any case, the authors' aim is not to provide a detailed chronicle of those events but to answer and analyze certain questions raised by the intifada: Why did it break out when it did? What were its immediate causes? Why were both the Israeli authorities and the PLO leadership surprised by the outbreak of the intifada as well as by its tenacity and staying power? Who leads the intifada, and what is the relationship between the local grassroots leadership and the national Palestinian leadership outside the Occupied Territories? What is the relative importance of the Islamic fundamentalist trend in the Gaza Strip and the West Bank, compared with

Review of *Intifada* by Ze'ev Schiff and Ehud Ya'ari (in Hebrew) (Tel Aviv: Schocken, 1990), 383 pages. English edition, *Intifada: The Palestinian Uprising—Israel's Third Front* (New York: Simon & Schuster, 1990), 337 pages.

Published as "Intifada," in *Journal of Palestine Studies* 20, no. 1 (Autumn 1990): 129–34. Published by the University of California Press. The intifada discussed here was later referred to as the "first intifada."

the nationalist (PLO) trend? What has the intifada achieved, and what is its lasting effect on the Palestinian-Israeli conflict likely to be?

On all these questions the authors provide important factual and critical analytic insights, which makes their book indispensable reading to anyone seriously interested in the conflict.

Of course, the reader should not expect these authors to be politically and morally impartial. They are staunch Zionists, albeit of a relatively moderate color, and their chief concern is Israel's own interests (or what they perceive these interests to be).

The "solution" they advocate is a Palestinian political entity within a Palestinian-Israeli-Jordanian confederation. The Palestinians, represented by the PLO, would have to sign away the right of return as well as any claim to full independence. The Palestinian entity would be completely demilitarized, and "Israel would have to insist upon adjustments along its eastern frontiers. These changes are necessary . . . primarily because uncontrolled drilling on the western slopes of the Samarian mountains can cause severe damage to Israel's most important underground water reserve." (Note how the underground water of the whole of Palestine is regarded as "*Israel's* reserve.") Other, smaller, territorial concessions would be demanded "for security reasons" (*Israel's* security, of course; the authors do not worry about the Palestinians' security).

As far as value judgments are concerned, the authors' bias is reflected in their terminology—a tendentious use of language characteristic of most Israeli journalists. This is particularly blatant when reporting incidents in which there is loss of human life. When a Palestinian kills an Israeli or a Palestinian collaborator, the verb "kill" is used in the active voice ("x killed y"). Moreover, such acts are often described as "murder," even when the casualties are armed soldiers in uniform, or adult male settlers engaged in a provocative armed demonstration in the middle of Hebron. But when Israelis kill Palestinians, the authors prefer to use the passive voice ("y got killed by x"), and add an explanation that is apparently designed to make the killing partly excusable. For example, "a schoolgirl from the Gazan town of Dir al-Balah was shot to death by a Jewish settler after his car had been stoned."

Nonetheless, when it comes to reporting and analyzing the major facts, this book is anything but an apology for the authorities. On the contrary, the main concern is to expose and criticize the blunders of the political leadership and the conceptual myopia that has led to these blunders, in order to jolt the Israeli public and politicians toward ending the occupation through dialogue with the PLO. It is evident that they make a genuine effort to provide an accurate account of the events of the intifada and the processes that underlie these events. From their point of view, any attempt to minimize the importance of the intifada and to belittle its achievements would have been counterproductive.

They are, of course, limited by their sources of information—mostly in the Shin Bet and other branches of the Israeli security and military machine. They also seem to have quite good sources in the American and Jordanian establishments, and some contacts with leading Palestinians. But they have little, if any, direct access to the grassroots leadership in the Gaza Strip and West Bank that played such a central role in the intifada. However, this limitation is perhaps inevitable, and they seem to have made the best of the material available to them. (Of course, this does not mean that all the claims made by the authors are necessarily correct. The reader should bear this in mind when reading the lines that follow.)

Among the most interesting topics covered in the book are the following:

- The relationship between the Israeli government and the upper echelons of the army. The authors claim that the former, more precisely some ministers of the Likud, kept trying to push the generals toward using more brutal measures, some of them plainly illegal, to crush the intifada, and that the latter have often resisted this pressure.

- The description of the process of trial and error through which the Palestinian masses invented new strategies and forms of struggle; first the method of violent but unarmed mass confrontation with the forces of occupation, and then a long-term campaign of civil disobedience. As in all truly popular revolutionary struggles, the initiatives always came from below, from the grass roots. The local leadership of the struggle—the Unified National Command (UNC)—was itself led by the rank and file almost as much as it led them.

- The dialectic of the complicated relationship between the UNC and the PLO leadership in Tunisia. According to the authors, there were several factors that counteracted the natural tendency of the UNC to display and exercise independent initiative vis-à-vis the PLO leadership. First, the Israeli repressions—the mass arrests, and the deportation of several important local leaders. Second, the UNC itself did not wish to play into Israel's hands by seeming to present itself as an alternative to the PLO. Third, the authors claim, the PLO leadership regarded the UNC as a potential threat to its own authority and took steps to cut it down to size. (On this point they make some rather unflattering remarks concerning the jealousy with which the PLO leaders, especially Yasser Arafat, guard their own prestige.)

- The importance of the social factor among the immediate causes leading to the outbreak of the intifada is one of the most interesting points made by the authors. According to them, what motivated the masses in the Gaza Strip during the early phase of demonstrations in December 1987 was not so much the spirit of nationalism and the desire for national self-determination as feelings of deep resentment against their miserable social conditions, their superexploitation by Israel, coupled with a burning bitterness against the constant personal humiliation at the hands of Israeli soldiers, officials, settlers, and employers. A whole chapter, entitled "The Enraged Proletariat," is devoted to this topic.

Even if the intifada were to be crushed tomorrow, it is almost certain to be rekindled in the future. Besides, it has already achieved certain irreversible gains. Schiff and Ya'ari list some of these (p. 331):

> By their uprising, the Palestinians have smashed the status quo beyond repair. Although unable to impose a new order, they have been able to open a third front against Israel: the front of regular warfare and the front of terror [i.e., armed guerrilla struggle] have now been followed by the front of mass civilian warfare, using means of violence other than firearms.
>
> Moreover, the occupied territories can no longer be viewed by Israel as a purely positive military asset.
>
> [The intifada has] shown the importance of the fact that [these] territories are not unpopulated, and the need has arisen to weigh the advantages of holding on to them against the disadvantages. The territories are undoubtedly important for Israel's security, but it is necessary to balance against this the price of the resulting cancer that is devouring the body of Israeli society.
>
> During the course of the uprising, the Palestinians have succeeded in retaining the initiative and in gaining partial achievements; from their point of view the two most important strategic victories were Jordan's renunciation of its claim to the territories and the American recognition of the PLO. They have been able to win power over themselves, to wrest control over the Palestinian population from Israel's hands; they have crystallized the patterns of a mobilized society prepared to make great sacrifices, and have dictated to the PLO changes in its positions.
>
> [But] in the last analysis, although a new local leadership has begun to emerge, this has not undermined the PLO's authority; on the contrary, the latter's command and superiority over its rivals, such as Hamas [the Islamic Resistance Movement], in leading the struggle against Israel have been demonstrated. In brief, the intifada has shown that the PLO cannot be bypassed on the road to a settlement.[1]

◆ ◆ ◆

An English version of *Intifada*, edited and translated by Ina Friedman, has been published by Simon & Schuster. I must devote some space to this, if only to warn the would-be reader of the book that the English version differs from the original in significant respects. The changes are of three kinds.

First, the material has been quite radically rearranged. Some of these changes are beneficial, resulting in greater coherence and clarity.

Second, twelve pages of photographs, a three-page glossary, and thirty-two pages of documentary appendixes have been omitted. These omissions are serious defects, especially in the case of the documentary appendixes. Most of these are of great interest, including, for example, a leaflet in Hebrew issued by the UNC of the intifada and aimed at Israeli soldiers.

Finally, there are a number of changes clearly designed to adapt the text to the requirements of Zionist propaganda in the West. Thus, factual descriptions that are apparently considered to be "inconvenient" are frequently toned down or simply omitted. Here are three typical examples:

1. On page 139 in the Hebrew text, the authors tell us that the Israeli army in the Occupied Territories "forces elderly Arabs, in a humiliating way, to erase PLO slogans from walls." In the English version (p. 142) the reference to humiliation is omitted.

2. On page 188, in a quotation from a document published by Hanna Siniora, editor of the daily *Al-Fajr*, there is a demand for "the release of all prisoners of the intifada, particularly the children." In the English version (p. 206) the word "children" is replaced by "minors." In Hebrew there is an exact equivalent of "minors," *qtinim*, which means "persons under 18." But the authors do not use this word in the Hebrew original. They use *yeladim*, children, because in Israel it is well known that many Palestinian children—yes, children—are held in detention by the Israeli authorities. Ms. Ina Friedman and the people who employ her services evidently do not wish readers outside Israel to know this fact.

3. On page 302 in the original the authors refer to TV shots "showing Israeli soldiers cruelly beating Arab youths." In translation (p. 296), the word "cruelly" has been omitted.

In some cases, the edited translation goes much further than such relatively gentle massaging of the text. For example, on page 229 the authors state that, contrary to the practice of the Islamic fundamentalist groups, "the organizations belonging to the PLO have meticulously refrained from any shade of anti-Semitism." This evidently faced the translator-editor with a problem: Zionist propaganda claims that anyone opposed to Zionism is anti-Semitic. How did she solve this problem? Very simply; the translation (p. 227) reads: "*More attuned* to *Western sensibilities*, the PLO avoided any hint of anti-Semitism." The words in italics do not appear in the Hebrew original. More attuned to the dictates of the Zionist propaganda machine than to the ethics of truthful and accurate translation, Ms. Friedman is telling the Western reader, in effect, that the PLO, for purely tactical reasons, merely *pretends* not to be anti-Semitic.

This is by no means the only—or even the worst—case of outright falsification. Let one last example suffice. On page 272 of the Hebrew version, in the middle of a paragraph listing the harsh measures introduced by [Defense Minister] Rabin during 1988 in the hope of curbing the intifada, the authors say: "Changes in the instructions on opening fire—particularly after plastic bullets were brought into use in August 1988—increased the number of fatalities." From these words themselves, as well as from the context of the whole paragraph, it is quite clear that the increase in the number of Palestinians killed was not unintended by those who issued the orders.

In the English version (p. 261), the sentence in question appears at the beginning of a new paragraph, *not* dealing with Rabin's harsher measures, and it reads: "Changes in the army's guidelines on opening fire, after plastic bullets were introduced in August 1988, *did not lessen* the number of fatalities" (italics added). The impression that these words are meant to create—contrary to what the original text plainly says—is that the new instructions were intended to reduce the number of fatalities, but—alas—failed to achieve that humanitarian aim. This deceptive impression is further reinforced by a special footnote, added in the English version, which explains that plastic bullets "are designed to wound rather than kill, but at short ranges they can be as lethal as live ammunition." Note also that the English version links the new instructions for opening fire *exclusively* with these plastic bullets, whereas the Hebrew original makes it quite clear that some of the new instructions (which actually made it easier for soldiers to open fire) were issued *before* plastic bullets were introduced.

The examples quoted above are only some of the changes I have discovered between the Hebrew original and the English translation. However, I have not made a systematic effort to uncover all the differences between the two texts. Perhaps this project—not an easy one, due to the drastic reordering of the material—should be undertaken by someone who has more time and patience than me. The results can then be published in a booklet under the title *Some Facts That Zionist Propaganda Wishes You Not to Know.*

30

Misinformation as "News"

This book contains a fascinating, impressive, and meticulous study by the Glasgow University Media Group of how the main [British] TV news channels (BBC1 and ITV) misrepresent the Palestinian-Israeli conflict and misinform the great British public. It is therefore essential reading from two distinct viewpoints, on two important topics.

First, it is a must-read for anyone interested in the Middle East, arena of what is arguably the most dangerous and intractable conflict in our present-day world. Second, it can and should also be read as a case study, using the Middle East issue as an illustration, of how public political ignorance and confusion, packaged as "news" and "information," is spread and fostered—an essential prerequisite for the preservation of the existing order.

The book begins with a ninety-page historical introduction, outlining the evolution of the conflict from the inception of the Zionist colonizing project in the late nineteenth century up to the end of 2003. Quite properly, the narrative gets progressively more detailed as it approaches the present. Although the authors make no attempt to disguise their own opinions, they carefully report how each side to the conflict views those facts that are in dispute—that is, virtually *all* relevant facts. Fittingly, the heading of this chapter is "Histor*ies* of the Conflict."

Unfortunately, this account—which inevitably depends entirely on secondary sources—is marred by several inaccuracies. Politically, the only really serious error is the treatment of the program for a "Democratic State of Palestine" put forward by the PLO "[i]n the years after 1967." Referring the reader to a book published by the

---

Review of *Bad News from Israel* by Greg Philo and Mike Berry (London: Pluto Press, 2004), 304 pp. An edited version of this book review was published in *Race & Class* 47, no. 1 (2005). A second, updated and much-enlarged edition of this book has since been published as *More Bad News from Israel* (London: Pluto Press, 2011).

journalist David Hirst in 1977, the authors tell us (p. 43): "The brainchild of the PLO planner and negotiator Nabil Shaath, the Democratic State of Palestine would involve the dismantling of the Israeli state and its replacement with a non-sectarian bi-national Palestine in which Christian, Muslim and Jew would live together in equality."

In fact, the PLO explicitly rejected the idea of a binational Palestine as a "misconception." In a programmatic article—unsigned, but to my certain knowledge written by Nabil Sha'th himself—we are told that "[t]he call for a non-sectarian Palestine should not be confused with . . . a bi-national state" and that in the reality of Palestine "the term bi-national and the Arab-Jewish dichotomy [are] meaningless, or at best quite dubious." Moreover, the article stresses that "[t]he liberated Palestine will be part of the Arab Homeland, and will not be another alien state within it"; and looks forward to "[t]he eventual unity of Palestine with *other Arab* States."[1]

The whole point of the programmatic formula "*Secular* Democratic Palestine" proposed at that time by Fatah, the dominant component of the PLO led by Yasser Arafat, was to present the Palestinian-Israeli conflict in *confessional* terms and to propose a future Palestine in which Jews would have individual equality and freedom of religious worship in a country whose nationality would be Arab.[2] At that time, Palestinian nationalist ideology was coming to terms with the painful realization that the Israelis were there to stay, and had to be accommodated in a future free Palestine. But it denied the highly inconvenient fact that Zionist colonization had given birth to a new Hebrew (Hebrew-speaking Israeli Jewish) nation—a fact that is indeed an enormously complicating factor in the conflict. The adjective "secular" in the formula "Secular Democratic Palestine" encoded this denial.[3]

However, with this sole exception, the errors in the historical outline are quite minor, ranging from a couple of amusing solecisms[4] to wrong transliteration of names and slight factual inaccuracies that do not affect the basic validity of the account. Indeed, a corrected version of this historical outline could perhaps be republished separately and serve as a highly recommendable and much-needed brief introductory reading on the complex Palestinian-Israeli conflict. This should be accompanied by a glossary, whose absence in the present book must make some passages in it quite puzzling to a reader with little previous knowledge of the subject.[5] As the authors themselves point out (p. 99): "what may seem obvious to the researcher or the journalist may not be so to all members of the audience."

The remaining four chapters (with three appendixes) contain the authors' original findings. The material presented here is devastating.

Chapter 2 ("Content Studies") deals with the production of misinformation: it is an extensive account of the authors' analysis of BBC1 and ITV news reports on the conflict during four periods: September 28–October 16, 2000 (outbreak of the second intifada), October–December 2001, March 2002, and April 2002 (Israeli onslaught on Jenin). The authors rightly confine themselves to these media because for the great majority of the British population these are the main, if not only, sources of information on foreign affairs.

Chapter 3 ("Audience Studies") is concerned with the consumption side: here the authors report research they conducted using fourteen small focus groups of viewers (averaging seven members), selected on the basis of income, age, and gender. Members of these groups were presented with questions probing their understanding of the news, following which there was a group discussion, led by a moderator who posed supplementary questions. Some of these discussions were attended by journalists and broadcasting professionals. In addition, two samples of students (one numbering 300, the other 280), whose ages ranged from seventeen to twenty-three, were presented with an abbreviated version of the same questionnaire on two successive occasions, one year apart (in October 2001 and October 2002). For the sake of comparison, the same questionnaire was also given to a group of German high-school students, and a group of US university students studying journalism or communications.

The headings of the final two chapters, Chapters 4 and 5, "Why Does It Happen?" and "Conclusions," are self-explanatory. The detailed evidence presented in Chapters 2 and 3 and the Appendixes leaves no room for doubt that BBC1 and ITV news are massively biased in favour of the official Israeli narrative.

In part, this is the effect of general structural causes, to do with the way *all* news is packaged and presented on TV. As one of the journalists, George Alagiah, confirmed, reporters are "constantly being told [by news editors] that the attention span of our average viewer is about 20 seconds" (p. 213). This leaves no room at all for explaining the background of the current events being reported. A BBC journalist told the authors that "he had been instructed not to do 'explainers' by his own editor" (p. 215). With the total absence of historical background, many viewers are not aware that since 1967 the West Bank and Gaza Strip have been under oppressive Israeli *military* occupation, which is regarded by most international observers as illegal. (The term *Occupied Territories* is often used in news reports, but in the absence of any further explanation many viewers interpret this in the same sense as a house or a bathroom being "occupied," and so conclude that it is the Palestinians who are the "occupiers"!) Nor is it explained that a great many of the Palestinians in these territories were displaced in the 1948 war from their homes in what became Israel, or are descended from the original refugees. Viewers are left with the impression that the conflict is a symmetric quarrel between two nations over some bits of land along their mutual border. Moreover, in the absence of explanation how it came about, the status quo is automatically made to appear legitimate and "natural"; and since it is the Palestinians who are resisting it, they are automatically seen as causing the trouble and starting each "cycle of violence." The Israeli occupation forces are seen as keeping order or restoring it, albeit by overly harsh means.

But there is also incontrovertible evidence of explicit and specific pro-Israeli bias in what is actually said and shown on TV news. There is a great imbalance in interviews: Israelis are allowed to speak to the camera much more than Palestinians (as measured by lines of transcript text).

In a period when Palestinian fatal casualties outnumbered Israeli ones more than threefold, the coverage of deaths was roughly reversed: the former was given in total about one third of the airtime devoted to the latter. It is hardly surprising that a majority of viewers are consequently unaware of the true facts.

Reporters and presenters of news tend to use Israeli explanations and terminology not only when quoting official Israeli sources but also when speaking on their own behalf. Thus, Israeli assassinations and violent attacks are regularly reported as acts of "retaliation" or "response," but such motivation is very rarely offered to explain Palestinian attacks, which are therefore seen as starting the "cycle of violence." So, unlike a mathematical circle, this cycle appears to be far from perfectly round: the Palestinians start while the Israelis "respond." A typical example of this is the reporting of events in October–December 2001, a period of intense violence, during which Palestinian casualties, as usual, far outnumbered Israeli ones (pp. 160–61). On December 2, 2001, a journalist commented on BBC1: "This cycle of violence began six weeks ago when an Israeli cabinet minister was shot." That was a reference to the assassination of Rehav'am Ze'evi, Israel's minister of tourism and a notorious open advocate of ethnic cleansing, by the Popular Front for the Liberation of Palestine (PFLP). BBC1 neglected to report that the PFLP had justified their action as revenge for the assassination, seven weeks earlier, of their West Bank political leader, Abu-Ali Mustafa, at age sixty-four. (The PFLP assassins daringly infiltrated a Jerusalem hotel in pursuit of their victim. The Israeli uniformed assassins took no similar risk: they fired missiles from a helicopter into the PFLP's Ramallah office.)

Another typical example is the way in which ITV news reported the emblematic incident in which the twelve-year-old Muhammad al-Durrah was shot dead by an Israeli marksman, while crouching behind his father who was desperately trying to shelter him. Newscasters and journalists parroted the Israeli official spin that the boy was "caught in the crossfire"—which according to eyewitnesses was a blatant lie: the boy was murdered in cold blood (p. 149).

TV news presenters and reporters also use emotionally charged terms that betray strong pro-Israeli prejudice. Descriptions such as "horrific attack," "brutal murder," "savage cold-blooded killing," and "lynching" are used about Israeli deaths, but not when Palestinians are killed in ways that could also be so described. Terms such as "mass murder," "carnage," and "slaughter" are regularly used to describe incidents in which, say, six or ten Israeli civilians are killed, but not when an even greater number of Palestinian civilians are killed by the Israeli occupation forces.

The authors report and analyze many more examples of grossly inadequate and biased reporting. They also show convincingly that members of the public are indeed affected by this: they are confused due to the lack of background information and misinformed about the actual facts of the conflict, especially if TV news is their only source of information.[6]

What are the reasons for this marked bias? Again, some are generic and operate in other comparable circumstances, when a regular army of a modern capitalist state is involved on one side of a conflict. In the present case, Israel controls access to the Occupied Territories. Therefore journalists, who in any case naturally tend to live in the safer and technically more convenient Israeli side (especially in West Jerusalem), find it much easier to interview Israelis. The far greater slickness and professionalism of the Israeli spin machine, as compared to its Palestinian counterpart, also contributes to the imbalance.

There is also some racist stereotyping at work. Journalists—and probably even more so editors—find it easier to identify with Israel, a modern capitalist country, and with Israelis, especially members of the Ashkenazi elite, than with Palestinians. This outweighs sympathy for the Palestinians as underdogs. Widespread guilt feeling toward Jews, overcompensating for the endemic anti-Semitism of previous generations, is no doubt an added factor.

Then there is the heavy pressure, not to say emotional blackmail, applied by the efficiently orchestrated and well-organized pro-Israeli lobby and the many fanatic friends of Israel in the Jewish community, who habitually vilify as "anti-Semitic" even relatively mild criticism of Israel, self-appointed state of all Jews. Journalists and TV officials can be intimidated by such smear tactics.

Finally, there is American influence. The United States gives Israel, its chief Middle East junior partner and bully-boy, enormous support in finance, arms, and political protection.[7] These facts are not explained on TV news. But when BBC1 and ITV interview a third-party "expert" or politician on the Palestinian-Israeli conflict, it is usually an American who, in the guise of expertise or objectivity, advocates the Israeli position. Amazingly, these British TV channels interview US politicians twice as often as British ones on the topic in question! This is no doubt part of the process of harnessing Britain slavishly to the American imperial chariot—a process that both requires and results in systematically misinforming the British people.

31

A Peace Activist on the Border

The opening sentences in the author's preface are: "This book is not a work by an historian or a study of the Israeli-Arab conflict. Nor is it an autobiography."

A very apt observation. If you are looking for your first read on Israel/Palestine, don't start with this book. On the other hand, while not an autobiography, it is wholly autobiographical: a subjective account by a peace activist, deeply involved in bridging what is arguably the world's most intractable conflict.

Michel Warschawski (nicknamed "Mikado" because of his supposedly "Japanese" features) was born in 1949 in Strasbourg, son of that city's chief rabbi. At the age of sixteen he moved to Jerusalem to study in a yeshiva (Talmudic college—the Jewish equivalent of a madrassa). Unlike almost all his fellow students, who combined religious fervor with extreme chauvinism and virulent racism, he had an antifascist and antiracist upbringing: Rabbi Max Warschawski had been a member of the Maquis resistance during the Second World War, and later sympathized with the Algerian struggle for independence.

Confronted with the oppressive Israeli regime of occupation following the June 1967 war, Mikado felt visceral sympathy with the oppressed, and eventually joined the Israeli Socialist Organization (ISO), better known by the name of its journal, *Matzpen* (compass)—a small but highly militant revolutionary group founded in 1962. Eschewing the sectarianism that cripples the radical left almost everywhere, Matzpen included members (both Jews and Arabs) of various Marxist persuasions, united by thorough internationalism and, consequently, opposition to Zionism.

The 1967 war brought the issue of Zionist colonization and the nature of the Israeli state into the limelight. But during the preceding decade this topic had lain

Review of *On the Border* by Michel Warschawski (translated from the French by Levi Laub), Pluto Books/South End Press, 2005, 247 pages. This review was first posted online by *Iran Bulletin/Middle East Left Forum*, 2007, www.iran-bulletin.org/book%20review/MikadoRev.htm.

dormant backstage and was largely ignored in Israel itself as well as abroad. In this respect Matzpen was exceptional: it developed a detailed critical analysis of Zionism as a colonizing project and of Israel as a settler state of a specific kind. So, when the 1967 war erupted, Matzpen was prepared: armed with a theory that allowed it to face the difficult struggle in conditions of virtually total isolation.

What gave this small embattled group considerable encouragement was the up-surge—precisely in the post-1967 period: in the late 1960s and the 1970s—of a new wave of the international left, of which Matzpen rightly saw itself as part.[1]

During that heyday of the international left, Mikado shared with many others an exhilarating optimism, looking forward to a world revolution, "unfolding now or at least in the very near future. The Palestinian resisters were the catalysts of the soon-to-come uprising of the workers of Cairo and Damascus, which would reunify the Arab nation under socialism after overthrowing the reactionary regimes of the region, including, clearly, the Zionist state" (p. 38).

But even in those heady times he felt he was paying a high emotional price (or perhaps so it seems to him now, in retrospect): "that internationalism . . . involved voluntarily giving up an identity, a step that rather quickly proved to be politically sterile and personally destabilizing. . . . Having chosen to be citizens of the world, or members of an international class, we willingly cut off the roots that bound us to our society and our culture" (p. 39). So, when his naive revolutionary socialist optimism was frustrated, he reverted to embracing the spiritual identity of what he feels to be his real community.

This ideology that he now espouses is not so much Israeli-Hebrew patriotism—which he criticizes for its "tribalism," but a "diasporic" Jewish identity, an ideology that (for lack of a better term) may be described as "ethno-patriotism."

Like all patriotic ideologies, this is a form of false consciousness, made up in large measure of nostalgia and wishful thinking: in historical reality, the dominant trends in diasporic Jewish tradition have been no less tribalist, not to say xenopho-bic.[2] But Mikado's idiosyncratic construction has some saving grace: it enabled him to cling to what has proved to be the most stable progressive element in his makeup: antiracism and solidarity with the oppressed.

So, while discarding his erstwhile socialist revolutionary militancy and even his presumed atheist outlook, both of which proved to be less firmly rooted,[3] he rein-vented himself as a combative and courageous peace activist, founder of the Alternative Information Center,[4] and an anti-Zionist dissident. (In Israel he is still described as being on the "radical left." But that is due to the special meaning this term has acquired in Israel: contrary to its usage everywhere else, it has no necessary socioeconomic con-notation, and refers only to a person's position on war and peace and the Israeli-Pales-tinian conflict. In the book under review, "left" is used in this specifically Israeli sense.)

Of course, the shift from revolutionary socialism to the peace activism of an ethno-patriot involves a significant change in perspective and attitude.

Genuine socialists are profoundly committed to supporting all struggles for human liberation—including of course the liberation of any oppressed national group. But this support is proffered from a socialist platform, which is quite different from nationalism, and by no means involves concessions to any nationalist ideology—not even to that of an oppressed nation. Socialists are—or ought to be—aware of the ambiguous role and unreliable nature of a petty-bourgeois nationalist leadership, and keep their critical faculties on full alert. On the other hand, joint action, genuine comradeship, and personal friendship between socialists belonging to oppressed and oppressing national groups is not only possible but in fact fairly common, because they share a common socialist outlook and an overriding internationalist commitment, and regard their respective national identities as a matter of mere accident of birth rather than of positive active choice.

But where this common overriding commitment to socialist internationalism is lacking, matters are quite different. A person who actively embraces Jewishness as a primary identity and a Palestinian nationalist are not equal partners in a common struggle. The former, even if s/he is anti-Zionist, can at best extend solidarity and support to the latter, but must refrain from offering any programmatic opinion and advice, lest it be interpreted as a colonialist patronizing the colonized. The two remain politically separated by the Border—hence the title of the book!—even when trying to bridge it. And in such circumstances "an intimacy in personal relations that does away with ethnic or religious belonging, and which one can call friendship, is almost impossible to achieve" (p. 63).

The difference between socialist internationalism, to which Mikado had formerly subscribed, and his present ethnic identity–based peace activism is illustrated by his account of the following episode (p. 139):

> A few months after the signing of the Oslo accords, in 1993, in the course of a discussion that included activists of the Palestinian and Israeli far left, I heard an Israeli woman militant explain, like a teacher presenting a lesson to her students, that accepting a Palestinian state in the West Bank and the Gaza Strip was pure and simple treason.
>
> She received a curt response from a Palestinian militant who had been in all the battles and had spent years in prison: "Why do you take it upon yourself to refuse us an independent state, even a tiny one, in less than 22 percent of our national territory? Are you going to endure fifty more years of occupation and violence?"
>
> But it was the insensitive response of the Israeli militant that needs to be pondered: "I see that even the Palestinian left has lost the desire to fight . . ."

Now, even if we take Mikado's account at face value, as factually accurate—which is by no means safe, given his numerous deviations from strict adherence to veracity (of which more anon)—the fact remains that the Oslo Accords were indeed a monumental monstrous confidence trick played by the Israeli government on a politically submissive or at best gullible Palestinian petty-bourgeois leadership. The unnamed Israeli militant surely had a clearer insight (based on something like inside knowledge) into the true intentions and devious modus operandi of "her own" government than did the Palestinian veteran of battles and prisons. He was under the false impression that the Oslo Accords would provide the Palestinians with an independent state, albeit a tiny one. Was it not her duty to warn him against falling into the trap of this illusion?

More generally, the difference between a radical socialist perspective and that of Mikado's latter-day ethno-patriotic peace activism is reflected in the politics and personalities of the Palestinians with whom he allies himself, as reported in this book (which include some unsavory members of the venal elite of the Palestinian Authority). A leftist radical would confine his close alliances to like-minded leftists.

Also, his position on Zionism seems to have softened. Somehow, this book creates the impression that Zionism acquired its colonizing character following the 1967 war, rather than being a colonizing project from its inception.

I have alluded above to the book's many misstatements. This is an unfortunate failing on which it is a reviewer's unavoidable duty to dwell. While it makes interesting reading, full of fascinating—albeit often quite subjective and debatable—observations about various aspects of Israeli society, the book cannot be treated as a dependable source of facts. Any factual statement or report found in it must be taken with a large pinch of salt, pending its verification with more reliable sources. A considerable number of these, which I have been able to check either from direct first-hand knowledge or from the evidence of several highly trustworthy witnesses, have proved to be extremely unsound if not largely fabricated.

Apart from many factual errors due to simple carelessness, the more significant departures from factual accuracy are mainly of three kinds. The first, which is of least importance and which an indulgent reader may most easily pardon, is the author's persistent tendency to inflate his own role in various events and activities. These exaggerations, accompanied by name-dropping so relentless as to be comical, are actually quite unnecessary and counterproductive: even reduced to their true proportion, Mikado's contributions—involving real personal sacrifices—to the struggle against injustice deserve considerable respect.

A second group of misleading statements—of much greater importance and interest to the general reader—are on matters concerning the Israeli-Palestinian conflict and the so-called Peace Process. Here are a couple of outstanding examples:

On page 152 the author states: "According to Oslo, the system [of closures] would disappear within five years and give way to an independent [Palestinian] state possessing territorial continuity, real borders, and thus, sovereignty."

In fact—and as Mikado must surely know—the Oslo Accords said nothing of the kind. They promised no such thing. True, at the time there was much informal and unofficial chatter about a sovereign Palestinian state having territorial contiguity; but the crucial fact is that Israel studiously avoided making any formal commitment to any of this.* Nor did it commit itself to removing its illegal settlements from the

---

* Indeed, in his last speech in the Knesset (October 5, 1995), when presenting the Oslo Accords for ratification, Rabin stated explicitly that Israel's policy is that the Palestinians would "get an entity which is less than a state."

Palestinian territories occupied in 1967, or even to halting the process of colonization of these territories. The sad truth is that Yasser Arafat signed on the dotted line, if not as a conscious act of capitulation then as a result of self-delusion, encouraged by nods and winks of inveterate political con artists such as Shimon Peres. At the time, many Israeli peace activists shared this wishful thinking, and encouraged Arafat in going along with it; but this does not justify spreading such alternative misinformation long after the event.

On page 165 the author tells us that only after the assassination of Prime Minister Yitzhak Rabin in 1995: "The previously minority ideas of the right had become official *policy*, particularly with regard to the settlements. . . . The colonization of the West Bank and Gaza became one of the components of the new consensus, the only debate being the question of the number of new settlements. It explains why so many Labor voters and activists had no problem shifting heir vote to Sharon a few years later." (Emphasis in the original.) This is simply untrue. The colonization of the territories occupied in 1967 was initiated immediately—when the guns were still smoking— under a Labor-led government, and with its full complicity and encouragement: first in Jerusalem and a large area around it; in the Golan Heights (where it was accompanied by major ethnic cleansing); slightly later in Hebron. Then it proceeded to the rest of the West Bank, the Gaza Strip, and the north of the Sinai Peninsula (which was subsequently returned to Egypt by the first Likud government led by Menachem Begin).* Plain statistics, which are freely available, show that the metastasis of colonization spread, and the number of settlers increased, at a steadily accelerating pace under *all* Israeli governments since then—including the Labor-led government headed by Rabin. While that government was negotiating the Oslo Accords, as well as after they had been signed, this colonization continued relentlessly.[5]

Indeed, anyone who was paying close attention to what the Rabin government was doing on the ground could have realized that they had no serious intention of allowing the creation of a truly sovereign and territorially contiguous Palestinian state. Their aim was evidently the creation of a kind of Indian reservation, or a disconnected set of such reservations, policed on Israel's behalf by Arafat and his CIA-trained security forces. I suspect that the unnamed Israeli militant, whom Mikado excoriates for her "insensitive" warning to the Palestinian veteran, realized all this and deserves Mikado's apology.

A third group of systematic distortions concerns Matzpen. This may not be of much interest to the general reader but only to those wishing to know the detailed history of the revolutionary left in our region. However, as a founding member of Matzpen, I feel duty-bound to set the record straight. A reader who is not curious about these minutiae may stop reading the present review at this point.

* Commitment to Zionist colonization of the Occupied Territories was included in the platform of the Labor Alignment for the 1969 elections to the Knesset. The Alignment, led by Golda Meir, formed the government at the end of that year. See also the end of chapter 21 in this book.

The evident common aim of these prevarications and evasions is to make it seem as though the group that Mikado joined after the 1967 war—the ISO (Matzpen)—was from the start a wholly or largely Trotskyist organization. Indeed, this myth is widely repeated in Trotskyist circles, and has even found its way to the French version of Wikipedia in Mikado's native language: the entry devoted to "Michel Warschawski," claims: "*En 1967, il adhère au mouvement trotskiste anti-sioniste Matzpen aujourd'hui disparu.*"*

This is, as the French say, a canard. When Matzpen was founded, in 1962, it had not a single Trotskyist member. A handful of Trotskyists, led by the Arab Marxist intellectual Jabra Nicola, joined the group more than a year later, on the understanding that they could keep their individual ties with the Brussels-based Fourth International, provided they did so openly; but the group as such would not affiliate to that organization. The majority resolutely opposed such affiliation, and we all agreed that it was important to keep the broad nonsectarian unity of various shades of Marxist opinion.

The story Mikado tells on pages 24–25 about the creation of Matzpen (when he was still a schoolboy in Strasbourg) is carefully crafted to give wings to that canard. It could serve as a nice illustration to the comment made by Catherine, the heroine of Jane Austen's *Northanger Abbey*, about historical writing: "It is very tiresome: and yet I often think it odd that it should be so dull, for a great deal of it must be invention."

To make the invention somewhat less dull, he embroiders it with some of his choicest hyperboles. Thus, a Trotskyist comrade, an office worker in the Haifa refineries, who kept such a low profile as to be almost invisible, is transmogrified into "a well-known and respected leader of workers in the Haifa bay area." To be fair, these exaggerations are not confined to Trotskyist comrades. One of the founding members, who as a young man had taken part in the epic seamen's strike of 1951 as an ordinary striker, is described, quite ludicrously, as "one of the leaders" of that strike. A few pages later (p. 30), the present reviewer is described as a "brilliant orator"; I wish.

But the most astounding untruth in the whole tall tale is one of omission: the one political leftist group that Mikado actually founded and led *jusqu'à ce qu'il ait disparu* is never mentioned by name: the Revolutionary Communist League (RCL), the Israeli section of the Brussels-based Fourth International; nor is a single word said about its creation.[6]

Here is a brief account of what happened. By 1972, Mikado was apparently convinced not only that the world revolution was at hand but also that it was going

---

* See "Michel Warschawski," *Wikipedia* (French), http://fr.wikipedia.org/wiki/Michel_Warschawski. Since this review was posted and circulated, this has been corrected to: "*En 1967, il adhère à l'Organisation socialiste israélienne, plus connue sous le nom de Matzpen, le nom de son journal mensuel.*"

to be orchestrated by the said Brussels HQ. He therefore pressed for the ISO (Matzpen) to affiliate itself to the Fourth International. As he could not gain sufficient support for this move, he engineered a destructive sectarian split—as a result of which, instead of one nonsectarian group whose size was just above the critical mass that enabled it to make a significant mark on the Israeli political scene, there were now two groups of roughly equal size, both below that critical mass. By then Jabra Nicola—the one Trotskyist comrade who, with his profound understanding of the Arab East, made a valuable contribution to Matzpen's political theory—had moved to London and was in bad health. Opposed to the split, he was unable to prevent it. (His ashes must now be turning in their urn at the political twists of his disciple: he despised petty-bourgeois Palestinian nationalism and until his death in 1974 kept warning us against its impending betrayal.)

The splinter group led by Mikado, the Jerusalem-based RCL, wished to appropriate the political prestige won by Matzpen among the radical left in Israel and abroad, and therefore claimed this name for themselves. As they had no legitimate right, let alone legal ownership, over the journal *Matzpen*, they published their own rival journal, *Marxist Matzpen*. (It sounded better than "Trotskyist Matzpen.") They rightly assumed that the ISO, which of course remained in existence and continued to publish the original *Matzpen*, would not sue them in a Zionist court for misappropriation of the title. Thereafter, the RCL was usually referred to in Israel as "Matzpen Jerusalem," while the original group, the ISO, was referred to as "Matzpen Tel-Aviv."

Mikado may well believe that his sect had some moral title to the name "Matzpen"; although in my opinion this view is mistaken, it is understandable that he should hold it. But the honest thing to do would have been to tell the reader that after the split (and until the demise of the RCL) there were two groups using that name, and make it clear to which of the two he is referring. He deliberately avoids doing this, and for this reason suppresses all mention of the split he engineered and of the official name of the group he founded and led. This economy with the truth is designed to create the false impression that there was always one Matzpen, and it was a Trotskyist group.

Such behavior can only be described as devious and reprehensible. And it has some absurd consequences.

On page 41 he tells an amusing little story about the strange practices of the (unspecified) "Matzpen":

> One of my duties was to lead a small cell in the village of Tira. Once or twice a week there, I tried to organize the political work of a dozen Palestinian activists, who, although they shared our radical critiques of Zionism and Israeli policy, found it hard to adapt to the rigid rules of an organization in which Leninism was embodied in a maze of hierarchical structures (from the political bureau to branch secretaries—despite the fact that our active membership never exceeded 50!). Politely, the activists regularly voted on the resolutions submitted by the central committee, only to do exactly as they pleased once the meeting was over.

Here is the reinvented Mikado, no longer a revolutionary militant, commenting sardonically on the follies of the group in which his former youthful Leninist self was an activist. What he neglects to tell the reader is that the Matzpen that he originally joined, the ISO, had very different structure, culture, and ethos: open and nonhierarchical; and that he himself split Matzpen-ISO precisely in order to install in his groupuscule the kind of caricature Leninism he now so wittily derides.

Read this book—not as a sound factual record but as a series of sometimes insightful observations, and a subjective account of Mikado's peace activism and the work of the AIC, which has played a very positive and commendable role in fighting injustice and disseminating information about the occupation.

One final note about the translation: it is fairly competent and fluent, but contains quite a few Gallicisms that should have been corrected. Hebrew and Arabic terms and names are usually given in their French rather than English transcription, and acronyms are kept in their French form (thus for example on page 171 "National Religious Party" is abbreviated as "PNR").

32

Zionist Myths Debunked

This is a somewhat paradoxical book: undoubtedly important—yet it contains little that is new. Written by a professional academic historian, it is about history and historiography—but not in his established field of expertise.

Shlomo Sand is professor at Tel-Aviv University, specializing in modern European, particularly French, history. He is not even in the "right" academic department to concern himself with the subject of this book: in Israeli universities, Jewish History and "General" (!) History are taught in two quite separate departments.

In this book, Sand sets out to debunk widespread Zionist myths about the origin of the Jews, and who they are.

Zionism modeled itself on nineteenth-century Eastern and Central European nationalisms: it regarded itself as the nationalism of the Jews. The ideological project of any nationalism is to invent, as it were, the nation for which it claims to speak: to provide it with a narrative of common origin, homeland, and destiny. This is then used to claim possession of, and sovereignty over, the homeland.

In one crucial sense, Zionism had to be more inventive than any of its European models. Each of the latter had a ready-made objective raw material: a community inhabiting a roughly discernable contiguous territory, speaking a more-or-less distinct vernacular (in many cases also using a highbrow version of it as a secular literary language), and sharing a distinctive secular culture. The project of nationalism was to unify this inchoate nation-in-itself (*an sich*) and forge it into a nation-for-itself (*für sich*). This was, at least in principle, a secular project: a modern nation need not share a common religion. Since the American and French Revolutions, modernity regarded religion as a private matter, whereas the nation—and hence nationalism—are nothing if not public and collective.

Review of *The Invention of the Jewish People* by Shlomo Sand, translated by Ya'el Lotan (London, Verso, 2009), 332 pages. Edited version published in *Race & Class* 52, January 2011.

By the end of the nineteenth century, the largest cluster of Jewish communities, the Yiddish-speaking Ashkenazim of Eastern Europe, did possess to some extent the objective attributes of a nation-in-itself. This was good enough for the Jewish Labor Bund. Founded in 1897, this socialist party demanded equal rights and linguistic-cultural autonomy for the real quasi-national Jewish minority in the Russian Empire and on its fringes; but it never aspired to national sovereignty over a territory. And it only addressed itself to Jewish workers in Russia, Poland, and Lithuania; it was not concerned with distant Jewish communities. It therefore had no use for an elaborate pan-Jewish national myth.

This was precisely what the Zionist movement did need. Although founded (in the same year as the Bund) and led by Ashkenazim, it was in principle pan-Jewish, and like its European nationalist models it aimed at establishing a nation-state: its foundational text was Theodor Herzl's *Der Judenstaat* (1896).

But the *only* thing that all Jewish communities had in common was, precisely, their religion: Judaism.[1] They were scattered across the world, and shared no common vernacular or secular culture. So if (as claimed by Benedict Anderson) all nations are imagined communities, the nonexistence of a pan-Jewish nation-in-itself meant that Zionists had to perform an exceptionally prodigious leap of imagination.

However, once this extraordinary feat of positing worldwide Jewry as a single nation had been performed, the ideological task of constructing for it a narrative of common origin, homeland, and destiny was easier than for Zionism's European nationalist models: a ready-made ancient sacred narrative of history and eschatology offered itself. Jews already "knew" that they were all direct descendants of the patriarchs Abraham, Isaac, and Jacob, who was renamed "Israel" by God.[2] Thus they were all "literally" Bnei Yisrael (Sons of Israel). Their God-promised and God-given homeland was Eretz Yisrael (Land of Israel), covering a huge area "from the river of Egypt unto the great river, the river Euphrates."[3] The ancient Jewish kingdom reached its early zenith, ruling the whole of that area, under King Solomon, son of David. Eventually—to cut a long story short—the Jews were punished "for their sins" and were exiled from their homeland by the Romans. But at the End of Days God will send his *Mashiah ben-David* (anointed scion of David), who will ingather the exiled Jews and return them to their homeland, the Land of Zion.

All that remained for Zionist ideology to do was to secularize this sacred narrative. The eschatological bit, the "return" to Zion, was converted into a political colonizing project—hence its very name: "Zionism"—with the impressively bearded Theodor Herzl as secular messiah or his herald. The creative task of bringing the divine history down to earth was undertaken by the early Zionist historians.

These historians had a formidable fudging job cut out for them. Archaeological and documentary evidence fails to corroborate essential elements of the sacred narrative, and on some vital points flatly contradicts it.

As for the descent of latter-day Jews, there is copious evidence of numerous and geographically widespread conversions of Gentiles to Judaism. The converts were assimilated into Jewry, and soon became notional "descendants" of the patriarchs.[4] In addition to countless individual proselytizations, there were also mass forcible or voluntary conversions. One of the earliest was the forcible Judaization of the Edomites toward the end of the second century BCE. (Herod the Great, Roman client king of Judea, was of Edomite extraction.) Judaism dominated the Himyar kingdom in southern Arabia during most of the period from the end of the fourth century CE to the rise of Islam. The Yemenite Jews are almost certainly descendants of Himyarite converts. There was extensive conversion to Judaism among the Berbers of North Africa, and there is good evidence that the Muslim invaders of Iberia early in the eighth century were joined by allied Jewish Berber regiments. But the best known and numerically most important case of mass conversion was that of the great Khazar kingdom, wedged between the Byzantine and Muslim Empires, which adopted Judaism, probably in a gradual process, between the mid-eighth and mid-ninth centuries. The Ashkenazi Jews of Eastern Europe are in large part descended from Khazars.

As for the huge and mighty kingdom of Solomon the Wise—there is no mention of it in the extensive documentary material from the ancient Near East. Nor is there any archaeological evidence for it, and in particular for the magnificent Temple of Solomon, although there are substantial material remains in situ from both earlier and later periods in Jerusalem's history.

But, perhaps most damaging for the ancient narrative, there is no evidence that Jews were ever exiled en masse from Judea and the Galilee, whether following the Great Revolt and the fall of Jerusalem to the Roman army under Titus (70 CE) or after the defeat of the Bar-Kokhba uprising during the reign of Hadrian (135 CE). No doubt, thousands of captives were taken to Rome as slaves. But the surviving mass of the population, overwhelmingly rural, remained in place. The Romans did not have the means for deporting hundreds of thousands of peasants. Nor was it in their interest to depopulate the countryside: the peasant population was a valuable source of revenue for Rome. The same applies to other empires, before and after the Roman. Ironically, the Palestinian peasants have a greater claim than today's Jews to be descendants of the ancient Israelites.

Shlomo Sand's book is a highly readable account—more readable in the excellent English translation by the late Ya'el Lotan than in the original inelegant Hebrew of the author—of the historical facts outlined above and of the attempts of Zionist historiography to wriggle its way around or out of them.

Does all this really matter? In some sense it hardly does.

From an unbiased viewpoint, even if it were true that present-day Jews are descended from an ancient people forcibly exiled from Palestine, it would clearly not justify Zionist colonization and the "repossession" of the country after two millennia from its long-standing inhabitants. This is the epitome of chutzpah coming from Zionists, who deny the right of return to the Palestinians they evicted and exiled sixty-two years ago.

For committed Zionists, the secularized mythical ideological legitimation of Zionist colonization and the Israeli settler state may have outlived its usefulness. It has largely been superseded by a more bare-faced legitimating ideology, based on the "right" of actual possession ("nine points of the law"); on the self-righteous persuasiveness of might ("the strong do what they can, and the weak suffer what they must"); and on self-pitying cynical manipulation of the world's bad conscience following the Nazi genocide. The original Hebrew version of Sand's book was a best seller in Israel, but I don't expect it to change the minds of very many Zionist readers. In his review, written in a perceptibly wounded tone, Professor Israel Bartal, a senior member of the Department of Jewish History at the Hebrew University of Jerusalem, complains that Sand has maligned Israeli Zionist historians, especially those of more recent vintage: they are provably not ignorant of the historical facts he adduces, and are on record as admitting as much in their academic publications.[5] Bartal does have a point: Sand's accusations against recent Israeli historians are incorrect or at best exaggerated. However, it is true that these historians have made no special effort to disabuse the Israeli hoi polloi and Zionists abroad of the naïve belief in the scientifically discredited narrative.

Yet, at another level this book does matter. It is an exemplary exercise in debunking a particular nationalist myth, and by implication all nationalist myths. It contains a concentrated account of fascinating episodes in the history of the Jews, many of which are not widely known. It is an enjoyable read. Recommended.

Part VI
FINAL ANALYSIS

33

Israelis and Palestinians: Conflict and Resolution

Preface

On November 30, 2006, I had the great privilege of delivering the Barry Amiel and Norman Melburn Trust Annual Lecture. The event took place at the Brunei Gallery lecture theater, in London University's School of Oriental and African Studies.

My predecessors in these Annual Lectures have included some very illustrious men and women; and I am deeply grateful to the Trustees for the honor of being added to that distinguished line, and for offering me this invaluable opportunity to share with a large and lively audience thoughts on a subject that has been engaging me these fifty years.

I am indebted to the trust administrator Willow Grylls, and to the lecture organizer Ariane Severin, for their most efficient work in setting up and organizing the event.

Special thanks are due to one of the trustees, Tariq Ali, who chaired the meeting with great skill and insight into the subject. No choice of chairperson could be more fitting: in 1969, an article coauthored by the late Palestinian Arab Marxist Jabra Nicola (writing under the pen name A. Sa'id) and me, in which some of the main ideas contained in my lecture were first outlined in English, was published in the journal *Black Dwarf* edited by Tariq.*

In this connection I would like to pay tribute to the memory of my comrade and friend, Jabra Nicola (1912–74). He joined the Israeli Socialist Organization (Matzpen) a few months after its foundation, and his analysis of the impact of Zionism on Palestine and the Arab East greatly influenced our thinking on the subject. In particular, we owe to him the insistence on the regional context of the Palestinian problem and its eventual resolution—which is a central theme of my lecture.

---

* See chapter 4 in this book.

What follows is a somewhat expanded version of the lecture. I have added here a few observations and clarifications—mainly suggested by questions or comments from members of the audience—as well as some source material that I had no time to quote during the lecture. But I have tried to preserve the discursive and informal style of an oral presentation.

I am grateful to Ehud Ein-Gil, Zvika Havkin, and Tikva Honig-Parnass, who read a draft of this text and made some helpful comments.

Preamble: How to Think about the Conflict

How should we think about the Israeli-Palestinian conflict? Please note: *how* comes before *what*. Before coming to any substantive conclusions—certainly before taking sides—we must be clear as to how the issue ought to be approached.

It would be a mistake to start in normative mode. A moral value judgment must be made: I would certainly not advocate avoiding it. But we must not *start* with moral value judgments.

Assigning blame for atrocities is not a good starting point. In any violent conflict, both sides may—and often do—commit hideous atrocities: wantonly kill and maim unarmed innocent people, destroy their homes, rob them of livelihood. And of course all these atrocities must be condemned.

Now, it is quite easy to show that Israel commits atrocities on a far greater scale, greater by several orders of magnitude, than its Palestinian (or other Arab) opponents. But this in itself is not a sufficient basis for taking sides. Israel does much greater harm, commits far greater atrocities, because it *can*: it is much stronger. It has an enormous war machine, one of the world's biggest in absolute terms, and by far the most formidable relative to its size. So the balance of atrocities doesn't automatically imply that Israel is in the wrong.

Also, asking "who started it?" is not helpful. Each side claims that it "retaliates" for crimes perpetrated by the other. The media refer to it as the "cycle of violence"; actually it is not really a cycle but a spiral chain. How far back do you go? And even if we go as far back as "far back" goes, and find who fired the first shot—so what? Perhaps the one who fired the first shot was justified in doing so?

We should first address the issue in descriptive and analytic mode. We must ask: what is the nature of the conflict; what is it about? Understanding ought to precede judgment. When we understand what it is all about, then each of us can apply his or her moral criteria and pass judgment. And only then, having understood the nature of the conflict and passed moral judgment, we can work out what would constitute a resolution of the conflict, and try to figure out what it would take to achieve that resolution.

1. Analysis of the Conflict

1.1 Colonizing Project in a Regional Context

History is important. You cannot understand the conflict by taking a snapshot of its present state: you have to rewind the tape.

The conflict did not begin in 1967; then it only entered a new phase with Israel's military occupation of the West Bank, the Gaza Strip, and the Syrian Golan. Nor did it begin in 1956 with the Israeli attack on Egypt, in collusion with France and Britain. And it didn't begin in 1948 with the establishment of Israel and the precipitation of the Palestinian Nakba (calamity), in which most of the Palestinian Arab people of what became Israel were turned into refugees.

The conflict began a century ago, and became acute following the First World War. In *general* terms: it is part of the complex of unresolved problems bequeathed to the region by the Western—British and French—imperialist powers in the way they broke up and carved up the Ottoman Empire. We are witnessing other components of this complex legacy in Iraq, Lebanon, and throughout the region.

This all-important regional context will be a leitmotif in what follows.

But *specifically*: it is a conflict between the Zionist project of colonizing Palestine and the indigenous people of that land, the Palestinian Arabs. In 1948 it became a conflict between Israel—the settler state that is a product of the Zionist colonization project—and the Palestinian Arab people.

Saying that Zionism was and is a colonizing project and Israel is a settler state, a colonist state, is not a matter of value judgment but a plain statement of fact. I don't use these terms as invectives. In fact, the Zionist movement, in its internal discourse, used the term "colonization" (and later its Hebrew equivalents).

It is possible to argue—and some do argue—that colonization and the establishment of a settler state are morally acceptable—in general or in this specific case. This *is* a value judgment, which depends on one's moral criteria. But it is not intellectually tenable to deny the fact that Zionism is a colonizing project and the State of Israel is a settlers' state.

There are of course many settler states, established by colonists from Europe who settled in various parts of the world. Israel is in this sense by no means unique. But Zionism and Israel are exceptional in several important respects, three of which I will point out in what follows.[1]

1.2 Late to Start—and Still Ongoing

The first exceptional feature of Zionist colonization is that it was historically the last colonization project to get off the ground. And it is the last and currently the only one to remain active—active as in "active volcano," as opposed to an extinct one.

Other settler states have fulfilled their "manifest destiny" (to use an American

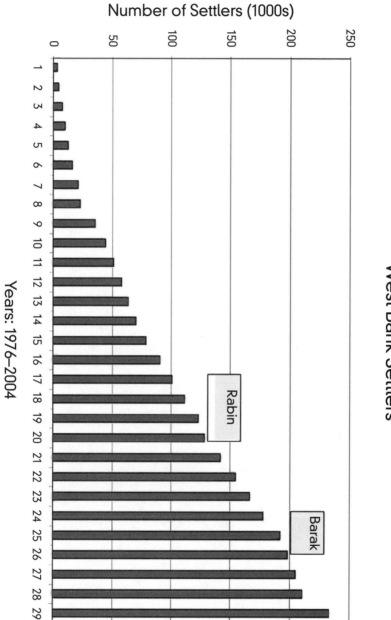

Number of Settlers (1000s)

West Bank Settlers

Years: 1976–2004

term, popular during the expansion of the United States). Colonization there is over and done with.* Not so in the present case.

---

* With perhaps some residual exception, such as the US semi-annexation of Puerto Rico.

Present-day Israel is not only a *product* of the Zionist colonization project but also an *instrument* for its further extension and expansion. Colonization is ongoing. It continued in 1948–67 in the territory then ruled by Israel, within the Green Line.[2] Land belonging to Palestinian Arabs—including those who remained within the Green Line—was expropriated and given over to Zionist colonization. And soon after the 1967 war colonization continued in the newly Occupied Territories (OTs). This happened under all governments: Labor-led, Likud-led, and grand coalitions.

There is much controversy about what the Israeli government headed by Yitzhak Rabin really intended when it signed the Oslo Accords of 1993, and what Prime Minister Ehud Barak meant by his so-called generous offer at the Camp David (2000) summit. I would advise you: do not listen to politicians' spin, for politicians generally—not only our own Tony Blair—are presumed prevaricators: they lie when it suits them. Look at facts on the ground, for they do not lie.

Let us look, for example, at the graph "West Bank Settlers." It shows the number of Israeli settlers in the West Bank in the years 1976–2004.[3] On the time axis, Year 1 is 1976 and Year 29 is 2004. We can see for ourselves that colonization—planned, conducted, and subsidized by the Israeli government, and given military protection by its army—was relentless. Now, I have marked on this graph the periods of the Yitzhak Rabin and Ehud Barak Labor-led governments, 1992–95 and 1999–2000/01, respectively. Can you detect any slowdown? Any change at all?[4] Look also at the settlement maps on the B'Tselem—The Israeli Information Center for Human Rights in the Occupied Territories website.* So what intentions did the Israeli government—*all* Israeli governments—harbor regarding these Israeli-occupied Palestinian territories? Please draw your own conclusions.

1.3 Ben-Gurion's Doctrine

On February 16, 1973, General Moshe Dayan delivered a programmatic speech at a meeting of the Israeli Bar Association. The daily *Ha'aretz* (February 18, 1973) reports that Dayan "surprised his listeners": the lawyers who had invited him expected that, as minister of defense, he would talk about military matters. Instead, he read a prepared ideological lecture in which he expounded the "doctrine" of his mentor, the founder of the State of Israel, David Ben-Gurion. The latter was still alive at the time—he was to die at the end of 1973—and it is fair to assume that Dayan was certain of his approval. (Indeed, it is not too fanciful to suppose that Ben-Gurion was delivering a message to the nation through his favorite protégé.)

Dayan quoted what Ben-Gurion had said many years before, in internal debates about the Peel Commission report,[5] but he stressed that those words, spoken in 1937, were "pertinent also today." This is the gist of Ben-Gurion's doctrine, as quoted by Dayan:

---

* B'Tselem—The Israeli Information Center for Human Rights in the Occupied Territories, "Maps," www.btselem.org/maps.

> Among ourselves [the Zionists] there can be no debate about the integrity of the Land of Israel [i.e., Palestine], and about our ties and right to the whole of the Land. . . .
>
> When a Zionist speaks about the integrity of the Land, this can only mean colonization [*hityashvut*] by the Jews of the Land in its entirety.
>
> That is to say: from the viewpoint of Zionism the real touchstone is not confined to [the question of] whom this or that segment of the Land belongs to politically, nor even to the abstract belief in the integrity of the Land. Rather, the aim and touchstone of Zionism is the actual implementation of colonization by the Jews of all areas of the Land of Israel.[6]

This is the Zionist counterpart of the doctrine of "manifest destiny." Let me spell out what it implies: *any partition of Palestine, any "green line," any accord or treaty that shuts off any part whatsoever of the "Land of Israel" to Jewish colonization is from the viewpoint of Zionism at best a transient accommodation—accepted temporarily for tactical or pragmatic reasons, but never regarded as final.*

Of course, this does not mean that the expansion of Zionist colonization is unstoppable. What it does mean is that it will be pursued—as a matter of highest priority—so long as the balance of power makes it possible.

1.4 Writing on the Wall

Zionist colonization of Palestine is the root cause of the conflict; ongoing colonization is the persisting impetus that drives the conflict on. For this reason I confine myself in this analysis to discussing the Zionist project, which is the proactive side in the conflict. For lack of time, I shall say very little about the Palestinian struggle, which was a predictable reaction.

That the implementation of Zionism's political project would inevitably provoke resistance by the indigenous Palestinians, and inexorably lead to a violent conflict, was obvious from the outset. It was recognized by the most clear-sighted and openly admitted by the most uninhibited and outspoken Zionists.

None was less inhibited than Vladimir Jabotinsky (1880–1940), the political and spiritual progenitor of five Israeli prime ministers: Menachem Begin, Yitzhak Shamir, Binyamin Netanyahu, Ariel Sharon, and Ehud Olmert.[7]

The following are extensive excerpts from his justly famous article, "The Iron Wall" (*O Zheleznoi Stene*), published in 1923 in the Russian-language journal *Rassvyet* (dawn):

> Compromise between the Palestinian Arabs and us is out of the question at present, and in the foreseeable future. I express this inner conviction of mine so categorically not because of any wish to distress nice people [i.e., moderate Zionists] but, on the contrary, because I wish to save them distress. All those nice people, except the congenitally blind, have long since understood the utter impossibility of ever obtaining the willing consent of Palestine's Arabs to transforming that same Palestine from an Arab country into a country with a Jewish majority.
>
> Every reader has some general idea of the history of the colonization of other countries.[8] I suggest that he recall all known instances; let him go through the entire

list and try to find a single instance of a country colonized with the consent of the natives. There is no such instance. The natives—whether they are civilized or un-civilized—have always put up a stubborn fight against the colonizers—whether they are civilized or uncivilized . . .

Any native people, whether civilized or savage, view their country as their na-tional home, of which they will be the complete masters. They will never voluntarily accept not only new masters but also new co-owners or partners.

This applies also to the Arabs. Compromisers amongst us try to convince us that the Arabs are fools who can be tricked by a "toned down" formulation of our true goals, or a venal tribe who will abandon their birthright to Palestine for cultural and economic gains. I flatly reject this view of the Palestinian Arabs. Culturally they are 500 years behind us, spiritually they possess neither our endurance nor our willpower; but apart from this there are no inherent differences between us. They are as subtle psychologists as we are, and exactly like us have had centuries of training in crafty *pilpul* [Hebrew for casuistry]. Whatever we tell them, they can see through us as well as we can see through them. And they have for Palestine the same instinctive love and intrinsic fervor that the Aztecs had for their Mexico or the Sioux for their prairie. . . . Every people will struggle against colonizers as long as there is a spark of hope of ridding itself of the danger of colonization. This too is what the Palestinian Arabs are doing and will go on doing as long as there is a spark of hope. . . .

Colonization has only one goal; this goal is unacceptable to the Palestinian Arabs. This is in the nature of things. To change that nature is impossible . . .

Even if it were possible (which I doubt) to obtain the consent of the Arabs of Baghdad and Mecca, as if Palestine were for them some kind of small, insignificant borderland, then Palestine would still remain for the Palestinian Arabs not a bor-derland, but their only homeland, the centre and basis of their own national exis-tence. Therefore it would be necessary to carry on colonization against the will of the Palestinian Arabs, which is the same condition that exists now. But agreement with non-Palestinian Arabs is also an unrealizable fantasy. In order for Arab nation-alists of Baghdad and Mecca and Damascus to agree to pay what would be for them such a high price, agreeing to forego preservation of the Arab character of Pales-tine—a country located at the very centre of their [future] "federation" and severing it in the middle—we would have to offer them something just as valuable. Clearly, this could mean only two things: either money or political assistance or both. But we can offer neither. As for money, it is ludicrous to think we could finance Mesopotamia or Hejaz, when we do not have enough for Palestine. . . . And political support for Arab nationalism would be totally dishonest. Arab nationalism sets itself the same aims as those set, say, by Italian nationalism before 1870: unification and political independence. In plain language, this would mean expulsion of Eng-land from Mesopotamia and Egypt, expulsion of France from Syria and then per-haps also from Tunisia, Algeria and Morocco. For us to support such a movement, even remotely, would be suicide and treachery. We are operating under the English Mandate; in San Remo, France endorsed the Balfour Declaration. We cannot take part in a political intrigue whose aim is to expel England from the Suez Canal and the Persian Gulf, and totally annihilate France as a colonial power. We cannot play such a double game; we must not even think about it. They will crush us—with well-deserved disgrace—before we can make a move in that direction. . . .

Conclusion: we cannot give anything to the Palestinian or other Arabs in ex-change for Palestine. Hence their voluntary agreement is out of the question. Hence those who hold that such an agreement is an essential condition for Zionism can right now say "*non*" [French in the original] and renounce Zionism. Our colonization must either be terminated or proceed in defiance of the will of the native population. This colonization can therefore continue and develop only under the protection of a force independent of the local population—an iron wall which the native population cannot break through.

This is the sum total of our policy toward the Arabs. . . . What is the Balfour Declaration for? What is the Mandate for? To us they mean that an external power has committed itself to creating such security conditions that the local population, however much it would have wanted to, would be unable to interfere, administratively or physically, with our colonization.

1.5 Rampart against Asia

A second rather exceptional feature of Zionist colonization is that the settlers were not nationals of a European Power who sent them on their colonizing mission and protected them. It was therefore clear from the outset to the founders of political Zionism that it was vital for their project to obtain the sponsorship of a Great Power—whichever Great Power was dominant in the Middle East—that would provide them with an "iron wall," behind which Zionist colonization could proceed. Without such sponsorship—which early Zionist discourse referred to as a "charter"—colonization of Palestine would be a nonstarter.

Of course, Great Powers are no philanthropists. Their protection is not given for nothing, but in exchange for services. And from the outset it was clear what these services would be. The founder of political Zionism, Theodor Herzl (1860–1904), put it like this in his programmatic book *Der Judenstaat* (The Jewish State) published in 1896: "For Europe we would form there part of the rampart against Asia, serving as an outpost of civilization against barbarism. As a neutral state, we would remain in contact with all Europe, which would have to guarantee our existence."

Not so much a "clash of civilizations" as a clash of the one-and-only civilization with barbarism.

So it's a deal, a matter of quid pro quo. In exchange for the vital protection of the "iron wall" against the Palestinian Arabs that Western imperialism would help to erect, the Zionist colonizers—and eventually their settler state—were to provide their sponsors with a "rampart" against the "barbarians" of the Middle East. (The practice of Zionism is replete with walls and ramparts; but they appear even earlier in Zionist discourse: in the beginning was the word.)

A necessary consequence of this historic deal has been that it *regionalized* the conflict. The clash of the Zionist project (and eventually Israel) with the indigenous Palestinians was extended into a conflict with the people of the entire region. This is due not only to the national solidarity of Arabs throughout the region with their fellow Arabs in Palestine but also to the active role of Zionism (and Israel) as partner of Western exploitation and domination of the Middle East.

By the 1880s Germany under Kaiser Wilhelm II had replaced France and

Britain as "friend and military adviser" of the decaying Ottoman Empire. Palestine was then part of that empire, so Herzl tried to sell his idea to the German kaiser. But he was rebuffed; the kaiser passed on the proposed deal.[9]

1.6 "A Little Loyal Jewish Ulster"

Chaim Weizmann had much better luck with the Lloyd George government toward the end of the First World War. The Charter of Zionist aspirations was granted in the form of the Balfour Declaration (November 2, 1917).[10]

In his memoirs, Sir Ronald Storrs—the brain behind Lawrence of Arabia, and the first British governor of Jerusalem—made the following comment on the logic behind the Balfour Declaration: "Even though the land could not yet absorb sixteen million, nor even eight, enough could return, if not to form the Jewish State (which a few extremists publicly demanded), at least to prove that the enterprise was one that blessed him that gave [Britain] as well as him that took [Zionism] by forming for England 'a little loyal Jewish Ulster' in a sea of potentially hostile Arabism."[11]

The Balfour Declaration was part of a package. Another part of the package was the sculpting of Palestine as a separate political entity.

During nearly thirteen centuries of Muslim rule—interrupted only by the Crusades—Palestine had never been a distinct, let alone separate, administrative entity, but was an integral part of Greater Syria (consisting roughly of present-day "little" Syria, Lebanon, Jordan, Israel, the West Bank, and the Gaza Strip). In the Ottoman Empire, the southern half of Palestine constituted a special district of Jerusalem, subject directly to the High Porte in Istanbul; the northern half consisted of two districts, which were part of the province of Beirut.

Now, when the ravenous imperialist powers tore up the carcass of the Ottoman Empire, Palestine was one of the limbs grabbed by Britain. In 1922 Britain got the League of Nations to grant it a mandate over Palestine; and the Balfour Declaration was included verbatim in the text of the mandate, together with several detailed provisions for facilitating Zionist colonization.[12]

It would hardly be an exaggeration to say that Palestine, carved out of the Arab East, was purpose-made for Zionist colonization, irrespective of the wishes of its actual inhabitants. Indeed, as the American King-Crane Commission discovered in 1919, these inhabitants had no particular wish for a separate Palestine, but were quite content to be included in Greater Syria. Moreover, this carving out involved considerable trimming. The Palestine Mandate originally embraced also a large mostly arid territory to the east of the Jordan River, but Britain was allowed to "postpone or withhold" application of the provisions promoting Zionist colonization to this eastern territory. Thereupon Britain instituted it as a separate emirate of Transjordan, under its Hashemite protégé Abdullah. This later became the kingdom of Jordan. From 1923, "Palestine" meant the territory west of the Jordan, to which the Balfour Declaration applied fully under the League of Nations Mandate. It existed as a distinct and separate political entity for twenty-five years.

1.7 "A Kind of Watchdog"

In the 1930s the relations between the Zionist movement and its erstwhile British protector cooled down. Their aims and interests began to diverge. Eventually a serious rift opened up between them, developing after the Second World War into a violent conflict. I cannot go here into the detailed causes of this conflict. Suffice it to say that—among other things—the Great Uprising of the Palestinian Arabs made it clear to Britain that the cost of imposing the terms of the mandate would take too great a toll of its limited power and influence. Meanwhile, the Zionist project had outgrown the role of a mere "little loyal Jewish Ulster" and was ripe for assuming state sovereignty. But in any case Britain was losing its dominant position in the Middle East; Zionism needed a new imperial patron.

Michael Assaf, a Labor-Zionist Orientalist put it as follows:[13] "In those very years of struggle [between Zionism and British imperialism] there took place a process of a beginning of a new attachment: instead of England-Zion, America-Zion—a process that depended on the fact that the US was penetrating the Middle East as a decisive world power."

From the moment of its establishment in 1948, Israel continued this process of reattachment. It was seeking a new alliance—protection in exchange for services—with the United States. But the shift to the new imperialist sponsor was gradual and went through several stages. At first, Britain still retained some influence in the Middle East. This is reflected in the following assessment of Israel's regional role:[14]

> The feudal regime in these [Middle Eastern] states must be mindful to such a great extent of (secular and religious) nationalist movements that sometimes also have a decidedly leftist social hue, that these states are no longer prepared to put their natural resources at the disposal of Britain and America and allow them to use their countries as military bases in case of war. True, the ruling circles in the countries of the Middle East know that in case of a social revolution or Soviet conquest they would surely be physically liquidated, but the immediate fear of the bullet of a political assassin outweighs for the time being the impalpable fear of annexation to the Communist world. All these states are . . . militarily weak; Israel has proved its military strength in the [1948–49] War of Liberation against the Arab states and for this reason a certain strengthening of Israel is a rather convenient way for the Western Powers for keeping a balance of political forces in the Middle East. According to this supposition Israel has been assigned the role of a kind of watchdog. It is not to be feared that it would apply an aggressive policy toward the Arab states if that would be clearly against the wishes of America and Britain. But if the Western powers will at some time prefer, for one reason or another, to shut their eyes, Israel can be relied upon to punish properly one or several of its neighboring states whose lack of manners toward the West has gone beyond permissible limits.

The period 1948–67 was a delicate phase for Israel in its quest for attachment to the new dominant imperialist power: the United States was interested, agreeable, but not too enthusiastic. It gave Israel significant financial and political support, but its commitment to Israel was by no means total. The usefulness of Israel as a regional enforcer was by no means proven; it was not obvious to US policy makers.

For closer political alliance and for military equipment, Israel turned in the 1950s to France, which was then fighting a colonial war in Algeria. Arab nationalism—led by the charismatic Egyptian president Gamal Abdul-Nasser—was the common enemy.

In the 1956 Suez war Israel indeed proved its military prowess, its usefulness as a local Rottweiler—but to the wrong imperialist boss. France and Britain were spent forces as colonial powers. The United States was not amused by their gauche unauthorized attempt at a comeback and imperiously scotched it. Israel too was told in no uncertain terms to withdraw from its conquests, which Prime Minister Ben-Gurion had been too hasty to declare "part of the Third Kingdom of Israel."[15] However, Israel did make a considerable gain from the episode. At the secret conclave at Sèvre, where the Suez collusion was hatched, Ben-Gurion, Dayan, and Peres extracted from France a prize for Israel's crucial role in starting the war: a French promise to build a nuclear reactor in Israel and supply it with fissile material. This eventually led to Israel becoming the world's fifth nuclear power.[16]

In 1967 Israel made sure to obtain prior US approval for its attack on Egypt and Syria. It used this opportunity also to occupy the remaining part of Palestine, which Abdullah had grabbed in 1948, by a secret agreement with Ben-Gurion's government.

Israel has rendered many important services to the West, particularly to the United States; but the most valuable of these was its help in defeating secular Arab nationalism, which was rightly regarded by the West as a danger to its interests, and which never recovered from its 1967 military debacle. Israel has become the staunchest and most reliable US ally and enforcer in the region.[17]

1.8 Is It Apartheid?

Israel is often compared to South Africa as it was under apartheid. The term "apartheid" is widely used to characterize the Israeli settler state, and especially the Israeli regime in the territories occupied since 1967.

I think the reason for this widespread usage is that South Africa under apartheid is the only other settler state that was actively pursuing its colonizing project until recently, in most peoples' living memory. It is the only other active settler state that most people can recall. So they use the term "apartheid" as an invective, or as a generalized label for an oppressive regime of racist discrimination.[18]

But, analytically speaking, this label does not strictly apply to Zionist colonization. And it can be misleading: using "apartheid" as invective may be a satisfying way of venting one's feelings, and can perhaps serve as effective propaganda shorthand, but it is dangerous because people begin to believe that Israel is another South Africa, and therefore the Israeli-Palestinian conflict is similar and can be resolved in a similar way.

There *are* of course many similarities: South Africa under apartheid and Israel belong to the same genus: *colonial settler state*. Colonization necessarily involves dispossession of the indigenous people, harsh racist discrimination against them, and brutal measures to suppress their resistance. In actual fact, while the Palestinian Arabs inside the Green Line (who are citizens of Israel) suffer from severe institutionalized discrimination, they are not quite as badly off as were the nonwhites under apartheid. On the other hand, the Palestinians in the 1967 OTs are in many ways more brutally treated by the Israeli military and settlers than were the nonwhites under apartheid.

But my point is not about a comparison of the *degree* of oppression. There is an important *qualitative*, structural difference between the two settler states: they belong to the same genus but to different species of the genus. Precise characterization must not only state the proximate genus but also pinpoint the specific difference.[19]

Here I invoke Karl Marx's profound insight: the key to understanding a society, a social formation, is its political economy, its mode of production.[20] And this means primarily the source of surplus product, and the form of its extraction.[21]

In all colonizations, the indigenous people were dispossessed. But what was to become of them?

Speaking somewhat schematically, we can distinguish two species, two main models, of colonization and settler societies. The crucial difference is whether the indigenous population is harnessed as a labor force to be *exploited*, a source of surplus product; or *excluded* from the settlers' economy—marginalized, exterminated, or expelled, ethnically cleansed.

South Africa belonged to the former species. It didn't start this way, but with the development of capitalist industry and mining it evolved into a system in which Black Africans were the main source of surplus value. Apartheid was a system designed to keep the nonwhites at hand, as an essential resource of the economy—but without civil rights.

Zionism deliberately, consciously, and explicitly chose the other model: use of indigenous labor power was to be avoided. The Palestinian Arabs are not regarded as a useful exploitable *source* of surplus labor—but are *themselves* surplus to requirement. They are not needed to be at hand or even at arm's length, but are to be moved out of the way. They were to be ethnically cleansed or—in Zionist parlance—"transferred."

Transfer was envisaged right from the very beginning of political Zionism. On June 12, 1895, Theodor Herzl confided to his diary: "We shall try to transfer the poorer section of the [indigenous] population across the border, without raising noise, by giving them employment in the transit countries, but in our own country we shall deny them all work."

It would be tedious to quote here the vast stack of evidence for the planning of transfer, and accounts of its implementation—by pressure, intimidation, or forcible expulsion—when the opportunity arose. I refer you to the literature.[22]

In this respect—in excluding the indigenous Palestinians from the settlers' economy before 1948, and in planning and implementing their transfer—"left-wing" or "labor" Zionists were the most diligent.[23] They thought in class terms and so knew perfectly well that, as in any other political economy, the direct producers would be the majority. Zionism could not achieve a Jewish state, with a predominant Jewish majority, except by excluding the Arabs. The work had to be done by Jews: by idealistic European Jewish pioneers, and (since there were not enough volunteers) by destitute, mostly darker-skinned, Jews ingathered from the four corners of the earth.

On the whole, Zionism and Israel adhered to this model, minimizing reliance on Palestinian labor, with only a partial and brief deviation in the 1970s and '80s.[24] At present, Israeli capitalist high-tech enterprises established in the OTs on colonized Palestinian land prefer to employ superexploited Israeli-Jewish workers rather than Palestinian Arabs.[25]

Zionist/Israeli strategy has always had a twofold aim: *maximize Jewish colonization of land, minimize its Arab population.*

There is a degree of tension between these two goals. Yosef Weitz—a "labor" Zionist, a most ardent architect of transfer plans before the 1948 war, and one of the chief practitioners who engineered it during that war and its aftermath—got worried after the 1967 war:

> [W]hen the UN resolved to partition Palestine into two states, the [1948] War of Independence broke out, to our great good fortune [*sic*], and in it there came to pass a double miracle: a territorial victory and the flight of the Arabs. In the [1967] Six-Day War there came to pass one great miracle, a tremendous territorial victory, but the majority of the inhabitants of the liberated territories remained "attached" to their places, [a fact] which is liable to destroy the foundation of our State. The demographic problem is the most acute, especially when to its numerical weight is added the weight of the refugees.[26]

The wet dream of expanded colonization is troubled by a nightmare of demographic danger.

Different Zionist currents balance the two aims in different ways. Some prioritize the imperative of territorial expansion above absolute ethnic purity; others are petrified by the demographic peril: there are too many Arabs in Palestine, and they have a high birth rate.

Ideally—they all agree—if the Palestinians were somehow to disappear, the problem would disappear with them. But major ethnic cleansing can only be perpetrated at what Zionist discourse calls an "opportune moment" (*she'at kosher*). Pending such opportunity, the dominant strategy is to confine the Palestinians to easily contained, preferably self-policing, pockets. These differ from concentration camps inasmuch as the inmates are very welcome to leave, provided they emigrate. Nor are they bantustans, because the main purpose of the bantustans was to serve as nominally independent dormitories for a reserve labor force on which the settlers' economy depended.

What they most resemble are Indian reservations in the United States. And the various Israeli "peace plans" and accords with willing Palestinian leaders are not unlike the famous Indian Treaties.

◆ ◆ ◆

The fact that Zionist colonization follows this model—based not on exploiting the labor of the indigenous people but aiming to exclude and expel them—has some very important consequences.

First, the danger of further massive transfer is never far away. An "opportune moment" may arise, for example, during an extreme emergency or war—a prospect that is ever present in this volatile region.[27] Israel may even help to provoke such an opportunity. Meantime, slow-motion transfer proceeds by the salami tactics, using economic, administrative, and physical harassment.

Moreover, ethnic cleansing, expulsion, is evidently much harder to undo than relations of exploitation and racial discrimination.

Therefore those of us who are opposed to this injustice must act *with great urgency* to arouse world public opinion and mobilize civil society, so as to make it as difficult as possible for Israel to expand its colonization and perpetrate transfer.

1.9 The National Dimension

Another extremely important consequence that follows from the specific nature of Zionist colonization is that the conflict crystallized as a *national* one.

Whereas in the exploitative model of colonization the conflict between settlers and indigenous people assumes the form of a quasi-class struggle, in the other model—the one followed by Zionism—the colonists form a new settler nation. So also Zionist colonization resulted in the creation of a new nation: the *Israeli Jews*, or modern *Hebrews*.[28] They have the essential attributes of a nation in the modern sense of this word: territorial contiguity; a complete class structure (similar to that of other modern capitalist nations); a common language of everyday discourse (which is unique to them); and a secular culture, both "high" and popular.

Note that the Jews at large—those of today's Diaspora—lack *all* these attributes.[29] They do not constitute a nation in the current modern sense of this term.[30]

Adoption of the new national identity is as rapid as in the case of other immigrant settler nations. Those born in Israel to Jewish immigrants from Russia or an Arab country are members of the Hebrew nation: they are no more Russian or Arab than an American of Italian or Polish descent is an Italian or a Pole. Their parental origin is not erased but recedes into the background.

Ironically, Zionism—like a father denying the existence of his unwanted child—denies the existence of this Hebrew nation, newly created by Zionist colonization. For according to Zionist ideology, all the Jews around the world constitute a single nation. The true homeland of every Jew is not the country in which s/he may have been born and in which his or her family may have resided for generations. The homeland of this alleged nation is the biblical Land of Israel, over which it has an ancient inalienable—indeed God-given—national right.[31] Non-Jews living in the Jewish homeland are mere foreign interlopers. Zionist colonization is justified as "return to the homeland"—a right possessed by Jews but denied to those foreign interlopers, the Palestinian refugees, who have been legitimately evicted from the Jewish homeland. There is no Hebrew nation but merely members of the worldwide Jewish nation who have already returned to their homeland, an advance guard of their brethren in the Diaspora, who have a right—indeed a sacred duty—to follow the vanguard and be "ingathered" in the Land of Israel.

◆ ◆ ◆

Here I wish to point out yet another exceptional feature of Zionist colonization. In the exploitative model of colonization, the colonists ended up as a relatively small minority, an upper crust or quasi-class exploiting the labor power of the indigenous people. The latter comprise the bulk of the direct producers, and therefore remain the great majority of the population. On the other hand, in most colonizations that followed the other model, in which the colonists formed a new settler nation, the indigenous peoples, if not completely pulverized, were swamped or at any rate marginalized. Their distinct separate national identities have been overlaid by that of the settler nation. Their languages and cultural traditions, if not obliterated, have persisted as folk relics—"underground" or in remote rural areas—while the language and culture of the settler nation predominates elsewhere.

Not so in the case of Zionist colonization: here the clash between oppressor and oppressed—colonists and indigenous people—has assumed the form of a *national conflict between two discrete and quite well-defined national groups, of roughly equal size.*[32]

Despite its efforts, the Israeli state has so far been only partly successful in "transferring" the Palestinian Arabs from their homeland. The 1967 war was too brief for ethnic cleansing to be repeated on anything like the massive scale of 1947–49. Besides, the Palestinians had learned the bitter lesson of that Nakba, and—as Yosef Weitz ruefully notes*—remained tenaciously "attached" to their places. At the same time, the Arabs' higher rate of natural increase has to some extent balanced the influx of Jewish immigration to Israel.

The Palestinian Arabs' national identity, far from dissolving under the impact of colonization, crystallized and has been reinforced through the conflict with it. They have kept their language and developed a lively national cultural production.

This remarkable vitality is largely due to the regional context. Most Palestinians are located in close proximity to, or are dispersed as refugees in, a vast and populous Arab world sharing a common literary language (as well as its less formal version used by the media) and a glorious cultural heritage. Their spoken dialect is very close to those of other parts of the former Greater Syria, and not too distant from

---

* See p. 182 in this volume.

those of neighboring countries of the Arab East. Cultural exchanges are easy. Even the Palestinian Arabs who eluded the ethnic cleansing of 1948 and remained as an oppressed minority in Israel were able to tune in to broadcasts from the Arab world. Conversely, a poem or novel composed by a Palestinian in Haifa can be read and appreciated by many millions, from the Atlantic Ocean to the Arabian Sea.

Moreover, due to the historical "lateness" of Zionist colonization (see section 1.2), by the time it got going it encountered Arab national identity and a nascent Arab nationalism, which emerged at about the same time. Exceptionally, a colonization project was confronted from its very beginning by an emergent national movement. Note the worried reference to Arab nationalism and its aspiration to a regional federation in Jabotinsky's *Iron Wall* (section 1.4).

The analogy Jabotinsky draws between Arab nationalism and pre-1870 Italian nationalism is also quite apt. In Italy, alongside "pan-Italian" national identity and nationalism—which had yet to achieve political unification—there existed distinct local mini-national identities and local patriotisms: Venetian, Tuscan, Roman, Neapolitan, Sicilian, et cetera. In fact, they survive to this day.[33] Likewise, in the Arab world there are two tiers of national identity and nationalism: alongside pan-Arab identity and aspiration for unification or federation, there are local identities and patriotisms: Egyptian, Iraqi, Syrian, and so on—and of course Palestinian, formed through a common calamitous experience and in the struggle to survive and overcome. There is some tension between these two tiers of national identity, but they need not be mutually antithetical; they are capable of being compatible and even complementary.

While Arab governments and ruling elites merely pay lip service to the ideal of Arab unity, genuine commitment to it is widespread among the masses; and a central component of this commitment is a deep-seated solidarity with the Palestinians.

◆ ◆ ◆

Any cogent projection of a resolution must start from this understanding of the nature of the conflict. It is a violent colonial confrontation between two nations that have taken shape through this very conflict: a colonizing Hebrew nation and its oppressing Israeli settler state, and an oppressed indigenous colonized Palestinian Arab nation. The former is allied to the imperialist Power dominating the entire region; the latter is a component part of the greater Arab nation of the region.

2. Resolution—Principles and Preconditions

2.1 Normative Principles

In thinking about *resolution* of the conflict, we ought to start in normative mode. It is pointless to try to evaluate any proposed specific formula before establishing some general principles that a genuine just resolution must satisfy.

In several other settler states belonging to the same species of colonization, the settlers have succeeded in eliminating the entire indigenous population or in reducing it to small and relatively insignificant remnants. The conflict between colonizers and colonized ended with the overwhelming and virtually total victory of the former, and was in this sense "resolved."

Such an outcome is very unlikely in the case of the Israeli settler state. To be sure, the historical record suggests that Israel's Zionist leaders will exploit any opportunity for further territorial expansion and ethnic cleansing. Moreover, the more daring among them will attempt actively to create such opportunities. But however far this process may realistically be pushed, Israel will always find itself surrounded by Arabs, by the Arab nation, of which the Palestinian Arab people is a constituent part.

In the end, the conflict in this case can only be resolved by accommodating the two national groups directly involved: the Palestinian Arabs and the Hebrews.

Note that what I propose to discuss here is *resolution* rather than palliatives. There are of course various steps that can be taken to ameliorate the present dire situation, in which great suffering is caused to millions of human beings—mostly to Palestinians, but also to many Israelis. I am certainly not arguing against such palliative measures; on the contrary, I think public opinion should be mobilized to demand them. Above all, pressure must be applied on Israel to end its military occupation of the West Bank, the Gaza Strip,[34] and the Syrian Golan Heights. But we must not confuse palliatives with cure and amelioration with resolution: that would be a dangerous illusion. So long as its causes are not eliminated, the conflict will persist; any amelioration is likely to be no more than a lull, followed by another violent eruption.

◆ ◆ ◆

What then are the essential elements that a lasting resolution must embody? First and foremost, *equal rights*. By this I mean not only equal *individual* rights for all— this goes without saying. But also, no less important: equal collective rights, *national* rights, for the two national groups actually involved: the Palestinian Arabs and the Israeli Hebrews. This is a minimal necessary condition because its absence means, by definition, that one of these groups will be underprivileged, subjugated, and oppressed. National oppression inexorably leads to national struggle—the very opposite of resolution.

Second, *the right of return*: recognition of the right of the Palestinian refugees to return to their homeland, to be rehabilitated and properly compensated for loss of property and livelihood. This is so self-evidently just that it needs no elaborate justification. Indeed, the only argument voiced against it is that it would jeopardize the "Jewish character" of Israel, or, in plain language, its ethnocratic constitution as a settler state. But to accept this argument would amount to capitulation to Zionist ideology. Which brings me to my next point.

The third and most fundamental element in a genuine resolution is removal of the fundamental cause of the conflict: *the Zionist colonization project must be superseded.* This means not only de-Zionization of Israel but also repudiation of the Zionist claim that the Jews at large, constituting a "diasporic nation," have a special right in—let alone over—the "Land of Israel." For this claim amounts not only to a retroactive legitimation of past Zionist colonization, but, in effect, demands an acceptance of an alleged *continuing* right to future further "ingathering"—which implies further colonization and expansion. Such an impossible claim precludes a true resolution of the conflict.

2.2 Two States? One State?

In principle—that is, conceived abstractly, without regard to actual realities such as the present balance of power—an equitable resolution satisfying the principles I have just outlined could be implemented within various state-institutional frameworks.

One can imagine Palestine divided into two states: Israel and a Palestinian Arab state. Or one can envisage a single state in the whole of Palestine. And one can think of other setups, which I will mention later. But clearly the crucial point is not the number of states, but whether the essential principles of genuine resolution are satisfied. For a two-state setup to satisfy them, Israel would have to be de-Zionized: transformed from an ethnocratic settler state into a democratic state of all its inhabitants. Also, resources—including land and water—would have to be divided justly and shared equitably by the two states. And neither of them should be allowed to dominate the other. On the other hand, a single state would have to be not merely democratic (and hence secular) but have a constitutional structure that recognizes the two national groups and gives them equal national rights and status.[35]

But in fact none of this is feasible at present. Indeed, no genuine resolution is possible in the short or medium term, because of the enormous disparity in the balance of power. The Palestinians, economically shattered, lightly armed, and enjoying little effective international support, are facing a dominant modern capitalist Israel, a regional hegemonic nuclear superpower, a local hatchet man and junior partner of the global hyper-power. So long as such gross imbalance of power persists, any settlement will inevitably impose harsh oppressive conditions on the weaker side. To expect anything else would be wildly unrealistic.

In these circumstances any "two-state settlement" is bound to be a travesty: not two real sovereign states (let alone two equal ones) but one powerful Israeli state dominating a disjointed set of Palestinian enclaves similar to Indian reservations, policed by corrupt elites acting as Israel's proxies. This was the real prospect even under the Oslo Accords of 1993; and since then the situation has deteriorated much further, with the virulent malignant metastasis of Israeli colonization, and the weakening of the Palestinian Authority under Israeli pounding and international strangulation.[36]

Faced with the evident present infeasibility of an equitable two-state setup, many people of genuine goodwill have reverted to the "one-state" formula. This is, abstractly speaking, an attractive proposition. The trouble with it, however, is that a truly equal one-state setup is no more feasible in the short or medium term than an equal two-state one—and for exactly the same reason. Given the actual imbalance of power, a single state embracing the whole of Palestine will be no better than an extension of direct Israeli military occupation and subjugation.

A flaw common to both "two-state" and "one-state" formulas is that they are confined to the "box" of Palestine—the territory of the British Mandate from 1923 to 1948. They differ in that the former proposes to repartition it, while the latter proposes to resurrect it as a single distinct political entity. Ironically, as I pointed out earlier, this box was purpose-made for Zionist colonization, the root cause of the conflict. Can it serve as an insulated container for the conflict's resolution?

2.3 Resolution in a Regional Context

No balance of power lasts forever. A genuine resolution of the conflict will become possible in the longer term, given a change in the present balance of power. It is impossible to foresee *exactly* how this change may come about. But it seems quite certain that it will not be confined to the relationship between Israel and the Palestinians, while all else remains as it is: it will necessarily involve tectonic movements in the entire region, as well as international global shifts.

Two interconnected and mutually reinforcing processes will be vital for changing the present balance of power. First, the decline in American global dominance, and in particular in the ability of the United States to go on backing Israeli regional hegemony without incurring unacceptable economic and political costs. Second, a radical-progressive social, economic, and political transformation of the Arab East, leading to a degree of unification of the Arab nation—most likely in the form of regional federation.

It is pretty pointless to discuss the resolution of the Israeli-Palestinian conflict as though it would take place in an isolated Palestine box—whether partitioned or in one piece—while ignoring the rest of the region, and failing to factor in its transformation, without which that resolution is in any case impossible. Set in its proper regional context, our vision of resolution involves a change of focus. It would be a mistake to insist on a piece of "real estate"—Israel in its 1948–67 borders or Palestine in its 1923–48 borders—as the data given once and for all. Rather, the true primary data are human: the two national groups that are directly involved in the conflict, and that will continue to exist for a very long time to come: the Palestinian Arabs and the Israeli Hebrews. And the task will then be to accommodate these two groups in the regional union or federation. Borders will become internal demarcations within the federation, and will be drawn accordingly. We cannot foresee what they will be, but they need by no means conform to those that have existed so far.

◆ ◆ ◆

It would be foolish to claim that at present the prospect looks bright. American dominance still seems solid, as is total US backing for its Israeli regional enforcer. The Arab East is ruled by corrupt and craven elites. It has not as yet recovered from the defeat of secular Arab nationalism. Even in its relatively progressive Nasserist form, Arab nationalism was unable to break out of its petty-bourgeois limitations and mobilize truly active mass democratic self-organization. Its later degeneration under murderous rival Ba'thi regimes, pretending to uphold "socialism" and "Arab unity," managed to give both ideals a bad name in the region. The subsequent emergence of Islamism holds a false promise. While it poses a challenge to Western domination, it is backward-looking and inherently unable to deliver progress. Nor can it possibly be a uniting force: on the contrary, it is deeply divisive as between Sunnis and Shi'is, and has no attraction whatsoever for non-Muslim and secular Arabs (including Palestinians), let alone Hebrews.

While there are few grounds for immediate optimism, there are some hopeful signs pointing to the longer term. American economic and political power, outwardly robust, is beset with symptoms of decline. US military power is of little avail and is overreaching itself. Meanwhile, a new radical progressive counter-globalization movement is gathering momentum in parts of the third world. It is yet to take off in the Arab East. But much depends on all of us.

Appendix: Israel as US Strategic Asset

The following are excerpts from an article by General Shlomo Gazit, former head of Israel's Military Intelligence, published in the daily *Yedi'ot Aharonot* on April 27, 1992, under the title "No Demise as a Strategic Asset."

> Israel's main task has not changed at all [despite the end of the Cold War], and it remains of crucial importance. The geographical location of Israel at the center of the Arab-Muslim Middle East predestines Israel to be a devoted guardian of stability in all the countries surrounding it. Its [role] is to protect the existing regimes: to prevent or halt the processes of radicalization, and to block the expansion of fundamentalist religious zealotry. . . .
>
> [One of Israel's "red lines" is to foil] threats of revolt, whether military or popular, which may end up by bringing fanatical and extremist elements to power in the states concerned. The existence of such threats has no connection with the Arab-Israeli conflict. They exist because the regimes [in the region] find it difficult to offer solutions to their socioeconomic ills. But any development of the kind described could subvert the existing relations between Israel and one or another of its neighbors. . . .
>
> Israel's red lines signal to its neighbors that Israel will not tolerate anything that might encourage the extremist forces to go all the way, following in the footsteps of the Iranians in the east or the Algerians in the west. . . .
>
> In the aftermath of the disappearance of the USSR as a political power with its own interests in the region, a number of Middle East states have lost a patron guaranteeing their political, military and even economic viability. A vacuum has thus been created, with the effect of adding to the region's instability. Under such condi-

tions, the Israeli role as a strategic asset in guaranteeing a modicum of stability in the entire Middle East, far from dwindling or disappearing, has been elevated to the first order of magnitude. Without Israel, the West would have to perform this role on its own, when none of the existing superpowers could really perform it due to various domestic and international constraints. For Israel, by contrast, the need to intervene is a matter of survival.

The following article was published on May 12, 2005, in the English-language online version of *Yedi'ot Aharonot*, under the title "Two-Way Independence." The writer, Yoram Ettinger, is a consultant on US-Israel relations, chairman of special projects at the Ariel Center for Policy Research and frequent contributor to *Yedi'ot Aharonot*.

In Many Ways, Israel Is the Giver and the US Is the Receiver

Statements made by, and the conduct of, Israel's leaders since 1993 create the false impression that Israeli-American ties constitute a one-way relationship.

The presumption is that America gives and Israel receives, leading to Israel's inferior position and the alleged compulsion to follow the State Department dictates.

However, former Secretary of State and NATO forces commander Alexander Haig[37] refuted this claim, saying he is pro-Israeli because "Israel is the largest American aircraft carrier in the world that cannot be sunk, does not carry even one American soldier, and is located in a critical region for American national security."

On our 57th Independence Day, Israel and the United States enjoy a two-way relationship. Israel is like a start-up company that enjoys the kindness of the American investor, but yields much greater profits than the investment.

Every day, Israel relays to the US lessons of battle and counterterrorism, which reduce American losses in Iraq and Afghanistan, prevent attacks on US soil, upgrade American weapons, and contribute to the US economy.

Senator Daniel Inouye recently argued Israeli information regarding Soviet arms saved the US billions of dollars. "The contribution made by Israeli intelligence to America is greater than that provided by all NATO countries combined," he said.

Yoram Ettinger then lists some of the ways in which Israel is the "giver." They include the following:

- According to information provided by the VP of the company producing the F16 fighter jets, the company owes Israel 600 improvements in the fighters' system, worth billions of dollars.
- Israel's use of US arms boosts the US military industry. Israeli purchase and improvement of US arms also helps to persuade other countries, such as Japan and South Korea, to buy arms from the United States rather than from the UK or France. In fact, Israel is regarded as a successful research and development provider for both military and civilian US industry.
- In the 1967 war, Israel caused a major setback to the radical Arab regimes that "threatened to bring about the collapse of pro-American

Arab regimes and disrupt oil supply."

- In 1970, Israel caused the withdrawal of Syrian forces from Jordan, thus saving the pro-US Hashemite regime of that country, and preventing "a possible domino effect that could have reached Saudi Arabia and the Gulf states."
- In 1977 Israeli intelligence helped to foil Gaddafi's plan to assassinate Egypt's president Anwar Sadat, a loyal US protégé.
- In 1981, Israel bombed the Iraqi nuclear reactor, thus preventing Iraq acquiring nuclear weapons and making it safe for the United States to invade it in 1991 and 2003.
- In 1982, Israel shared with the United States the lessons it acquired in destroying Soviet anti-aircraft batteries in Lebanon, which had been thought to be immune to American weapons. Ettinger claims that these lessons were not only "worth billions of dollars" but also changed the global balance of power and contributed to the eventual disintegration of the Soviet Union.
- In 2005, Israel provided the United States with "the world's most extensive experience in homeland defence and warfare against suicide bombers and car bombs."
- Israel provides American soldiers with training facilities.
- Israeli-made drones are used by the United States in Iraq and Afghanistan.

He ends his article by pointing out that "Congress leaders, Vice-President Cheney, and Secretary of Defense Rumsfeld are aware of Israel's unique contribution to US interests."

34

Resolution of the Israeli-Palestinian Conflict: A Socialist Viewpoint

This article is not written as a polemic against Zionists, social-imperialists, and purveyors of similar reactionary ideologies; nor is it aimed at a broad liberal or progressive audience. It is addressed specifically to genuine socialists. I can therefore take certain things for granted.

I will take for granted the analysis of the Israeli-Palestinian conflict I have expounded elsewhere, especially in my 2006 Amiel and Melburn Trust lecture.[1] But I would like to elaborate on the second part of that lecture, which dealt all too briefly with resolution of the conflict.

I will also take it for granted that we, socialists, reject not only any ideology of colonization and oppression but also all nationalism, including the nationalist ideology of an oppressed people struggling for national liberation. This latter precept, while accepted in principle by all genuine socialists, is not always adhered to in political practice. It is all too easy to slide from support for a national liberation struggle—which is our unwavering duty as socialists—into accommodation with the bourgeois or petty-bourgeois nationalist ideology of the leadership of that struggle. Wishing—quite correctly—not to appear patronizing by preaching from afar to the oppressed masses how to conduct their struggle and presenting them with a pre-packaged program, socialists often forego an independent critical socialist viewpoint and are content to tail behind this or that brand of radical nationalism. Independent positions such as those advocated in the present article, which were formerly held and defended by significant sections of the revolutionary left, have been abandoned or simply forgotten. They need to be reaffirmed.

An edited version of this article was published in *Weekly Worker* 757, February 19, 2009.

Principles

Let me start with the least controversial part: the principles on which a just and lasting resolution of the Israeli-Palestinian conflict must be based, the minimal conditions it must satisfy.[2]

The most fundamental element in a genuine resolution of the conflict is removal of its fundamental cause: the Zionist colonization project must be superseded. This means not only de-Zionization of Israel but also repudiation of the Zionist claim that the Jews at large, constituting an alleged "diasporic nation," have a special right in—let alone over—the "Land of Israel." For this claim amounts not only to a retroactive legitimation of past Zionist colonization, but, in effect, demands an acceptance of an alleged persisting right to future further "ingathering"—which implies further colonization and expansion. Such an impossible claim precludes a true resolution of the conflict.

This fundamental negative condition must be supplemented by the following positive ones.

First and foremost, equal rights. This includes not only equal individual rights for all but also, no less important: equal collective rights, national rights, for the two national groups actually involved: the Palestinian Arabs and the Israeli Hebrews. We must insist on this as a minimal necessary condition because socialists cannot ever tolerate any national privilege, any national inequality.

Second, the right of return: recognition of the right of the Palestinian refugees to return to their homeland, to be rehabilitated and properly compensated for loss of property and livelihood. This is so self-evidently just that it needs no elaborate justification. Indeed, the only argument voiced against it is that it would jeopardize the "Jewish character" of Israel, or, in plain language, its ethnocratic constitution as a settler state. But to accept this argument would amount to capitulation to Zionist ideology.

How can these principles be implemented? What political framework will be needed for this?

In addressing these questions I do not presume to offer the Palestinian masses unsolicited advice as to what they should be struggling for. I do not propose to emulate the habit of some leftist sects of self-appointed vanguards, who dispense from afar off-the-peg one-size-fits-all programs to movements that have not asked them for this service.

But socialists cannot be content with echoing demands raised by this or that Palestinian national leadership. We must perform our own independent analysis of the problem and come to our own conclusion as to which resolution of the conflict we ought to uphold and which demands we should raise.

In particular, it is incumbent on us to be clear about the relationship between the liberation of the Palestinian Arab people and the struggle for socialism. Are these two separate issues or are they connected; and if so, how?

From One State to Two, and Back

The Palestine Liberation Organization (PLO) was originally created in 1964 by the League of Arab States, and was an empty shell manipulated by the Arab regimes until February 1969, when it was taken over by Fatah (the Movement for the Liberation of Palestine), led by Yasser Arafat. Under Arafat's chairmanship, the PLO became an umbrella body of the secular Palestinian liberation movement, including Fatah and several other smaller groups.

From 1969 until 1974, the PLO unambiguously called for the liberation of the whole of pre-1948 Palestine—including not only the West Bank and the Gaza Strip occupied by Israel since 1967 but also Israel itself—and establishing in it a unitary "secular democratic state."

However, from 1974 the PLO began to shift its position, and by the 1980s accepted a "two-state solution": an independent Palestinian state in the West Bank (including the eastern part of Jerusalem) and the Gaza Strip, which would exist alongside Israel. Thus the PLO was resigned to giving up—at least for the foreseeable future—the Palestinian claim over 78 percent of the territory of pre-1948 Palestine, and making do with the remaining rump of 22 percent.

This led eventually to the 1993 Oslo Accords between the PLO and Israel. These accords reflected the enormous disparity in the balance of power between the two sides. Although the impression created was that the accords would lead to the establishment of a sovereign Palestinian state, this was not actually stated in the text, and in fact Israel made no such commitment. The accords merely established a "Palestinian Authority" and Israel accepted an obligation to a staged withdrawal from an unspecified part of the territories it occupied in 1967. Agreement about the final borders, the status of Jerusalem, and the issue of the Palestinian refugees was deferred to a later date. In the meantime Israel retained control over the vital water resources of the whole of Palestine, including the parts from which it would withdraw. It also retained control over the population of the areas administered by the Palestinian Authority: it continued to exercise a veto over who would count as a legitimate resident of these areas. Most crucially, Israel made no commitment to halt its colonization of the Occupied Territories. In fact, the colonization of these territories (except for some areas administered by the Palestinian Authority) continued apace and even accelerated during the years of the "Oslo process."

Already before the assassination of Yitzhak Rabin (November 1995), Israel stalled in fulfilling its part of the bargain and made no further withdrawal from the Occupied Territories. After his assassination, the Oslo Accords became a dead letter. The Palestinian Authority was reduced to impotence and its only remaining role is to police the Palestinian population on behalf of Israel.

By now, the Gaza Strip has been turned into the world's largest open-air prison; and the ever-accelerating Israeli colonization of the West Bank has cut it up into a series of separate Palestinian enclaves surrounded by blocs of Israeli settlements.[3] As there is little likelihood that any Israeli government in the near future will be willing and able to reverse these facts on the ground, there is no longer any realistic prospect of a contiguous Palestinian state with true sovereignty even on the remaining 22 percent rump of Palestine. Any so-called Palestinian state that may be created in the present circumstances will in effect be no more than a series of Indian reservations, under total Israeli domination.

This has led a growing number of Palestinians to revert to the idea of a unitary state in the whole of pre-1948 Palestine.

The Palestine Box

Most socialists around the world—just like most liberal supporters of Palestinian rights—have been content to uphold either one of these slogans: some call for a "two-state solution" in a partitioned Palestine, with a Palestinian Arab state alongside Israel; whereas others call for a "one-state solution" in an undivided Palestine.

Supporters of either formula generally fail to think carefully through such questions as to whether, and under what circumstances, their favored "solution" is likely to be implemented in a way that provides a genuine resolution of the conflict. They are content to stay at a high level of abstraction.[4]

Thinking abstractly, it is indeed quite possible to visualize a just and equitable resolution in a "two-state" as well as a "one-state" framework.

As for a "two-state" framework, it would have to be very different indeed from any settlement that has even a remotely serious prospect of being implemented in the short or medium term. What is currently proposed and desultorily negotiated by the powers that be as a "two-state" setup is really nothing of the kind. It is more like one-and-a-quarter states: a dominant Israel, possessing the lion's share of the land, controlling virtually all the vital water resources; and a disconnected set of Palestinian enclaves incapable of more than token sovereignty. This would provide no possibility for implementing the Palestinian refugees' right to return to their homeland. Nor would it address the racist nature of Israel: an ethnocratic Jewish state in which the Palestinian Arab minority (comprising about one fifth of the population) is severely discriminated and underprivileged.

But of course it is possible to visualize a totally different picture: two states of comparable size and equitable shares of resources, in which the Palestinian refugees attain their due rights, and national equality is implemented.

As for a "one-state" framework, it is not currently a realistic option, except of course in the present extremely oppressive form in which one state, Israel, rules the whole of Palestine, with the West Bank and the Gaza Strip under military occupation.

But again it is possible to visualize a very different undivided Palestine, in which the conflict is truly resolved. Some people have indeed attempted to produce a detailed blueprint of this kind, including a draft constitution of a future undivided Palestine.

Here it must be pointed out that the "secular democratic state" as proposed by the PLO in 1969/70 would not provide a genuine lasting resolution of the conflict.

Some of those who repeat this formula as a mantra don't stop to think about the strange and apparently redundant combination "secular democratic." How could a democratic state be anything *but* secular? Surely, a theocratic state cannot be democratic. But the bourgeois nationalist Fatah ideologues who coined this formula meant something very specific by the adjective "secular." What it was intended to convey is the vision of an Arab Palestine, in which "Jews" (along with Christians and Muslims) would be accorded equal individual status and freedom of worship as a *religious denomination*, but would not be recognized as a nationality. This was the meaning encoded by "secular": it was counterposed not to "theocratic" but to "binational."[5] So the formula was designed to evade the reality of the Hebrew nation.

However, it is quite possible to imagine an undivided Palestine in which both national communities are recognized and enjoy equal collective rights as such.

An Instructive Analogy

In my opinion both formulas—the so-called two-state solution and one-state solution—are misguided, and socialists should refrain from echoing either of them.

In arguing for this thesis I would like to invoke an analogy. I do so not to clinch the argument: analogies cannot settle anything conclusively. Rather, I hope that it will make it easier for socialists to follow the analogous *logical structure* of my argument.

All genuine socialists (which of course excludes Stalinists) understand that the slogan of "socialism in one country (Russia)" was disastrous. In fact it was used as cover and justification for some of the most monstrous atrocities of the twentieth century; but even without having foreknowledge of this, it was a grave error for socialists to uphold this slogan when it was first raised.

But why? What was wrong with a vision of a socialist Russia, even if it was isolated? Surely, socialism in one country is preferable to no socialism anywhere?

Well, of course there was nothing wrong with that vision *as such*, and it would have been very good to achieve socialism even in an isolated Russia—if such a thing were possible. But it was *not* possible; it was from the start a purely utopian formula, and because of this any attempt to implement it was bound to end disastrously.

Socialism in one country, Russia, was a doomed Utopia for two interconnected reasons.

First, the socioeconomic level of development and the balance of class forces within the Russian Empire were adverse to the establishment of a socialist order there.

Second, capitalism is in any case a global system, which cannot be overthrown in a single country, but only—at the very least—in a large region of the world.

Now, the analogous argument I wish to put forward is that both the "two-state solution" and the "one-state solution" to the Israeli-Palestinian conflict are fundamentally flawed. Although each of them, in a suitable version, may present an acceptable and even attractive vision, they are equally abstract and utopian, because no just and lasting resolution of the conflict is possible within the confines of pre-

1948 Palestine. Whether repartitioned into two pieces or reconstituted as a single piece, the Palestine box itself is not a container within which the conflict can be justly and lastingly resolved. This is so for two interconnected reasons.

First, the balance of power within pre-1948 Palestine—between the two nationalities, the Hebrew settlers and the indigenous Palestinian Arabs—is adverse to any just resolution of the conflict.

Second, in any case the conflict is deeply imbedded in the regional context of the Arab East, and cannot possibly be resolved in isolation from it and in the absence of a profound transformation of the entire region.

The Internal Balance of Power

Let me put it very bluntly. Socialists must not accept without protest, let alone uphold, any unjust arrangement or project. But proposing a just blueprint that is purely utopian is of little use, and may well be irresponsible.

So it is incumbent on anyone proposing a just resolution of the Israeli-Palestinian conflict to provide, or at least to outline, a strategy for getting both nationalities to abide by it. By far the more problematic is the stronger side, the Israeli Hebrews.

In a much-quoted account, Thucydides reports the Athenians' chilling remark to the Melians: "The strong do what they can and the weak suffer what they must." We may question the second half of this statement if it means accepting oppression without struggle, without resistance; even the weak can take defensive action. But the first half is undoubtedly true.

How may the Hebrew nation, or a majority of it, be induced to give up its present oppressive privilege and overwhelming dominant position? What means of coercion or persuasion, what combination of pressures and promises, what sticks and carrots can achieve this?

Sadly, no such combination exists; no sufficient means are available within pre-1948 Palestine, which is at present entirely under Israeli rule.

In order to make this point clearer, let me contrast the situation there with that in South Africa toward the end of the apartheid era. Elsewhere I have analyzed the differences between the two models of colonization and settler state in terms of their fundamentally different political economies.[6] This underlying difference has entailed profound consequences regarding the balance of power.

South African colonialism, based on exploiting the labor power of the indigenous people, resulted in the settlers emerging as a quasi-class of exploiters, a small minority of the total population. The oppressed were the overwhelming majority. The liberation movement did engage in some armed resistance; but this did not play a critical role in ending apartheid. In a sense, it didn't need to. The huge numerical superiority of the nonwhites was in itself a massive if implicit threat that the settlers could not indefinitely ignore or hope to defeat. Moreover, the latter depended on the labor power of the former. Despite the pretensions of apartheid, the colonial conflict was *internal*, within the South African socioeconomic system. Economically, the settlers could not exist on their own. Thus they were vastly outnumbered by a population that could not indefinitely be suppressed, but was economically indispensable. In this situation, the settlers' leaders could not refuse the generous deal offered to them by the liberation movement.

In contrast to South Africa, Zionist colonization deliberately chose not to rely on the labor power of the indigenous people; instead they were to be excluded and whenever possible ethnically cleansed. As in other countries where a similar model of colonization was pursued, the settlers emerged not as a relatively small quasi-class but as a new settler nation, with its own class structure similar to that of other modern capitalist societies.

During the 1947–49 war, the majority of the Palestinian Arab inhabitants of what became Israel were ethnically cleansed, so that within the Green Line (Israel's de facto borders from 1949 to 1967) Palestinian Arabs are a minority (at present about 20 percent of the population). In the entire area currently ruled by Israel, there is rough numerical parity between the two nationalities: the Israeli Hebrew settlers and the indigenous Palestinian Arabs.

Israel has been colonizing the best lands in the occupied West Bank, whose Palestinian Arab population has been isolated in several enclaves. Israeli policy aims to contain and control these, as well as the separate densely populated enclave of the Gaza Strip. Wherever possible, this is done by proxy, using a compliant elite of collaborators. The people confined in these enclaves have little or no economic leverage against Israel, as they play no significant part in the Israeli economy, except as a captive market.

The prospect facing these enclaves is, at best, to be declared a nominal "Palestinian state"; at worst, Israel will use any suitable opportunity to ethnically cleanse them.

To a considerable extent, Israel has been able to *externalize* its conflict with the Palestinians, so that it can be managed using its vastly superior physical force. Palestinian resistance—whether armed or nonviolent—may be able to put up a defensive struggle, but *on its own* it has no realistic prospect of inducing Israel to give up the Zionist colonizing project and share Palestine on equal terms, be it in two states or in one.

Given the great disparity of internal forces, a major section of the bourgeois and petty-bourgeois Palestinian leaders have put their hope and trust in external pressure, to be applied on Israel by the big powers. Actually, the only big power that could conceivably apply decisive pressure on Israel is the United States, the hegemonic world power, whose influence in the Middle East is unrivaled, and on whom Israel depends for vital economic, political, and military support.

As advance payment for pressure on Israel, these Palestinian leaders have sought American patronage and have become US camp followers. But the returns have been very meager indeed. This is no accident: Israel is the main henchman of the United States in the Middle East, a junior partner and regional enforcer, who helps to keep the regimes of the Arab East in abject subservience to American imperialism.[7] Given this relationship between the United States and Israel, the former may prevail on the latter to make a few relatively minor concessions; but these will fall far short of giving up Israeli domination and accepting Palestinian rights, without which the conflict cannot be resolved.

It is impossible to escape the conclusion that all schemes for resolving the conflict within the narrow confines of Palestine are exercises in futility. They are also historically myopic.

Creation of the Palestine Box

Palestinian bourgeois and petty-bourgeois nationalist ideology fetishizes the Palestinian homeland as a Lost Paradise, to be regained. But the prosaic historical fact is that Palestine, as a separate entity, is itself a major part of the problem. The Nakba, the Palestinian catastrophe, occurred in the 1947–49 war, with the botched *partition* of Palestine. But its roots go back to the imperialist *creation* of Palestine in two earlier acts of partition. This half-forgotten history is of crucial importance, and I must recapitulate it briefly.

From late antiquity until the First World War, "Palestine"—from the Latin Palæstina—was a term used almost exclusively by European Christians.

During twelve centuries of Muslim rule,[8] Palestine did not exist as a distinct geographic or administrative, let alone political, entity. It was an integral part of Syria (al-Sham); even the name Filastin (Arabized form of Palæstina) was very rarely used.[9] In the final period of the Ottoman Empire, roughly the southern half of what would later become Mandate Palestine was a separate district (*sanjak*) of Jerusalem, directly under the Sublime Porte in Istanbul; the northern half consisted of two districts, subdivisions of the province (*vilayet*) of Beirut. All three districts, together with what are now Syria, Lebanon, and Jordan, were part of a single country (*eyelet*): Greater Syria or Şam (pronounced "Sham").

Following the First World War, the British imperialists reneged on their promise to allow the former Arab provinces of the defeated Ottoman Empire to unite (as demanded by the nascent Arab nationalist movement). Instead, they and the French imperialists carved up and rearranged the former Ottoman possessions according to their own interests and designs. In particular, Greater Syria was partitioned into two parts. In 1922 the League of Nations was "persuaded" to grant France a mandate over the northern part (present-day Syria and Lebanon); while Britain was granted a mandate over the southern part, which was christened "Palestine." ("Christened" is apposite here, as the name, and the very concept of a country of this name, were part of a European Christian tradition, not a local one.)

This was the first fateful partition. But at that point Palestine still included also a sizable, albeit mostly arid, territory east of the Jordan River—Transjordanian Palestine.

It is important to note that the resolution of the League of Nations, adopted on July 24, 1922, granting Britain a mandate over Palestine, specified explicitly that Britain was to facilitate Zionist colonization. In the text of the resolution, the Balfour Declaration was quoted verbatim. In fact, the whole text reads as though a principal purpose of the mandate—and by implication the creation of the country referred to as "Palestine"—was the establishment of a Jewish "national home."[10]

However, Article 25 of the mandate makes an exception of Transjordanian Palestine: there "the Mandatory shall be entitled, with the consent of the Council of the League of Nations, to postpone or withhold application of such provisions of this mandate as he may consider inapplicable to the existing local conditions." Based on this exception, the British secretary of state for the colonies, one Winston Churchill, partitioned Palestine in May 1923.

This was the second act of partition. The Transjordanian part was made into a separate emirate (principality) of Transjordan under Britain's protégé Abdullah bin al-Husayn. This is the present Kingdom of Jordan. The remaining (Cisjordanian) part—consisting of only 22.6 percent of the short-lived Greater Palestine—to which the mandate's provisions of Zionist colonization fully applied—was henceforth referred to exclusively as "Palestine" *tout court.* That imperialist creation, carved and trimmed expressly as the domain of Zionist colonization—existed as a single country, under the British Mandate, for a mere twenty-five years: 1923–48. Ironically, this is what is sometimes referred to, with astonishing lack of historical awareness, as "historical Palestine"!

The Nakba of 1947–49 is indelibly seared into Palestinian collective memory. But the ad hoc imperialist territorial arrangements that were imposed on the region a mere generation earlier and prepared the ground for the Nakba should also not be forgotten. Talk of "historical Palestine" tends to foster the false impression that it was an authentic entity sanctified by long duration.

Arab National Unification

So, the creation of Palestine was part of the imperialist dispensation following the First World War, which deliberately prevented the unification of the Arab East, thus reneging on promises made by Britain during that war. A divided Arab world suited the interests of the imperialist powers: a divided nation is easier to dominate and exploit.

A divided Arab nation is also a vital interest of the Zionist project; and it is this common interest that lies at the basis of the close alliance between Zionism (and the Zionist state) and its successive imperialist sponsors and senior partners. This was clear from the very beginning. In his famous article "The Iron Wall" (1923), the right-wing Zionist leader Vladimir Jabotinsky wrote:

> Arab nationalism sets itself the same aims as those set, say, by Italian nationalism before 1870: unification and political independence. In plain language, this would

mean expulsion of England from Mesopotamia and Egypt, expulsion of France from Syria and then perhaps also from Tunisia, Algeria, and Morocco. For us to support such a movement, even remotely, would be suicide and treachery. We are operating under the English Mandate; in San Remo France endorsed the Balfour Declaration.[11] We cannot take part in a political intrigue whose aim is to expel England from the Suez Canal and the Persian Gulf, and totally annihilate France as a colonial power.

Preventing Arab national unification has been a cornerstone of Israeli political-military strategy. This is why Israel did its damnedest to defeat secular Arab nationalism, led by Gamal Abdul-Nasser, who had raised the anti-imperialist banner of Arab unification, enthusiastically acclaimed by the Arab masses.

In reflecting on the Sinai Campaign—Israel's name for the 1956 Suez war—David Ben-Gurion, then, as in 1948, Israel's prime minister wrote:

> Another aim of the Sinai Campaign was to diminish the stature of the Egyptian dictator, and the importance of this should not be underestimated. Being in charge of security since before the foundation of the state, one grave worry preyed on my mind. We know about the inferior state and corruption of the Arab rulers, which is one of the main causes of their military weakness. But I was always concerned that there might arise an exceptional man, as there had arisen for the tribes of Arabia in the seventh century, or for Turkey following its defeat in the First World War, Mustafa Kemal, who uplifted the spirit of the nation, increased its self-confidence and made it into a fighting nation. This danger still persists, and it seemed as though Nasser was that man. It is no simple matter that in various Arabic-speaking countries the children hold his portrait aloft. And diminishing Nasser's stature is a great political deed. His stature has been diminished in his country as well as in the other Arab countries, and in the Muslim countries and throughout the world.[12]

In actual fact, Israel failed to achieve this aim in 1956, but tried again and succeeded in 1967.

However, the failure of petty-bourgeois Arab nationalism to unify the Arab nation cannot be entirely blamed on Israel. The experience of the short-lived and ill-fated attempt to unify Egypt and Syria—the United Arab Republic (UAR), 1958–61—illustrates the inability of the Arab middle classes to lead a truly democratic, lasting unification.[13]

Thus national unification, which in Europe was achieved by bourgeois revolutions, remains to be accomplished in the Arab world (along with other democratic tasks) by a future revolution, to be led by the working classes.

Unification is prescribed not only by past history, by the fact that the Arab world constitutes a single, albeit diverse, linguistic-cultural domain, whose cultural unity is already a reality, greatly reinforced by modern communication media. It is also a vital economic necessity, as the Arab world in its present divided and fractured state suffers from an uneven distribution of population and resources, which need to be brought together to provide the basis for balanced development, realizing the enormously rich potential of this region. By the way, in the coming era of gradual depletion of light and easily extracted oil, the value of the region's large remaining deposits will go on increasing.

It is of course impossible to foresee the exact form that Arab national unification may take. But some general predictions can be made. It is quite clear that a democratic Arab union must be fairly decentralized and have federal structure, with a suitable measure of local autonomy. This is so for two reasons.

First, notwithstanding all the historical, linguistic, and cultural features common to the entire Arab world, there is in it a great deal of local diversity, on which a centralized state structure cannot be superimposed democratically. For this reason, too, the union may have to take the form of a confederation linking two distinct sub-federations: one of the Arab East (Mashreq) and the other of the North-African Arab West (Maghreb).

Second, there is a great disparity in population size between the various Arab countries. The population of Egypt alone is 82 million (and counting . . .)—constituting about one third of the population of the whole Arab East. The population of Sudan is about 40 million. Thus roughly one half of the population of the Arab East (and about one third of that of the entire Arab world) are concentrated in and around the Nile Valley. On the other hand, some Arab countries, with their own dialects, customs, and history, have small populations. A centralized state structure would therefore be unacceptably lopsided, overwhelmed, and dominated by one great population center, and inevitably resented by other regions. The miscarriage of the ill-conceived UAR is a cautionary object lesson.

Framework for Resolution of the Conflict

A successful Arab revolution, and the national unification that it must bring about, offers the one prospect for changing the balance of power, radically redressing its present inequality. It is Zionism's nightmare. The settler state will no longer be facing a fragmented Arab world, ruled by corrupt and abject elites subservient to Israel's own imperialist patron. Instead, it will find itself in the very midst of—and almost surrounded by—a united Arab nation. The enormous energy latent in the Arab masses will have been released and mobilized in solidarity with the captive Palestinian section of the Arab nation. The closest and most ardent ally of the Palestinian masses is the great Egyptian working class as well as the working classes of Iraq and other Arab countries. This giant, unchained, will be a formidable force.

It is not a matter of dealing Israel a decisive military defeat. Even if this were possible, it would not by itself bring about a resolution of the Israeli-Palestinian conflict. We know from historical experience that a defeated nation that is offered no better prospect than extirpation or subjugation can go on resisting almost indefinitely. That would not resolve the conflict, merely invert its terms.

Nor is an actual shattering military defeat necessary for fatally undermining the Zionist project. Rather, it will be sufficient to achieve a position of equilibrium, when Israel is no longer a hegemonic local power able to dominate the region. When this point is reached—well before crushing Israel militarily can even be contemplated seriously—the Israelis, and primarily the Israeli working class, can be attracted by an offer they would be foolish to refuse: since you cannot beat us, join us and share with us in the great things we can achieve together.

The Israeli-Palestinian conflict can then be resolved by accommodating both national groups within the regional federal union. The Palestinian Arab people will take its place alongside the other components of the Arab nation. And the Israeli Hebrews can be offered equal membership with full national rights, on similar terms as the other non-Arab nationalities located within the Arab world (Kurds, South-Sudanese).

Will the disposition envisaged here be a one-state or a two-state setup? It will be both and it will be neither. It will be a one-state setup—in the sense that both national groups will be accommodated, as federated members, in one state. But that one state will not be Palestine; it will be a regional union. And it will be a two-state setup in the sense that each of the two national groups will have its own canton (in the Swiss sense) or Land (in the Federal German sense), where it constitutes a majority of the population. However, no purpose will be served by interposing between these cantons and the federal state an intermediate political entity—let alone one whose borders are those of the so-called historical Palestine, created by the British imperialists in 1923. The resolution of the Israeli-Palestinian conflict will not re-create that ill-starred territory as a unitary or binary entity but will supersede it—as it will also supersede the Zionist State of Israel.[14] The true liberation of Palestine cannot be accomplished short of a regional revolution—which will liberate "historical" Palestine by consigning it to history.

As for borders, it would be a pointless premature exercise to attempt to draw them now; but they need not coincide with any demarcation lines that have existed so far. When the time comes, they will be determined democratically according to economic, demographic, and administrative considerations operative at that time.

It may be objected that this vision puts off the resolution of the Israeli-Palestinian conflict to a distant time horizon. If so, the "fault" lies not with the vision but with objective reality. Shortcuts proposing liberation within the box of Palestine are illusory.

This is by no means a predicament unique to this conflict or to the Middle East. Revolutionary socialists surely realize that the most fundamental problems in all parts of our present-day world, including some conflicts that inflict untold suffering and stunt many millions of human lives, can only be resolved by a socialist revolution that cannot triumph in a single country. Easy fixes are an ideological con; and shortcut solutions are a reformist illusion.

And in the Meantime . . .

This does not mean that we have nothing to do now but wait with folded arms for a regional revolution led by the working class.

An immediate task is to mobilize solidarity and support for the Palestinian people's struggle against the extreme oppression and atrocities to which it is subjected. In the short and medium term, this is essentially a defensive struggle, but vitally important for all that. What is at stake is no less than preventing the worst: ethnic cleansing of the Palestinian Arab people, which remains a strategic aim of the Zionist settler state. World public opinion, civil society everywhere, must be mobilized in defense of the Palestinian people, by subjecting Israel to boycotts, disinvestments, and sanctions. Socialists have a special role in mobilizing the workers' movement to lead this campaign.

The demands to be raised in this campaign are: an immediate and unconditional end to the Israeli military occupation; and removal of all impediments preventing the exercise of Palestinian self-determination.

A further demand is the abolition of all discrimination against the Palestinian Arab citizens of Israel, and turning it from an ethnocratic Jewish state into a democratic state of all its citizens.

It would be unrealistic to expect these demands to be satisfied to a truly significant extent so long as the present balance of power is not radically changed. Any Israeli military withdrawal is likely to be nominal rather than real. And any Palestinian independence or autonomy is unlikely to be more than a sham. Also, so long as Zionism is not overthrown, Israel will continue to be discriminatory. Nevertheless, raising these demands is important—as a benchmark against which to measure and criticize actual conditions.

Beyond these demands, socialists must proclaim and uphold the principles (outlined earlier in this article) that must govern any genuine resolution of the Israeli-Palestinian conflict: de-Zionization; equal individual rights for all; equal national rights for the two national groups directly involved; the right of return of the Palestinian refugees.

Finally, Arab and Israeli socialists have a special historical responsibility. A revolution doesn't happen by itself; and when it does break out it can take a disastrous turn if it is hijacked by regressive forces. In order to ensure that an Arab revolution can resolve the Israeli-Palestinian conflict in the benign way envisaged here (along with the other great problems of the region), we must start working and organizing now in a democratic and nonsectarian way. We must closely coordinate our thinking, strategy, and activity; and form organizational links on a regional scale, prefiguring the future in the present.

35

Israeli Socialism and Anti-Zionism: Historical Tasks and Balance Sheet

This talk is dedicated to the memory of my late friend and comrade, the Arab Marxist Jabra Nicola (1912–74).

The terms "right" and "left" as used in Israel are misleading: they do not denote a socioeconomic position (as they do elsewhere, especially in Europe). They denote attitude to Israeli policy toward Palestinians, toward war and peace.

I will avoid this confusing usage. I will talk not about the "left" but about socialism. My theme is the correlation—if you like, the dialectical relation—between the struggle for socialism and the struggle against Zionism. My main theses are two sides of the same medal:

1. In Israel the struggle for socialism must be part of a regional struggle; and it necessarily implies a struggle to overthrow Zionism.

2. Conversely, a *defensive* struggle against the worst effects of Zionism can be waged on its own as a series of one-issue campaigns, by single-issue groupings; but Zionism cannot and will not be overthrown in this way. It can only be overthrown as part of a socialist transformation of the entire region, the Arab East. And it requires an organization set up according to this strategy.

1. Socialists Must Struggle against Zionism

I will be brief on this part of the thesis. I will say just this: Capitalism is a structured world system, in which individual states have specific roles. Israel is a capitalist country, but it is not "like any other capitalist country" (in fact, no capitalist country is like any other . . .).

Talk delivered on February 28, 2010, at the conference "The Left in Palestine/the Palestinian Left," School of Oriental and African Studies, London.

Israel's articulation in the world capitalist system is specifically as a Zionist state, a colonial settler state, with a regional role as a local enforcer of imperialism.

Therefore the struggle for socialism in Israel, against capitalism, necessarily involves resolute opposition to Zionism. Thus for socialists in Israel opposition to Zionism goes beyond a purely moral position. It includes, but cannot be reduced to, supporting Palestinian national rights and national liberation.

We in Matzpen understood this from our early days. Matzpen was founded in 1962. At that time, in the period between the Suez war of 1956 and the 1967 war, the Israeli-Arab conflict was at its least acute phase. Matzpen was not formed specifically around this issue but as a revolutionary socialist group. However, it was clear to us that we had to confront the nature of Zionism as a colonizing project, and the Israeli state as a settler state. It was clear to us that we must support Palestinian national liberation and the right of return.

You can find all this, for example, in a statement we published in May 1967: "The Palestine Problem and the Israeli-Arab Conflict."*

Before the 1967 war, when we expressed an explicitly anti-Zionist position and described Israel as a colonizing settler state, we were met with puzzled incomprehension. I recall my former comrades in the Communist Party (from which I had been expelled in 1962) saying: "A Zionist settler state? What on earth are you talking about? This is just history!"

2. How Can Zionism Be Overthrown?

I will say a bit more about the converse part of my thesis: what is required for resolution of the conflict?

As it is caused by colonization, resolution requires *decolonization.* In this specific case, as the cause is *Zionist* colonization, what is required is *de-Zionization,* overthrow of the Zionist project and its state.

I will argue that this can only be achieved as part of a regional socialist transformation—which requires an organizational setup designed for the struggle for socialism. And I will further argue that in this long-term endeavor socialists in Israel have a crucial role to play.

Let me stress: what I am talking about is *resolution of the conflict*—as distinct from resistance against the current effects of Zionist colonization. Such resistance is both necessary and possible, and indeed is taking place in Palestine/Israel as it is now, in the region as it is now, in the world as it is now.

This resistance is waged by the Palestinian masses and is aided by a whole range of single-issue solidarity campaigns and coalitions, in Israel, in the region, and throughout the world.

---

* Chapter 3 in this book.

Engaging in this struggle does not necessarily need to be conducted under a socialist banner. To engage in it you don't necessarily need to be a socialist. It helps if you are a socialist, but you don't have to be one.

But in my opinion it is an illusion to believe that this struggle by itself—even intensified as much as it is possible to intensify it—can lead to decolonization, de-Zionization, overthrow of Zionism and its machinery.

"But why not?" I hear many people say, "Decolonization has been achieved in many places, especially after the Second World War, in the second half of the twentieth century." The most recent example, that of South Africa, is often cited.

If South-African apartheid could be overthrown within the present global order and without a socialist revolution, why not Zionist apartheid?

Here it is vital to make an observation that to Marxists is elementary and almost obvious, although it is usually ignored by those to whom colonialism is only a moral issue.

Marxists distinguish two types, two models of colonization and colonial settler states. The difference is a structural one, regarding the political economy of the colonization project and the resulting settler state.

In all places where decolonization occurred in the twentieth century, the settlers' economy depended on exploiting the labor power of the indigenous people. As a result, the settlers were a relatively small minority, far outnumbered by the indigenous people; and the settlers needed the indigenous people, without whose labor they could not exist.

Thus the conflict was an *internal* one, a quasi-class struggle within a common economy.

Despite superficial appearances, the balance of power was not favorable to the settlers; they could only impose their domination by using force—against the very people whose presence was vital to their political economy. This was unsustainable in the long term.

In contrast, I know of no case of successful decolonization in places where colonization followed the other model: not exploiting the indigenous people as a source of labor power, but excluding them, ethnically cleansing them.

Historically, in all such places the settlers became a new settler nation, whereas the indigenous people, if not exterminated, were pulverized or at best overwhelmed and marginalized. At any rate, they were *externalized*.

Significantly, in the original US Constitution (article 1, section 2, subsection 3), in counting the number of persons in each state of the Union, an African slave counted as three-fifths of a person; but a so-called Indian counted as zero, a nonperson.

The remaining indigenous people of Australia or North America, for example, cannot hope to reclaim their ancestral homeland. The best they can hope for, and do indeed struggle for, is for equal rights and for the freedom to foster and preserve their old languages and traditions—but in a national framework dominated by the language and culture of the settlers.

We can say that in such places the conflict between settlers and indigenous people was in some sense resolved—but resolved in favor of the former, the settlers.

This is quite different from what happened in places where colonization followed the exploitative model.

This is why the analogy of South Africa is very misleading when applied to Palestine/Israel.

Of course, this does not mean that the fate of the North American and Australian aborigines necessarily awaits the indigenous Palestinian Arab people in this last remaining unresolved colonial conflict. I do not argue such determinism.

However, we must be honest, even if this forces us to pessimism of the intellect.

This analytical observation should make us see that the danger is very real—including the danger of another major wave of ethnic cleansing. This is why the defensive resistance struggle, and campaigns of solidarity with it, assumes an extreme importance and great urgency.

But as I said, this struggle by itself cannot lead to a just resolution of the conflict, to the overthrow of Zionism.

Within the confines of the box of Palestine, and within the existing regional and global order, the balance of power is vastly in favor of the Zionist state, which is backed by its imperialist senior partner and by the camp followers of that imperialist power, trading under the name "the international community."

In *this* situation there is no realistic prospect of a combination of external and internal forces capable of overthrowing Zionism.

What is required for a just resolution is a major change in the balance of power, which can only be achieved by a major social transformation of the entire region of the Arab East.

Here I would like to point out one exceptional feature of this conflict, which gives the Palestinian Arab people a definite advantage, an asset, compared to all other colonized people that were subjected to ethnic cleansing.

In all cases that belong to this exclusionary type of colonization, the settlers formed a new nation. In *this* Zionist colonization is *no* exception: despite itself, and in refutation of its own ideology, it resulted in the formation of a new Hebrew nation.

But what is exceptional, unique as far as I know, is that the indigenous people, the Palestinian Arabs, forged under the hammer blows of Zionist colonization a single national identity expressed in its own language—not the language of the colonizers—and modern culture, which has made notable contributions to world poetry, literature, drama, cinematography, music, and graphic art.

What is the cause of this remarkable exceptional phenomenon?

I have no doubt that the main reason for this is that the Palestinian Arab people are a component part of a larger national entity: the Arab nation—a huge world civilization, with a rich cultural heritage, old and living.

Imagine: if the Palestinian Arabs, like other ethnically cleansed colonized people, had their own isolated languages (or even one language) spoken by no other people, their own isolated civilization and cultural heritage—then in all probability their identity would have been extinguished, overwhelmed, or become an endangered relic.

Upon being exiled, the Palestinian refugees did not find themselves among foreign people speaking a foreign language. And those who remained inside Israel could tune in to broadcasts in Arabic from nearby stations. And of course, this was a two-way traffic.

The Arab regimes of the countries into which the Palestinian refugees were exiled did the Palestinians few favors; but among ordinary people, and especially radical oppositional forces, the Palestinians won a great deal of sympathy and solidarity.

This points toward the process that is capable of achieving a major change of the balance of forces, against Zionism and in favor of Palestinian rights.

In my opinion, the only way in which the balance of power can change to a sufficient extent to enable a favorable resolution of the Palestinian problem is a radical transformation of the region, which will overthrow the corrupt and repressive regimes, subservient to Zionism's imperialist sponsor; and will unify the Arab East as a progressive entity, strong enough not to be cowed and terrorized by the Zionist state; and at the same time able to offer the Hebrew masses, primarily the Israeli working class, an attractive alternative prospect—integration in this progressive federal regional union.

Let me make it clear: external pressure *by itself* cannot lead to a just resolution of the conflict. Zionism cannot be destroyed purely from the outside, even if and when the balance of power changes, so that Israel can no longer dominate the region. Its Hebrew population is militarized, and Israel is a nuclear power. It would resist to the death any purely external onslaught—not only its own death, but of many others. It would commit the most horrendous suicidal explosion in history.

But, given a change in the balance of power, the Israeli masses, primarily the working class, could be attracted by a generous offer from a progressive Arab East: "Since you can no longer dominate us, join us; give up Zionism and accept equal rights, including the right to express your national identity within a regional federation."

In this way the Zionist state can be overthrown: this can be achieved from the inside—given favorable external circumstances.

It will be like an egg: hatched from the inside, but only if it is warmed from the outside. Something must sit on it. . . .

Neither political Islam nor bourgeois Arab nationalism is capable of uniting the Arab East; and most certainly neither of them is able to offer the Hebrew masses an attractive internationalist alternative to Zionism.

This task can only be led by the working class. This is the historical agent of regional transformation and unification that can provide the regional framework for resolving the Palestinian problem.

And in such a framework not only the Zionist state can be superseded but also the box of a separate Palestine, created by the imperialist powers following the First World War, explicitly for the purpose of Zionist colonization—this too will be superseded.

3. The Role of Socialists Inside Israel

This is clearly a long-term project. And here I come finally to the bottom line: the crucial role of a *true* left, a socialist movement within Israel.

Its role is crucial because in order for the Hebrew masses to respond favorably to a transformed region, the ground must be prepared long in advance by a socialist movement inside Israel, working patiently on this project of long duration. It is a long-term strategy.

Such a movement must be patient, as it cannot expect great success in the short or even medium term. But it must prefigure the future in the present, and be organized in an internationalist way, without any national or ethnic barriers, and it must be allied to a regional socialist network.

Matzpen tried to do this. It made a promising start and worked quite well from 1962 to the early 1970s. Then it started splitting and eventually fell apart.

The splits were partly caused by a disease of the international left: sectarianism, a petty-bourgeois propensity to prioritize relatively small doctrinal differences above the need for unity.

But beyond this there was the objective difficulty of keeping together the two sides of the medal, which ought to be inseparable.

Some among us fixed their view on the long-term socialist aim and on the class struggle, and—regarding Israel as a more or less "normal" capitalist country—neglected the immediate tasks of struggle against Zionism.

Others among us, conversely, lost sight of the long-term socialist aim, and engaged exclusively in anti-Zionist activity and solidarity with the Palestinian national movement.

And some vacillated between one partial view and the other.

Consequently, there does not currently exist in Israel a viable nonsectarian socialist organization embodying the above points. What is left of Matzpen is some militants faithful to these ideas and a valuable heritage of analysis, found on the Matzpen website. (See http://matzpen.org/index.asp.)

Let me end with optimism of the will: one must hope that, given the present global crisis and discrediting of capitalism, some movement along these lines can be revived.

As I said, it is a project of long duration. But it needs to start now.

Acknowledgments

A s I have stated in the preface, I am indebted to all my Matzpen comrades (not only to those who coauthored some of the items in this book) who formed the collective environment within which my ideas originally took shape.

In selecting the material for this book, I consulted the following friends and comrades: Gilbert Achcar, Ehud Ein-Gil (who is also one of my coauthors), Arie Finkelstein, Zvika Havkin, Toufic Haddad, and Tikva Honig-Parnass. I am deeply grateful to them for taking the trouble to look at the material, as well as for the advice they have offered, which I considered very seriously. Needless to say, I alone am responsible for the final decision.

I owe a lifelong inestimable debt of gratitude to my wife, Ilana, for her patient and loving support.

Finally, it is a pleasure to acknowledge the invaluable encouragement and help I have received from Anthony Arnove, Dao X. Tran, Julie Fain, and Ahmed Shawki of Haymarket Books.

Acknowledgments of journals where articles included in this book were first published are noted in footnotes in the respective chapters.

Notes

Chapter 1: Why I Am Not an Israeli Peace Activist

1. After writing these words, I looked up "cast lead" in *Wikipedia* and was redirected to an entry headed "Gaza War." The *hasbarah* machine employs a special corps whose task is to edit entries in *Wikipedia* and tilt them closer to the Israeli official narrative.

2. A similar view was propagated by the *hasbarah* machine regarding the *Mavi Marmara* incident on May 31, 2010. The armed Israeli commandos, who invaded the ship on the high seas, were depicted as defending themselves against violence initiated by a mob of "terrorist supporters," in the course of which the commandos were forced to kill nine of their "attackers."

Chapter 5: Arab Revolution and National Problems in the Arab East

1. By the "Arab East" or "Mashreq" we mean the Arabic-speaking world east of Libya, that is, the old historical Mashreq plus Egypt.

Chapter 8: The Middle East—Still at the Crossroads

1. Many Zionists would in principle include the East Bank of the Jordan in the Land of Israel, and some would go much further. But in practice the great majority of Zionists think of the Land of Israel as the territory that at present comprises Israel, the West Bank, and the Gaza Strip—which is precisely what most people, including Palestinians, refer to as "Palestine."

2. The name "Hebrews" is particularly appropriate, as it refers to the most obvious attribute of this national group: use of Hebrew as an everyday language.

3. For example, one of the most important results of the Palestinian uprising that broke out at the end of 1987 [subsequently known as the "first intifada"] was its contribution to the crystallization of Palestinian nationhood. Even the smallest and most isolated rural communities in the West Bank, whose consciousness had previously been almost purely localist, became imbued with nationalism.

4. Until not so very long ago, even some of the most conciliatory ideologists of the PLO were toying with various schemes of encouraging Israelis, particularly those whose origin is in Arab countries, to re-emigrate. See, for example, Nabil Sha'th, "Toward the Democratic Palestine" in *Fateh* 2, no. 2, Lebanon, January 19, 1970.

5. We can approximate this usage by referring to the Arabs as a whole as a "nation," and to each of the subgroups as a "people." But there is no convenient way of distinguishing in English between the two levels of nationalism.

6. It is reasonable to assume that this federal structure will have to be rather complex, with the Mashreq

and the Maghreb constituting two distinct parts of the federation, and each of these two parts sub-divided into autonomous regions.

7. An excellent English-language source is the article by Nabil Sha'th mentioned in note 4, on which the following exposition is based.

8. Hypothetical but not entirely imaginary. In fact, just before the outbreak of the Palestinian uprising there was a widespread feeling that a situation of this kind was approaching. The uprising itself was perhaps, at least in part, a heroic reaction to the onset of this mood.

Chapter 13: The Class Nature of Israeli Society

1. *Statistical Yearbook* [of the Israeli Government] (Jerusalem, Israel's Central Bureau of Statistics, 1969).

2. Moshe Dayan, reported in [Hebrew daily] *Davar*, May 2, 1956.

3. The vast majority of those who immigrated before 1948 were of European origin; between 1948 and 1951 the proportions were about equal; and since then the majority of immigrants have come from outside Europe. By 1966 only half of the Israeli population were of European origins.

4. Reported in *Le Monde*, July 2, 1969.

5. Oscar Gass, [untitled] review, *Journal of Economic Literature* (December 1969): 1177.

6. This law was passed in 1959.

7. These figures are taken from N. Halevi and R. Klinov-Malul, *The Economic Development of Israel* (Bank of Israel and Frederick A. Praeger, 1968). The category "other sources," included under "long-term capital transfers," has been omitted from the figures for both long-term and unilateral transfers taken together.

8. D. Patinkin, in *Ma'ariv*, January 30, 1970.

9. Quoted in *Yedi'ot Aharonot*, September 30, 1970. Out of a total of $1,034 million in US military aid to foreign countries excluding Vietnam during 1970, Israel received $500 million.

10. Early in December 1970, Sapir presented the budget for the period 1970–71; 40 percent was de-voted to military purposes. This included: the purchase of arms, partly covered by the $500 million promised by Nixon; the development of the arms industry and military research; and the everyday costs of national security operations.

11. See "Why This Nation Does Buy British," *Times* (London), March 28, 1969.

12. The term "Zionist establishment" is that conventionally used in Israel to denote the ruling group present in the interlocking set of Zionist institutions.

13. In January 1970 there were ten daily Hebrew papers in Israel, of which seven were subsidized party papers; these included the Labor papers *Davar* and *Lamerhav*, and the Mapam paper *Al-Hamishmar*. The three privately owned papers were *Ma'ariv* and *Yedi'ot Aharonot*, both evening papers supporting expansionist policies, and *Ha'aretz*, a more liberal morning paper owned and run by Gershom Shocken. Military censorship operates in Israel.

14. Poless (pen name of Dr. Shlomo Gross), "The Harlot of the Sea Ports and Us—Thoughts on the Eve of [Jewish] New Year 5712," op-ed, *Ha'aretz*, September 30, 1951.

15. The opposition movement in Israel, particularly among high-school students, was discussed in Akiva Orr's "Israel: Opposition Grows," *Black Dwarf*, June 12, 1970.

16. Africa Research Group, "Israel: Imperialist Mission in Africa," *Tricontinental* 15, 1969.

17. Arnold Rivkin, *Africa and the West* (Cambridge, MA: MIT Press, 1962).

18. *International Supplement on the Jubilee of the Histadrut, 1920–70.*

19. Ibid.

20. Full details of Israel's military aid to Africa in Africa Research Group, "Israel, Imperialist Mission in Africa: The Untold Story of Israel's Counterrevolutionary Role in Africa," *Tricontinental* 15, 1969.

21. Reported in *Der Spiegel*, November 3, 1969.

22. Theodor Herzl, *Selected Works*, vol. 7, book I (Tel-Aviv: Newman Edition, 1928–29), 86.

23. *Falk Institute Report*, 1961–63. The remainder was owned in approximately equal proportions by the state and by the Histadrut.

24. Joseph Waschitz, *The Arabs in Palestine* (in Hebrew) (Sifriat Po'alim, Merhaviah: 1947), 151.

25. Union dues are collected by special collection offices that the Histadrut has set up throughout Israel, and local branches receive their funds from the center, not from their local membership. This severely limits their independence. The Histadrut employs a permanent staff of thirty thousand and its bureaucracy has a very tight hold on its members; indeed the Histadrut building in Tel-Aviv is known as "the Kremlin."

26. *International Supplement on the Jubilee of the Histadrut*, 1920–70.

27. *Mo'ed* (in Hebrew), Yehuda Gotthelf and Tzvi Arad, eds. (Tel Aviv, Department of Culture and Education of the Histadrut, 1960), 3.

28. Waschitz, *The Arabs in Palestine*, 173.

29. The secretary-general of Histadrut Enterprises, the industrial wing that controls 25 percent of the economy, told a group of Zionist businessmen in Los Angeles in early 1969 that Histadrut Enterprises was no different from any other capitalist organization, despite its trade union links; it was expected to make a profit and show a decent return on capital just like any private firm (reported in *Sunday Times* [London], July 27, 1969).

30. See Elie Lobel, "L'escalade à l'intérieur de la société israélienne," *Partisans*, no. 52, (March/April 1970).

31. The kibbutzim never contained more than 5 percent of the Jewish population of Palestine or Israel. Hence, whatever their other limitations, they cannot be said to constitute Israeli society or to be evidence for Israel being a socialist country.

32. J. Amitai, editor, in *Siah*, no. 5, August 1970.

33. Statement in *Zo Haderekh*, September 2, 1970.

Chapter 14: Zionism and "Oriental" Jews

1. Broadly speaking, the Mizrahim—the term is Hebrew for "Orientals"—are Jews belonging to, or originating from, communities that have lived for several centuries in Muslim countries. They should not be—but often are—confused with the Sephardim: Jewish communities originating from the Iberian peninsula, from which they were expelled at the end of the fifteenth century by the Catholic kings. Those Sephardim who migrated to Mediterranean Muslim countries lived there alongside Mizrahi communities and partly merged with them, but largely preserved their distinct cultural identity and Ladino (Judeo-Spanish) language.

2. Broadly speaking, the Ashkenazim—the term is Medieval Hebrew for "Germans"—are Jews belonging to, or originating from, Yiddish-speaking communities that lived in Central and Eastern Europe.

3. For a recent typical example of this kind of narrative by an Israeli, see Smadar Lavie, "Colonialism and Imperialism: Zionism," in the *Encyclopedia of Women and Islamic Cultures*, vol. 6 (Leiden: Brill, 2007). A seminal text in this line of narrative is Ella Shohat, "Sephardim in Israel: Zionism from the Standpoint of Its Jewish Victims," *Social Text* nos. 19/20 (1988): 1–35. For a Palestinian leftist acceptance of this claim, see Adel Samara, "Why the Socialist Solution in Palestine: and Why the Secular Democratic State Will Serve the Zionist and Arab Comprador Solution," *Kana'an e-Bulletin* 8, no. 1592 (2008), available online at www.kanaanonline.org/articles/01592.pdf.

4. We are speaking here of Zionism in the proper sense: the political movement that arose at the end of the nineteenth century—not of earlier Jewish messianic movements that are sometimes described as "proto-Zionist." Of these, the two most important ones were led by non-Ashkenazim: David Alroy (twelfth century) was an Iraqi Jew and Shabbetai Tzvi (seventeenth century) was a Romaniot (member of the ancient Greek Jewish community).

5. Raphael Shapiro, "Zionism and Its Oriental Subjects," *Khamsin*, no. 5 (1978), 5–26; reprinted in *Forbidden Agendas*, ed. Jon Rothschild (London: Saqi Books, 1984), 23–48. By recommending Shapiro's article we do not imply that we agree with everything he says. A more impassioned but analytically far less rigorous account is given by Shohat, "Sephardim in Israel," who totally ignores Shapiro's earlier article.

6. Alex Bein, *Toldot Ha-Hityashvut Ha-Tzionit* [History of the Zionist Colonization] (Tel-Aviv, Massada, 1970), 97–98, quoted in Haim Hanegbi, "Hatteymanim" ["The Yemenites"], *Matzpen*, no. 58 (1971), available online at www.matzpen.org/index.asp?p=Temanim, and by Shapiro, "Zionism and Its Oriental

Subjects," and Shohat, "Sephardim in Israel," also quotes Thon (whose name she misspells as "Tehon").

7. In the event, the immigrants from Yemen did not quite fulfill the hopes of the Palestine Office. They were mostly artisans, unused to agricultural labor, and were unable to compete with the indigenous Palestinians employed by Jewish colonists. The Palestinians were themselves peasants, for whom wage labor was a supplementary source of income and so could manage even if employed for very low wages. The Yemenites had no other source of income, yet were expected to work for the same low wages. This created great poverty and distress; the women were forced to work as domestic servants for the colonists and the children had to start working from an early age.

8. Shapiro, "Zionism and Its Oriental Subjects," 19–20.

9. Government of Israel, *Statistical Abstracts* (Jerusalem: Central Bureau of Statistics, 1967); quoted by Moshe Behar, "Palestine, Arabized-Jews and the Elusive Consequences of Jewish and Arab National Formations," *Nationalism and Ethnic Politics*, no. 13 (2007), 585.

10. See Sergio DellaPergola, "Demography," in *Encyclopaedia Judaica* (Philadelphia: Coronet Books, 2006), table 2.

11. True, not all Mizrahi immigrants were Zionists: some must have immigrated to Palestine out of other motives. But the same must be true, to at least the same extent, also of Ashkenazi immigrants, especially after the rise of fascism and Nazism in Europe.

12. Acronym for Plugot Mahatz ("Strike Companies").

13. During the first three months of the 1947–49 war (November 30, 1947–February 29, 1948)— that is, well before the State of Israel came into existence—378 Jews, all volunteers, were killed in active service, of whom 73 (19.3 percent) were Mizrahim according to their biographies in the official memorial site of Israel's Ministry of Defense, available online at www.izkor.gov.il.

14. Acronyms, respectively, for Irgun Tzva'i Le'umi ("National Military Organization") and Lohamei Herut Israel ("Combatants for Israel's Liberty"). Both were described as "terrorist" by the British Mandate authorities. Lehi—also known as the "Stern Gang"—described its own activities as "terroristic" in a notorious document in which it offered to collaborate with the Third Reich: see Lenni Brenner, ed., *51 Documents: Zionist Collaboration with the Nazis* (Fort Lee, NJ: Barricade, 2002), 302. Ya'akov Bannai (Mazal), *Hayyalim Almonim: Sefer Mivtza'ei Lehi* [Anonymous Soldiers: The Book of Lehi Operations] (Tel-Aviv, Hug Yedidim, 1958), lists 119 Lehi members killed in action, of whom 34 (28.5 percent) may be identified by their names as Mizrahim.

15. See Hebrew *Wikipedia* page, "Olei Haggardom," commemorating Jewish Underground members executed under the British Mandate, http://tinyurl.com/yrvlsf.

16. See Abbas Shiblak, *Iraqi Jews: A History of Mass Exodus* (London: Saqi Books, 2005).

17. The first outbreak was in the Ein-Shemer immigrant camp on February 14, 1950. This soon spread to other camps of immigrants from Yemen: Beit-Lid, Rosh-Ha'ayin, and Be'er-Ya'akov. The outbreaks kept erupting sporadically until the end of May and approached the scale of an uprising, suppressed by large police forces. On April 8, the immigrant Salem ibn-Salem Ya'qub Jarafi was shot dead by a guard. There was another outbreak on October 25, 1952, in the Yemenite transit camp in Emeq Hefer (Wadi Hawarith). After a force of 25 policemen had been attacked and forced to leave the camp, the police reacted as an army of occupation: 200 policemen, armed with batons and seven rifles, encircled the camp in the early morning, declared a curfew in Hebrew and Arabic, and then made house-to-house searches for suspects. Initially, 450 men were arrested, of whom 105, including 13 soldiers on leave, were detained; 39 suspects—"mostly Yemenites, the rest Iraqis and Persians"—remained in custody after questioning (see report in *Ha'aretz*, October 27, 1952).

18. See "Wadi Salib riots," *Wikipedia*, http://en.wikipedia.org/wiki/Wadi_Salib_events.

19. This involvement was widely reported and somewhat sensationalized by the Israeli press. Thus, for example, a headline in *Ha'aretz* of March 3, 1971: "Jerusalem Police Arrested 13 Youths Known as 'Black Panthers' and Members of Matzpen." See also report "Demonstration of the 'Panthers' in the Capital" in *Yedi'ot Aharonot* of March 4, 1971; "Night of the Panthers in the Streets of Jerusalem" in *Yedi'ot Aharonot* of May 19, 1971. An editorial by Uri Avnery in *Ha'olam Hazeh* of May 19, 1971, excoriates Matzpen for trying to manipulate the Panthers and foster the dangerous illusion that the struggle of the Mizrahim is going to overthrow Zionism.

20. For a typical example, see Samia Dodin and Sami Shalom Chetrit, "Culture, Identity and Borders: Samia Dodin, a Palestinian American, Interviews Israeli Poet and Author Sami Shalom Chetrit on Israel and Arab Jewish Identity," *Sephardic Heritage Update*, no. 132 (2004), Palestine: Information with Provenance (PIWP database), http://cosmos.ucc.ie/cs1064/jabowen/IPSC/php/art.php?aid=10964; Lavie, "Colonialism and Imperialism: Zionism," *Encyclopedia of Women and Islamic Cultures*, vol. 6 (Leiden: Brill, 2007), speaks of "the first wave of Arab Jewish labor migration from Yemen to Palestine" in 1882.

21. Authored by Nabil Sha'th, "Toward the Democratic Palestine," *Fateh* 2, no. 2 (1970). *Fateh* was the English-language newspaper published by the Information Office of the Palestine Liberation Movement.

22. By the way, the claim that a majority of Israeli Jews are Mizrahim, which was correct in 1970, has often been repeated by various authors long after it ceased to be true due to the immigration to Israel of about a million Jews from the former Soviet Union. By 2000, only 47 percent of all Israeli Jews were Mizrahim: see Sergio DellaPergola, "Sephardic and Oriental Jews in Israel and Western Countries," in *Studies in Contemporary Jewry*, no. 22: *Sephardic Jewry and Mizrahi Jews* vol. XXII, ed. Peter Y. Medding (New York: Oxford University Press, 2008).

23. Thus Behar, "Palestine, Arabized-Jews," is correct in referring to them as "Arabized Jews" in this cultural sense.

24. In traditional Arabic discourse, the term "Arab" had quite a different connotation from its modern national sense. Thus the translator of *The Muqaddimah*, the monumental fourteenth-century sociological work by the great Ibn Khaldun, notes: "As a sociological term, 'Arab' is always synonymous with 'Bedouin, nomad' to Ibn Khaldun, regardless of racial, national or linguistic distinctions." Ibn Khaldun, *The Muqaddimah: An Introduction to History*, vol. I (London: Routledge & Kegan Paul, 1967), 250. Five centuries later, the term "Arab" was still used to describe the Arab Bedouin tribes (by others and by themselves). The rest of the Arabic-speaking masses normally self-identified according to their locality or religious community. See Adeed Dawisha, *Arab Nationalism in the Twentieth Century: From Triumph to Despair* (Princeton, NJ: Princeton University Press, 2003).

25. An extreme special case is that of the Algerian Jews, who were granted French citizenship in 1870 under the *décrets Crémieux*. Although indigenous Algerians, the vast majority regarded themselves as French, took no part in the Algerian liberation struggle, and finally—like the European colonists— chose to leave en masse.

26. See Dawisha, *Arab Nationalism in the Twentieth Century*.

27. What we say here applies at least to the vast majority of Jews in Arab countries. This was in stark contrast to the important role played by their Christian compatriots in the Arab nationalist movement, as well as to the significant participation of Jews in the communist parties in several Arab countries, principally Iraq and Egypt.

28. Behar, in "Palestine, Arabized-Jews," 591f, is right in contending "that in so doing such Arab nationalists effectively embraced the Zionist conflation between Judaism and Zionism." He is right in pointing out that in principle the Arab nationalists could have made a different choice.

29. In this list, only the most senior positions held by each person are mentioned. Amir Peretz was succeeded as chairman of the Histadrut—a key political position—by Ofer Eini (father born in Iraq, mother in Libya).

30. The ancestral Yiddish language and culture of the Ashkenazim were also frowned upon and disparaged by the Zionist leadership.

Chapter 17: Summing Up Our Position on the National Question

1. The quotes from Borochov are taken from chapter 8 of *Our Platform* (originally published in Russian in 1906) and chapter 9 of *On the Question of Zion and a Territory* (originally published in Russian in 1905), B. Borochov, *Works* vol. I, L. Levité and D. Ben-Nahum, eds. (Israel: Hakibutz Hameuchad and Sifriat Poalim, 1955).

2. Authored by Nabil Sha'th, "Toward the Democratic Palestine," *Fateh*, no. 2 (1970).

3. The whole of the discussion above refers, of course, only to the official PLO position. On the other

hand, there are well-known persons in the PLO who explicitly recognize the existence of the Hebrew (Israel-Jewish) people, and accept some of what this implies. Among these, the late Sa'id Hammami deserves special mention. (See Matzpen pamphlet, *Conversation between a Member of Matzpen and the PLO Representative in London*, November 1975, http://www.matzpen.org/index.asp?p=report.) It appears as well that the Democratic Front for the Liberation of Palestine, which is included in the PLO, has also moved toward this position.

4. One of these ideologues is the writer A. B. Yehoshua. See Avi-No'am's article, "A B Yehoshua and the right to rob" (Hebrew), in *Matzpen* no. 75, November–December 1975, available at www.matzpen.org/index.asp?p=articles_ab-75.

Chapter 21: The Zionist Left and the Palestinian Resistance

1. *Al Hammishmar*, August 29, 1969.
2. Even though the two cases are by no means similar in all respects.

Chapter 22: Borochovist "Revival"

1. There were even cases of young people being expelled from Mapam's youth movement for trying to propagate Borochovist ideas.
2. As we shall show, the claims that Mapam is a legitimate heir to Borochovism are unfounded.
3. Y. Ben-Aharon, "Toward Reevaluation of Relations between Israel and the Diaspora," *Ot* no. 2 (February 1967). The writer is a prominent Israeli Labor Party ideologist and at present secretary general of the Histadrut. [This article is discussed in chapter 18 of this book.]
4. We use the term "Jewish people" as a collective name for the Jews throughout the world, without making any theoretical commitment as to their constituting a national entity or not.

Chapter 24: Zionism and Its Scarecrows

1. Cf. Alfred Moos, *links*, no. 33 (1972). A Hebrew translation of Moos's article was immediately published in Israel by the Zionist group that had split in 1965 from the Israeli Communist Party, Maki (today: Moqed), in its organ *Qol Ha'am*, no. 32 (1972) under the title "Zionism, the Scarecrow." This group had taken upon itself to back the Israeli state by accusing "from a communist point of view" all opponents of the Zionist policy of anti-socialism and by seizing most gratefully on any political or apologetic contribution from abroad. These people revised socialist positions not only by putting forward the classical Zionist arguments but by historicist constructions that use the actual events and negative trends in the international communist movement and in the Soviet Union to come to the conclusion they desire—that socialist opposition to Zionism is just another negative trend, which, like the Stalinization of the Soviet Union and the Comintern, is to be condemned and repudiated. In what follows, when we quote the position of "left-wing" Zionists without further attribution, we are referring to this article by A. Moos.
2. The original Hebrew text of the Matzpen article mentioned here appeared originally in the Tel-Aviv organ *Matzpen*, whose editors presumed that the reader was familiar with the organization's analysis of the history and nature of Zionism, as put forward in many articles since 1962. It is obvious that these analyses cannot be repeated in detail here. They partly appear in Arie Bober, ed. *The Other Israel: The Radical Case against Zionism* (New York: Doubleday, 1972); cf. also Nathan Weinstock, *Zionism: False Messiah* (London: Inklinks, 1978).

    We shall only go into historical questions here as far as it is necessary to disprove the argument of the "left-wing" Zionist criticism of anti-Zionism.
3. Speech by Esther Maria Frumkina in *Der 2. Kongreß der Kommunistischen Internationale. Prot. der Verhandlungen vom 19.7. in Petrograd und vom 23.7. bis 7.8.1920 in Moskau* (Hamburg: Verlag der KI, 1921), 198.
4. David Ben-Gurion, *Memoirs*, Part 1 (Tel-Aviv: Am Oved, 1971), 245 (in Hebrew).
5. Cf. for example, in *Qontres*, organ of Ahduth Ha'avodah, no. 47, Tel-Aviv, 1920 (in Hebrew).

6. Yaakow Meiersohn, *Nach der 5. Poalei-Zion-Konferenz—Brief an die Genossen der Sozialistischen Arbeiterpartei in Palästina* (in Yiddish) (Vienna, 1920), reprinted in Mario Offenberg, *Kommunismus in Palästina—Nation und Klasse in der antikolonialen Revolution,* (Meisenheim/Glan: BRD, 1975).

7. Aharon Cohen, *Israel and the Arab World* (Merhaviah: Sifriat Po'alim, 1964), 259 (in Hebrew).

8. R. Meinerzhagen, *Middle East Diary* (London: Cresset Press, 1958), 49.

9. *The Diaries of Theodor Herzl,* (London: Gollancz, 1958), 6.

10. Leo Pinsker, *Auto-Emancipation* (New York: Rita Searl, 1947), 33; and M. Hess, *Rome and Jerusalem* (Tel-Aviv, 1935), 25–26.

11. Cf. Y. Elam in "New Premises for the Same Zionism" in *Ot,* organ of the Israeli Labor Party (Ma'arakh), no. 2, Tel-Aviv, 1967 (in Hebrew).

12. This quotation comes from a book that appeared in Berlin in 1934. The author, Joachim Prinz, was at that time one of the leading Zionists in Germany and became a leading Zionist in the USA and chairman of the international leadership of the—Zionist controlled—World Jewish Congress. Cf. J. Prinz, *Wir Juden* (Berlin: Erich Reiss, 1934), 154 (emphasis in original).

13. Cf. *Die Nürnberger Gesetze,* 5th ed., official publication of the government of the Third Reich, 1939, Central Zionist Archives, Jerusalem, 13–14 (our italics).

14. Isaac Deutscher, *The Non-Jewish Jew* (London: Oxford University Press, 1968), 67.

15. Y. Elam, *Introduction to Zionist History* (Tel-Aviv: Levin-Epstein, 1972), 113, 122 (in Hebrew).

16. A. Tartakower, *The Jewish Worker's Way to Zionism: Zionism and Socialism* (New York: 1954), 63.

17. Reprinted from the minutes of the meeting in Elam, *Introduction to Zionist History,* 123.

18. Elam, *Introduction to Zionist History,* 122. "Yishuv" was the term for the Jewish community in Palestine, dominated by the Zionist movement, before 1948. On the "transfer" deal see Shaul Esh, *Iunim beheqer ha-sho'ah ve-yahadut zmanenu* (Institute of Contemporary Judaism, the Hebrew University of Jerusalem, 1973), 108ff.

19. Herbert Lucht, report from Vienna in the Berlin daily *Der Tagesspiel,* January 1, 1975.

20. Viktor Polski in Dov Goldstein, "Interview of the Week," *Ma'ariv,* (December 27, 1974).

21. Cf. reports in *Le Monde,* December 20, 1974; and *Der Tagesspiegel* (Berlin), December 21, 1974.

22. Cf. A. Hoder, "Russian Jews, Black Jews and Non-Jewish Jews," in *ISRACA* no. 5 (1973), 16–25.

23. Abraham Tirosh, report in *Ma'ariv,* January 10, 1973.

24. Quoted from Elam, *Introduction to Zionist History,* 122.

25. Ibid., 111. The Israeli historian S. B. Beit-Zvi shows in his recently published monograph—*Post-Ugandan Zionism in the Crucible of the Holocaust* (Tel-Aviv: Bronfman, 1977) (in Hebrew) [translated into English as *Post-Ugandan Zionism on Trial,* 1991]—how "As a result of narrow-mindedness and fear of the danger of territorialism [i.e., the "danger" that the Jewish problem might be solved by migration to some territory other than Palestine] the Zionist movement in a number of cases acted against attempts of Jews and non-Jews to save the lives [of Europe's Jews]. As time went on this intervention [against rescue of Jews] grew in scope and energy. . . . In fact, the intervention against attempts to save Jews, to the extent that they were not connected with immigration to Palestine, continued up to the end of the [Second World] War" (ibid., 458). Even Y. Grienbaum, who in 1935 had demanded that the Zionist movement participate in the struggle for the rights of Europe's Jews, opposed in 1942 demands that Zionist funds (devoted to the colonization of Palestine) be used to finance projects for saving the lives of Jews. Beit-Zvi quotes Grienbaum as saying, "When I was asked whether the money of the Zionist Construction Fund may not be used for saving Jews, I said 'No,' and I now repeat, 'No.' I know that people wonder why I found it necessary to say this. Friends tell me that even if what I say is right, there are things which must not be revealed in a moment of sorrow and anxiety such as this. I cannot agree with this. In my view, the wave which relegates Zionist activities to second place must be resisted" (ibid., 110).

On the same subject see also Ben Hecht, *Perfidy* (New York: Messner, 1961).

26. Quoted in Elam, *Introduction to Zionist History,* 125–26. The historical background was the revolt of the Palestinian Arabs against British rule, which Great Britain had a hard time putting down. The British government did not want to antagonize the indigenous Arab population too much at that

time by allowing a large wave of Zionist colonization and were supported in this by anti-Zionist Jews.

27. Report in *Davar*, February 5, 1945, emphasis in the original.

28. Isaac Deutscher, *The Non-Jewish Jew*, 49–50.

29. A. Moos, in *links*.

30. Cf. reports in the weekly *Ha'olam Hazeh*, April 20, 1966, and June 1, 1966. This operation is of course denied by Zionists. Cf. Y. Me'ir, *Children of the Desert, Underground Organizations in Iraq 1941–1951* (Tel Aviv: Ma'arakhot, 1973), 204f (in Hebrew).

31. Moos, in *links*.

32. Quoted in Elam, *Introduction to Zionist History*, 73–74.

33. Quoted in *[Minutes of] The XII Zionist Congress in Karlsbad, September 1–14, 1921* (Berlin, 1922), 70.

34. L. Gaspar, *Histoire de la Palestine* (Paris: Maspero, 1970), 104, 119.

35. See Sabri Jeries, *The Arabs in Israel* (Beirut: Institute for Palestine Studies, 1969), 55–90, for a detailed account.

36. Ben-Gurion, *Memoirs*, 117.

37. Cf. the speech of Saskin, member of the subcommittee for colonization in the Zionist Executive at the XII Zionist Congress, *Minutes*, 104.

38. A. Bonné, *Palästina: Land und Wirtschaft* (Berlin: Josef Singer Verlag, 1935), 154–55.

39. Meiersohn, *Nach der 5. Poalei-Zion-Konferenz*.

40. Quoted from the statement of the Union Department of the PCP, October 1924; reprinted in Offenberg, *Kommunismus in Palästina*, 336–37.

41. Ben-Gurion, *Memoirs*, 275, 299–300, and 339.

42. Ben-Gurion, *We and Our Neighbours* (Jaffa: Davar, 1931), 81–82 (in Hebrew).

43. Y. Ben-Zvi in *Achduth* no. 16 (1912). [Ben-Zvi was to be Israel's second president.]

44. Theodor Herzl, *Diaries* (Berlin: Jüdischer Verlag, 1922), (in German).

45. Joseph Weitz, *Diaries*, vol. 1 (Israel: Masada, 1965) (in Hebrew), quoted by the author in "Solution to the Refugee Problem: The State of Israel with a Small Arab Minority," *Davar*, September 29, 1967.

46. Moos, in *links*.

47. A. M. Hyamson, *Palestine under the Mandate* (London: Methuen, 1950), 87–88.

48. Cf. C. Sykes, *Crossroads to Israel* (London: World Publishing, 1965), 119. Details of the complicated dodges used by the Zionists to evade government regulations enacted to protect tenants are given by Weitz in the preface to his *Diaries*, xxii–xxviii. Many illustrations can be found throughout these *Diaries*.

49. Cf. *A Survey of Palestine*, vol. 1 (London: HMSO, 1945–46), 296; and *Palestine Royal Commission Report* (London: HMSO, 1937), 239–40.

50. General Moshe Dayan, report in *Ma'ariv*, July 7, 1968.

Chapter 25: Abominable Warmongering on the Left

1. Having written this paragraph, I took a coffee break and picked up today's (August 4, 2008) *Guardian*. I found in it an article by the bourgeois journalist Max Hastings, entitled "Negotiating with Iran Is Maddening, but Bombing Would Be a Catastrophe," in which he observes: "Jerusalem and Washington are talking seriously about a possible Israeli strike, for which American collusion would be indispensable." He goes on to observe that Israel would need not only the consent of the present lame-duck US president (G. W. Bush), but also that of his likely successor: "Even if Obama does not yet sit in the White House, no Jerusalem government could lightly defy America's likely next president on an issue of such gravity."

2. "How Israel's Nuclear Secret Just Slipped Out," *The Age* (Australia), July 23, 2005, available online at www.tinyurl.com/684co4.

3. Warner D. Farr, LTC, US Army, "The Third Temple's Holy of Holies: Israel's Nuclear Weapons," *The Counterproliferation Papers*, Future Warfare Series no. 2, USAF Counterproliferation Center, Air War College, Air University, Maxwell Air Force Base, Alabama, September 1999, available at www.tinyurl.com/25jpwp.

4. For a fascinating virtual 3D tour of this installation, see www.tinyurl.com/64glofs.

5. For detailed analysis of Zionism, see my article "Israelis and Palestinians: Conflict and Resolution" [chapter 33 in this book].

Chapter 26: Zionism: Propaganda and Reality

1. These "facilities" were in fact an unfinished and unused building, which may possibly have been originally intended for processing nuclear material but was later abandoned—which explains why it was undefended and unguarded.
2. See "Excusing Catastrophe," *Weekly Worker*, September 4, 2008.
3. "Iranian Nukes Mean End of Zionism," *Jerusalem Post Internet Edition*, September 9, 2008.
4. Article in *Ma'ariv*, April 19, 1972.
5. Article in *Ha'aretz*, March 19, 1972.
6. Its limits are fuzzy, but they include in any case not only Israel and the Palestinian and Syrian territories occupied by it since 1967 but also parts of Jordan and Lebanon.
7. A serious contender was the highland part of Kenya. [On the so-called Uganda Plan, see footnote to the section "Continual Warfare," in chapter 23 in this book.]
8. See, for example, the report in the *Daily Telegraph* of September 12, 2008: "Iran Is a Threat, but the West Can't Afford to Have Israel Bomb It—Yet," available online at www.tinyurl.com/3gogrb.

Chapter 27: Things Bad Begun . . .

1. To give one tiny example: he quotes the date of the Bolshevik overthrow of the Kerensky government as "November 17" (p. 104). This cannot be a misprint, because he goes on to say that this was "two weeks" after the Balfour Declaration [dated November 2, 1917!].
2. "Kassem" is an acceptable, though unscientific transliteration of what should be rendered as "Qasim." But "Kfar" is a chauvinistic mistake: it is the Hebrew word for "village," while the Arabic is "Kafr." There is no reason to refer to an Arab village in English by a half-Hebraized name. Another ideologically inspired use of language is "Sinai War" for what the whole world knows as the "Suez war." The aim is to deny the collusion between Israel and its two colonialist partners in that war.
3. M. Pa'il, in *Yedi'ot Aharonot*, April 4, 1972.
4. For a quote from Ben-Gurion, dating from 1927, in which he makes clear that the true content of Zionism is the desire for a Jewish state, see Machover and Offenberg, "Zionism and Its Scarecrows" [chapter 24 in this book].

Chapter 28: Exploded Myths

1. Among his rare deviations is the cosmetic way in which he presents the policies of his own party, Mapam, and its precursor, Hashomer Hatza'ir (see p. 20). Also, in translating Hebrew words he sometimes tones down their harshness, perhaps unconsciously. Thus on page 114 he refers to the committee set up by Ben-Gurion to coordinate the eviction of the Palestinians as the "Committee for Removal and Expulsion." The Hebrew word that he translates as "removal" is *aqirah*, which actually means uprooting, not removal.
2. Two technical faults must, however, be pointed out. First, the transcription of Hebrew and Arabic names is a bit erratic, and sometimes simply wrong. Second, in Maps 2 to 6 the Litani River is inexplicably shown as flowing along the Israeli-Lebanese border, whereas in fact it is about twenty miles further north.
3. This impression is confirmed in an interview he granted to the Tel-Aviv newspaper *Ha'ir* on October 21, 1988.

Chapter 29: Lost in Translation

1. The foregoing paragraphs are translated from the Hebrew original by the reviewer; the corresponding passages in the English version are found on pages 328 and 329.

Chapter 30: Misinformation as "News"

1. Authored by Nabil Sha'th, "Toward the Democratic Palestine," *Fateh* 2, no. 2 (1970). My emphasis. *Fateh* was the English-language newspaper published by the Information Office of the Palestine Liberation Movement.

2. Incidentally, elsewhere the authors of the book under review rightly note that "to reduce the conflict to 'religion' . . . can be misleading" (p. 127).

3. Ironically, this denial is also shared by Zionist ideology, which refuses to recognize the existence of the new nation created by Zionist colonization, because it insists on the fiction that there is one worldwide Jewish "nation," with the Land of Israel as its God-given "homeland."

4. On page 2 we are told that from the 1830s onward some rabbis "stressed the need for Jews to return to the Holy Land as a necessary prelude to the Redemption and the second coming of the Messiah." The authors do not seem to realize that the rabbis are one coming behind: as far as they are concerned the first (and only) coming is still awaited, Jesus was an impostor, and his alleged first coming is a blasphemous fib.

5. How is such a reader to know that the Yom Kippur War referred to at the bottom of page 47 is the same as the October 1973 war mentioned earlier on that page?

6. Reports based on focus groups display interesting differences in this respect along both class and gender lines. Middle-class males and professionals (mixed groups) tend to be best informed (p. 210). But middle-class women tend to be very ill-informed, worse than low-income mixed groups (p. 272).

7. The United States never votes against Israel in the UN and habitually vetoes any resolution of the Security Council condemning Israel for violations of human rights and international law, no matter how serious.

Chapter 31: A Peace Activist on the Border

1. For information on Matzpen and its history and political positions, see www.matzpen.org/index.asp?p=100.

2. For a more erudite and critical view see Israel Shahak, *Jewish History, Jewish Religion: The Weight of Three Thousand Years* (London: Pluto Press, 1994).

3. One of the most puzzling and significant lacunae in this book (which devotes much space to the author's mental struggles) is the lack of any account of what had persuaded him to become a Marxist, and later a Trotskyist. Another astonishing lacuna is the absence of any account of what made him lose his religious faith in the late 1960s. He now describes himself not as an atheist but as an "agnostic" (p. 66). Significantly, the solidarity meeting with Mikado, on the eve of his imprisonment in November 1989, took place in a synagogue. He asks the reader: "is this a paradox or a symbol?" (p. 129). In the opinion of this reviewer it is an apparent paradox and a true symbol.

4. See www.alternativenews.org.

5. See my article, "Israelis and Palestinians: Conflict and resolution" [chapter 33 in this book, especially the table "West Bank Settlers," p. 265].

6. The name is mentioned in the English version of *Wikipedia*: see "Michel Warschawski," http://en.wikipedia.org/wiki/Michel_Warschawski.

Chapter 32: Zionist Myths Debunked

1. Jews who convert to another religion are generally regarded by their former coreligionists as non-Jewish. True, by the late nineteenth century there were in Europe and America many "secular" Jews, who no longer practiced Judaism but did not convert to another religion. But these are better described as persons of Jewish origin or background. Their "Jewishness" somehow dissipated after a couple of generations: you would have been hard put to find a person who identified as a Jew but did not practice Judaism and had no parent or grandparent who had practiced that religion. This is still true today everywhere outside Israel.

2. Genesis 32:28.
3. Genesis 15:18.
4. Symbolically, individual male converts often adopt the name Ben Avraham (Son of Abraham).
5. I. Bartal, "Jewish History: Inventing an Invention," *Ha'aretz,* July 6, 2008.

Chapter 33: Israelis and Palestinians: Conflict and Resolution

1. See sections 1.2, 1.5, and 1.9.
2. Significantly, Israel never officially defined its own international borders. The green line drawn on its maps during that period was its de facto border.
3. This excludes the (enormously enlarged) area within the municipal jurisdiction of Jerusalem. In the years 1967–76, the main thrust of Israeli colonization was in the Syrian Golan Heights and in Greater Jerusalem. The major drive of colonization in the rest of the West Bank started in 1976, as shown in the chart.
4. Similar relentless trends appear clearly in the data on area in Occupied Territories given over to colonization, and numbers of settlers' housing units built. See, for example, *Gezel Haqqarq'ot: Mediniyyut Hahitnahalut Baggadah Hamma'aravit* (Robbery of the Lands: The Policy of Colonization in the West Bank) report by B'Tselem—The Israeli Information Center for Human Rights in the Occupied Territories, May 2002. Posted on http://www.btselem.org/topic/settlements (where updated data can also be found).
5. The Palestine Royal Commission of Inquiry, headed by Lord Peel, was set up by the British government in 1936, following the outbreak of the Great Uprising of the Palestinian Arabs, and asked to propose changes in the status of Palestine. In 1937 the commission recommended partition of the country between Arabs and Jews. Ben-Gurion reluctantly accepted the plan; but—as Dayan clearly implies—did so for tactical reasons, with the expectation that Zionist colonization could continue in the whole of Palestine.
6. Report in *Ha'aretz,* February 18, 1973. Words in brackets here and in subsequent quotations are added by me.
7. Begin was founder of the Herut (Freedom) party, the direct post-1948 incarnation of the "Revisionist" Zionist movement founded by Jabotinsky. Herut combined with smaller parties in 1973 to form the Likud (Consolidation). Following Begin's resignation, Likud was led by Shamir, Netanyahu, and Sharon. In 2005 Sharon broke away from Likud to form a new party, now [2006] led by Olmert. The new party's name, "Qadimah" (often transliterated as "Kadimah")—meaning in Hebrew both "forward" and "eastward"—was an homage to Jabotinsky, who had founded in 1904 a Zionist publishing house by that name. The same Hebrew word was also inscribed in the insignia of a Jewish volunteer unit— set up after much lobbying by Jabotinsky—in the British Army during the First World War.
8. Some current English translations of this article translate (here and in the sequel) "settlement" instead of "colonization"; but the Russian original is unmistakable: *ob istorii kolonizatsii drugikh stran.*
9. See photograph at the Central Zionist Archive, Jerusalam: Herzl (left) propositioning the Kaiser during the latter's visit to Palestine, 1898. Actually this famous photo is a fake, a photomontage; but it is significant as wishful thinking.
10. Arthur James Balfour was foreign secretary. The "declaration" was in a form of a letter addressed to Lord Rothschild (Walter Rothschild, second Baron Rothschild), a leader of the British Jewish community, for transmission to the Zionist Federation. Other British Jewish leaders were opposed to Zionism and to the declaration; they included Edwin Samuel Montagu, secretary of state for India, who was the only Jewish member of the British Cabinet.
11. Ronald Storrs, *Orientations,* definitive edition (London: Nicholson & Watson, 1943), 345.
12. The mandate was drafted two years earlier at the League of Nations conference held in San Remo. Hence the reference to San Remo in the passage quoted above from Jabotinsky's "Iron Wall."
13. M. Assaf, *Davar,* May 2, 1952.
14. Poless (pen name of Dr. Shlomo Gross), "The Harlot of the Sea Ports and Us—Thoughts on the Eve of [Jewish] New Year 5712," op-ed, *Ha'aretz,* September 30, 1951.
15. Message to the Israeli forces in Sharm al-Sheikh, November 6, 1956, quoted in *Davar,* November 7,

1956. Amazingly, Ben-Gurion was oblivious to the sinister connotations of the term "Third Kingdom."
16. See *Yedi'ot Aharonot*, December 23, 2005. Shimon Peres hinted at this deal in an article entitled "This War Has Taught Us That Israel Must Revise Its Military Approach," published in the *Guardian* on September 4, 2006: "Fifty years ago I had the privilege of introducing new arms systems to the Israel Defence Forces that provided Israel with a powerful deterrent that is still valid."
17. On Israel's importance as a Western strategic asset, see Appendix, p. 281ff.
18. In much the same way, the term "fascism" is often misused as a generalized label for any authoritarian right-wing regime.
19. According to the classical maxim: *Definitio fit per genus proximum et differentiam specificam.*
20. "The mode of production of material life conditions the general process of social, political and intellectual life." Karl Marx, preface to the *Critique of Political Economy.*
21. This point is made forcefully by G. E. M. de Ste. Croix, *The Class Struggle in the Ancient Greek World* (Ithaca, NY: Cornell University Press, 1981).
22. See, for example, Nur Masalha, *Expulsion of the Palestinians: The Concept of 'Transfer' in Zionist Political Thought, 1882–1948* (Washington, DC: Institute for Palestine Studies, 1992); Ilan Pappé, *The Ethnic Cleansing of Palestine* (London: Oneworld, 2006).
23. "Labor" Zionism dominated the Zionist movement from the early 1930s and led all Israeli governments until 1977.
24. By the end of that period, well over a hundred thousand (possibly twice as many) workers from the West Bank and the Gaza Strip were employed inside the Green Line, mostly in menial and badly paid jobs. See Emmanuel Farjoun, "Palestinian Workers in Israel: A Reserve Army of Labor," in *Forbidden Agendas*, ed. Jon Rothschild (London: Al Saqi Books, 1984). Since the outbreak of the first intifada (end of 1987), these workers have largely been replaced by migrant workers from faraway countries.

According to Kav La'oved (Worker's Hotline) estimates, the number of West Bank Palestinians currently employed by Israelis in the West Bank itself (excluding Jerusalem) is twenty thousand: most of them in industrial parks, the largest of which is Barkan near Ariel. There are also up to ten thousand employed in construction according to demand, inside settlements (mainly the urban ones) but also in roads and even in constructing the notorious separation wall. These current numbers are very small in proportion to the total Palestinian workforce, let alone the Israeli one.
25. For an excellent eye-opening case study, involving the exploitation of docile ultra-Orthodox Jewish women, see Gadi Algazi, "Matrix in Bil'in—Capital, Settlements and Civil Resistance to the Separation Fence, or, A Story of Colonial Capitalism in Present-Day Israel," http://www.taayush.org/new/fence/matrix-bilin-en.html.
26. Yosef Weitz, "Solution to the Refugee Problem: The State of Israel with a Small Arab Minority," *Davar*, September 29, 1967.
27. For a detailed scary scenario of this sort, see "Sharon's Plan Is to Drive Palestinians across the Jordan," by the leading Israeli military historian Martin van Creveld, in the *Sunday Telegraph*, April 28, 2002.
28. I prefer the latter term, as it avoids any religious connotation and focuses on the most salient attribute of this group: their language.
29. Arguably, the Jews of Eastern Europe before the Nazi genocide did possess these attributes to a considerable extent, and constituted something like a national community.
30. What then do they constitute? This is a notoriously complex question, into which I cannot and need not enter here in any depth. Let me just make two fairly simple observations. First, the term "Jewish" has several different, albeit partly overlapping, meanings. Second, although Diaspora-Jewishness cannot be analytically reduced to Judaism (the Jewish religion), the latter is, empirically speaking, a vital constituent of the former, in the following sense: Without Judaism, Jewishness somehow dissipates after a couple of generations: outside Israel you would be hard put to find a person who self-identifies or is regarded by others as a Jew but does not practice Judaism and has no parent or grandparent who practiced Judaism. Among the Hebrews, on the other hand, you will find quite a few third-generation atheists.
31. As someone—I can't remember who—observed: a Zionist doesn't have to believe that God exists but does have to believe that He promised Palestine to the Jews.

32. This exceptional feature of the present conflict is pointed out by Nira Yuval-Davis in her conclusion in *The Challenge of Post-Zionism*, ed. Ephraim Nimni (London: Zed Books, 2003), 182–96.
33. Arguably, they are further reinforced thanks to the EU's Principle of Subsidiarity.
34. Israel's "withdrawal" from the Gaza Strip in 2005 did not end its military occupation but merely changed its form—mostly for the worse.
35. As I have shown elsewhere, the formula that proposes a unitary "secular democratic Palestine" is inadequate and was devised in order to evade the national dimension of the conflict (analyzed above, in section 1.9) and present it as an interconfessional conflict. [See chapter 8 of this book.]
36. Some advocates of a "two-state settlement" argue that even this travesty is preferable to the continuation of the present direct military occupation. Arguably, it is a lesser evil; and there are situations of extreme duress in which a lesser evil must be accepted. But what is imposed under duress ought to be met with protest—not embraced, advocated, and recommended as though it were the greatest good or a genuine resolution.
37. Alexander Haig was Richard Nixon's White House chief of staff (1973–74), NATO supreme Allied commander (1974–79), and Ronald Reagan's secretary of state (1981–82).

Chapter 34: Resolution of the Israeli-Palestinian Conflict

1. "Israelis and Palestinians—Conflict and Resolution" [chapter 33 in this book].
2. See ibid., section 2.1.
3. See "Maps," B'tselem—The Israeli Information Center for Human Rights in the Occupied Territories website, http://www.btselem.org/English/Maps/Index.asp, and "Analysis of the map of the West Bank," http://www.btselem.org/english/Settlements/Map_Analysis.asp.
4. One of the rare exceptions is Jack Conrad, "Zionist Imperatives and the Arab Solution," *Weekly Worker* 753, January 22, 2009. Conrad supports a two-state configuration, but in a very different form from that proposed by the US-led "international community"; and he addresses the question of the circumstances and forces needed for implementing it.
5. See "Toward the Democratic Palestine," *Fateh* (English-language newspaper published by the Information Office of the Palestine Liberation Movement) II, no. 2. This official programmatic article explicitly rejected the idea of a binational Palestine as a "misconception": "[t]he call for a non-sectarian Palestine should not be confused with . . . a bi-national state." Moreover, the article stresses that "[t]he liberated Palestine will be part of the Arab Homeland, and will not be another alien state within it" and looks forward to "[t]he eventual unity of Palestine with *other* Arab States."
6. See chapter 33.
7. For a brief account of Israel's services to US interests, see the appendix in chapter 33.
8. From 630 to 1918, interrupted by Christian Crusader rule from 1099 to 1187.
9. Thus, for example, the great fourteenth-century Arab traveler Ibn Battutah does not mention Palestine by that name, although he visited it. He refers to Gaza as "the first of the towns of Syria on the borders of Egypt."
10. Of course, the British imperialists had larger strategic reasons for wishing to rule that country.
11. This refers to the San Remo conference of April 1920, in which the victorious imperialist Entente powers (Britain, France, Italy, and Japan) decided the fate of the Middle East.
12. David Ben-Gurion, *Al mah lahamnu, madu'a pinninu, mah hissagnu* (What We Fought for, Why We Withdrew, What We Achieved), pamphlet published by the Central Committee of Mapai, March 1957. "Mapai" is an acronym for the Hebrew name used at that time by the Israeli Labor Party.
13. For a brief outline of this abortive attempt and the causes of its failure, see Conrad, "Zionist Imperatives and the Arab Solution."
14. Of course, there is no reason why the Palestinian-Arab canton should not be called "Palestine" and the Hebrew canton "Israel." Both names have been used in antiquity for variously and variably defined domains.

Index

"Passim" (literally "scattered") indicates intermittent discussion of a topic over a cluster of pages.

A

Abdullah I, 11, 63, 233, 234, 270, 272, 292
Africa, 84–86, 89. *See also* North Africa;
    Ethiopia; Kenya; Mozambique; South
    Africa; Uganda
African Americans, 184, 299
Afro-Asian Institute, 85–86
Ahad Ha'am, 180
Ahdut Ha'avodah, 138n, 165, 202
Ahmedinejad, Mahmoud, 211
aid, foreign, 80–86, 153, 280, 281. *See also*
    military aid
Alagiah, George, 246
Al-Fatah. *See* Fatah
Algeria, 49, 122, 123, 230–31, 249, 272
Algerian Jews. *See* Jews, Algerian
Al Hammishmar, 158
Alignment, 138n, 163
Alliance for Workers' Liberty (AWL), 210, 216
Al-Sa'iqa, 31
Alsop, Joseph, 29–30
Alterman, Nathan, 148–49
American Indians. *See* Native Americans
American Jews. *See* Jews, American
Amiel and Melburn Trust Lectures, 262–83
ancient history, 258–59

Ancient Rome, 259
annexation of territory. *See* territory annexation
anti-Semitism, 139–42, 154–55, 179, 191–94
    passim, 199, 224; Borochov and, 172;
    overcompensation for, 248; PLO and, 242;
    simulation and creation of, 200
anti-Zionist left, 95, 190
apartheid, 3, 51, 126, 127, 134, 272–73,
    289–90, 299
"Arab" (term), 308n24
Arab Awakening (2011), xiv
Arab Communist Parties, 46
Arab East. *See* Mashreq
Arabic language, 45, 106, 126, 277, 301
Arab-Israeli War (1948), 15, 16, 63, 148, 182,
    229–30, 290; Mizrahim and, 307n13; myths
    about, 233; Weitz on, 204. *See also* Nakba
Arab-Israeli War (1956). *See* Suez war
Arab-Israeli War (1967). *See* Six-Day War
Arab-Israeli War (1973). *See* Yom Kippur War
"Arab Jews" (label), 103–5
Arab revolt in Palestine (1936–39). *See*
    Palestinian Revolt (1936–39)
Arabs, Palestinian. *See* Palestinian Arabs
Arab states: national unification, 19–21, 44–47,
    66, 280, 292–94; Palestinian Arabs and,
    15–18 passim, 31, 294; Syria and, 30. *See*
    also Maghreb; Mashreq
Arafat, Yasser, 36, 39, 54–56 passim, 128, 253,
    286
Aref, Aref al-, 208
arms trade, 282
Ashkenazim, 99–109 passim, 129, 258, 306n2

317

Federation. See Histadrut
federation, regional, xi, 28, 47, 111, 150, 280,
    295, 301, 304–5n6; Arab, 27, 268, 277,
    280, 290; Uri Avnery and, 156
fighter jets, 282
Flapan, Simha: *The Birth of Israel*, 332–37 passim
forced transfer. See eviction and deportation
foreign aid. See aid, foreign
foreign capitalization: of Israel, 80–84, 88,
    186–87; of the PLO, 55
Fourth International, 7, 9, 254–55
France, 119–23 passim, 184, 211, 268, 272,
    291, 293; Algerian Jews and, 308n25; arms
    trade and, 282; Egypt and, 12
Freedom party. See Herut
French Mandate for Syria and Lebanon, 291
Fried, Erich, 2–3
Friedman, Ina, 241–42

G

Gaddafi, Muammar, 283
Gahal. See Herut-Liberal Bloc
Garvey, Marcus, 184
Gass, Oscar, 80, 187
Gaza, 156, 240, 286, 316n34
Gazit, Shlomo, 281–82
General Zionists, 94
German Jews. See Jews, German
German reparations, 80
Germany: Nazi-era laws, 118, 119, 193; Nazi
    occupation of Netherlands, 153; World
    War II, 198–99. See also Holocaust; Nazism
    and Zionism
Golan Heights, 253, 278, 314n3
Goldmann, Nahum, 194
Great Britain, 86, 176, 184–85; arms trade and,
    282; Falklands and, 226; Iran and, 226;
    Israeli capitalization and, 81–82; Jewish
    workers in, 175; national oppression in,
    116; Palestinian Revolt and, 230; police
    actions, 207, 307n17; South Africa and,
    152; television news bias, 244–48; "trans-
    fer" and, 236. See also imperialism: British;
    London
Greater Israel movement, 127, 189
Greater Syria, 27, 28, 43, 233, 234, 270, 276, 291
Great Powers, 269
Great Uprising. See Palestinian Revolt (1936–39)
Green Line, 51, 100, 266, 290, 314n2
Grienbaum, Yitzhak, 194, 310n25

Gulf War, 55
Gush Shalom, 1
Gvati, Haim, 90–91

H

Ha'aretz, 87, 186, 305n13
Haavara Agreement. See Zionist-Nazi transfer
    agreement
Haganah, 102, 230
Haig, Alexander, 282, 316n37
Hakohen, David, 209
Halevy, Ephraim, 219, 220
Hamas, 178n, 241
Hammami, Sa'id, 308–9n3
Hammeqasher, 67
Ha'olam Hazeh, 61, 70, 74
Ha'olam Hazeh–New Force, 61–75
Hashomer Hatza'ir, 96, 165
Hastings, Max, 311n1
health insurance, 88
Hebrew Immigrant Aid Society (HIAS), 196
Hebrew language, 23, 49, 106, 154, 304n2
Hebrew nation. See Israeli Jews
Hebrew nationalism. See nationalism: Hebrew
Hebron, 253
Hecht, Dinah, 156
"heroic" (word), 58
Herut, 94, 147, 185, 314n7
Herut-Liberal Bloc, 94
Herzl, Theodor, 87, 142, 169, 179–80, 258;
    anti-Semitism and, 192, 194; in faked
    photos, 314n9; *Judenstaat*, 139, 184, 258,
    269; on "transfer," 180, 204, 273
Hess, Moses, 192
HIAS. See Hebrew Immigrant Aid Society
    (HIAS)
Hillier, Bill, 111n
Hirst, David, 244–45
Histadrut, 81, 85–93 passim, 228, 306n25
Histadrut Enterprises, 306n29
history, ancient. See ancient history
Holland. See Netherlands
Holocaust, Jewish. See Jewish Holocaust
homeland, 41–42, 186, 215, 223, 257, 258,
    275–76; Palestinian Arabs and, 268, 291
human rights, 120, 125–26, 131, 134, 135,
    197, 278, 285
Hussein, Saddam, 55
Hussein I, 36
Husseini, Hajj Amin al-, 160

Palestine Royal Commission of Inquiry. *See* Peel
Commission
Palestinian Arabs, 19–22 passim, 27, 31–33,
42–53 passim, 111–14 passim; Arab states
and, 15–18 passim, 31, 294; Borochov
on, 177; collective punishment, 229;
Jabotinsky on, 267; Mizrahim and, 108–9;
national identity and culture, 276–77,
300–301; national oppression and, 123,
126; partition and, 232–37; population in
Israel, 287; racist discrimination and, 117,
118, 122; Sharon and, 54–56. *See also*
intifada; Oslo Accords; right of return for
Palestinian Arabs
Palestinian Arab workers, 88–90 passim, 100,
107, 315n24; boycott against, 206–9 passim
Palestinian Authority, 1, 252, 279, 286
Palestinian declaration of independence, 39
Palestinian National Covenant, 31, 128
Palestinian refugees. *See* refugees: Palestinian
Palestinian Revolt (1936–39), 230, 271,
310n26, 314n5
Palestinian state, 28–30, 48–52 passim,
135–36, 279–80, 286–89 passim, 295,
316n5; Avnery and, 64; Egypt and Syria
and, 234; Hebrew self-determination and,
111–14 passim; Matgamna on, 215; PLO
and, 39, 128–30, 244–45; Rabin govern-
ment and, 253; Rakah and, 37; Zionist
leadership and, 233
Palestinians. *See* Palestinian Arabs
Palestinian territories. *See* Occupied Territories
Palestinian uprising (1936–39). *See* Palestinian
Revolt (1936–39)
Palestinian uprising (1987–93). *See* intifada
Palma, 102
pan-Arabism. *See* nationalism: Arab
Partition Plan for Israel. *See* United Nations:
Partition Plan for Israel
patriarchs, Jewish (ancient history). *See* Jewish
patriarchs (ancient history)
patriotism, 250
peace accords. *See* Camp David Accords (1978);
Oslo Accords
peace and peace activism, 1–4, 162–63, 234,
249–56, 274
Peace Now, 1
Peel Commission, 29, 63, 266, 314n5
Peled, Matityahu, 221
Peres, Shimon, 54, 253, 272, 314–15n16
Persian Gulf War. *See* Gulf War

petite bourgeoisie. *See* lower middle class
petroleum. *See* oil
Philo, Greg: *Bad News from Israel*, 244
photographs, faked. *See* faked photographs
Pinsker, Leo, 192
plastic bullets, 242
PLO. *See* Palestine Liberation Organization (PLO)
Po'alei Smol, 165, 166, 171
Poland, 140, 193
police actions, 207, 307n17
Polish Jews. *See* Jews, Polish
Polski, Viktor, 195
Popular Front for the Liberation of Palestine
(PFLP), 155, 247. *See also* Democratic Popular Front for the Liberation of Palestine
(DPFLP)
population "transfer." *See* eviction and deportation
*Post-Ugandan Zionism in the Crucible of the
Holocaust* (Beit-Zvi), 310n25
Poujadism, 75
private enterprise, 73
private property, 73
privatization, 92n
proletariat. *See* working class
propaganda, 2, 43, 141–42, 147, 151–57, 189,
191, 203; Avishai book as, 228–29; books
countering, 232–37; Borochovism and, 165,
167; Mapam and, 163; Matgamna and, 212,
221–22, 225; Soviet Jewish emigrants and,
195; in translation, 241–43; *Wikipedia* and,
304n1–2
proportional representation, 94
protests. *See* demonstrations and protests
punishment, collective. *See* collective punishment

Q

Qaddafi, Muammar. *See* Gaddafi, Muammar
Qadimah, 314n7

R

Rabin, Yitzhak, 29–30, 242, 253, 266, 286
racism, 100, 101, 115–30 passim, 134–35, 248
Rafi, 95
Rakah, 32–33, 37, 39, 97
Ramadan War. *See* Yom Kippur War
Ramleh, 106, 148
Ratosh, Yonatan, 128
refugees, 63; Jewish, 100, 140, 198; Palestinian,
11, 12, 55, 114, 183, 235–36. *See also*

Also from Haymarket Books

Boycott, Divestment, Sanctions:
The Global Struggle for Palestinian Rights
Omar Barghouti

Gaza in Crisis: Reflections on Israel's War on the Palestinians
Noam Chomsky and Ilan Pappé

Diary of Bergen-Belsen, 1944–1945
Hanna Lévy-Hass, foreword and afterword by Amira Hass

False Prophets of Peace: Liberal Zionism and the Struggle for Palestine
Tikva Honig-Parnass

A Little Piece of Ground
Elizabeth Laird with Sonia Nimr

Midnight on the Mavi Marmara:
The Attack on the Gaza Freedom Flotilla and
How It Changed the Course of the Israel/Palestine Conflict
Edited by Moustafa Bayoumi

Between the Lines: Readings on Israel,
the Palestinians, and the U.S. "War on Terror"
Tikva Honig-Parnass and Toufic Haddad

The Pen and the Sword: Conversations with Edward Said
David Barsamian

The Struggle for Palestine
Edited by Lance Selfa

The Palestine Communist Party, 1919–1948: Arab and Jew in the Struggle for Internationalism
Musa Budeiri

what i will tell my jewish kids: and other poems
Kevin Coval

About Haymarket Books

Haymarket Books is a nonprofit, progressive book distributor and publisher, a project of the Center for Economic Research and Social Change. We believe that activists need to take ideas, history, and politics into the many struggles for social justice today. Learning the lessons of past victories, as well as defeats, can arm a new generation of fighters for a better world. As Karl Marx said, "The philosophers have merely interpreted the world; the point, however, is to change it."

We take inspiration and courage from our namesakes, the Haymarket Martyrs, who gave their lives fighting for a better world. Their 1886 struggle for the eight-hour day, which gave us May Day, the international workers' holiday, reminds workers around the world that ordinary people can organize and struggle for their own liberation. These struggles continue today across the globe—struggles against oppression, exploitation, hunger, and poverty.

It was August Spies, one of the Martyrs targeted for being an immigrant and an anarchist, who predicted the battles being fought to this day. "If you think that by hanging us you can stamp out the labor movement," Spies told the judge, "then hang us. Here you will tread upon a spark, but here, and there, and behind you, and in front of you, and everywhere, the flames will blaze up. It is a subterranean fire. You cannot put it out. The ground is on fire upon which you stand."

We could not succeed in our publishing efforts without the generous financial support of our readers. Many people contribute to our project through the Haymarket Sustainers program, where donors receive free books in return for their monetary support. If you would like to be a part of this program, please contact us at info@haymarketbooks.org.

Order these titles and more online at www.haymarketbooks.org or call 773-583-7884.

About the Author

© Haymarket Books

Moshé Machover was born in 1936 in Tel-Aviv, Palestine. As a teenager he joined the left-Zionist youth movement Hashomer Hatza'ir, from which he was expelled in 1952 for questioning its ideology. As a student, he joined the Israeli Communist Party, from which he was expelled in 1962 together with a small group of party dissidents who challenged the ICP's lack of internal democracy and its subservience to the Soviet Union.

In the same year they founded the Israeli Socialist Organization (better known by the name of its journal, *Matzpen*, and later renamed the Socialist Organization in Israel), an independent radical left group.

Moshé Machover is a mathematician. He taught at the Hebrew University of Jerusalem, the University of Bristol, and at King's College, London; he is emeritus professor at London University and has been living in London since late 1968.

Apart from academic books and papers on mathematical logic and social choice (the mathematical theory of collective decision-making), he has written extensively on socialist theory, particularly as applied to Israel, the Middle East, and the Israeli-Palestinian conflict.

With Akiva Orr he co-authored *Peace, Peace Where There Is No Peace* (1961) on the Israeli-Palestinian conflict (Hebrew; English translation available online: (http://www.akiorrbooks.com/files/PEACE.pdf). With Emmanuel Farjoun he coauthored *Laws of Chaos: A Probabilistic Approach to Political Economy* (Verso, 1983), a critical reconstruction of Marxian political economy using a stochastic approach borrowed from statistical mechanics.